Soul of the Man

Soul

OF THE Man

BOBBY "BLUE" BLAND

Charles Farley

UNIVERSITY PRESS OF MISSISSIPPI • JACKSON

www.upress.state.ms.us

The University Press of Mississippi is a member of the
Association of American University Presses.

First printing 2011

∞

Library of Congress Cataloging-in-Publication Data

Farley, Charles, 1945–
  Soul of the man : Bobby "Blue" Bland / Charles Farley.
    p. cm. — (American made music series)
  Includes bibliographical references and index.
  ISBN 978-1-60473-919-0 (cloth : alk. paper) —
  ISBN 978-1-60473-920-6 (ebook)
1. Bland, Bobby. 2. Singers—United States—Biography.
3. Blues musicians—United States—Biography. I. Title.
  ML420.B647F37 2011
  782.421643092—dc22
  [B]   2010036218

British Library Cataloging-in-Publication Data available

The stories that I was telling during that time, I didn't know how strong they really were until I got a little older and then listened to them over again and in those stories was pretty much my life.

BOBBY BLAND

Contents

Acknowledgments

First, thanks to the many friends and associates of Bobby Bland, especially B.B. King, Willie Mitchell, and Wolf Stephenson, who generously gave their time, recollections of the artist, and their support for this project. Conspicuous by his absence on the list of those consulted is Bobby Bland himself, who, despite repeated requests, declined to be interviewed for this account. Obviously, he has given scores of interviews over the years, many of which are referenced herein, but none in support of a complete biography, on which he is reluctant to collaborate.

In addition to these interviews, many other sources have been consulted in piecing together the Bobby Bland story found here. Of these, the single best at addressing his early and mid-life career is Peter Guralnick's "Little Boy Blue," which first appeared in the July-August 1978 issue of *Living Blues* and is also included in his fine book, *Lost Highway: Journeys and Arrivals of American Musicians*, originally published in 1979 by David R. Godine, Publishers, Inc. In addition, Charles Keil's 1966 *Urban Blues*, published by the University of Chicago Press, captures the spirit of B.B. King and Bobby Bland at the height of their popularity in the early 1960s. Both Guralnick's and Keil's works are indispensable in any examination of Bobby Bland and are quoted and cited extensively.

Roger Wood's *Down in Houston: Bayou City Blues* (University of Texas Press, 2003), Alan Govenar's articles and books, and Galen Gart and Roy Ames's *Duke/Peacock Records: An Illustrated History and Discography* (Big Nickel Publications, 1990) are particularly useful in chronicling Bobby Bland's many years at Duke Records. James M. Salem's *The Late, Great Johnny Ace and the Transition from R&B to Rock 'n' Roll* (University of Illinois Press, 1999) provides excellent primary material and research on the Beale Streeters and the early days of Duke/Peacock Records, both in Memphis and Houston. And Rob Bowman's *Malaco Records: The Last Soul Company* (Malaco Records, 1999) tells the Malaco story with style and humor.

There are many other useful and valuable sources which are cited here, including material from the French publication *Soul Bag*, which was proficiently translated by Elaine Fisher. Other blues music critics and writers, particularly Jim and Amy O'Neal, Bill Dahl, Robert Gordon, Dave Hoekstra, Barney Hoskyns, and Jon Pareles, have followed and reported on Bobby Bland faithfully and fairly throughout his career.

The photographs of Bobby Bland and his colleagues that are included here are made possible by the creative efforts of especially Ernest C. Withers, Ray Flerlage, Ebet Roberts, D. Shigley, David Corio, Sylvia Pitcher, Gene Tomko, Andy Fallon, and Patricia Kuhn.

Much of the material cited would not have been uncovered, of course, without the unflagging, unflappable, and unassailable help of librarians and archivists at many institutions, including especially the University of Mississippi's Blues Archives, the Memphis and Shelby County Room of the Memphis Public Library and Information Center, the Ned R. McWherter Library at the University of Memphis, the Huntsville–Madison County Public Library, and the Los Angeles Public Library.

Special thanks goes to David Evans, Robert Pruter, and Dick Shurman, who know more about the blues than just about anyone, and the others who have read and critiqued this story as it has been ponderously and painstakingly put together and placed before you.

Because Bobby Bland represents such a commanding presence in modern popular music, and because the Internet provides a readily available platform for everyone to post anything, anytime, anywhere, an overabundance of information about Bobby Bland is available online. In an attempt to consolidate some of this information that is particularly accurate and useful, Patricia Kuhn, a consummate Bland fan and crackerjack web designer, has graciously lent her formidable talents to organizing a web site dedicated to Bobby Bland and his distinguished career.

On her web site, in addition to a much briefer biography of Bland than is found herein, you can peruse photos, consult a complete session discography, check out performance descriptions and schedules, and find links to other pertinent online sources: www.souloftheman.com.

Soul of the Man

Last of the Great Masters

Yes. I, too, have said that I would exchange all the blues to save one starving child. I was wrong, not only because the exchange is not in my power, but because this singing of the Lord's song in so strange a land has saved more children than anyone will ever know, and the beginning is not yet in sight.

JAMES BALDWIN

Why I am a Poet, #7

getting drunk on dreamy horny summer Friday nights
45 rpm records with the big holes dripping rhythm and blues onto
   the turntable
Jimmy Reed and Bobby Blue Bland and Little Richard,
God bless them all,
They saved my life I thank them I praise them

BOBBY BYRD

Introduction

The Man

When bandleader Joe Hardin introduces Bobby "Blue" Bland at one of his live performances as "the world's greatest blues singer," one might presume it to be typical show-business hyperbole. But then Bobby Bland opens his mouth and starts singing, and one is hard put to name another who can paint a blues palette, from dirges to jump and all shades of shuffles and ballads in between, as beautifully as Bobby "Blue" Bland. There are certainly other bluesmen who can play an instrument better than Bland (who plays no instrument at all), and others who can write better blues lyrics (seeing that he seldom writes a song), and still more who can dance better (he hardly moves at all when he performs), but none sound better than the man with "the voice of satin," as his friend B.B. King acclaims, when he sings a popular song in any form.[1]

When Bobby Bland hit the charts in 1957 as his first hit, "Farther Up the Road," skyrocketed to number one on the Rhythm and Blues chart, no one was prepared for the phenomenal success that would follow. Bland himself was least prepared. Despite several previous years of performing, he remained at heart a shy, country boy from rural Tennessee. But throughout the 1960s Bland "could do no wrong," fellow bluesman Little Milton Campbell remembered. "Whatever he did was a smash . . . he was invincible."[2] Hit after hit ensued, making Bland as ubiquitous on black radio station airwaves as James Brown, Ray Charles, and the Temptations, and selling more records than B.B. King, Sam Cooke, and the Impressions, all contemporaries who ultimately became better known than Bland in the broader, paler, popular culture.[3]

Still, of Bland's sixty-three R&B hits, more than forty crossed over onto the pop charts, and, as he continued to perform more than three hundred shows a year, throughout the rest of the century, he finally began receiving the recognition that he had earned and so richly deserved. He was inducted into the Blues

Foundation's Hall of Fame in 1981, became a member of the Rock and Roll Hall of Fame in 1992, was recipient of Lifetime Achievement Awards from both the National Academy of Recording Arts and Sciences (the Grammy Awards) in 1997 and the Blues Foundation in 1998, recipient of the Pioneer Award by the Rhythm & Blues Foundation in 1992, and the unprecedented winner of the Blues Foundation's Soul/Blues Male Artist of the Year award seven times running.

Yet it was always more than the voice and the many awards that placed Bobby "Blue" Bland in the pantheon of modern blues greats. It was also another part of his upper anatomy that enabled him to turn a trifling lyric into a work of art. Few have a better blues ear than Bobby Bland. And despite the great influence of his collaborator and arranger at Duke Records, Joe Scott, as well as others in later years, it was Bland himself who could take a tune, often no more than a simple rhythm track and a few words, and massage them to fit his ear and his voice for the most compelling blues delivery imaginable. It was this impeccable ear for what was the right way to sing a song, as much as anything else, that made Bland such a long-lasting voice in popular music in the second half of the twentieth century.

Bland's fans would seldom analyze his wide and ever-present appeal to this degree. To them, Bobby's stature was more attributable to his overall style than to his voice, his record sales, his awards, or his ear. It was a way of performing, of carrying himself, of living. To borrow a fashionable word from that era, Bobby was "cool." He was suave yet sincere, strong but nurturing, sometimes smiling and, at others, sad—in a word, human; but always just a bit above it all so he could confidently tell his audience just how life and love really were, all through the simple songs that spoke to so many for so long.

Through the years, Bland has been described not only as "the world's greatest blues singer" but also as "the lion of the blues," "the crown prince of the blues," and "the Sinatra of the blues."[4] But his story has never been fully told, and his music remains not that widely known, particularly outside the older African American community where his name remains as familiar as cornbread and collard greens. There are many reasons for this, a few of which will be explored later, but perhaps J. B. Figi summed it up best when he wrote in *Down Beat* that "the more subtle reason why Bland's popularity has not spread beyond its natural boundaries has to do with the very personal, romantic nature of his appeal. His fans tend to keep it quiet, the way a man won't flaunt his wife as he may have done earlier his girlfriends. But casually mention his name, and you'll discover a legion. They're all about; people soft on Bobby who cherish his music, for whom his voice has somewhere been a backdrop to their lives."[5]

Among the legion you'll find not only Little Milton and B.B. King, who calls Bland his favorite blues singer, but also countless other blues, jazz, and rock artists who have proclaimed Bobby as one of their prime influences: stars such as Johnnie Taylor, Tyrone Davis, Freddie King, Boz Scaggs, Van Morrison, Rod Stewart, Mick Hucknall, among many, many more.

Dan Penn sums it up well. Penn wrote some of the greatest R&B hits of all time, including Aretha Franklin's "Do Right Woman, Do Right Man," James Carr's "Dark End of the Street," and James and Bobby Purify's "I'm Your Puppet." As he told interviewer Les Back in *The Oxford American*: "Bobby Bland was just the Man. You wanted to be like him, at least I did—just a great, great singer. He had exceptional delivery and understanding. He made you *understand* what the song means to him. He didn't just shuffle through, you know—it's also blood and guts. The r&b records that I loved are not prominent or in your face. Listen to *Share Your Love with Me*, the one with the strings— that's my favorite. That one, and *Two Steps from the Blues* are the two that stick out for me. I have to say that I've never heard records any better than those. No gimmicks, just pure blues pop. Nobody's ever beat 'em. . . . I can't say enough good things about Bobby Bland. I guess that's what it comes down to, don't it? It's like, well, who had the best voice? Bobby Bland did."[6]

Here is his story.

A young Robert Bland at the microphone at WDIA in Memphis, Tennessee, ca. 1950.
Copyright Ernest C. Withers Estate, courtesy Panopticon Gallery, Boston, MA.

Memphis Monday Morning

1945–1948

When fifteen-year-old Robert Bland walked down Beale Street for the first time after his family moved to Memphis in 1945, he found a city filled with hope, racial division, and the music that would change America.

Robert was a shy country boy who was old enough and bright enough to know that Memphis held a whole new world of opportunity for him compared to the tiny rural cotton towns where he had grown up. Thankfully his mother agreed; she, in fact, was the one who had hatched the plan of moving to the city in the first place. She had experienced all her life the hard, daily grind of small-town, Jim Crow southern living and instinctively knew, especially with young Robert's aversion to books and school, that he would likely end up in the cotton fields forever unless she did something soon. The only thing the boy seemed to enjoy doing was singing, and she thought perhaps he could best take advantage of this affinity if they moved to Memphis where there seemed to be music everywhere, even if a lot of it was not the church music that she so very much preferred.

So, soon after Mrs. Bland's parents moved to Memphis and World War II ended with Japan's surrender on August 14, the Bland family—young Robert, his mother, Mary Lee, and his stepfather, Leroy—made the twenty-two-mile move southwest from Barretville, Tennessee, to Memphis. The city on a bluff above the Mississippi River was now, according to the *New York Times*, "the cultural as well as the social and commercial capitol of a huge area of near-by Tennessee, Mississippi, Arkansas and Missouri."[1] They first lived with Mary Lee's parents on Hill Street on Memphis's north side, but soon moved to their own apartment downtown at 398 Vance Avenue, when Mary Lee found a job at the Firestone Plant on Thomas Street and Leroy landed a position at a foundry on the north side. Later, Leroy worked as a laborer at Samuel Furniture until he found easier work repairing juke boxes at Joe Cuoghi's on Summer Avenue. Joe Cuoghi later became one of the founders of Hi Records, where Leroy's stepson would make records in 1967 with the legendary soul producer Willie Mitchell.[2]

However, before all that was to occur, Robert had first to find his way in his new home town. His parents urged him to return to school. Booker T. Washington High School was not far from their apartment and recognized as one of the best secondary schools for young African Americans in the South. But Robert would have none of it. He had made it through only third grade in Rosemark, where the family had lived before moving to Barretville, and it had been a struggle to do that. The truth was that, between picking and chopping cotton almost year-round, he had attended classes only sporadically and had never even learned to read or write. So, in this pre-GED/adult education era, to a self-conscious adolescent newcomer, it seemed either entering high school, as unprepared as he was, or returning to elementary school, as old as he was, would be far more embarrassing than suffering the occasional indignities of living a life of illiteracy.

Besides, by now Robert was used to working and earning his own spending money, and school, he reasoned, would afford him little immediate opportunity to find a job that would help to support him and his family while he tried to forge some kind of career in music. So he scraped up enough to buy a second-hand bicycle and found a job delivering groceries from the little store on the corner of Vance and Hernando Streets, a few blocks from the Blands' apartment. The job didn't pay much, but with tips he made enough to begin saving for a car. The job also gave him the opportunity to explore his new neighborhood.[3]

Fortunately for Robert and his family the economy in Memphis was thriving. The price of cotton had doubled in the past five years.[4] Robert and the veterans returning triumphantly from World War II looked on Memphis as *the* place in the mid-South to make their marks and to escape the cotton fields and rural poverty of the Delta's Depression in which many of them were raised before the war. Here, they found a bustling, vibrant city of hope and possibility. Their hopes were not unfounded, as it turned out. By 1955, according to David L. Cohn, a Mississippi native who wrote in the September 4, 1955, issue of *The New York Times*, Memphis was "the nation's largest inland cotton market, largest inland hardwood lumber market, largest producer of cottonseed products, and the country's tenth largest wholesale center, with the prosperous population of nearly a half million."[5]

But unfortunately not all of Memphis was equally affluent. Whereas the median income for white Memphis families in 1950 was $2,264, it was only $986 for black families (figures similar to Atlanta, Birmingham, and New Orleans).[6] A 1940 WPA survey noted that 77 percent of Memphis's black population lived in substandard housing, compared to 35 percent of the white citizenry, and less than 11 percent of black families had an indoor bathroom.[7] The reality was that the black Memphis that young Robert Bland encountered in 1945 was largely cut off from the white majority of about 63 percent who actually owned, controlled, and ruled the city. "Like a whole city of Ralph Ellison's invisible men and women, they were out of sight and out of the minds of most white people," wrote Louis Cantor in his *Wheelin' on Beale*.[8]

And while the South's nasty brand of segregation was nothing new to Robert, he was surprised at some of Memphis's racial peculiarities. Once he had mistakenly entered Jim's Barber Shop, at the corner of Beale and Main, next to the Malco Theater, to get his hair cut, but was quickly ushered out, since Jim's only cut the straight hair of white people even though all its employees were black.

He also soon learned that he could have lunch at one of the downtown department stores, Kress's 5 & 10 or the Black and White Department Store, but he had to eat at a separate black-only counter. In 1947, Jackie Robinson would become the first African American to play major league baseball, winning the National League Rookie of the Year Award after a stellar season with the Brooklyn Dodgers, but in Memphis Robert was not allowed to watch the Memphis Chicks, the all-white Southern Association baseball team. Instead he often took in a Memphis Blues game at the African American Martin Stadium where the Blues hosted Black Southern Association rivals such as the Atlanta Black Crackers, the Birmingham Black Barons, and the Chattanooga Choo-Choos.[9]

Still, despite the economic and social inequalities that this separation of the races created, it also spawned an extraordinary breeding ground for African American creativity not only in the sports and entertainment worlds, but also in the arts, music, and business fields. And at the heart of this southern black renaissance was the street where Robert was to reside and grow into manhood during the next seven years. From the small apartment on Vance, the family moved the next year, 1946, to a larger unit at 304 Cynthia Place, just three blocks off Beale Street, the famous street that begins at the Mississippi River and runs east for about a mile.[10]

When, earlier in the twentieth century, the steamboats docked at the foot of Beale, passengers and roustabouts needed only walk a few steps to be met with dance halls, cafes, honky-tonks, booze, and blues. The street soon would be known worldwide, thanks primarily to a young man from Florence, Alabama, named W. C. Handy who immortalized Memphis and its rowdy thoroughfare in 1912 with his "Memphis Blues," and in 1916 with his "Beale Street Blues." Until its decline in the 1960s, Beale Street was the focal point of the Mississippi Delta and "the Main Street of Negro America," observed George W. Lee, a Memphis insurance executive and author. "There are many other streets upon which the Negro lives and moves," he wrote, "but only one Beale Street. As a breeding place of smoking, red-hot syncopation, compared to it, Harlem, State Street, and all the rest of the streets and communities of Negro America famed in story and song are but playthings."[11]

Indeed, by the time a wide-eyed young Robert Bland was cycling around his neighborhood delivering groceries, Beale Street and its nearby environs was the one thing that southern African Americans could call their own—a community in which they felt comfortable shopping, entertaining, and communicating. It was a refuge for Robert and other southern black people from the daily degradation of the deep South's humiliating stripe of segregation. "To Handy and untold other blacks," Beale Street observers Margaret McKee and Fred Chisenhall wrote, "Beale became as much a symbol of escape from despair as had Harriet Tubman's underground railroad. On Beale you could find surcease from sorrow; on Beale you could forget for a shining moment the burden of being black and celebrate being black; on Beale you could be a man, your own man; on Beale you could be free."[12]

At first Robert's mother feared for her son's safety in the bustling city whose rough reputation as a city of sin was widely recognized. During Prohibition, Memphis was run by the political machine of E. H. "Boss" Crump who turned a blind eye to vice, gambling, and partying in the African American neighborhoods around Beale Street—as long as necessary payments were made, racial segregation was maintained, and nothing untoward spilled over into white sections of the city. But by the time the Blands took up residence in the city, it was no longer the South's center of homicide and corruption. In response to state investigations of his alleged manipulation of black voters, Crump had clamped down on the violence, gambling, and prostitution that his political machine had largely protected in the earlier years of its reign. Now the city was relatively tame, although it seemed to young Robert, accustomed to the serenity of country living, that the party was still going on.

"Well, to say it lightly, there's nothing light to say about Beale Street," Bland recalled about the street. "It had everything that you would probably want to get into, from a good thrashing to all the fun you could handle and all the whatever. Beale Street was the place because if you were an out-of-towner you had always heard about Beale Street—the good and the bad, basically the bad, you know, something that travels faster than good. But it was a learning process for a lot of things. All the theaters were down there. You know, you couldn't go Downtown because if you go to the Princess you've got to sit upstairs and also the Malco—they call it the Orpheum now. So didn't too many travel up there because it was too high, actually. You could pay a quarter and go to the New Daisy and stay all day. You could stop at the One Minute and get five or six hot dogs and go in there and enjoy all the westerns because they played all day Saturdays. But, Beale Street, as I said, was a learning process for a lot of people and it's got all the history in the world that you can think of—some good and some bad—but I can appreciate what I learned from the area."[13]

Rufus Thomas was one of Robert's best teachers. At the time he was em-cee for the weekly Wednesday night amateur shows at the Palace Theater, and in 1986 he described the earlier scene like this: "But, talking about Beale Street—every neighborhood had its roughness, and Beale Street was no worse than any other. You didn't have to go to Beale Street to die from a killing. But the collection of people that went to Beale Street was different. Beale was not a rich-man's neighborhood. Nobody on Beale, the clientele, were rich. Now, they wore good clothes. They wore the best clothes that money could buy. Shoes shined to the bone—and whatever dress was fashionable at that time. Both man and women dressed up. The clothes I remember, they called 'em drapes. They had all those pleats in the front and pants legs were small at the bottom. They had big hats and they wore a long watch chain and they used to stand on the corner and twirl that chain. It was the zoot suit, the drape, we called it. I went on the radio, WDIA, in the 1950's, and Beale Street was still flourishing. . . ."[14]

It was a perfect place for a young man like Robert Bland who was bored and fed up with his previous rural life and immediately heard something in the tone and tunes of Beale Street musicians that represented a feasible fu-ture for the ambitious teenager. One of the first performers that Robert met was another country boy, five years Robert's senior, who was trying to forge a musical future in Memphis himself. His name was Riley B. King, later to be known as B.B. King, who recalled in his autobiography:

On Beale Street, you could get the whole meal for 20 cents. Beale Street had chili, best in the world, thick and rich and spicy delicious. Belly washers were huge quart bottles of flavored soda pop—cream or grape or peach—for washing down the chili. Grab you some chili at Mitchell's Hotel or the One Minute Café. Or go to Johnny Mills' Barbecue on the corner of Beale and Fourth . . .

There was a caring feeling on Beale Street. Musicians would talk to each other, exchange ideas, listen long and hard to each other. I learned so much just hanging 'round the park. Folks were friendly. They sensed your eagerness and opened their hearts, shared their experiences. I made some friends I've kept for life. Bobby Bland was one. He's one of the only people I've stayed close to for over fifty years. He's my favorite blues singer. Man can sing anything, but he gives the blues, with his gorgeous voice of satin, something it never had before. He lifts the blues and makes them his own. I got started a little before Bobby, but when he came 'round Beale Street I loved having him sit in with those little bands of mine. Bobby was one of the joys of Beale Street.

> *Beale Street was like WDIA. They were the hot spots for people who loved music and wanted to get somewhere. Seemed like these were the only places where the races really got along. They were islands of understanding in the middle of an ocean of prejudice.*[15]

WDIA was a small, ailing radio station in Memphis when in 1948 its white owners, Bert Ferguson and Don Kern, in desperation, decided to switch its all-white format to a completely black format and become the first all-black radio station in the United States. And, although the station remained white-owned, the first black-hosted show aired at 4:00 p.m. on October 25, 1948, and by the end of 1949, there was not a white voice to be heard at 730 on most black Memphians' AM radio dials. As Louis Cantor recounts in his excellent history of the station, *Wheelin' on Beale:* "Claiming to reach an incredible ten percent of the total black population of the United States, WDIA was a celebration of firsts: the first radio station in the country with a format designed exclusively for a black audience; the first station south of the Mason-Dixon line to air a publicly recognized black disk jockey [Nat D. Williams]; the first all-black station in the nation to go 50,000 watts [in 1954]; the first Memphis station to gross a million dollars a year; the first in the country to present an open forum to discuss black problems; and, most important, the first to win the hearts and minds of the black community in Memphis and the Mid-South with its extraordinary public service. For most blacks living within broadcast range, WDIA was 'their' station."[16]

It was also at WDIA where B.B. King got his start in 1949 as a disk jockey, and where B.B. and Robert would appear, initially without pay, in order to plug their own shows at local clubs. When the station went from being a local 250-watt, dawn-to-dusk operation to a 50,000-watt, 4:00 a.m.-to-midnight regional powerhouse in 1954, it claimed to be reaching 1,439,506 listeners in 115 counties in Arkansas, Mississippi, Missouri, and Tennessee. Performers, who may have enjoyed only local fame, were now being catapulted into national black consciousness. In addition to B.B. King and Bobby Bland, Rosco Gordon, Earl Forest, Joe Hill Louis, Willie Love, and Willie Nix were soon to gain national recognition, largely attributable to their airplay on WDIA. "WDIA did more to help the bluesmen of the Delta," blues historian Mike Leadbitter has written, "than anything else."[17]

Bland remembers gratefully the support of the station's first black deejay and black Memphis community leader. "Nat D. Williams, one of the greatest people I've ever known. You know, Nat D. was actually a teacher at Booker T. Washington High School and he gave everybody a break. So far as music information, he could keep your head straight and whatever. He helped in so many ways. You know you couldn't talk to him like you could Rufus and Moohah [other WDIA on-air personalities]. He was a little more business. But he was good people."[18]

WDIA's owners were not the only white people to recognize and appreciate the rich distinction of African American culture right there in their midst. Rufus Thomas recalled: "Now they've gone and fixed up Beale Street. Well, we didn't expect Beale Street to be like it used to be anyway. Everybody goes to Beale Street now. But during the old days, the clientele on Beale Street was black. Whites went down only on special occasions like the *Midnight Rambles.* When a road show would come to the Palace Theater, which was the showplace of the South, they would have matinees and two night shows. But on Thursday they'd have a third show at midnight that was for whites. They added a little spice to it. Have the girls strip and when they get right to the point, the lights would go out. You never saw anything. They'd tell spicy jokes and that sort of thing. That's what made it the *Midnight Rambles.* That was the only nights the whites came."[19]

One of Thomas's favorite lines aptly summarizes both the allure and his own celebration of the famous street: "Beale Street was heaven for the black man. You'd come up from the Delta and go to Beale Street, don't owe nobody, no nothin'. I told a white fella on Beale Street one night, I said, 'If you were black for one Saturday night on Beale Street, you never would wanna be white anymore.'"[20]

But even more surprising to Robert and his Memphis neighbors than the emergence of WDIA and the *Midnight Rambles* was the appearance in 1948 for the first time ever of black postal clerks in the city. Even this news, which made the front page of the black Memphis *World,* was overshadowed by the sight of black policeman on Beale Street and the surrounding neighborhood. While the first thirteen black Memphis police academy graduates were not permitted to arrest white lawbreakers (they could hold them until white policemen arrived), they did receive the same salary paid to white officers, and, according to both local and national black newspapers, were unanimously greeted by the black community as a major advancement in Memphis race relations at the time, even though their main job was to keep peace in black Memphis, particularly in the blues and jazz spots in the Beale Street area—Club Tropicana, the Hippodrome, Club Handy, and others.[21]

Among the first group of black police officers hired was Ernest C. Withers, a World War II veteran born in Memphis in 1922. While serving on Saipan during the war he had developed an interest in photography, and earned beer money by making photos that fellow soldiers could send home. After three years on the police force, Withers quit to pursue a full-time career as a photographer to the Memphis black community, first taking publicity photos for the clubs he had patrolled and musicians who played in them, and later as a photo journalist for the *Tri-State Defender*, Memphis's new black newspaper, as well as *Ebony* and *Jet* magazines. His photographs chronicled not only the Memphis music scene, in which Robert Bland was soon to play a major role, but also the civil rights struggle throughout the South and black middle-class life and Negro League baseball in and around Memphis. His stark, powerful photography, which he continued to pursue until his death in 2007, is collected in several books that represent in bold detail the life and times of a people otherwise ignored, confined, and isolated by the white Southern establishment.[22]

Young Robert seemed to thrive in this relative isolation. He soon graduated from delivering groceries on his bicycle to a more lucrative position at Bender's Parking Garage at Beale and Third streets. His stepfather, Leroy, had taught him how to drive at an early age, and soon after earning his first driver's license he was working fifteen hours a day parking cars for Peabody Hotel guests for $27 a week. He soon developed a reputation in the neighborhood as a sober and reliable driver—at a time and place where not many working men knew how to drive or could afford to buy a car. In 1945 the level of auto ownership in the United States was just 0.69 per household nationwide.[23]

Later Robert was hired to drive laborers from downtown Memphis to the Delta cotton fields of Mississippi and Arkansas. With his earliest childhood memories still vivid and with these daily trips, he was soon convinced that this was as close as he ever wanted to be to cotton fields and the back-breaking work required to maintain them. When he had saved enough money and with his stepfather's help he purchased his first car, a 1949 Ford. And with it, he earned $5.00 and a tank of gas for each round trip from Memphis to West Junction, chauffeuring customers to the bootleggers who sold their wares there.[24]

When he was not driving, Robert was helping his mother, who by 1950 had saved enough money to buy an established soul food restaurant named the Sterling Grill. The family moved to an apartment above the Grill and Goodlett's Drug Store at 280½ South Third Street, on the east side of the street between Linden and East Pontotoc, just half a block from what is now the FedEx Forum. Robert did not care much for working in the restaurant, clearing tables and washing dishes. He would rather be driving or out listening to music at night, but his mother insisted and Robert did as he was told. After all, his mother was the one constant in his life, the one person he could depend on, the one who had raised him, taken care of him, even encouraged his love of music and brought him to Memphis to give him more opportunity. It was true, Robert knew, that he was a "mama's boy," but he didn't care. He loved his mother and he had grown accustomed to and relied on her always being there for him. Besides, her restaurant sported a new Wurlitzer juke box and on it played the most popular hits of the day. The Sterling Grill became a popular hangout (and remained so until 1961) for downtown workers and musicians, and there Robert met some of the people making the music that was percolating everywhere around him into an innovative, intoxicating brew.[25]

These more urban sounds of the jukebox and Beale Street were soon to replace as his favorites the country songs he had learned to love and sing from the radio back in Barretville. But his first musical love was not so easily superseded: on Sundays, as he always had, Robert attended church with his mother and grandmother, and soon he was singing in the choir at his family's Baptist church in Memphis; eventually he joined a gospel group. "This is my background, all the way up to the blues that I'm doing today," Bland told Jim O'Neal in a 1970 interview for *Living Blues*. "It's a spiritual background, because I started in the choir. This was in Memphis, Tennessee. During that time the Pilgrim Travelers was a very, very, very hot group, and so we called ourself the Miniatures, what you would have called the local Pilgrim Travelers. We had five guys together and we never did anything professional, like on records, but it did start, it originates, from the church. And after that I just started out. I love to sing, always, and I find myself doing rhythm and blues, rock 'n' roll, what have you, but I still have the spiritual thing in all the tunes that I do." On the radio, he listened to the latest gospel hits from not only the Pilgrim Travelers but also the Highway QC's, the Mighty Clouds of Joy, the Soul Stirrers, and his favorites, Ira Tucker and the Dixie Hummingbirds.[26]

When he was not singing in church, working and listening to the juke box in his mother's restaurant, or driving someone somewhere, Robert was on Beale Street, where he could hear a wide variety of music. All the theaters typically had movies during the week and live entertainment on the weekends—the Malco (originally and currently the Orpheum) at Main and Beale, the Old Daisy at 329 Beale, the New Daisy right across the street, and the largest black entertainment venue in the South, the Palace Theater, which had once been affiliated with the Theater Owners' Booking Association (TOBA). The TOBA organization brought national tours into the Palace, including Alberta Hunter, Ma Rainey, and Bessie Smith. Some performers claimed TOBA really stood for Tough On Black Asses because of the low pay and shabby conditions on the circuit. Later, after the demise of TOBA, the Palace continued to host top touring acts like Duke Ellington, Count Basie, and Ella Fitzgerald.[27]

At the corner of Beale and Hernando is Handy Park, where Robert often stopped to listen to the musicians who played for tips there. It was dedicated to W. C. Handy by Boss Crump on March 29, 1931, to placate blacks on whose votes he relied heavily, and to keep other facilities white. This was mostly blues and jug band territory at the time; Beale Street clubs featured jazz and the more urbane blues style just emerging.[28]

Around the corner, at Union and Second Street, is the Peabody Hotel, completed in 1925, and in whose opulent lobby it is said that the Mississippi Delta begins.[29] Furry Lewis, Charlie McCoy, Speckled Red, and other area bluesmen were first recorded at the Peabody by northern record companies in the 1920s and 1930s. But by the time Robert arrived in Memphis, no black music was played at the Peabody, except occasional performances by the Jubilee Singers, a choral group composed of the hotel's waiters, maids, and laundry workers.[30] Other black music in Memphis was performed by trained musicians who could read scores and play a wide variety of music upon request or as accompaniment to traveling shows at the Palace and other Beale Street theaters.

Memphis jug bands were also popular for dances around Memphis in the 1920s through the 1940s, playing a mixture of blues, ragtime, minstrel tunes, and pop music upon request. They usually consisted of a mixture of found, homemade, and legitimate instruments, including kazoos, banjos, guitars, harmonicas, and washtub or jug basses. Two of the most frequently employed jug bands were Gus Cannon's Jug Stompers and the Memphis Jug Band, who would regularly make more on tips from drunken partiers than they would from fees.[31]

In the late 1940s Robert could still hear plenty of down-home blues in Memphis: in Handy Park, wafting from the gambling dens, pool halls, and juke joints in his neighborhood, and especially across the river, via the new Memphis–Arkansas Bridge that opened in 1949. West Memphis, Arkansas, was where the funkier, electrified blues of Howlin' Wolf and Sonny Boy Williamson (Rice Miller) was being blasted in clubs like the Little Brown Jug, the Sixteenth Street Grill, and the Cotton Club, a white nightspot that hired black blues bands. In 1949 Sonny Boy Williamson (Rice Miller) and Howlin' Wolf were also broadcasting over West Memphis's KWEM radio station, often hosting guest appearances by the likes of Robert Lockwood, Joe Willie Wilkins, and Elmore James.[32]

"At that time," Rufus Thomas recalls, "the bigger and better black clubs in Memphis had a big band and a floor show. We had people like Duke Ellington and Count Basie coming through with their bands and playing in some theaters. The blues, with harmonica and guitar and so on, that was in the juke joints. Now I was born in the country, but I never lived there. I was raised in town. A person like me might want to go out and dig some blues occasionally. People from the so-called best families did that from time to time. It was just a part of living. But that would be what they called slumming. When you decided you wanted to go slumming that's when you went out to dig some blues."[33]

Many of these electrified juke bluesmen, direct descendants musically of the Delta country bluesmen ("I took the old-time music and brought it up to date," Muddy Waters said), eventually hopped Illinois Central trains north to Chicago and Detroit, where they played their down-home style for other Southerners who had migrated there. Muddy Waters, born McKinley Morganfield, in Rolling Fork, Mississippi, left Clarksdale for Chicago in May 1943, stopping in Memphis only long enough to change trains. Howlin' Wolf, born Chester Arthur Burnett in West Point, Mississippi, stayed awhile longer in Memphis, but joined Muddy and scores of other Delta bluesmen, including Elmore James, Robert Jr. Lockwood, and Jimmy Reed in Chicago by the mid-1950s, where they worked the factories by day and the South Side juke joints and lounges by night. John Lee Hooker, Sonny Boy Williamson, Eddie Burns, and Eddie Kirkland developed the sound in Detroit, where Southerners both black and white were finding jobs on the automobile assembly lines.[34]

They expanded their country sound to compete with the larger, noisier city crowds by electrifying their traditional instruments—guitar and harmonica—and adding piano, drums, and bass. Their sound came to be known as juke blues or Chicago blues, which is still enjoyed today, primarily by white audiences, in several Chicago clubs and venues elsewhere throughout the world.

Young Robert Bland, like Rufus Thomas, spent more time listening to the more urbane, jazz-inflected sounds in Beale Street clubs than to the gritty blues in Handy Park and the dingy bars of West Memphis. Among the most popular singers at the time were Amos Milburn, Charles Brown, Lowell Fulson, T-Bone Walker, Louis Jordan, and Jimmy Witherspoon—all of which Robert, at one time or the other, has said influenced him. Many of these performers had national R&B hits that Robert listened to on WDIA and on the jukebox in his mother's restaurant. Some regularly toured the South and Midwest and stopped in Beale Street clubs, where Robert enjoyed them live.

Charles Keil, in his 1966 classic *Urban Blues*, postulates that the foundation of these singers' styles, and subsequently that of B.B. King's and Robert Bland's, originated not on Beale Street but in the clubs and dance halls of Kansas City, where, before the demise of the Pendergast machine in 1938, all-night jazz and blues clubs were in rambunctious abundance.[35]

If Memphis was run by Boss Crump, Kansas City was run by the Pendergast machine. And, as in Memphis, almost anything went as long as the machine was paid and white supremacy and complacency maintained.[36] The bands that provided the music in these wide-open Kansas City clubs were called Territory bands, because they not only played in Kansas City but also traveled regularly throughout Missouri, Kansas, Oklahoma, Texas, Arkansas, and Tennessee, including Memphis—the so-called Territories. Keil points out: "The key men of the swing era and the golden age of jazz (Bennie Moten, Walter Page, Alphonse Trent, Troy Floyd, Jesse Stone, Hot Lips Page, Count Basie), the seminal figures in what came to be known as bebop (Buster Smith, Tommy Douglas, Lester Young, Charlie Christian, and Charlie Parker), the leaders of today's jazz avant-garde (Ornette Coleman, Don Cherry, Charlie Mingus, and many other young men whose families migrated from the Territories to Los Angeles), the originators of modern or urban blues and its more commercial offshoots rhythm and blues and rock and roll—all were Territory men."[37]

In addition to Kansas City and Los Angeles, the Territory sound was soon spreading, not just throughout the Territories and the West Coast but in every major American city with a sizeable black population. Texas, the biggest state in the Territories and future home of Bobby Bland, claimed more than its share of Territory band talent. Jazz greats Gus Johnson, Gene Ramey, Alphonse Trent, Eddie Durham, Herschel Evans, Oran "Hot Lips" Page, among many others, all hailed from the Lone Star State.[38] Atlanta, Nashville, New Orleans, Oklahoma City, St. Louis, Tulsa all boasted Territory stylists, and, in Memphis, Robert enjoyed the swinging sounds of Rufus Thomas and Gatemouth Moore who were adding a more southern country and gospel slant to the mix.

All these Territory bands, whether based in Memphis, Kansas City, Dallas, or transplanted to and imitated in Los Angeles and other major cities, combined blues and jazz in ways not heard previously, and the musicians who developed the sound did not draw a distinction between the two genres. Vocalists Jimmy Witherspoon and Al Hibbler, originally with the great Jay McShann band, saw the two as one entity, as did other Kansas City–based singers such as Jimmy Rushing, Joe Turner, and Walter Brown.

Jay McShann put it this way: "Back in them times these cats were so good at jazz [that] they tried to look down on the blues players, ya know. But I always played jazz and blues together. I thought they went together, heh heh. I did. I always felt that the blues was set there so that when ya got through with this other stuff you had it to come on and fall back on, fall back on the blues. Ya get tired of playin' jazz. Somebody call out, 'Hey, man. Play the blues.' Heh, heh, they start all that hollerin' and screamin' and stuff. Or he says it in a relaxin' manner. So you relax and play the blues."[39]

B.B. King recalls as a child peeking through the slats of Jones Night Spot in Indianola, Mississippi, to see the preeminent Territory band of Count Basie: "I'd heard of Count Basie on the radio; I knew the band came from Kansas City and sounded good. But listen here: This was better than good. With brass blaring and saxes moaning, they played 'One O'Clock Jump' and 'Jumpin' at the Woodside' and 'Taxi War Dance' and had a short man fat as Santa Claus singing 'Evil Blues.' Later I'd learn the singer was Jimmy Rushing. Mr. Five by Five. He had a high nasal voice that brought home his message. I think of him now as the Henry Ford of the blues, one of the true inventors. I ran my eye over the band members dressed in matching green suits—the saxist holding his horn horizontally was Lester Young, the light-handed rhythm guitarist Freddie Green, the bass player Walter Page, the drummer Papa Jo Jones. In a few years, I'd read these names in magazines. As a teen, though, I could only identify the round-faced man at the piano as Count Basie and the music he projected as modern and swinging and beautifully loud, as bluesy as anything I'd heard in the Delta. I believe I listened harder than anyone in the history of listening."[40]

However, two other Territory bands had the greatest influence on King, Bland, and many other young mid-century Memphis musicians, those of Louis Jordan and T-Bone Walker. Jordan, a talented saxophonist and singer, originally from Brinkley, Arkansas (about an hour from Memphis), developed his style playing in the Earl Hines and Billy Eckstine *Blue Ribbon Salute* shows in the early 1940s. He later formed his own band, the Tympany Five (actually with six, seven, or eight members), a so-called "jump band" that played up-beat, swing music, usually with a strong saxophone line and humorous, often double entendre lyrics. "I made the blues jump," said Jordan. His bouncy music and flagrant self-promotion made the territory-style music popular nationally and provided the precursor to modern rhythm and blues and rock 'n' roll. During the 1940s he was the undisputed leader of the R&B charts, having nearly a third of all the top black hits, many of which crossed over to the pop charts. He was the only African American musician to do so consistently besides Fats Waller and Louis Armstrong.[41] "I could play a white joint this week and a colored next," Jordan boasted. Between 1938 and 1946 he recorded five million-selling 78s, due in part to a device called a nickelodeon which combined a juke-box with a screen and a tape loop of a brief portion of Jordan's live show—the precursor of modern music videos.[42]

T-Bone Walker, reared in Dallas and relocated to California in 1934, brought the guitar into prominence as part of the band and show and, at his height in popularity, fronted a big band that represented the ultimate in Territory styling, sparkle, and showmanship. His electric guitar playing featured string bending and long sustained notes, jazz techniques he had learned from fellow Texans Eddie Durham and Charlie Christian. Walker started out working with the legendary Blind Lemon Jefferson in Dallas during the 1920s. Jefferson's string bending and his improvisational and harmonic approach to the guitar, with jazz embellishments, were applied by Walker in a big band setting, creating a unique confluence of blues, jazz, and pop music.[43]

Call it what you want—"urban blues" as Charles Keil named it; "soul blues" as blues historian David Evans refers to it; "southern soul" as it is often termed today by *Living Blues* magazine and others; or simply "modern blues"—the twelve-bar country blues was complemented by the eight- and sixteen-bar patterns of gospel and popular music. The basic recipe, emanating in Kansas City, crafted in Memphis, and perfected by B.B. King and Bobby Bland goes something like this: Start with a big combustible bouillabaisse of Territory jazz/blues band, add a pinch of sharp, sustained electric guitar, mix in a tad of howling horns, stir in a dollop of good old down-home Delta blues, and top it off with a gospel-inspired vocalist, with just a touch of smooth country twang. Here you have the makings of the new rhythm and blues sound, the foundation of soul music, the sound that dominated black popular music for the next three decades until rap and hip-hop emerged in the 1980s, and that remains to this day the only true blues music that African Americans still listen to.

The Beale Streeters: Robert Bland, Earl Forest on drums, Adolph "Billy" Duncan on tenor saxophone, and John Alexander (Johnny Ace) on piano, at Memphis radio station WDIA, ca. 1949. Copyright Ernest C. Withers Estate, courtesy Panopticon Gallery, Boston, MA.

2

Loan Me a Helping Hand

1949–1952

The prominent A&R (Artist and Repertoire) head of Atlantic Records, Jerry Wexler, coined the term "rhythm & blues" in 1949. Later that year, in its June 25th issue, *Billboard* substituted that term for the word "race" in a chart labeled since 1945 as "The Top 15 Best Selling Race Records," and previously since 1942 as the "Harlem Hit Parade." The change was made not only in recognition that *race* held derogatory social implications, but also because the music of black America had changed dramatically since the term "race records" was initially coined in 1922, from vaudeville and country blues to jump bands, jazz, shouters, and crooners.[1]

Among the most influential young musicians who developed this rhythm & blues sound in Memphis during the 1950s was a loose affiliation of performers who later became known as "the Beale Streeters." The group included at one time or another vocalist and guitarist B.B. King, vocalist Bobby Bland, vocalist and pianist Johnny Ace, vocalist and drummer Earl Forest, and saxophonist Adolph "Billy" Duncan.[2]

Exactly how they became acquainted is open to conjecture. Charles Keil admitted that, in researching *Urban Blues*, "I am still confused about developments in Memphis during this period, largely because none of the principal innovators is eager to re-examine the 'wild oats' phase of his career. Jr. Parker's comment is typical: 'I can't really tell you much about the other blues singers in those days, but I can remember a whole lot of good telephone numbers from my little book.'"[3]

B.B. King recalled, in an interview with Arnold Shaw, that he first performed alone on WDIA, and then later added pianist John Alexander (later to become Johnny Ace) and drummer Earl Forest to form a trio. Still later, saxophonist Adolph "Billy" Duncan was added,[4] replacing Richard Sanders, King's first saxophonist.[5] "I guess you could say this was the first little-bitty B.B. King band," King writes in his autobiography.[6] Ernestine Mitchell, who ran the Mitchell Hotel on Beale Street, remembered Rosco Gordon as an occasional member of the group as well,[7] although Gordon and King both deny that there ever was a formal group called the Beale Streeters at this point.[8]

They no doubt heard each other at local clubs. B.B. King mentions talking with other musicians in Handy Park. Bobby remembers B.B. frequenting his mother's restaurant. "All the musicians coming through would stop at Mrs. Bland's place," Bobby said in an interview with Robert Gordon. "B.B. King was a regular customer there. I idolized him and I still do. This was before B.B.'s first record came out. We were on Amateur Nights together on Beale Street."[9] Indeed, Bobby and all of the so-called Beale Streeters recall two Memphis gathering spots, above all others: the Wednesday Amateur Nights at the Palace Theater and the late night jam sessions at Mitchell's Hotel.

The largest crowds at the Palace Theater on Beale were for Amateur Night, begun in 1935 as a revival of the amateur shows that the old minstrel men held years before on Beale. At eight o'clock every Wednesday night, the lights would go down, the curtain would part, and the spotlight would center on the master of ceremonies, Nat Williams, until 1940, when Rufus Thomas took over. The orchestra would blast out "Beale Street Blues" as a line of anxious amateurs waited in the wings.[10]

The Palace's Amateur Night audiences were said to be the world's most demanding. At New York's Apollo Theater, the amateur night audience was so tough, "they would boo their own mama off the stage," according to Rufus Thomas. "But they weren't as tough as Memphis."[11] There were one-legged dancers, jugglers, comics, glass eaters, and blues singers of all ages and ilk. If the audience did not like the performer, they threw paper bags in winter, tomatoes in summer. No simple hook like the Apollo; if the would-be star was booed and pelted and still would not give up, the audience would raise such an uproar that the "Lord High Executioner" would leap from the wings and shoot him with a pearl-handled revolver. Usually one blank shot would do it, but the Executioner would not hesitate to empty his gun if necessary to remove the reluctant amateur.[12]

All the Beale Streeters, at one time or another, competed, with varied success, on Amateur Night at the Palace. The first was a skinny blues singer from Mississippi named Riley King, who debuted in 1946. Rufus Thomas recollects:

> First they had the movies and then the amateur, which was the bottom hour, and then it was back to the movies. I reached back and got a friend of mine, his name was Robert Counts, they called him Bones, and we were together for eleven consecutive years at the Palace Theater every Wednesday night. I tell you, you wouldn't believe this, but we were making five dollars a night, and you had Al Jackson's band—that was Al Jackson, Sr.—and I found out that they were only

making twenty-five dollars, and they had a big band, too. Course the show was only a nickel then, but the place was packed. In the beginning we used to have $5, $3, and $2 prizes, but then they cut that out and everybody who come up on stage would get a dollar. B.B. used to come with holes in his shoes, his guitar all patched up, just to get that dollar. There was no graduation as such, but after he made "Three O'Clock," B. didn't come back to the Amateur Show no more. Well, you know, same with Bobby. I wrote one of the first songs that Bobby Bland ever sung, and he has promised me through the years that he would record that tune, but he hasn't recorded it yet. 'I got a new kind of loving that other men can't catch on / While they losing out I'm steady holding on.' It was a good tune. Bobby sang it on the Amateur Show and won first prize.[13]

In addition to singing Thomas's tune at the Palace, Bobby also recalls covering the popular hits of the day: "I was doing things off the jukebox. I had a lot to choose from, because they had good artists like Charles Brown, T-Bone Walker. You had B.B. King, you had Lowell Fulson, you had Jimmy Witherspoon, you had Big Joe Turner—just thousands of people that was a big hit in my surroundings. So I could just pick and choose. Roy Brown was one of the guys that kind of struck my fancy."[14]

"The first concert," Bobby recalls about his early days in Memphis, "would be Rufus Thomas, Rufus and Bones. They had an amateur show every Wednesday night on Beale Street at the Palace Theater, and people who thought that they could sing, like myself, could go in and try out. They would pay $5 for the top winner, $2 for the second, or whatever it was. I managed to win a couple of nights in a row, and then I had to kind of lay off because you can't win every night—people would think they have it fixed."[15]

Bobby also remembers one particularly important night at the Palace, "Was a scout out that night on the 27th of June in '51, because this was the first time I got a contract for a recording company."[16] The scout was WDIA's production manager/program director, David James Mattis; the following year, Mattis would launch Duke Records, and he was affected enough by Bobby's performance that night to sign him as one of the label's first acts.[17]

If there was a resident father figure for all these aspiring young musicians it had to be Andrew "Sunbeam" Mitchell. He was born in Memphis in 1906 and operated the Mitchell Hotel, which occupied the third floor above Abe Plough's Pantaze Drug Store ("You Never Pay More, Often Less") at the corner of Beale and Hernando.[18] Mitchell loved musicians, especially blues musicians, and kept the Beale Streeters and others fed when times were tough.

"The street had a spirit best represented by Sunbeam Mitchell, patron saint of Memphis musicians," recalls B.B. King. "Sunbeam owned Mitchell's Hotel on the third floor and a lounge, called the Domino, on the second where he had jam sessions during the week and name bands on the weekends. That was the place to hear the heaviest dudes. I call Sunbeam a saint 'cause he'd give you a room and board for free if you had a halfway decent story or could play halfway decent blues. Sunbeam loved music and cared for the folks who made it."[19]

The Mitchell Hotel opened in 1944 and was billed as "Memphis' Leading Colored Hotel." Mitchell also owned the Mitchell Grill at 195 South Third and the Club Ebony at 500 Beale Street. Since the musicians who played in his night clubs were not allowed to stay at the Peabody or other whites-only hotels, it was only natural for the entrepreneurial Mitchell to enter the hotel business. Mitchell's wife-to-be, Ernestine McKinney, managed the hotel, which had thirty rooms and boasted "gas heat and modern baths."[20]

In the late 1940s the Mitchells changed the name of their lounge from the Domino to the Club Handy, on the second floor of the building that dated back to 1896, with an entrance at 195 Hernando. Club Handy continued to be one of the most popular blues and jazz venues in Memphis, featuring the likes of Lionel Hampton, Dizzy Gillespie, Sonny Boy Williamson, and B.B. King, and was the last to close before Urban Renewal in the 1970s. In his book *Elvis*, Albert Goldman reported that even the King was a frequent visitor to the Club Handy and one night sang "Good Rocking Tonight" and "wore the place out."[21] (The Center for Southern Folklore moved to the building in October 1996 and spotlighted the hotel/club in its award-winning documentary film *All Day and All Night: Memories from Beale Street Musicians*.)[22]

Mitchell recalled:

> *I got started with Mitchell's Hotel on top of the Pantaze Drug Store at Beale and Hernando. Then I put in the old Club Domino up there and later changed the name to the Club Handy. The old musicians—Roy Brown, Sonny Boy Williamson, Ray Charles, Joe Tex, people like that—would play in the club on the second floor and stay in the hotel on the third floor.*
>
> *Little Richard stayed at the hotel for weeks when he didn't have any money. He would come down and eat chili with us every day because we fed him free. I helped B.B. King when he went out on his first professional date. He didn't even have a car at the time. Joe Tex stayed with me a whole year at the hotel. All of them knew they could come to Memphis and be taken care of in those days.*[23]

The Mitchell Hotel was the usual place to end the day for Bobby and the other Beale Streeters. There they could find other musicians, a good bowl of chili, and a friendly place to unwind, to perform, and to try out new ideas. "We never did close because somebody was constantly coming in," Ernestine Mitchell remembers. "Like all the fellows play gigs someplace else? When they got off they'd come and get some chili. I don't care if it was West Memphis or wherever they was, they would come. I don't care how far they was, all of them, carloads of them, would stop by. Then they'd get to talking, drinking, then jamming. That was just a nightly thing."

"I can remember many nights sitting back and watching the great jam sessions," B.B. King says, "because after the show usually everybody would go to Mitchell's." Rufus Thomas recalls that the young players would arrive with their instruments and listen awhile to the jam session before deciding whether to join. If it was "too hot for him, he would take that horn and ease right back out the door."

The house band for the Club Handy was led by Bill Harvey, an accomplished alto sax man, who had worked his way through Tennessee State University.[24] He and his band would later work as studio musicians for Peacock and Duke Records and provide members for the road bands of B.B. King, Johnny Ace, and Bobby Bland. "Harvey was a learned musician with a passion for teaching," Charles Sawyer reported, "and the Club Handy was a kind of Academy of Rhythm and Blues. . . . The joint was small, and it was combined with limited hotel accommodations; in fact, some of the sleeping rooms opened directly into the bar room itself. Harvey's musicians lived in the hotel and ate in Mitchell's kitchen, while Harvey schooled them in basic musicianship. Over the years, dozens of young musicians cut their chops in Harvey's makeshift school."[25]

"He did a lot for Memphis musicians," according to B.B. King. "Harvey stayed at Mitchell's Hotel and played there. He had the freedom to do what he wanted with the arrangements. Everybody came to him, Joe Scott, Calvin Owens, Phineas Newborn . . ."[26] Bill played a band like Willie Mays played the outfield. He had it covered."[27]

"Well, I couldn't say enough about Sunbeam," Bobby said, "for the simple reason that Sunbeam has helped any entertainer who ever did anything—who came through Memphis at one time or another. Sunbeam and Mrs. Ernestine Mitchell, who is his wife, helped me first of all. I used to worry 'em to death every weekend, in fact. Bill Harvey had the band during that time and when they'd see me coming in the room they'd say, 'Aw, here he comes, he wants to sing.' And they wanted to play basically jazz, you understand what I'm saying? They weren't really into it until Sunbeam would say, 'Well, let him sing.' You know, that type of thing, and he had been that way for anybody. Every entertainer that has come through Memphis, Sunbeam has helped them one way or the other. They had Mitchell's Hotel there and if you didn't have a place to stay, Sunbeam and Mrs. Ernestine had a place for you to stay and something for you to eat. But you had to work 'cause Ernestine did not take no jive!"[28]

It was here at Mitchell's that the Beale Streeters often performed for "five dollars a night and all the chili they could eat," according to Bobby,[29] and where Bobby approached B.B. one night: "I said B., why don't you let me help you with your stuff? To drive or whatever. So he'd take me with him to small towns near Memphis if I didn't have anything to do—which was all the time. I learned a lot just standing around."[30]

"To be honest with you, I don't remember the first time I met Bobby," B.B. admitted. "I do remember going to his mother's café, but I knew Bobby before I started going in there. I knew him in '49, cause, I remember, I had a '49 Chevy and Bobby had a '49 Ford. The radio station that I worked for [WDIA] leased the Chevy for me because it had the call letters on it."[31]

B.B. King was born Riley B. King on September 16, 1925, in a sharecropper's cabin near the tiny Delta town of Itta Bena, Mississippi. His grandfather was a bottleneck guitarist and his cousin (actually his mother's cousin) was the famous bluesman, Bukka White, who young Riley lived with for ten months when he first arrived in Memphis in May, 1946, with $2.50 in his pocket. In the Delta, B.B. was already well-schooled in gospel music, singing in church choirs and quartets. As a teenager, he began teaching himself how to play guitar. He listened carefully to the radio and local juke boxes and his ear became more attuned to the stylings of lead guitarists like Lonnie Johnson and T-Bone Walker than area Delta players. In the late 1940s, B.B. learned timing and chording techniques from Robert Lockwood in West Memphis, as well as the single-string lead style that B.B. already favored. Along the way, B.B. was also influenced by the leading jazz guitarists of the time, Charlie Christian and Django Reinhart, as well as Memphis guitarist Calvin Newborn. But given all this jazz influence, B.B. was still a Delta boy at heart and his gospel-tinged singing and blues song selection would never betray these early roots.[32]

By 1948, B.B. was good enough to pull in a regular gig at the Sixteenth Street Grill in West Memphis, and was performing on Sonny Boy Williamson's radio show on KWEM, a West Memphis station famous for featuring the electrified blues of Howlin' Wolf.[33] But his big break came later that year when he walked into the studios of WDIA, the new black radio station in Memphis.

According to WDIA chronicler Louis Cantor, B.B. showed up at the door of the radio station one rainy day soaked to the bone with his old guitar wrapped in a newspaper to keep it dry. Apparently he had walked from the Greyhound bus station downtown, all the way to the WDIA studios at 2074 Union Avenue, a distance of several miles. There, according to B.B., he stood, dripping wet, in his army fatigue jacket—"That was about all I had in my wardrobe at that time"—looking through the window into the studio where Nat D. Williams was on the air. B.B. waited patiently until Williams turned off his microphone and then he knocked on the studio door. B.B. remembers that Nat's first words were: "What can I do for you, young fellow?" To which B.B. replied that he'd "like to make a record and go on the air."

For some reason, Williams was intrigued by the young man and asked Bert Ferguson and Don Kern, the station's white owners, to come and meet him. "Mr. Ferguson came up and took a look at me," B.B. recalls. "You know how he looked through those glasses." Ferguson told him, "We don't make records, but it is possible that we might be able to use you."

So they took him into a studio and auditioned him right then and there. Ferguson and Kern were so impressed that they decided to put him on the air that same afternoon for ten minutes. Soon after, he was given a live ten-minute segment on Nat's Jamboree, singing his own songs and a jingle that he wrote for the show's sponsor, the tonic medicine, Peptikon—"Peptikon sure is good. You can get it anywhere in your neighborhood."[34]

As he developed a larger and larger radio audience, he promoted his club dates over the air, and then plugged his radio show wherever he and the Beale Streeters played live. As his popularity grew, B.B. was given a longer show, called *The Sepia Swing Club*, and a new name, "Beale Street Blues Boy," later shortened to "Blues Boy," and finally to "B.B."[35] By 1950 and 1951, B.B. and his band had become, according to Nick Tosches, "the premier band of Memphis."[36]

While Bobby did accompany B.B. on some gigs, he was never really a part of the group until B.B. left it. "It's not true," King insists, "Bobby was never my driver or my valet. Not that I know anything about. He never did work with me. We'd jam a lot and might be singing with the same band at a jam session, but we never actually worked together. He was the good singer though, not me."[37] But Bobby still learned a lot about performing from B.B., as well as gaining some first-hand experience on how to lead and manage a working band—both lessons that would prove invaluable to him in the years ahead.

"Then I got a chance to run into Rufus Thomas," Bobby recalls. "He and B.B. King were doing a couple of tunes on Saturday at WDIA. He was advertising Peptikon. So he would invite me—and he didn't have much time for himself. That's the reason why I say that I love him as a person and also a friend. He'd let me do a partial tune or at least one, or I'd either do something with him."[38]

B.B. remembers that at about this time Bobby gave him a nickname that he still uses to this day. "Bobby calls me Doc," King laughed. "When I was on the radio, once there was a guy who had a band called Doc Sausage. The guys tried to get me by calling me Doc. I think Bill Harvey started it, but Bobby always called me Doc with respect. Don't think he ever calls me B."[39]

In 1949, King cut his first four recordings for the Bullet Recording and Transcription Company, which was owned and operated by Jim Bulleit, a former Grand Ole Opry radio announcer for WSM in Nashville. Bulleit started out by making country records, then expanded to the so-called race-record market with his Sepia series, and eventually to the pop market, where he hit it big with Francis Craig's "Near You," a chart-topper in 1947. Bullet's most popular R&B act was the blues shouter, Wynonie Harris. Meanwhile, back in Memphis Sam Phillips was looking to get started in the recording business and sold an interest in his own start-up company to Bulleit, which Bulleit later sold back to Phillips.[40]

Such convoluted transactions were not uncommon at the time, as the record business was spawning a whole new flock of independent labels, like Bullet and later Sam Phillips's Sun, which would discover, record, and distribute the new R&B and rock 'n' roll performers that the three major labels—Decca, Columbia, and RCA-Victor—were all but ignoring. These new entrepreneurial record companies came about as the result of three independent factors: World War II, a musicians strike, and new recording technology.

The main ingredient in early record discs, shellac, was made from the secretions of an insect called the lac beetle. Unfortunately, this lac beetle refused to live anywhere outside of Southeast Asia, and the Japanese occupiers of that region didn't see why they should continue shipping shellac to a country that was shooting at them. So, faced with a shortage of shellac throughout World War II, the major labels cut production of anything other than mainstream pop music, leaving an opening for smaller, independent labels to fill the void.

Then, during 1942 and 1943, a strike by the American Federation of Musicians against the record industry virtually closed the recording studios. The union charged that the records were replacing live music in clubs and on radio and thereby threatening the livelihoods of its members. The major record companies waited out the strike, relying on their back lists to keep them going. But once the strike was over, the new independent labels were a lot faster and nimbler in signing new talent and getting records out to the record-starved public.[41]

World War II did, however, bring one major benefit to the floundering record industry. American audio engineer, John T. Mullin, working with (Bing) Crosby Enterprises, used captured German sound recorders to develop the first commercially developed tape recorder, the Ampex 200, launched in 1948. With magnetic tape, music could be portably, easily, and relatively cheaply recorded, erased, and re-recorded on the same tape as many times as needed, and recordings could now be precisely edited by cutting the tape and rejoining it at any given location. While portable disc recording machines were becoming more readily available in the 1940s, this new tape technology had the effect of opening up the recording business even more, to about anyone who could afford the $4,000 for the new device and could locate a quiet place to use it.[42]

Which was pretty much what happened. Even though many important independent record labels were launched prior to 1948, between then and 1954, it is estimated that more than a thousand new record labels went into business.[43] Not only sound engineers, but also record store owners, radio repairmen, broadcasters, club owners, juke box suppliers, and even musicians could and did launch their own record labels in every major city of the U.S.[44] Among these pioneering independent R&B labels:

In Chicago, Aristocrat, was started in April 1947 by Charles and Evelyn Aron, Fred and Mildred Brount, and Art Spiegel. In September of that year, Leonard Chess invested in the company, and, by 1950, Leonard and his brother Phil, former night club owners, had gained full ownership of the company and changed its name to Chess. With its subsidiaries, Checker and Cadet, Chess produced hits by Muddy Waters, Howlin' Wolf, Chuck Berry, Etta James, Bo Diddley, Otis Rush, and many more.

In Cincinnati, King Records was started in 1945 by Syd Nathan, a former department store owner, who recorded, in addition to country records, on King and its subsidiaries–Queen, Bethlehem, Federal, and DeLuxe–Bill Doggett, Lonnie Johnson, Little Willie John, Ivory Joe Hunter, the Dominoes, and, of course, James Brown.

In New York, Ahmet Ertegun and Herb Abramson, two college students, started Atlantic Records in 1947, ultimately becoming the most successful independent label founded during this period, recording the likes of Solomon Burke, Ray Charles, the Drifters, the Coasters, the Clovers, Ruth Brown, LaVern Baker, Aretha Franklin, Percy Sledge, the Temptations, and Mary Wells, as well as a plethora of famous rock and pop acts.

In Los Angeles, the Specialty label was launched in 1946 by Art Rupe, a former part-owner of short-lived Atlas Records; Specialty produced popular records by Wynona Carr, John Lee Hooker, Little Richard, Percy Mayfield, and Lloyd Price.

In Newark, New Jersey, Herman Lubinsky, a former record store owner, started Savoy Records in 1942, and recorded Little Esther, Big Maybelle, Varetta Dillard, Nappy Brown, J.J. Johnson, as well as many jazz and gospel greats.[45]

B.B. King's initial four recordings for Bullet enhanced his local reputation, but they did not score nationally. They did, however, draw the attention of another independent record company based in Los Angeles's Watts district. Modern Music was founded in 1945 by Jules, Joe, and Saul Bihari, whose father had moved them in 1941 from Oklahoma, where he was a feed grain farmer and salesman. Joe Bihari recalled in an interview with Arnold Shaw: "My brother Jules operated juke boxes in all-black locations, and it was difficult to get R&B records at that time. His feeling of frustration was crystallized by the shortage of one particular record, Cecil Gant's 'I Wonder.' It was a monster. No matter how many copies he got, he still needed more. Finally, one day he said, 'Let's make records ourselves.'

"I was still in high school; Saul was at business college; but we all pitched in. We took the name Modern Music from a Galveston juke box company where brother Lester was working. I undertook the selling. Saul took charge of manufacturing and Jules handled the recording. He had been wanting to make records, and I guess the success of that ex-pressing plant worker who recorded 'I Wonder' in his garage gave him the confidence to try it."

Modern and its subsidiaries RPM, Kent, Crown, and Flair eventually grew to become one of the most successful of the 1940s independent labels, producing records by some of the biggest stars of the time, including John Lee Hooker, Pee Wee Crayton, Elmore James, Jimmy Witherspoon, and Etta James.[46]

To tap into the talent in the South, brother Lester set up shop in Memphis and hired a young man named Ike Turner from nearby Clarksdale, Mississippi, as Modern's talent scout in the area. Brother Joe recalls, "Ike wasn't more than sixteen then. He would send dubs of things he cut to us, and if we liked them we'd make a deal or sign the artist. That's how we acquired B.B. King."[47]

In the summer of 1949, Modern's RPM label released six B.B. singles that became local best-sellers and increased demand for appearances by B.B. and his band in the tri-state area—in clubs like Slackbritches in Birdsong, Arkansas; Club Casablanca in Blytheville, Arkansas; the Blue Flame in Covington, Tennessee; Stevens Lounge in Jackson, Mississippi; and Jones' Night Spot in B.B.'s hometown of Indianola, Mississippi—dives, juke joints, roadhouses, and dance halls of all description, where, besides the blues, drinking, gambling, and prostitution often thrived.[48]

In late 1951, RPM released B.B.'s seventh single, "Three O'Clock Blues," a Lowell Fulson song popular in Memphis then, featuring, in addition to B.B. on guitar and vocals, Billy Duncan and Richard Sanders on tenor sax, Johnny Ace on piano, Earl Forest on drums, and Tuff Green on bass. By the end of 1951, it had reached the number one position on the *Billboard's* R&B chart where it stayed for seventeen straight weeks.*[49]

King believes that the song was actually recorded in 1949,[50] and Modern's Joe Bihari remembered that "Three O'Clock Blues" was recorded at the Memphis YMCA on a new portable tape recorder. "They had a large room," he told Arnold Shaw, "with an out-of-tune upright piano. At that session, we cut Johnny Ace, Rosco Gordon, and Bobby Bland—possibly also Ike Turner. By then we were recording on tape, not disk. Apart from B.B.'s debut hit, we got 'No More Doggin' by Rosco Gordon, which came onto best-seller lists just as 'Three O'Clock Blues' was beginning to fade."

None of the numbers that Bobby recorded for Modern at this session were released. "When 'Three O'Clock Blues' became a hit and I started to work out of a booking agency called Shaw Artists Corporation and Universal, they didn't want me to have a band," said B.B. in 1979. "They wanted me alone. So

I left the band, and when I did, I gave it to Johnny Ace. And that's when he changed it. Instead of calling it the 'Blues Boys' as it had been, he started calling it the 'Beale Streeters.'"[51] At this juncture, Bobby took over the vocal duties for the group, sharing them occasionally with Johnny Ace, at gigs in and around Memphis.

But it was Bobby's dependability as a driver, not as a singer, that resulted in Bobby striking up a friendship with another of Modern's up and coming young stars, pianist and vocalist Rosco Gordon. "I wasn't important at all, really," Bland said later. "I mean, I was fortunate enough to be able to sing, but, you see, I was the one who had the car."[52]

Rosco Gordon was born in Memphis on April 10, 1928, although he said he was born in 1934. The youngest of eight children, Rosco learned to play the piano by imitating his sister who had the benefit of a teacher. In 1946, he moved to Chicago "after getting in trouble in Memphis."

He returned to Memphis in 1949, and the next year won first place in the Wednesday night Amateur Show at the Palace Theater. "I wasn't really a musician," Rosco remembered modestly, "but my friends knew I could sing. . . . We had no wine money." The five dollars prize money presumably remedied that, but not before Rufus Thomas, the emcee and WDIA deejay, invited Rosco to visit the radio station. Within a week, he had his own show.[53]

As a result, Rosco was suddenly in demand to play around town. "Rosco, at all those juke joints," Bobby remembered, "he'd come straight off the stage and head right to the gambling room in back. Do little tricks with the dice—roll them and they stay together, just like soldiers. It's dangerous if somebody catches you. I'd be over in the corner, out of the way of dancing. The guy with the corn liquor would be back there if you needed a shot, and the houseman called all the bets and held the money. They had some big people to settle any argument that would happen. We all were hicks."

Rosco tells about a night when Bobby drove him to a show somewhere in Arkansas: "Bobby started singing and said, 'I got the voice, but my timing's bad.' I said, 'All you got to do is say one, two, three, four, sing, two, three, four, shut up, two . . .' So this night I was dicing—if you didn't have money to shoot dice with me, I'd give you some—and I put Bobby on the stage. That night nobody came to get me because Bobby sang all night."[54]

Sometime in 1951, WDIA station manager, David Mattis, introduced Rosco to Sam Phillips, who had founded the Memphis Recording Service the year before. Phillips, born in 1923, was, like Rosco Gordon, the youngest of eight children. He was raised on a farm near Florence, Alabama, W.C. Handy's hometown, where he gained an appreciation of black music. "I never did see white people singing a lot when they were chopping cotton," Sam remembered, "but the odd part about it is, I never heard a black man that couldn't sing *good.*

Even off-key, *their* singing had a spontaneity about it that would grab my ear."[55]

Phillips discovered Beale Street in 1939 when he was still in high school. "I was 16 years old," he remembered, "and I went to Memphis with some friends in a big old Dodge. We drove down Beale Street in the middle of the night and it was rockin'! The street was busy. It was active—musically, socially. God, I loved it!"[56]

After high school, Sam went to Alabama Polytechnic Institute in Auburn, Alabama, where he studied engineering, particularly audio engineering for radio. Then he kicked around radio stations in Alabama and Tennessee, landing at WREC in Memphis in June, 1945. At WREC, he hosted the *Saturday Afternoon Tea Dance*, where he played jazz, blues, and pop music from the Skyway Room of the Peabody Hotel,[57] where he also managed the hotel's public address systems.

As if that weren't enough to keep him busy, in 1950, Phillips decided to open his own recording service. He rented a small storefront at 706 Union Avenue for $150 a month and built a recording studio from scratch. At first, just to pay the rent, he recorded anything anyone wanted recorded, providing acetate disks of speeches, weddings, funerals, and other local events—"We Record Anything-Anywhere-Anytime." In the summer of 1950, Saul and Jules Bihari of Modern Music came to Memphis and booked Phillips's studio to record B.B. King and Rosco Gordon. Sam, having already been introduced to B.B. and Rosco by David Mattis, was familiar with their talents, but he had not signed either to a contract, nor did he have anything in writing from the Biharis. Meanwhile, Leonard Chess of Chess Records made several field trips looking for Southern blues talent and when he was in Memphis asked Sam to send him masters for possible release.[58]

So, in August 1951, Phillips, a veteran audio engineer, but a novice record producer, invited Rosco and his friend, Bobby Bland, whom he had heard at the Palace Theater's Amateur Night and on Rufus Thomas's WDIA show, to record some songs in his new studio, hoping that either the Bihari brothers or the Chess brothers might be interested. Rosco brought along the Beale Streeter regular Billy Duncan, as well as Willie Wilkes, to play tenor saxophone, and John Murray Daley to play drums. With Rosco on piano, the band cut several songs composed by Gordon and others. Two of them, "Saddled the Cow (And Milk the Horse)" and "Booted," became hits within weeks of their release.[59]

Phillips recorded several takes of "Booted" and sent one to Modern and one to Chess. The Modern/RPM version reached number 1 by February 9, 1952, and remained on *Billboard's* R&B chart for 13 weeks.[60] On the B-side of the 78 rpm Chess version, Phillips placed Robert Bland's first recording, "Love You Till the Day I Die," which went largely unnoticed, particularly amidst the controversy of who owned the rights to the Rosco's A-side hit, "Booted"—Modern or Chess? Gordon remembers that "I wrote a tune called 'Love You Till the Day I Die' and Bobby performed and I performed it together. But the other side [Chess 1487] was "Booted." That was the hit. 'Love You Till the Day I Die' just died right there."[61]

Now, standard recording contracts prescribe that an artist should not record the same tune for more than one record label within a five year period, but neither Phillips nor Gordon, neophytes to the record business, were familiar with these precepts, and for that matter, neither were the Bihari or Chess brothers, who were only a little less new to the business than Sam and Rosco. After considerable wrangling, a settlement was finally worked out that resulted in Modern signing Rosco exclusively and Chess signing Howlin' Wolf whose exclusivity arrangement was also in dispute.[62]

"Yeah, they had a thing going there," Gordon recalled years later. "See, they kept it hidden from me. But, after that, Chess, he didn't record me no more. They wouldn't have anything to do with me. Chess wouldn't. But, I didn't know any better. You know I'm like 16 years old. What do I know about doing the same tune for different companies. I didn't know. . . . Now 'Booted' stayed number one for 13 weeks. Sam Phillips gave me one hundred dollars. One hundred. No royalties. No nothin'. But, I did it for the Biharis, now they gave me six hundred dollars. No royalties. No nothin'. But, like I say, I didn't know any better."[63]

In addition to this fine mess, Ike Turner became impatient with Phillips for not cutting a record of his own after he had delivered the huge hit, "Rocket 88," which used Turner's band, but featured Jackie Brenston on vocals. Phillips sent the song to Chess, instead of Modern, so Turner decided to join the Biharis' Modern/RPM label as a talent scout and producer, taking his band with him, except Brenston who stayed with Chess, but nonetheless denying Phillips a chance to record the entire band on a follow-up to "Rocket 88."[64]

Typical of the wild-west nature of the independent recording industry at that time is the story of how "Rocket 88," which rock historians have named as one of the first rock 'n' roll tunes, got its unique sound. It seems that on the band's way from Clarksdale, Mississippi to Memphis to record for Phillips for the first time on a rainy March 5, 1951, guitarist Willie Kizart's amplifier fell off the top of the car, breaking the speaker cone. Sam Phillips remembers that the band was very disturbed about the broken woofer, "I said, 'Look, if an amplifier is going to keep us from cutting a record that's worthwhile, then we're not very good in the first place!' I wasn't discouraged; I had brown paper for packaging, so I got me a handful of that paper, wadded it up real good and stuffed that cone with it." The effect was a fortuitous distortion every time Willie Kizart struck the bass strings of his guitar. Phillips boosted this distorted guitar track to feature it as the song's primary rhythm, along side Willie Sims's frenetic drumming. Jackie Brenston and Raymond Hill added a double sax barrage to accompany it, with Ike on piano, playing what he called "a mixture of boogie woogie with stuff that Jimmy and Joe Liggins was doing."

The song's message, based on Jimmy Liggins's "Cadillac Boogie," was also right for a new musical genre. Instead of the sadness and pain rhapsodized by the blues, this tune was a tribute to having fun, riding in big, fast cars, "gals will ride in style . . . sporting with me, riding all around town for joy." It was about freedom and possibility and youth and the car as sex symbol—"Ooh, going out, boozing and cruising along." In other words, it was about rock 'n' roll, although the term would not be coined for another two years.

The song was released in April 1951, hit number 1 in June, and became one of the biggest R&B records of the year, second only to the Dominoes' raunchy "Sixty-Minute Man." And although it did not cross over to the pop charts, it did, as Sam Phillips said, seem to capture "the ear of the white and the black youngsters" of the time. And there for a moment in that time and for the next few years this new music—this rock 'n' roll—did seem to be bringing the races closer together. Everyone would soon be listening to Chuck Berry, Fats Domino, Bo Diddley, Johnny Ace, and Lloyd Price.[65]

Despite the double release of "Booted" and the subsequent confusion, Rosco and Bobby were back in Phillips's studio again by the end of the year. With "Saddled" having faded and "Booted" not yet a hit, the same band as before recorded several numbers. Meanwhile, "No More Doggin," which Rosco had recorded at the same Modern session at the Memphis YMCA as B.B.'s "Three O'Clock Blues," would eventually peak at number 2 on the *Billboard* R&B chart by April 5, 1952. It would turn out to be Rosco's last hit until 1960, when his "Just a Little Bit" scored, peaking at number 2 and staying on the chart for 17 weeks.[66] The song, written jointly by Jimmy McCracklin and Gordon, has become a true blues standard, covered by many a star, including Little Milton, Jimi Hendrix, Etta James, Blue Cheer, Roy Head, Jerry Lee Lewis, and Elvis Presley. Unfortunately, Ralph Bass and other producers at King Records stole the song from a demo sent by Rosco and had it copyrighted before Rosco had a chance to file, costing Gordon thousands of dollars in royalties over the years.[67]

At the first December, 1951 session, Robert Bland cut "Crying" and then a few days later, on December 4, "A Letter From a Trench in Korea," which Phillips again leased to Chess who released them as 78 rpm Chess 1489, which again gained little attention. Also recorded at this session were songs entitled "Native Chant" and "Dr. Blue" that were never issued.

These initial Chess recordings demonstrate Bland's spirited, passionate approach to singing. There's nothing subtle here, his voice seemingly attacking the simple lyrics with a gusto and power that easily overshadows the small combos that backed him. There is only a hint of the more jazz-inflected style that was to follow on these straight-ahead blues songs; but, regardless of the rawness, there is that unmistakable voice that shouts and moans terrific talent and potent potential to be somehow harnessed ahead.

At these early recording sessions with his band and Bland, Rosco Gordon demonstrated a style of piano playing that Sam Phillips called the "Rosco Rhythm." It's a boogie-woogie style that emphasizes the off (or the up) of all four beats, combined with a wailing blues vocal with deliberately slurred words. When Jamaican artist Laurel Aitken heard it, he was inspired to write "Boogie in My Bones," which took the "Rosco Rhythm" a step further by exaggerating the off-beat even more. Aitken, and two other Jamaican artists, Owen Gray and Theophilus Beckford, used the same rhythm and added horns and guitar.

"Towards the end of the 50s Jamaicans got keen on rhythm and blues, particularly a record called 'No More Doggin' sung by Rosco Gordon," explained Island Records founder, Chris Blackwell. "They got hold of this beat, cheered it up a bit, added some lyrics and called it ska. . . . From 1959 onwards this was all the rage." Ska evolved into rock steady and then reggae. So, while to claim that Rosco Gordon invented reggae may be stretching it, he is certainly credited by many music historians as the inspiration behind this popular island sound.

Gordon moved to Queens, New York in 1962; there he recorded for ABC-Paramount, Old Town, Jomada, Rae-Cox, Caller, and Bab-Roc, which he owned with his wife, Barbara. In the 1980s, he was a partner in a dry cleaning business in Queens. When his wife Barbara died in 1984, and with their five children grown up, Rosco returned to recording and performing in the New York area.[68]

Rosco's *Memphis, Tennessee* album on the Stony Plain label was nominated for a W.C. Handy award in 2001. In May 2002, Rosco returned to Memphis one more time to participate in a Sun reunion with B.B. King, Ike Turner, and Little Milton. During the visit, Rosco participated in the making of Richard Pearce's acclaimed PBS documentary, *The Road to Memphis*. Six weeks after having finished his part of the film, on July 11, 2002, Rosco Gordon died of a heart attack at his apartment in Queens.[69]

Meanwhile, Ike Turner, still scouring the South for talent to record on Chess's rival Modern, walked into Mrs. Bland's Sterling Grill one day in early 1952. "His mother had a soul food restaurant and she told us her son could sing," Ike said. "We took him out to Tuff Green's house and recorded him."[70]

Tuff Green was a Memphis music teacher, bassist, and bandleader. He was known to select some of the city's top musicians for his band, the Rocketeers. And it was no accident that Green's band was picked to play on B.B. King's first recordings. "Tuff Green's was one of the best," King remembered. "Tuff was a bass player who put together a group with saxist Ben Branch, Phineas Newborn, Sr., a wonderful drummer, and Phineas' two sons—Phineas Jr. on piano and Calvin on guitar. They were both great. Junior, though, was more than great. He was a genius who could play Chopin and Mozart when he was only a child. Folks were calling him the new Art Tatum. Tuff's band never made records but didn't need to. They worked all over, just off their reputation. White people flocked to hear them play country; blacks came for swing or bebop. And Tuff was never ashamed to play the blues. When big names came through to work at Mitchell's—say, Cat Anderson from Ellington or Sweets Edison from Basie—Phineas Jr. might sit in and, after a tune or two, the cats would want to take him back to New York or Chicago. But Junior, like many of us, was tied to Memphis and its down-home hospitality."[71]

While Modern's Bihari brothers drove big new Cadillacs, they were known to be quite economical, even going so far as to sleep in the recording studios to keep from having to pay hotel bills. That is probably why they initially recorded at the YMCA in Memphis and at Tuff Green's house—for the early-January 1952 session, where they hung blankets on the walls to "soundproof" as best they could Green's living room. "Yeah, I remember those sessions at Tuff Green's," B.B. King recalled. "They'd put quilts on the walls to keep the sound in. Tuff's band had three horns and that's when I starting using horns, because Tuff Green's band had the horns. But I always loved Count Basie, Duke Ellington, Benny Goodman, Jimmy Lunceford, and the big band sound. They influenced me and those other early Memphis musicians a lot."[72]

Assembled for this initial Modern session were Beale Streeters Johnny Ace on piano and Earl Forest on drums, Tuff Green on bass, as well as guitarist M. T. (Matthew) Murphy, and harmonica player Little Junior Parker. Murphy, the first of several great guitar players to record with Bobby, moved to Memphis in the 1940s from Sunflower, Mississippi, where he was born on December 27, 1927. He played awhile with Howlin' Wolf and later in Tuff Green's band before becoming lead guitarist for Little Junior Parker's Blue Flames. Matt moved to Chicago later in 1952, where he played for seven years in Memphis Slim's band. In subsequent years he played lead guitar for Howlin' Wolf, Muddy Waters, and James Cotton. Of course, he is best known as Matt "Guitar" Murphy in the *Blues Brothers* films, where he was featured as Aretha Franklin's husband.[73]

Harp player and vocalist Herman "Little Junior" Parker was well-known around Memphis, and, of the Beale Street gang, probably held the best blues pedigree of them all. Born Herman Parker Jr. to Willie and Jermeter Parker in West Memphis, Arkansas, on March 27, 1932, and a cousin of soul great Al Green, Junior grew up singing in the church and picking cotton in the fields of Mississippi. He listened to *King Biscuit Flour Time*, a fifteen-minute radio program broadcast over KFFA in Helena, Arkansas, at noon every day. The show was hosted by blues guitarist extraordinaire Robert Jr. Lockwood, and harmonica player Sonny Boy Williamson (Rice Miller). Junior fell in love with Sonny Boy's harp playing and practiced obsessively in an effort to emulate him.[74]

In 1948, when he was just sixteen years old, Junior met Sonny Boy who was appearing in Clarksdale, Mississippi, where Junior was working in the cotton fields. Sonny Boy was so impressed with Junior's harp skills that he asked Junior to join his band whenever they worked around Clarksdale. Junior even filled in for his boss when Sonny Boy was traveling. The collaboration led to people believing that Sonny Boy and Junior were somehow related, so they tacked on the "Little" in front of Junior's name in contrast to Sonny Boy who was tall and lanky.

By 1949, Junior was playing for Howlin' Wolf's band, touring the mid-South with another great harmonica player, James Cotton. With Sonny Boy and Howlin' Wolf Junior traveled to Forest City, Arkansas, to buy air time on KYJK, like other performers at the time, to promote themselves and their shows. There they met David James Mattis, who would later become program manager at WDIA in Memphis and the founder of Duke Records.[75]

"We were kind of close," Bobby remembered his earliest times with Junior. "He was from West Memphis, and I was in Memphis. So we used to go on Eighth Street and play on weekends sometimes. It was our good chance to sit in, or whatever. And so it went on from there."[76]

The results of this initial Modern session were "Drifting from Town to Town," with Bobby on vocals, and "Love My Baby," with Parker taking the vocal and playing harmonica and Murphy serving up an impressive guitar solo. The Bihari brothers did not think much of them, and neither song was released as a single; however, both showed up later on LPs featuring various artists, issued by Modern's subsidiaries, Kent and United.

A few days later, on January 24, another session was arranged at Tuff Green's house, with a slightly different lineup of musicians. Ike Turner replaced Ace on piano, Beale Streeter Billy Duncan was added on tenor sax, and Earl Forest remained on drums, as did Matt Murphy on guitar. The session produced four 78 rpm singles: the mournful "Crying All Night Long" backed by the rocker "Dry Up Baby," with a searing guitar solo by Murphy, and another version of the moody "Drifting from Town to Town" backed by the swinging "Good Lovin'," featuring some rollicking boogie piano by Turner. Modern released them all under the name Robert Bland. As with the Chess releases, the records languished, prompting Modern's Joe Bihari to remark about Bland that "he'd better stop singing and buy a plow."[77]

These early recordings, released in 2000 on the Ace CD *The Original Memphis Blues Brothers*, demonstrate the potential of Bobby's keening blues voice, but they were rather raw and unpolished compared to his later records. To blues critic David Evans, "He sounded like a blues shouter but with elements of lead gospel singing and rural field hollers, along with falsetto cries."[78] Bobby himself admitted later, "I wasn't professional at all, really."[79]

Yet Bobby was determined. He reveled in the reaction of the Amateur Night audiences at the Palace Theater and at clubs around Memphis. It was not only his mother now who encouraged him. His friends B.B. King, Rosco Gordon, and Little Junior Parker were all behind him, not to mention Rufus Thomas and the folks at WDIA. People genuinely seemed to enjoy his singing and there was nothing he liked to do more. He was not ready to buy a plow quite yet. Somehow, he knew he could make it if he continued to work, to perform, and to pursue what by now had become his dream.

Bobby Bland and Rosco Gordon preparing for a performance in the early 1950s.
Copyright Ernest C. Withers Estate, courtesy Panopticon Gallery, Boston, MA.

3

Little Boy Blue

1930–1945

The seed of Bobby Bland's dream was planted in a cotton field sixteen miles north of Memphis in the little farming village of Rosemark, Tennessee, where Robert Calvin Brooks and his twin brother Maurice were born on the evening of January 27, 1930. Their mother, Mary Lee Brooks, the former Mary Smith, was born in nearby Kerrville, the daughter of Wesley and Bernie Hardy Smith. She was only sixteen at the time of Robert's birth, and his father, I. J. Brooks, a farmer, the son of Toney and Missouri Wright Brooks, originally from Dublin, Georgia, was eighteen. Mary Lee and I. J. had been married just a few months before in a hastily arranged ceremony on September 26, 1929.[1]

However, Mary Lee and her new twins stayed in Rosemark with her parents and seven siblings—Martha, 18; Josephine, 16; Beatrice, 14; Alphonse, 11; Blanche, 9; Dude, 7; and Nettie, 3—while the twins' father remained as a lodger in the home of eighty-five-year-old Mary A. Burns and her son and cousin down the road in Kerrville.[2]

The stock market had crashed only a few months before, but rural Tennessee was already feeling the effects. Work for the Brooks family was becoming increasingly scarce, as cotton farming became mechanized with tractors replacing mule teams and horses and, of course, some back-breaking human labor, mostly by blacks. Many southern African Americans migrated north to take jobs in the factories and foundries of Chicago, Detroit, Cleveland, and other major American cities. Between 1920 and 1930, there was a net population loss from the South of 773,400 through migration,[3] but, as the Depression deepened African Americans slowed their movement north, because employment for unskilled laborers was given first to the growing pool of unemployed whites. To many African Americans it was safer to take their chances in familiar places where family and church ties seemed more dependable than the unemployment lines in the cold North. Even some reverse migration occurred as blacks returned to the South when they could find no work or suitable housing. Northward migration was further discouraged by members of various organizations, like the Rural Industrial Association, which encouraged black farmers and sharecroppers to stay on the farm rather than to go north and compete for rapidly diminishing job opportunities.[4]

Kelly Miller expressed a common sentiment in a column in the September 18, 1931, issue of the Memphis *World:* "Give any Negro forty acres and a mule and he can succeed in raising a crop of cotton. There is no other industry in which the colored man is deemed indispensable unless he considers the comparatively small field of Pullman porter. In these two fields the black man is irreplaceable. . . . Notwithstanding the ugly face of things agricultural, the Negro's future will be mainly found on the farm and largely in the cotton industry."[5]

The Farm Security Administration was founded in 1937 by the federal government to provide low-interest loans to farm workers to help them start their own family-size farms. Indeed, over the next decade, 1930–40, net population loss through migration from the South decreased by more than half its previous level to 347,500.[6]

So, for the time being, the Brooks twins and their mother stayed put with Mary Lee's family in Rosemark. The prospects in and around the town did not go much beyond the surrounding cotton fields, but perhaps they were better than elsewhere in these tough times. Even in Memphis, during the 1930s, bread lines stretched for blocks along Beale Street, "the number of black retail establishments declined from 378 to 318, attorneys from 8 to 5, and physicians from 86 to 46," according to Roger Biles in his *Memphis in the Great Depression:* "With a leadership paralyzed by fear and subservient to a paternalistic ruling clique, the black community of Memphis wandered rudderless through the 1930s. Living conditions, never comfortable, worsened during the Great Depression, as unemployment, inadequate housing, and an unhealthy environment plagued the essentially helpless black masses. To be sure, some blacks avoided the relief rolls, and a handful of black-owned businesses survived the decade. But even for the more successful, living in the Bluff City meant segregation and second-class citizenship. The New Deal supplied a modicum of relief, but always under the watchful control of the resident machine—a machine imbued with the ethos of white supremacy. Washington largess helped a good number of destitute blacks make ends meet, a considerable accomplishment given the tenor of the times, but did little to augment changes in the racial caste system."[7]

Life was not easy anywhere in the rural South in the 1930s. Despite creeping modernization, it would be two more decades before cotton was routinely picked by machine.[8] It was still more profitable for most Delta plantation owners to hire cheap black labor than to incur the large debt needed to invest in expensive farm machinery.

Within a ten-mile radius of Robert's birthplace were four modest farm plantation villages, each centered around the tiny towns of Millington, Rosemark, Kerrville, and Barretville. Each was a self-contained little world consisting more or less of a long, tall cotton gin; a corrugated-tin-roof tool shed, where workers came for tools and mules (and, in the later 1930s, for tractors); a general store with a porch, a soda tub, and a gas pump in front; a white Presbyterian church and a small African Methodist Episcopal or black Baptist church; and, for the black sharecroppers and laborers, unpainted cabins, mostly shotgun shacks with back doors opening right out onto the fields—many insulated with newspaper and heated by wood-burning stoves, with no plumbing or electricity.[9] The Tennessee Valley Authority (TVA) was formed in 1933 to build a series of dams to control floods, prevent soil erosion, and provide affordable electricity to these rural Southern communities, but the effects of its efforts would be many years in coming.

It was not unusual for families to move or work among these nearby plantation villages and to name any one of them as home at any given time. So, while Robert's birth certificate, signed and filed by his mother about seven months after his birth, lists Millington, the nearest town of any substance, as the place of birth, Robert continued to live eight miles down the road in Rosemark with his mother's extended family for most of his formative years. As Bobby later described it, "Little country town. Period. Grocery store, a gin, a kind of Dr. [P.J.] Flippin, which has passed, he was the local doctor there [for 43 years]. Very small. Population, let me say, five hundred. Maybe . . ."[10] [We kids would] go to the cotton fields each and every day."[11]

Then, in the spring of 1930, Robert's twin brother, Maurice, fell ill of unspecified causes and died, despite the efforts of Dr. Flippin. Robert's father continued to live five miles away in Kerrville and never actually met Robert until Robert was eight, and then not again until he was 24.[12] And while Bland never talked about it much, the death of his twin and the desertion of his father were to have profound effects on young Robert and his mother, drawing them ever closer as they faced the pangs of Depression-era rural poverty and Southern racial intolerance together.

Some of these feelings of abandonment were salved when Robert was six and his mother remarried, to Leroy Bridgeforth Jr., who was three years younger than Mary and went by the last name of Bland.[13] However, the patterns of pulling together, us against the world, and the constant reliance on a strong maternal figure were solidly set for the bashful boy. Fortunately for Robert and his mother, his new stepfather was an industrious and mechanically inclined man who, when Robert was still in grade school, landed a job at the cotton gin in nearby Barretville, where he moved the family. A bit more prosperous than the neighboring towns, Barretville included a gin, a larger general store, a few churches, and even a bank—all owned, excepting the churches, by a Mr. Paul W. Barret, the overseer who later had Tennessee State Highway 385, from Millington to Arlington, named the Paul Barret Parkway after him.[14]

The Blands, like many families, and particularly black families, lived under constant strain and stress during these Depression years, with little money and hardly enough to eat. The strain and stress often became too much, causing families and relationships to break apart. Indeed, some of the blues' most heart-wrenching inspirations were born of these trying times. Take, for example, Bobby's 1966 hit "Poverty," penned by Dave Clark and Pearl Woods:

> *Up every morning with the sun,*
> *I work all day 'til the evening comes*
> *Busters and corns all in my hands*
> *Lord, have mercy on a working man*
> *I guess I'm gonna die, just like I live, in poverty*
> *My pay goes down and my tax goes up*
> *I drink my tea from a broken cup*
> *Between my woman and Uncle Sam,*
> *I can't figure out just what I am*
> *I guess I'm gonna die, just like I live, in poverty*
> *Oh Lord, it's so hard*

But Robert's mother was resolute. She was determined to keep her young family together and to give her son the best she could under the trying circumstances of discrimination and poverty that surrounded them. Bobby recalls his mother fondly: "Well, my mother was a great singer. I got my voice from her.[15] She came from the rural, you know, the countryside, and there weren't many opportunities, you know . . . And to hear her hum . . . I love being around her, period, because, you know, I'm a mama's child . . . My mother is all I had. And she's insisted several times that I work in a restaurant because even when I couldn't see it, I'd really work for about four days a week . . . So my mother knows what I need. So I want her home when I go to see her."[16]

It was also a time when every able-bodied member of most black families needed to work, if they could find it, to make ends meet. As a result, African Americans spent little time in schools. What little schooling they received was substandard and was conducted only during nonessential farming periods— "between chopping-cotton time and picking-cotton time." Typically, black children were educated either at home or in church.[17] So it is not surprising that Robert did not stay in the little one-room black school house in Barretville beyond third grade.[18] He was needed instead in the fields or at his stepfather's gin, where Leroy was a "gin master," although the title was seldom given to a black man at the time. Leroy basically ran the place, keeping the machinery running and the engines churning throughout the harvest. And young Robert helped out any way he could, earning change by watching draft teams and wagons waiting their turns to unload at the gin.

Later, he worked at Mr. Barret's bank, the Barretville Bank & Trust, cleaning spittoons at the rate of two for $1.00, and received a reward for retrieving any unclaimed coins he found on the bank's floor.[19] The bank had been recently rebuilt after it was burned in an unsuccessful robbery attempt in 1930, when the would-be burglars tried to use blowtorches to enter the bank vault.[20] Bobby recalls the period: "Basically, I didn't do anything but go to the grocery store and help clean up there, or go to the cotton gin, which my dad ran. I used to hang around there and hustle up quarters and dimes doing a little extra work with the people that brought the cotton to be ginned. So there wasn't really much to get into and nothing really exciting."[21]

The social center and spiritual anchor of every plantation village of the South was the church. The entire family attended the black community Baptist church in Barretville every Sunday and every Thursday evening for prayer meeting. Everyone sang, including Robert, and like many other blues singers before and after, here is where Robert first heard and began his appreciation of music. As Muddy Waters put it, in order to sing the blues you "had to go to church to get this particular thing in your soul,"[22] or as Bobby said, "You haven't did anything unless you've come through the church, because you don't know how to feel certain things."[23]

Bobby remembered: "I started liking music from an early age, which I started in the church, along with my grandmother. She used to do a lot of hymns, and I liked the way they sounded, the feel of 'em.[24] The hymns my grandmother used to sing while she'd be cooking—I got the feelings from there. I was just listening and asked what she was singing and she would tell me about the spiritual feelings she had. And I'm in there trying to steal a biscuit," Bobby laughed. "She had a beautiful voice. I learned how to approach a note, how to phrase it. The story you're telling, you have to feel it yourself to get it across to people. There are no fancy words for it.[25] Many times we would hold services right in our home and sing and pray. Singing religious songs was the first taste I had of any kind of music and I still like to sing hymns and spirituals."[26]

On the radio, Robert listened to CBS news and country music from Nashville's WLAC. There were no black radio stations yet, and the clearest channel in Rosemark and Barretville was the high-powered WLAC. The station played music by Ernest Tubb, Hank Snow, Eddy Arnold, and Hank Williams. He recognized immediately the truth of the stories that these country music pioneers sang. He understood the way they related stories from the lives of simple and direct people in simple and direct terms. He wanted to sing like them.[27]

"It's just a matter of wording," Bobby explains. "Like 'I love you, baby,' or 'Oh, Lord,' which I use in a lot of my records. It's a matter of phrasing. Spiritual blues and country and western are so close it's pathetic. A lot of good stories come from the country and western side. The greatest writer Hank Williams; Ray Charles did a lot of his material. Ernest Tubb had a blues feeling; 'Walking the Floor Over You' had the blues flavor. Some don't like the twang that country carries, but that's just the delivery they had. The lyric is what tells a story."[28]

Robert also recalls hearing his first blues music when he was growing up. An itinerant bluesman ("Mutt Piggee, don't ask me to spell it, I can't do no better than that") played around the area.[29] "This fellow named Mutt Piggee was a friend of my parents," Bobby recounts, "and summer months, he'd sing and play acoustic guitar. I was about eight years of age.[30] He played the guitar at juke joints and sang up in Tipton County in the red-light district. I used to hear him. He used to hang around my father a lot, worked at a cotton gin out there, and I used to sing along with him, all the old songs like Peetie Wheatstraw and Blind Lemon [Jefferson]."[31]

Recalling these childhood years, Bobby said, "I sang gospel and blues every day, but I wasn't allowed to sing the blues around older people. But I'd sing them in the field."[32]

While Robert appreciated all these styles of music that he grew up around—gospel, country and western, and blues—it was country music that would put him on his first "stage" on the front porch of the J. H. Barret & Son Store, where everything imaginable was sold and on Saturday became the social center of the community. Here, on the weekends, he would make up to eight or nine dollars a day in tips, a big sum in 1940, crooning the country hits he had heard on WLAC, accompanying himself on a jew's harp given to him by Mutt Piggee and an imaginary "guitar" that he had made from a flattened peach can. "Yeah, I sang for nickels, dimes, and quarters on Saturdays at the little grocery store there in Barret when I was around ten, eleven years old—mostly hillbilly tunes I heard on the radio. That was all the kind of music we could get," Bobby said.[33]

Robert sang these country tunes in a high falsetto, he recalls. But when he was fifteen, he had a tonsillectomy that, along with his developing puberty, no doubt, lowered his voice a couple of octaves, making it more mellow and malleable to different styles. "I had a falsetto until I got my tonsils out when I was fifteen and that lowered by voice," he said. "Most of my hits are sung in the key of G. But during that time after my tonsils came out I didn't know how to hit high notes and I was just singing smooth."[34]

Also, as Robert matured into a handsome but still baby-faced teenager, he realized that the birth father he had never really known was not how he wanted to be known, so he changed his surname to Bland (although he did not change it legally for another forty years or so, in 1985), in recognition of his stepfather who had been there for his mother and him since his early childhood. He liked his stepfather and he liked the sound of his name.[35]

When the United States entered World War II in 1941, Robert heard the marches and patriotic tunes that were broadcast on every radio station across the country. African Americans were drafted to help with the war effort, but only in segregated units, and seldom on the front lines. Over 2.5 million African Americans registered for military service during the war, but because of a strict quota system only 1.2 million actually served, including Elmore James in Guam and Howlin' Wolf in Seattle.[36] T-Bone Walker's flat feet kept him out of the war, but his continuing influence on African American music of the time was sustained through a series of USO shows. The Marines and the Army Air Corps did not accept blacks until later in the war. The Navy accepted them only as mess men. The Memphis Red Cross told blacks they could not donate blood. They later reconsidered, but kept black blood separate from white blood. The WAVES would not accept any black women, and the air corps limited the number of black men in its ranks. After a threatened march on Washington in 1941 by labor leader A. Phillip Randolph, blacks not serving in the armed forces were allowed to take jobs in defense plants.

When the war ended in 1945, many black veterans returned with a different attitude. They realized, having been welcomed and respected by Europeans and Australians during the war, that segregation and discrimination were not inevitable and they did not have to accept things the way they were. "We thought it was the way it was supposed to be," one returning soldier said. "We was dumb to the facts and didn't know."[37]

Despite the temporary optimism brought about by the war coming to an end, and despite the Bland family's obdurate ability to eke out a living no matter how hard the times, it became increasingly clear through Robert's childhood years that the cotton fields of West Tennessee did not offer many advantages or future beyond a lifetime of hard physical labor at low, subsistence wages. The Blands' weekly Saturday trips to Memphis and the fact that Mary Lee's parents now lived there made them believe that there might be more opportunity for them there than on Barret's plantation. Bobby explains: "You see, my mother wanted me to have a little more than what Rosemark had to offer. I always would tell her that some day I would make a lot of money and be able to take care of her. One of those things. I wasn't never really a bad kid."[38]

"My mother brought me [to Memphis]," Bobby continued. "She said she wanted something to be a little bit more handy for me to kind of move around and get choices and have an opportunity to do something and meet somebody and whatever, and to get a little bit more exposure."[39]

So, leaving the rural life behind, Bobby hoped for a better future in Memphis, but not as a blues singer. "I've always been concerned with singing," he said, "first spirituals and then white country blues—you know, what they call hillbilly. There used to be a morning radio show here in Memphis, Gene Steele, the Singing Salesman, and when I listened to him sing 'Take That Night Train to Memphis,' I got interested in hillbilly music and in coming to Memphis. Then I started listening to the Grand Ole Opry and singing hillbilly songs at the store there in Rosemark. That was kind of unusual, a black kid singing white songs. I made me some nickels and dimes. When I moved to Memphis, it was very, very tough. Not many places blacks could venture into. It was the wrong time and the wrong place for a black singer to make it singing white country blues."[40]

Bobby Bland (center) and his band at the Club Handy in Memphis, Tennessee, ca. 1950. Copyright Ernest C. Withers Estate, courtesy Panopticon Gallery, Boston, MA

Army Blues

1952–1954

Bobby Bland's first love, country and western music, was, at mid-century, the heart of the Nashville and southern white music scene, while the new rhythm and blues sound was becoming the soul of Memphis and the southern black music world. Bobby, of course, was in Memphis and at the center of the new black music, where his friends, B.B. King and Rosco Gordon, were making huge hit records. In 1952, at the age of twenty-two, Bobby Bland signed a recording contract with Memphis's new independent record label, Duke, a bond that would span the next twenty years and propel Bobby to the loftiest heights of black and pop music stardom.

The only other independent record labels in the South in 1952 were in Houston (Macy's, Freedom, and Peacock), Jackson, Mississippi (Trumpet), Nashville (Nashboro-Ernie Y and Bullet), and Gallatin, Tennessee (Dot). Also in 1952, Sam Phillips launched Sun in Memphis, after his earlier recording efforts had been leased or sold to out-of-town labels, primarily Modern and Chess.[1] His "handshake deal" with Chess had become strained. "I truly did not want to open a record label," he says, "but I was forced into it by those labels either coming to Memphis to record [Modern] or taking my artists elsewhere [Chess]".[2]

This still left a lot of available musical talent on Beale Street and in and around Memphis, or so thought WDIA program director, David James Mattis. He knew the Beale Streeters through the work of B.B. King, Rosco Gordon, and Johnny Ace at WDIA, and he knew WDIA's recording facilities were going to waste every evening when the station shut down at sunset, before it went to 50,000 watts and a 4:00 a.m. to midnight format in 1954. And most importantly, Mattis knew himself well enough to know that he was an out-and-out workaholic and a night owl who was up for most any challenge. "Routinely, when the control board operator arrived about 3:45 a.m. to turn on the equipment for the four o'clock sign-on," reported co-worker Louis Cantor, "it was not unusual to discover Dave—bright-eyed and bushy-tailed—still inside the station from the previous evening. He would have been up all night working on a Goodwill or Starlight Revue script.

"He claimed he did his best work in all-night sessions—especially when WDIA was off the air, from midnight until 4:00 a.m. The place cleared out, and he was not distracted; work tools were a bottle of gin and a typewriter."[3]

When Mattis proposed the idea of starting a record company to his wife, he remembers her saying, "Well, the kids need their teeth straightened, so let's take a shot at it."

"I went up to Forest City [Arkansas] in 1949," Mattis recalled in a 1984 interview with George Moonoogian and Roger Meeden. "I did a blues show. That's where I met Howlin' Wolf, Sonny Boy Williamson and Little Junior Parker. They used to come over and buy fifteen minutes once a week. They'd pay for this time. That was the standard thing in black radio. They'd make all that noise and leave happy. My wife liked [pianist-vocalist] Willie Love [probably Billy "Red" Love] because he'd always thank everybody for 'those lovely little requesses.' I always thought Sonny Boy Williamson was one of the cleverest of any of them and that Howlin' Wolf was the dirtiest! Rosco Gordon told me he was getting 'hosed.' It was just a do-gooder thing," Mattis said of his decision to start a record company.[4]

"Nobody paid us any royalties," Gordon explained. "All you got was front money. . . . You got as much as you could up front, because it was understood that nobody would pay you a dime once the record came out. Didn't matter if it was the biggest hit of the year. . . . Sure I cut for two people at the same time. Who wouldn't under those rules?"

So, David Mattis, with no previous record company experience but with lots of energy, local talent, and an empty recording studio, launched the Tri-State Recording Company in the spring of 1952, with the help of Bill Fitzgerald of Music Sales, a Memphis record distributor. Mattis put in $1,500, arranged to use the WDIA recording facilities at night, and established an accounting system that would pay union scale to the musicians, a generous practice that was unheard of in the recording business at that time.

"I was looking for a name for my company that had recognition and they had 'Queen' and 'King' and what was left was 'Duke' and I thought it was the best of the bunch," Mattis recounted. "Then I set about on the label itself which I made myself. Purple and gold were the signs of royalty and it was eye-catching. The design was simply the front end of a Cadillac: the two headlights, the V design. I bought myself a little drafting set and sat down and did it. It was a creative effort that was fun."

The fledgling label's first recording was in April 1952 of "God's Chariot" by the Gospel Travelers, led by Memphis's Eugene Walton. The second was by Bobby's friend Rosco Gordon, who cut a song called "Hey, Fat Girl," backed by "Tell Daddy." Because Gordon's "hosing" by Modern and Chess had left him leery about seeing any future royalties, Mattis paid him an undisclosed cash amount upfront, despite the fact that Rosco had condemned this practice when some of his previous recordings became hits.

The third session at the WDIA studio brought all the original Beale Streeters together except B.B. King, who by now had launched a lifetime of one-nighters on the strength of his first big hit, "Three O'Clock Blues." In attendance were Adolph "Billy" Duncan on tenor sax, Earl Forest on drums, John Alexander on piano, and Bobby Bland on vocals. Mattis had given Bobby the lyrics to a couple of songs a few days before the session was scheduled, but when Bobby arrived, Mattis was astounded to find that Bobby had not memorized the songs. Mattis did not know that Bobby was illiterate. "I got so damned pissed at Bobby because he couldn't learn the lyrics," Mattis recalled.

With plenty of studio time still left, Mattis had Earl Forest sing a couple of tunes and then heard pianist John Alexander playing around with a Ruth Brown number entitled "So Long" (Atlantic, 1949). "He sounded pretty good," Mattis recounted. "He said, 'I don't sing much,' and I said 'Go ahead and sing it.' I listened through the amplifier and said, 'Let's cut something right here. So I went back and got on the damned typewriter and wrote it out so that 'So Long' became 'My Song.' And 'My Song' is credited to me and Johnny Ace, John Alexander. We just changed it, the melody, enough to get by the damned copyright thing."

"My Song" became one of the biggest R&B hits of 1952, remained on the best-selling charts through the end of the year, and was named the Number Six R&B record of 1952 in the annual *Billboard* poll. Aretha Franklin covered the song for another hit in 1968. Mattis "renamed" the smooth-voiced crooner Johnny Ace by taking the first name of pop artist Johnnie Ray and combining it with the "Ace" in the Four Aces singing group.[5]

John Marshall Alexander Jr. was born in Memphis on June 29, 1929, one of ten children parented by the Rev. and Mrs. John M. Alexander. He was graduated from LaRose Grammar School and Booker T. Washington High School in Memphis and served in the Navy during World War II, even though he was underage. When he was "discharged from the Navy for being worthless and hopeless"[6] he returned to Memphis, only seventeen years old and ready to seek his fortune in music. He began hanging around the Mitchell Hotel and in 1949 joined B.B. King's band as its pianist. When B.B. began touring in 1952 to promote his big hit, "Three O'Clock Blues," he turned the band over to Johnny, who replicated B.B.'s formula of mutually reinforcing local performances and radio appearances over WDIA, where, of course, he met David Mattis.[7]

Mattis, once he heard the finished recording of "My Song," knew he had something special, but he also realized how ill-equipped he was to promote it.

Distributors were demanding "My Song," but not always paying when it was delivered. He told his partner, Bill Fitzgerald, "I've got five thousand dollars in this thing now and we're selling records, but nobody's paying. Either I'm going to go broke or I've gotta quit."[8] In addition, he was totally unprepared to launch what he believed to be a major talent—to build airplay, to distribute the records nationally, to secure public attention, to make Johnny Ace a real star. So he began looking for someone to help him.

A few days after the Ace session, he brought the Beale Streeters back into the WDIA studio to try again to cut some sides with Bobby. This time Bobby, embarrassed by his inability to read, had hesitantly enlisted some of the band members to help him with the lyrics and was ready, as were Billy Duncan on tenor sax, Earl Forest on drums, Johnny Ace on piano, an unidentified bassist, perhaps Tuff Green, and a guitarist listed as B.B. King on Mattis's session charge memo.[9]

The result was Duke 105, by "Bobby Blue" Bland and the Beale Streeters, doing "I.O.U. Blues" on one side and "Loving Blues" on the other. Both were typical slow blues numbers, featuring Billy Duncan's tenor sax and Ace's piano improvising, with King's uncharacteristically subdued guitar, around Bobby's unmistakable vocals. The record became a regional hit, selling particularly well in Memphis, Houston, Dallas, and New Orleans.[10]

All of Bobby's previous recordings for Chess and Modern named him Robert or Bobby Bland on the label. This was the first to use "Blue," although it was "Bobby Blue" Bland, not Bobby "Blue" Bland, as would be the case on records issued from 1955 to 1957, after which it was changed to just Bobby Bland. So apparently Dave Mattis originally coined the "Blue" moniker, not Don Robey, Mattis's future partner, as Bobby claims: "He said, 'We got to have some kind of slang for him.' So he said, 'Bobby Blue Bland.' We've tried to drop it several times, but it just wouldn't work. 'Bobby Bland,' and people'd say, 'Well, is that Bobby "Blue" Bland?'"[11]

Meanwhile, Mattis finally found someone who could help him promote Johnny Ace and the other Memphis artists he had signed, as well as provide a much needed influx of cash. In July 1952 he came to a partnership agreement with Don Robey and his Houston-based Peacock label, one of the few black-owned record companies.

Don Robey was born on November 1, 1903, the son of Zeb and Gertrude Robey, in Houston's Fifth Ward, a bustling African American community where Robey was to become streetwise and business-suave well before coming of age.[12] He dropped out of high school in the eleventh grade to pursue a career in professional gambling, where the ownership of a .45 caliber pistol was de rigueur. Before he was twenty he married and had a son, and to provide more reliable support for his new family he took a job as a salesman for a Houston liquor distributor, calling upon the same spots where he had previously gambled. But his real passion was music. At first he promoted ballroom dances in Houston, bringing in such big names as Louis Armstrong, Duke Ellington, Count Basie, Nat Cole, and Ella Fitzgerald.

In the late 1930s he moved to Los Angeles, where he ran the Harlem Grill night club for three years. When he returned to Houston in 1945, Robey started a successful taxi business that was the first in Houston to put radios in its eighteen cabs, overpowering the competition for several months.[13] Later that year, Robey opened the Bronze Peacock Dinner Club at 2809 Erastus Street, where he booked the top black musical talent of the day—Ruth Brown, Louis Jordon, Lionel Hampton, and T-Bone Walker, among others—placing him as one of Houston's "foremost black business wizards," according to the Houston *Informer*, the city's black newspaper.

The club was "the mecca of entertainment in the Southwest," claimed Robey's business partner, Evelyn Johnson. It was "Las Vegas in our category. There was everything but the chorus line at the Peacock. We had an emcee, comedian, band, featured singers, the whole nine yards. White people, important people came there. Segregation laws were not enforced with those people."[14]

The club soon became Houston's leading African American music venue and Robey sought other ways to invest his profits. He opened a record store, Peacock Records, in 1947, and later discovered and managed an unknown guitarist from San Antonio, Texas, Clarence "Gatemouth" Brown, who had taken over one night for an ailing T-Bone Walker at the Bronze Peacock. "I made $600 in fifteen minutes," Brown remembers, "from an all black audience. I didn't overdo it. Just a simple tune in E natural that I knew I could do. But it was a new sound and different from what T-Bone would ever have thought about. The people just rushed the stage, the women first, and if you can get a bunch of women in your corner, you've got it made."[15]

Frustrated by the way that Brown's white-owned record company was treating him, Robey decided in 1949 to launch his own label, naming it Peacock after his club. "I wanted him to have a record out," Robey told *Billboard*'s Claude Hall, "because he was playing in my club. But Aladdin waited until the last day of the year before releasing Brown's second record [per his two-record per year contract]. So I was mad."

He told his business partner, Evelyn Johnson, "We don't need Eddie Mesner [of Aladdin Records] to make records of Gatemouth Brown. We'll make them ourselves." Johnson said, "We will?" Robey answered, "Yes." Johnson said, "Tell me this. How do you make a record?" Robey said, "Hell, I don't know. That's for you to find out." "Robey didn't know a record from a hubcap," Johnson concluded.[16]

Using cash from his club and record store and the creative business skills of Evelyn Johnson, Robey eventually built his own modern recording studio, set up his own record pressing plant, and represented his own artists through his own Buffalo Booking Agency, named after Buffalo Bayou, Houston's main waterway where Houston's first black residents settled in the nineteenth century, and managed by his partner Evelyn Johnson. Gatemouth Brown went on to record two hits for Peacock in 1949, but the label ended up recording mostly gospel acts, including the Five Blind Boys of Mississippi, whose lead singer, Archie Brownlee, was said to have put the scream into soul singing, with "an unresolved falsetto shriek that conjured up images of witchcraft and bedlam"; the Dixie Hummingbirds, with Bobby's favorite lead singer Ira Tucker; the Sunset Travelers, with soul-sensation-to-be O. V. Wright; and the Tempo Toppers, a group from New Orleans with a vocalist named Richard Penniman, who later recorded for Peacock and Specialty Records as Little Richard.[17]

Since all the major black recording bands played Robey's Bronze Peacock Dinner Club, Robey was not above using them on his label. Lionel Hampton's band members were particularly adept at playing in various styles. To avoid exclusive recording contract conflicts, Robey simply changed the bands' names. Buddy Johnson's band became the Cherokee Conyers group (Johnson's sax player). Louis Jordan's Tympany Five would be the Caldonia Boys. Johnny Otis's band was Kansas City Bell's Band (Leard Bell).[18]

"In those days," Robey explained, "rhythm and blues was felt to be degrading, low, and not to be heard by respectable people. People twenty-five to forty years old believed that for years."[19] Nevertheless, Robey continued to seek ways to expand his empire. The next R&B singer to reach the charts for Peacock, after Gatemouth Brown, was Marie Adams who had a number 3 R&B hit with "I'm Gonna Play the Honky Tonks" in June 1952.[20]

Robey also recognized that something new and musically interesting was happening 600 miles east in Memphis. When he found out that Mattis had already signed the cream of the Memphis musical crop and was seeking investors, Robey did not hesitate to forge a deal with Mattis, which he promptly announced in a full-page ad in *Billboard:* "Peacock Proudly Introduces Duke Records . . . a hot rhythm and blues line, featuring Johnny Ace With the New Blues Sound, Rosco Gordon, Earl Forest," and a vocalist whom Robey listed as "Bobby Blue."

Within a few weeks of the agreement, in mid-August, Robey was in New York with Johnny Ace to promote "My Song" at a meeting of the National Association of Music Merchandisers, where he reportedly sold 53,000 copies before its release. It was there in New York that the Robey-Mattis partnership was formally signed. It quickly turned into a match made in hell.

Robey knew the business, Mattis did not, and Robey was not about to take the time to teach his inexperienced young partner anything. Instead, he was busy promoting "My Song" and taking charge of Duke's operations. He hated the amateur sound coming out of the ill-equipped WDIA studios in Memphis and promptly arranged for Duke artists to travel to Houston to record in Peacock's more modern facilities.[21]

But before Robey could completely move the Duke operations to Houston, Mattis continued to make records in Memphis, using both Memphis- and Houston-based musicians. His second and third sessions with Bobby Bland occurred, according to a Mattis memo dated November 2, before August 28, 1952. The first of these two was a split session with Johnny Ace, resulting in a cut called "Wise Man Blues," which would not be issued until 1981 on the British Ace label LP, *Woke Up Screaming* (CH 41), and "No Blow, No Show," which would be released later in 1953, as the flip side of "Army Blues" (Duke 115), by "Bobby Blue" Bland and Orchestra, recorded at Bobby's next session. Three other tunes were recorded at this session but never released.[22]

At these sessions, Beale Streeters Billy Duncan and Earl Forest were supplemented by an established Memphis group called the Johnny Board Orchestra, led by Board, a saxophonist who had previously performed with Coleman Hawkins, Lionel Hampton, and Count Basie and his Orchestra, as well as backing Peacock artists like Gatemouth Brown, particularly on Brown's 1953 "Gate Walks to Board." The band also included Peacock session musicians Paul Monday on piano, Milton Hopkins on guitar, C.C. Pinkston on vibes, Curtis Tillman on bass, Milton Bradford on sax, and Joe Scott on trumpet.[23] The resulting sound is much fuller than all Bobby's previous recordings and provides a powerful portent of the more sophisticated orchestral direction Bobby's brand of blues was to follow in the years to come.

"Wise Man Blues" is another slow blues with a prominent vibes accompaniment. "No Blow, No Show" is Bobby's first Duke attempt at a more up-tempo song and the train-based jump tune comes off well. Chances are that Bobby had received his draft notice when "Army Blues" was recorded because he does not sound too happy in this dirgelike goodbye. Of the song, Bobby recalls, "B.B. had me on [WDIA] one Saturday morning, and I sang a song I wrote, 'Army Blues,' about not wanting to go to the army. Well, I guess I wasn't the only one who didn't want to go to Korea. People started calling in to request the song, and it became [one of] my first recording[s]."[24]

This mournful farewell would turn out to be Bobby's last one for many Memphis friends, particularly saxman Billy Duncan, who did not make the move with Duke to Houston, but instead relocated to Chicago and later to Rockford, Illinois, where he died some years later. Drummer Earl Forest would go on to play drums in Johnny Board's band that backed Johnny Ace and Bobby and sang on several moderately successful Duke and Modern recordings in the mid-1950s. He also wrote songs for Little Junior Parker, Little Milton, and Bobby, including the standard "Next Time You See Me," recorded by Parker, James Cotton, and many others. Forest later composed songs with George Jackson for Johnnie Taylor and Bland at Malaco Records. He died of cancer at age 76 at the Memphis Veterans Affairs Medical Center on February 26, 2003.[25]

Soon after this final Duke recording session in Memphis, U.S. Army conscript Robert Calvin Bland left the Memphis area (and, more wistfully, his mother for the first time) and was on a bus to Fort Jackson, South Carolina, to begin basic training.[26]

Meanwhile, back in Memphis, David Mattis was growing impatient with Don Robey's failure to send him any of the Duke profits being made in Houston. So he decided to exercise the option in their partnership agreement that would allow him to become an active partner in the business. Here's what Mattis said happened: "I had $5,000 in the damned thing and it was getting kind of pinchy. . . . I wrote Robey, I guess around October or November [of 1952]. . . . I knew we were making some money. . . . So I wrote and said I'd like some advance on the property and he said he's not making any money. . . . He told me that I paid the artists too much! I had them for two-and-a-half cents per record. . . . It turns out that he was paying them one-half cent. . . . So I resigned from the radio station around November and went to Houston and said, 'I'm here to exercise my partnership,' and he said, 'They'll be nothing like that.' That's when the .45 came on the desk. . . . I called my brother-in-law, who's an attorney . . . and we decided we'd try to find a way to break this thing up. Well, this went on for about six months, and then we finally broke up."[27] By April 15, 1953, Robey had completely bought out Mattis for $10,000 and half of the $38,000 in Duke's bank account, and was now the sole owner of Duke Records, publishing royalties, master tapes, and artists contracts included.[28]

"I really enjoyed what I was doing," Mattis summed up his short-lived Duke experience. "Looking back now, I'm a bit cynical. I really don't think I accomplished a damned thing, but at the time it looked like we were causing this great black-white revolution to come about. . . . Then I found out later that to a lot of the blacks I thought were my bosom buddies, I was a 'honkie' and I can't blame them. Hell, I was such a snot-nose! . . . I ended up, the profits were $17,000 total, and I knew damned well that we'd had collections over $200,000. So what do you do? . . . I wanted to go back to the radio station and do the thing I did well. I just wanted out!"[29]

Mattis was not the first victim of Robey's tough management practices, nor would he be the last. Robey was no one's fool when it came to running a business and making money for himself. Evelyn Johnson, his longtime partner, doubts that Robey actually pulled a gun on Mattis, but she does admit that Robey "always wore a gun. I think he was impressing himself, because he had no notches in those guns. It was an image he was living up to."

Gatemouth Brown also tells a story about the time Robey pulled a gun on him. "When he pulled it on me, he got the shit whupped out of him, that's what happened," Brown says. "I tore his ass up." Then Brown, enraged, went home to fetch his own gun to finish Robey off, but fortunately someone called Brown's wife in time for her to hide Brown's gun before he got there.[30]

Rosco Gordon, who had joined Duke just before Bobby, remembered: "He [Robey] wanted me to record a particular song for him but the money wasn't right. I told him so. He threatened to kick me. So I opened my jacket and he could see I was carrying a gun. I told him, 'The very foot you kick me with, that's the foot I'm gonna shoot.' [Laughs] That was the end of that problem."[31]

Little Richard claimed that Robey beat him up at one point: "Ooh, yes! I knew Don Robey. He was a very rich black man in the South, he was a tycoon, really. People don't realize how rich he was. He called me in one day and beat me and Paul Monday. He had another gay guy named Paul Monday. He got me in there and he kicked me in my stomach and he went to hit Paul and 'OWWWWWW!' Paul hollered. And the only person he wouldn't beat was Big Mama Thornton, she'd run him outa there. He was scared of her. Whole lotta people was. She was a lady but she could fight. But he kicked me and I had a hernia in my stomach. They had to operate on me, you know, he just stomped me in my stomach. I wouldn't sign that contract. And I ended up signing it because he beat me so bad. I had ran away from home, I was a little boy, you know. And he took advantage of it."[32]

Evelyn Johnson disputes this, saying that Robey only slapped Little Richard once. There was no dispute, however, that Robey was one tough character whose formula of discovering the artists, cutting their records, copyrighting their songs, and then booking their live performances was an entrepreneurial, if not totally virtuous, brainchild.[33]

The Korean War began on June 25, 1950, and by the time Bobby was drafted in the fall of 1952, had pretty much reached a stalemate, with some large-scale bombing still continuing in the north and a few more major battles, most significantly the Battle of Pork Chop Hill in March–July, 1953, along the 38th Parallel, still to be fought. On November 29, U.S. President-elect Dwight D. Eisenhower fulfilled a campaign promise by flying to Korea to see if he could somehow influence the peace talks that had begun on July 10, 1951. Finally, on July 27, 1953, a cease-fire was established based on a proposal put forward by India.

By war's end, the conflict had claimed the lives of over one million North Korean, Chinese, and Soviet people and nearly half a million allied troops, including 36,516 Americans, about 5,000 of which were African Americans.[34] Unlike previous wars, African Americans, equaling about 8 percent of total U.S. manpower, were allowed to fight side by side with white military personnel in all combat operations. By the end of the war, approximately 600,000 African Americans had served in the armed forces all over the world. President

Harry S. Truman had issued an executive order integrating the armed forces in 1948 and, unlike President Roosevelt's similar order during World War II, this one was followed. In October 1951, the Army's all-black 24th Infantry Regiment, a unit established in 1869 that had served in every war since, was disbanded, effectively ending segregation in the U.S. Army and subsequently all other branches of service. As a result, hundreds of African Americans held command positions, served in integrated elite units such as combat aviation, and distinguished themselves in battles both on the ground and in the air.[35]

"By the end of the war, the military was the most integrated and racially advanced institution in the United States," according to Gerald Early, the author of *When Worlds Collide: The Korean War and the Integration of the United States.* "If for no other reason, this fact alone makes the Korean War one of the most important conflicts this country ever engaged in."[36]

After surviving basic training at Fort Jackson, Bobby was shipped all the way to Japan, where, near the end of his tour there, he was assigned to the same Special Services division as pop singer Eddie Fisher, who would later marry actress Debbie Reynolds (the couple's daughter Carrie would coincidentally play John Belushi's homicidal girlfriend in *The Blues Brothers*, among other film roles).[37] In the Special Services, Bobby worked with crooner Arthur Prysock and performed mellow songs by Nat "King" Cole, Charles Brown, and Floyd Dixon, taking the opportunity, now that he was thousands of miles from Beale Street expectations, to broaden his style beyond the wailing, southern manner of B.B. King, Roy Brown, and Lowell Fulson, which had characterized his recordings thus far.[38]

Bobby's final stint in the Army took him back to the United States at Fort Hood in Killeen, Texas, no more than 200 miles from the burgeoning Duke headquarters in Houston. On weekends, he continued to hone his musical skills by performing in amateur night contests at Johnny Holmes's Victory Grill in Austin, which, as at the Palace back in Memphis, he won often enough to eventually be disqualified. He considered the Victory Grill's manager, Valerie Cannon, his "play mother," Bobby recalls. "She put her arms around me and kept me out of trouble."[39]

Cannon, the first of many strong maternal substitutes in his life, helped ameliorate some of the boredom and loneliness of military life, for which, in the absence of Cannon and his real mother, whom he missed terribly, Bobby had begun using alcohol in Japan. The peer pressure was also strong, of course, but Bobby, under more familiar family circumstances back in Memphis, had withstood that before. Regardless of exactly how or why he acquired the fashionable habit, Bobby's wholesome mix of healthiness and youthful ambition were fortunately more than enough to counteract any ill effects from his drinking for several years to come.

Back in Houston, Don Robey was busy building and promoting his grow-
ing stable of Duke R&B artists. By the time Bobby returned from the Army,
Johnny Ace had tacked on six more top ten hits in addition to "My Song."
"The Clock," written by David Mattis under his pseudonym David James, with
"Johnny Ace and The Beale Streeters" on the label, reached number 1 on the
R&B chart and stayed there for five weeks. "You know the quality Johnny Ace
had," Mattis remembered. "He has that funny vocal surrounded by soft purple
sounds, ah, Nat Cole. It was a funny, fuzzy echo, hollow sound. It's not a style.
It's just something natural."[40]

Robey wasted no time promoting the label's biggest star and putting Johnny
on the road with the Johnny Ace Revue that showcased not only Ace but also his
popular labelmates Little Junior Parker and Willie Mae "Big Mama" Thornton.
Parker scored a number 5 R&B hit in October 1953, with "Feelin' Good" on
the Sun label before switching to Duke. Thornton's "Hound Dog," on Robey's
Peacock label, topped the R&B chart in April and May 1953, more than three
years before Elvis Presley's triple-platinum cover of the Leiber and Stoller tune
became Elvis's biggest hit in 1956. The revue with its band, known variously as the
Johnny Ace Band, the Johnny Board Band, and the C.C. Pinkston Orchestra,[41]
joined off and on by various other performers, like B.B. King, Johnny Otis,
Memphis Slim, and Faye Adams, was booked by Robey and Johnson's Buffalo
Booking Agency into one-nighters throughout most of 1953–54 all across the
country.

Big Mama Thornton recorded "Hound Dog" in a session in Los Angeles on
August 13, 1952, with only a rhythm section, including Johnny Otis on vibes.
It would be her only big hit, although she continued to cut sides for Peacock
into 1957, when the relationship ended she says because, "Peacock cheated me. I
didn't get my money. After they gypped me, I ups and quit, and stayed quit."

After working with Bobby on his initial recording sessions with Modern in
January 1951, Little Junior Parker made his own record for Modern in 1952 with
his group the Blue Flames. Ike Turner, still Modern's Memphis talent scout,
played piano and the session resulted in two sides: "You're My Angel" and "Bad
Women, Bad Whiskey." Junior then switched to Sam Phillips's new Sun label,
cutting four sides in late 1953. They are noteworthy because they included not
only Junior's first hit, "Feelin' Good," but also a tune called "Mystery Train."
Co-authored by Parker and Phillips, it too was covered by Elvis Presley the
next year and went on to become the first record released by RCA-Victor, in
November 1955, after RCA bought Elvis's contract from Phillips for $35,000.[42]
Don Robey was impressed enough by this time that he coaxed Junior away from
Sun, which resulted in a lawsuit by Sam Phillips that Phillips eventually won to
the tune of $17,500 and a 50 per cent writer's share of "Mystery Train."[43]

Bandleader and vibraphonist Johnny Otis paused briefly at Peacock before
moving on to Capitol and "Willie and the Hand Jive" fame, and Little Richard

recorded four undistinguished sides for Robey before he went on to Specialty Records and "Tutti Frutti" renown. Both were gone from Duke/Peacock by the time Bobby returned from the Army in early 1955.[44]

The Duke label also recorded a number of other artists, including Memphis Slim, Inez Andrews, Elmore Morris, Buddy Ace, and Floyd Dixon. All in all, the label was doing very well for a company just over two years old. Well enough that, in November 1953, Robey moved the Duke/Peacock headquarters from its original address at 4104 Lyons Avenue (which would later become the medical offices of Dr. Louis Robey, the son of the owner) to the site of the by then closed Bronze Peacock, at 2809 Erastus Street in the Fifth Ward. The club had become a legal and social headache as it grew in popularity, especially among white customers, and the recording operations desperately needed additional space. So Robey completely renovated the place to house the company's business offices, the yet to be completed recording studio, and a new record pressing and processing plant—the first such total record company operation in the South.[45] John Green, a Robey business associate and future Bobby Bland road manager, described the move: "They took it and converted it to the recording studio and the booking office. So Buffalo was there too. And they had a pressing plant in the back, and pressed the records right there. In '53 is when they converted it. . . . And that building was the base for all of Peacock [and Duke] until they sold out in '73." The building still stands, now as the F. W. McIlveen Educational Building of the Charity Baptist Church.[46]

Meanwhile, the Johnny Ace Revue continued its odyssey of one-night stands, rolling into Houston for the holidays just before the Thanksgiving of 1954. Everyone was tired and more than a little burned out by the months of miles that they had endured. A few days before, Earl Forest, the band's drummer, recalls that Johnny Ace purchased a .22 caliber pistol at a pawn shop in Tampa from a promoter named Boss "Pawnshop" Lewis. "[Johnny] bought a gun in Florida and treated it like a toy," bandleader Johnny Board recounted. "He and I were the only ones who could drive his car and when we stopped on the road sometimes to relieve ourselves in a field, he would take out the gun and shoot in the air like a child with a cap pistol." He seemed to be constantly playing with the gun. When he wasn't playing with it, he was turning it over to friends for safe keeping—"at least four times"—in the days just before Christmas.

Johnny Otis remembers a member of the tour coming to his hotel room in tears to complain while they were in Florida. "Man, he's doing that shit again," he told Otis. "He's got that goddamn gun and he spins the barrel and he points it at me and it just scares the shit out of me. He does it while we're riding along on the highway."

Johnny always seemed carefree and playful on the road, the band's guitarist Milton Hopkins remembered, "He loved to wrestle and horse-ass, and play around, and play the dozens, and all this kind of stuff, which I thought was good. And he was always jolly and full of pep and energy. And he loved to drink gin, and he liked women."

But B.B. King and Gatemouth Brown noted something darker in Johnny at this time. They were worried that the rapid success and the road-weariness were getting to Johnny, turning his playfulness in a dangerous direction. He didn't look right either. He had gained a lot of weight and added a new process hairdo and pencil mustache, almost obliterating the boyish charm persona that Robey was promoting. A few days before Christmas, the band was on the road in Johnny's Oldsmobile, Johnny at the wheel. According to Johnny Board, Ace ran a red light and bounced off a curb. Then he stopped the car, turned to Board, and said, "I don't know what's wrong with me. I shouldn't be driving. Take over the wheel, will you?"

On Christmas Eve, Johnny fired the gun out a window, drawing several complaints about the noise. On Christmas Day the Revue was booked into the Houston City Auditorium for a big "Negro Christmas Dance." Before the show, Johnny was still playing with the gun, at one point, taking a couple of rounds out of the gun and handing them to two little girls who were visiting backstage. "Here," he said. "If I fool around and kill myself, here's a souvenir."

At a break in the evening's performance, Ace, his girlfriend, Olivia Gibbs, and Big Mama Thornton were relaxing in the dressing room. Thornton, fed up with Johnny's constant antics with the gun, took it from him. But Johnny soon charmed her into giving it back. No sooner than he had it again, he aimed it at Big Mama herself. "Don't snap that thing on me," Big Mama demanded. Ace complied, but aimed it instead at Olivia. This angered Big Mama even more and she yelled, "Stop that, Johnny! You're going to get somebody killed!" Johnny again complied, but this time put the gun to his own temple and said to Big Mama, "There's nothing to worry about. Look, I'll show you," and squeezed the trigger for the last time.

His body was shipped back to Memphis where an estimated 5,000 mourners packed the Clayborn Temple AME Church, just off of Beale Street, to pay final tribute to the first of what was to become a long line of rock 'n' roll casualties.[47]

Brook Benton, Walter Bailey (future attorney for Bobby Bland), Little Junior Parker, Elvis Presley, and Bobby Bland backstage at Ellis Auditorium in Memphis for the WDIA Goodwill Revue on December 6, 1957. Copyright Ernest C. Withers Estate, courtesy Panopticon Gallery, Boston, MA.

5

Ain't It a Good Thing

1955–1957

Bobby was discharged from the Army in early 1955 and returned to Memphis to live with his mother and stepfather at their new home at 264 Pontonoc Avenue. "I think the army done quite a bit for me, though I didn't care for it much at that particular time," Bobby would later sapiently sum up. "I did two years, six months, and twenty-nine days; I had a little bad time to make up. But it grew me up into manhood, actually."[1]

Memphis had changed since Bobby had left. Popular music continued to be dominated by the easy listening sounds of Tony Bennett, Perry Como, Patti Page, Nat "King" Cole, and Eddie Fisher, but a group called Bill Haley & His Comets had a big hit with what they were calling rock 'n' roll, with "Shake, Rattle and Roll," a cover of Joe Turner's 1954 number 1 R&B hit. Elvis Presley was now in Memphis recording for Sam Phillips. And most of the Beale Streeters were in Houston working for Duke's new owner, Don Robey.

"I came back and I kind of relaxed for maybe a month," Bobby recalls. "Then I got a call from Don Robey in Houston. He said, 'You know I have you under contract.' So I said, 'Yeah, sure.' Then he said, 'You're under the Duke label, right?' I said, 'Yeah, but that's here in Memphis.' He said, 'No, I bought it from David James and I want you to start recording.' Oh, man, you're talking about butterflies. I said, 'Well, where are you?' He said 'I'm in Houston, Texas.' I said, 'Oh my gosh!' Then, he said, 'Well, I have a ticket for you.' Thirteen dollars and eleven cents—bus fare only—one way![2] So I was there for 18 years. It was a great move for me. I'm very thankful that he honored his list that he had of people that was on the label. So I'm happy that I was thought of and he gave me a chance to record."[3]

In Houston, Bobby looked up his old Memphis friends and found out that the 115-room Crystal Hotel on Lyons Street was the place for young African American musicians to stay in Houston. He booked a room there and started exploring the city. He found a bustling post–World War II boom town that was the fastest-growing city per capita in the country. The shipbuilding industry and the recent availability of air conditioning spurred growth throughout the city. The Fifth Ward, where Duke had relocated its headquarters to Erastus Street just a few months before, was dominated by the Lyons Avenue commercial corridor and the largest African American population in the city.

Like Memphis, Bobby found Houston to be very much segregated. Schools, parks, waiting rooms, drinking fountains, and lunch counters were all set apart by race. And like Memphis, Houston had separate white and black newspapers, theaters, and baseball teams. Alvia Wardlaw, a Houston art historian, remembered segregation in the city: "It was all around you. You knew what it meant from an early age. You encountered it at the grocery store. There was a colored water fountain and a white water fountain. Every adult in the community made you aware of segregation and discrimination, but at the same time you could forget about it when you were doing things that were part of the community, like going to the games and pep rallies, or hearing civil rights activists like Barbara Jordan or the Reverend William Lawson speak."[4]

While there was no ordinance against integration and blacks lived throughout the city, the majority lived in the city's Freedman's Town/Fourth Ward, where conditions were so crowded that neighbors could "stand in one house and hear the inmate in the adjacent house change his mind."[5] African Americans also inhabited the Third Ward, the Sixth Ward, and the Fifth Ward, northeast of downtown Houston, bounded by Buffalo Bayou on the south. There, as on Beale Street (but without the cultural cachet), were black restaurants, movie houses, schools, drug stores, saloons, churches, and clubs. Yet, despite the city's lack of a storied music history, Houston was a lively place to be for Bobby and his fellow Memphis musical transplants.

"Everybody wanted to get out, to go to the music—gospel in the churches, rhythm and blues in the city. The wages were low and the music talked to people," recalled bluesman Johnny Copeland about his native Houston in the 1950s. "There were hardly any televisions and only two black radio stations, KCOH and KYOK, but dances were held on Monday, Thursday, Friday, Saturday, Sunday, and sometimes Wednesday at the Eldorado Ballroom, Club Matinee, Diamond L Ranch, Club Ebony, Shady's Playhouse, Double Bar Ranch, and Club Savoy."[6]

"Most of the black clubs were small then," Houston bluesman and future Bland band guitarist Joe Hughes recalled. "A lot of houses were converted into clubs. That gave you basic two- or three-room structures, but there were many around the city. People felt the music more back then. And the musicians played with more feeling."

Bobby found Houston exhilarating and immersed himself in the local blues community that included Houston natives Lightnin' Hopkins, Johnny Copeland, and Jimmy Nelson, as well as jazz stars Illinois Jacquet, Arnett

Cobb, and Eddie "Cleanhead" Vinson. "A lot of people think that the blues is just a Southern thing," Bobby explained. "Just from Mississippi. And they think that all the people who made the blues popular in Chicago are just from Mississippi. Well, that's all wrong. You can argue that Texas was one of the first places the blues came from. You start with the old-timers like Blind Lemon Jefferson. These are the guys who invented the blues. God, the blues has been here since the beginning."[7]

As he had in Memphis and Austin, Bobby kept his stage act in tune by performing at the local amateur talent show, this time at the Club Matinee on Wednesday nights. And, of course, after winning the contest every time he appeared, he was eventually banned from the show.[8] The Club Matinee, with its always-open restaurant, and the adjacent Crystal Hotel were the closest spots in Houston to the Mitchell Hotel/Club Handy complex in Memphis. In addition to the club and hotel, owner Louis Dickerson also owned a taxicab operation, all on the Fifth Ward's main drag, Lyons Avenue. John Green, who would become Bobby's road manager in 1957, described the operation: "Club Matinee—oh yeah, that was the jumping-off place. That's where all the bands would come to stay, next door at the Crystal Hotel. Before integration, that's where all the entertainers, music or not, would go to stay, at the Crystal Hotel. Club Matinee stayed open twenty-four hours a day. You could get food there twenty-four hours, and you could get you a bottle of booze after hours, all night long. . . . All the guys brought the girls there"—including Bobby, who found the Texas women to be as sassy as they were beautiful. As a place for musicians to hang out and network, the complex was at the center of Houston's blues community. Hamp Simmons, Bobby's bass player for many years, remembers that Bobby stayed there when he was not on the road: "The Club Matinee, it was a point to meet. Bobby would stay there, at the Crystal Hotel. And we would meet up there, in the parking lot of the Matinee, to leave town. And when we'd come in, we'd come in to the Matinee. That was always the gathering spot for us—because they had that restaurant open all the time."[9]

Bobby checked in at Duke's new headquarters in the Fifth Ward and met Don Robey and Evelyn Johnson for the first time. Robey handed Bobby a new contract, which Bobby could not read, and helped Bobby sign his name on it. The original contract in Robey's file showed where Bobby had experimented signing. It read "r RRR, ooo, bbb BB . . ."[10]

Immediately after the contract signing, Robey put Bobby with bandleader Bill Harvey and arranger and trumpeter Joe Scott, both of whom had moved from their regular gig in Memphis at the Club Handy to Houston to become a part of Duke's regular session band. They worked on a few numbers and went into Duke's Houston studio for the first time on February 22, 1955, for a session shared with Little Junior Parker. The Bill Harvey Orchestra assembled for the session included Harvey on tenor sax, Scott on trumpet, Pluma Davis on trombone, Connie Mack Booker on piano, Hamp Simmons on bass, Sonny Freeman on drums, and a former Roy Milton band member, eighteen-year-old Roy Gaines on guitar.

They recorded two songs that first day, the mournful "Lost Lover Blues," which was relegated to the vaults until the British label Ace later issued it on the album *Woke Up Screaming* (CH 41), and the mid-tempo "It's My Life, Baby" (Duke 141),[11] which Bobby sings with an entirely new confidence, as if singing pop songs in the Special Services prepared him perfectly to front a brassy big band and to freely belt out the song's macho lyrics without hesitation. Roy Gaines's guitar work is impeccable on the cut, leading Bobby to shout spontaneously at one point, "Play that guitar, baby!"

The next session, held on February 26 with the same personnel, resulted in the jump-style "Honey Bee" (which also ended up on the Ace LP *Woke Up Screaming*) and the big band blues "Time Out," which backed "It's My Life, Baby" on Duke 141. A few weeks later, on April 22, 1955, the same group, with Clarence Hollimon replacing Roy Gaines on guitar, recorded the pretty ballad "You or None," and the swinging blues, "Woke Up Screaming," to create Duke 146. Also recorded at the session, but relegated to the vaults, was the mid-tempo blues "A Million Miles From Nowhere."

The band on all these cuts sounds tight and well-rehearsed, and Gaines's work again sets a high standard for future Bobby Bland band guitarists. Unfortunately, he soon got snatched up by Chuck Willis, whose road band he led for several years, before touring briefly with his hero T-Bone Walker in the 1970s, and pursuing his own successful recording career, receiving a W.C. Handy award *Living Blues* "Comeback Artist of the Year" award in 1999.[12]

The sound quality in Duke's Houston studio was a major improvement over Bobby's earlier recording efforts at Tuff Green's house and at the WDIA studios in Memphis. But there was still an amateur feel about it, as if no one had yet invented acoustic tiles, the music bouncing around like the band was in some little concrete-box roadhouse in West Texas.[13]

"It's My Life, Baby" by "Bobby 'Blue' Bland with Bill Harvey & His Orchestra" was released in April and by August was selling well, especially in Detroit and Chicago,[14] where Bobby worked for a while at around this time. The Windy City blues scene was really heating up in the mid-1950s, with Muddy Waters, Howlin' Wolf, Little Walter, Chuck Berry, and Bo Diddley churning out hit after hit, and Bobby wanted to be a part of it. He fondly remembers his first gig there: "Magic [Sam Maghett] and I worked together out on Madison and Damen for a good while. That was in the early years. Earl Hooker. You know about Earl Hooker? We worked together out at Cairo, Illinois. Magic Sam and all of us, we worked together out at Chuck's Place at Madison and Damen, on the West Side. Shit, I was just sittin' in for 15 a night. Earl got me the gig. I was doin' all that. I was gettin' naked damn near. I was crawlin' and"—Bobby imitates his gruff singing voice at the time—"'Do you believe, woaw, do you believe I'm a . . .'—all this. Shit, I was doin' everything."

He continued, "Look here. If anybody had somethin' to take pictures . . . you wouldn't believe some of the shit I was doin'. I lost weight doin' it. I was fat before, when I first come out here. I'm talkin' fat, fat, fat. Huge fat. Like Fatty Arbuckle. A big old huge nigger. And I was doin' 'I'm A Man,' what's this thing Muddy did, 'Got a Boy Child Comin.' I was crawlin', damn near gettin' undressed. I had the little girls goin' though."[15]

Bobby also met Otis Rush during these early days in Chicago and discussed with him the possibility of working with Cobra, Rush's record label at the time, if things did not work out with Don Robey at Duke. "Yeah, Bobby came by where I was workin'," Rush told Dick Shurman in 1976, "and he was digging those minor sounds that I was gettin'. That was before he started making these minor things, because he wanted to get into that. And I told him, 'Hey, you better off where you at. Cobra, it's no good either.' God damn, I got with who he was with—Duke—and he didn't do me any good. He [Don Robey] did Bobby some good, I guess they sort of went along smooth."[16]

"Woke Up Screaming," listed as by "Bobby Bland—Bill Harvey Orchestra" on the label, was issued in October and by the end of the year was selling well and receiving airplay in Cleveland, Baltimore, and Los Angeles. While none of these initial Houston cuts made the national charts, they sold well enough to convince Robey that he was on the right track with Bobby.[17] Bobby, on the other hand, was not so sure. He didn't like the boss hovering around the studio when he was working and had little confidence in Robey's musical ability. Knowing Robey's reputation for violence, Bobby approached Evelyn Johnson about his concerns. Apparently that was all it took, because from then on Bobby dealt with Evelyn and had very little interaction with Robey, except occasionally when Evelyn could not head off Robey before he snuck into the recording studio to deliver his insights.[18] "Basically, I dealt with Evelyn Johnson," Bobby recalls. "Robey was a business man and a hustling man. He upset me at the first session he came to and Evelyn took care of that."[19]

Born to a Creole family in Thibodeaux, Louisiana, on September 28, 1920, Evelyn Johnson moved with her mother to Houston's Fifth Ward when she was a young child. There, she was graduated with honors from Wheatley High School in Houston. She wanted to be an X-ray technician, but was denied the opportunity to take the certification exam because she was black. So she enrolled in the Houston College for Negroes, which later became Texas Southern University, where she took enough business courses that Don Robey was sufficiently impressed when she walked into his record store one early summer afternoon looking for work to hire her on the spot to help him run his Bronze Peacock Dinner Club.[20]

Johnson recalled, "The medical work was immediately out of high school. I walked out of high school into a doctor's—and to what was Houston College for Negroes. . . . In my earlier years, I worked with nothing but doctors, and that was good training for me in itself. . . . But I never received the type of professional training I needed to advance in my chosen career [as a radiologist]. There was a school for it. However, I was not permitted to take the state board in Austin. It was the same old thing: number one, I was too young, too dark, and too female. . . . Actually, while I was working in the medical field, I was in school in the business field. So I was working on a business education too, just in case."[21]

Before long Robey was depending on her to manage more and more of his growing business interests. She was not only smart and energetic, but also entrepreneurial and creative. If she did not know something, she would find out about it. Someone at the Library of Congress knew everything, and Johnson did not hesitate to pick up the phone and locate the right person there to give her the information she needed.

Evelyn established all the business systems needed to keep Duke/Peacock Records in operation. She learned about copyrighting and set up Lion Publishing Company to ensure that they received royalties for every song they recorded. When they could not find any agency to book Gatemouth Brown's personal appearances, it was left to Evelyn to apply to the American Federation of Musicians for a booking license in order to "act as agent, manager, or representative for members of the association," and it was Evelyn who named the agency the Buffalo Booking Agency.

She not only booked all the Duke/Peacock artists, but also added other top acts, including B.B. King, Earl King, and the Ike and Tina Turner Revue. At first she booked them into small towns in Texas, reasoning that, "Every little town has a dance hall, or a juke joint. Now every town has a band, because the band plays at the local club, so they are really high on the hog when they get somebody for a traveling band coming in. This is the way we started the agency and built from there." After a while she was booking acts in large and small venues throughout the South, and as far as California, St. Louis, Kansas City, and Chicago—a part of what was known then (and to this day still referred to) as the "chitlin circuit." Johnson recalled those days: "I booked Joe Hinton, B.B. King for nine years, Bobby Bland, Junior Parker, Johnny Ace, Willie Mae Thornton, Lloyd Price, Little Richard and the Tempo Toppers, one of the most terrific male groups that there ever was. I had the Buffalo Booking Agency. That was just my thing. It started with Gatemouth Brown. I finally gave it up because it was very unrewarding. It was a tough row to hoe. However, I can boast that I kept their heads above water until their time came. When I first met B.B. King, he couldn't move to the next town. I wasn't even interested in a contract on him. But we had nine nice years together. I remember them. I don't know who else remembers, but I do, and the United States Treasury, they remember very well."[22]

According to B.B. King, "Evelyn was one of the great women of her time. I don't think she gets enough recognition, because she was one of the pioneers." Gatemouth Brown agrees, recalling that "She was very important. She *made* Robey if you want to know the truth." Everyone who knew the business knew Evelyn Johnson was the key to its success, the real brains behind the operation. Although she did not deny this, she did comment on her partner's limited contribution, saying, "Don Robey had two things: guts and money."[23] In addition to these ever-expanding management responsibilities, she was also, in her words, "mother confessor, lawyer, doctor, sister, financier, mother superior, the whole nine yards" for the artists she represented. "What they needed, they asked for, and what they asked for, they got."[24]

"They [the musicians] did not trust men," she said. "As a matter of fact, many times I had to convey; I had to be the one between. They couldn't even discuss it together, the men. It was, many times, a conflict of interest for me. . . . So many times I had to be the go-between. There were times when they would not sign that record contract unless I presented it to them. That's the truth."[25]

Bobby remembers Evelyn as Duke Records—the person he went to if he had a problem, who kept Robey from interfering, who warned him about getting a swelled head, who even taught him how to read and write. She remembers Bobby as a timid young man with "a lot of complexes. When he hit the stage he was Bobby Bland, but offstage he was just Bobby. He was so shy, and he took no responsibility for anything. You had to lead him around. I was like a mother: 'Did you take a bath today, Bobby?' Even that thing about reading wasn't so severe; I think he pretended he couldn't read to avoid responsibility. He got a valet to do everything for him, so all he ever had to do was just perform onstage. Of course, people would go into a frenzy when he did."[26]

Bobby also met and became good friends with Duke/Peacock's promotion manager, Dave Clark, who ceaselessly pitched the company's products to record stores and radio stations throughout the country, as well as producing gospel records for Peacock's stable of outstanding gospel artists, like the Mighty Clouds of Joy, the Dixie Hummingbirds, the Five Blind Boys of Mississippi, and the Sensational Nightingales.

Clark was born on March 6, 1909, in Jackson, Tennessee. He was raised in Chicago, where he studied piano and violin, and later performed in traveling minstrel shows. He received his college degree from Lane College in 1934 and shortly thereafter began writing a jazz column called "Swing Row Is My Beat" for *Down Beat*. In 1939, he was graduated from the Julliard Conservatory of Music in New York City, where he became a song plugger of sheet music, including his own compositions, to popular big bands. During the 1930s he was also an advance man for the road shows of Billie Holiday, Lionel Hampton, Louis Armstrong, and others, traveling in advance to cities where they were going to perform and promoting the shows to black newspapers, radio stations, and jukebox operators.

In 1938 Clark went to work as an independent promoter for Decca Records, for whom he hawked records by Jimmie Lunceford and other Decca artists. Once, to get a Lunceford record played on New York City's WNEW radio station, he posed as a chauffeur to get in to see the station's deejays. Claiming he was the chauffeur for the station's owner, he told jazz deejay Martin Block that his boss wanted him to play Lunceford's "St. Paul's Walking Through Heaven with You." Block, of course, complied, making Clark the record industry's first promotion man—the first person to convince a deejay to play a record to increase record sales.[27] Later he worked as an independent, non-exclusive representative for a number of independent labels, including Aristocrat, Aladdin, Apollo, United, Vee-Jay, and Ronel. He joined Duke/Peacock in 1954 and worked as head of its promotion department, writing songs for B.B. King (such as "Why I Sing the Blues") and for Bobby Bland, as well as assisting him at recording sessions, until 1971.[28]

On the strength of Little Junior Parker's first hit, "Feelin' Good," and Junior's strong stage persona, Don Robey decided to have Junior break with the Ace-Thornton revue to form his own road show. So, in January 1954, Junior and Bill Johnson's Blue Flames—with Johnson on piano, Pat Hare on guitar, Hamp Simmons on bass, and Sonny Freeman on drums—were out on the "chitlin' circuit," performing across Texas and Louisiana. In March, the revue moved into one-night stands through the Midwest, and in April was joined by a young singer from Georgia who was billing himself as Little Richard. The revue continued its trek on and off throughout 1954 and 1955, playing clubs and dance halls in the South and Midwest, stopping occasionally in Houston to record and to backfill the band with more brass to attain the big band sound that Parker and Robey were now favoring.[29]

In early 1956, at Don Robey and Evelyn Johnson's suggestion, Bobby Bland joined the Junior Parker Revue for a series of one-nighters across the South with the full Bill Harvey band, including, in addition to the Blue Flames rhythm section, Connie Mack Booker on piano and the horn section of Harvey on tenor sax, Joe Scott on trumpet, and Pluma Davis on trombone. Bobby recalled: "Junior had the band. They were called the Blue Flames. Seven pieces.

Yeah, I started out, I was doing a little bit of everything. Doing the driving. Setting up the bandstand. Opening the show. Yeah, I think I was doing the right thing. You see, I didn't get a big hit until 1957, and even that wasn't enough to go out on your own at that particular time. What it was, normally Junior was a good business man, and he tried to teach me what he knowed, but I didn't have good enough ears at that time."[30]

The time on the road gave Bobby, Junior, and the band not only wider exposure but also a chance to work on new material. By March they had come up with a couple of new tunes that they liked and returned to Houston and the recording studio. There, Bobby and the Bill Harvey Orchestra, with the same personnel as on the tour, but with Clarence Hollimon on guitar, cut the loping blues "I Can't Put You Down Baby," and the catchy jump tune, "You've Got Bad Intentions" (Duke 153). It is obvious that Bobby was gaining still more confidence here, but the precise formula of simple phrases with big band pop had not yet been achieved. Nevertheless, the record became a top seller in Atlanta and fared well in most other southern cities.[31]

By this time, the combined Little Junior Parker and Bobby Bland road show was going so well that Don Robey and Evelyn Johnson decided to extend the trip to the West Coast in May and June. When the tour headed back east in October, they were joined by Buddy Ace—Johnny's younger brother, St. Clair Alexander—in an obvious attempt by Robey to continue cashing in on Johnny Ace's tragic demise.[32]

On November 10, 1956, Bobby returned to Duke's Houston studio to record with Onzie Horne's Orchestra, with Horne on piano and nineteen-year-old Clarence Hollimon on guitar, as well as a full band of unidentified brass and rhythm players. Onzie Horne was an Ellington alumnus and well-respected Beale Street band director, who arranged for B.B. King and later conducted and arranged for Isaac Hayes.

Why the sudden shift in band personnel is unclear, but the results are nonetheless swinging. The band sounds great, even though the chemistry starting to jell between Bill Harvey's group and Bobby is absent on both the up-tempo "I Don't Believe" and the Johnny Copeland blues "I Learned My Lesson."

The highlight on all these 1956 cuts is Clarence Hollimon's guitar work, which really shines on the two aforementioned tracks. Hollimon later recalled those early days: "He [Bobby] was a great person. He was real humble. During that time, he had just gotten out of the Army. So what they did, they just put a bunch of fellows together and made a studio band. I can remember Hamp Simmons, the bass player. Joe Scott was doing the writing and arranging. He was the A&R director around there. [Bobby] was a great guy. I met him, and we were the best of friends. I never did travel with him, but I did all the recordings with him from '55 to about '60. He called me 'Injun,' because both of us had big noses. So we called each other 'Injun.' That's how we really got tight. And then, he couldn't read. He couldn't read writing. People, they would laugh at him in the studio. So he kinda took up with me, and I kinda made him feel good by telling him things like, 'One day, these same people will be asking you for work.' And it happened!"[33]

By the beginning of 1957 Elvis Presley was a star and rock 'n' roll was overpowering the pop music charts with hits by Elvis, Fats Domino, Chuck Berry, and Bill Haley pushing aside established hitmakers like Frank Sinatra, Frankie Laine, Dean Martin, and Patti Page. But another appreciably different sound was coming out of Houston, epitomized by the Little Junior Parker tune "Next Time You See Me," which hit *Billboard's* R&B chart on March 16, rising to number 7, and to 74 on the pop chart. It remains a classic R&B song, later covered by the Grateful Dead among others, that provides an initial demonstration of just what tunesmith/saxophonist Bill Harvey, arranger Joe Scott, and Harvey's blasting band could produce given a catchy hook, a tightly arranged brass section, a sharp contrapuntal guitar, supplied here by Pat Hare, and an experienced vocalist like Junior Parker.

The same basic formula was applied to Bobby Bland's January 22, 1957, recordings, the smoky "I Smell Trouble," and the bar band and Johnny Winter favorite "I Don't Want No Woman," an apparent followup to "It's My Life Baby," only without the brass. Bobby sounds completely at home with both, at one point shouting an encouraging "Look out, Clarence!" to guitarist Clarence Holliman who provides the perfect melodic leadership to the hornless rhythm section of Connie Mack Booker on piano, Hamp Simmons on bass, and Sonny Freeman on drums. The short succinct phrasings are similar in these tunes and Bobby sounds more like he is in control of the outcome.

As *Blues Access's* Rooster put it: "His records from the '50s are full of fire, complemented in this case ['I Smell Trouble'] by Clarence Hollimon's down-in-the-alley guitar work. The song—another 'Deadric Malone' creation—is flat-out, searing blues. Bobby simply drives the lyrics, about a man who smells trouble 'way over yonder, up there ahead of me' right through the roof. It's a sound that presaged other, bigger hits that were soon to follow . . . All great, but none better than this one."[34]

Later that year, Bobby returned to the Houston studio to record two of the more interesting tunes of his growing repertoire. The first is a slow ballad *a la* Sam Cooke, "Sometime Tomorrow," featuring Bill Harvey on tenor sax, Sonny Freeman on drums, Pat Hare on guitar, and the "Joe Scott Singers" providing the background vocals. This first attempt to give Bobby vocal assistance is largely a failure, the singers getting in the way more than lending any lushness. The next song cut at this session was "Farther Up the Road," a conventional Texas shuffle with simple revenge love story lyrics that allows Bobby to tell a story and show off his growing vocal prowess. It became Bobby's first national hit, and a huge one at that, peaking at number 1 on the R&B chart, staying on the chart for fourteen weeks, and crossing over to number 43 on the pop chart.

"Joe Medwick wrote this first hit of mine, 'Farther Up the Road,'" recollected Bobby. "They'd kind of pick out the artists that they'd think they could write some good lyrics for and how you tell the story. They'd kind of write from that. They kind of specialized things for you." His first number 1 hit, after so many years of work, really boosted Bobby's confidence. "It was an opportunity, and I felt good about hearing myself on a record that was played every day, so it was quite a change," he said. "Something that you were not used to, but I was very happy about it."[35]

Dave Marsh picked it as one of his "1001 Greatest Singles Ever Made" (the subtitle of his book *The Heart of Rock & Soul*) and had this to say about it: "A virtually perfect Texas blues that became Bland's first pop chart single. Mel Brown's signature lick provides the missing link between T-Bone Walker and Eric Clapton; Bland's deep blues vocal and Scott's arrangement, which swings as hard as it rocks, link Ray Charles's big band R&B to more modern currents in Southern soul as well as the generation of British blues singers typified by Joe Cocker (and Clapton). The lyric beautifully suggests forties and fifties prototypes without a hint of cliché. Bland made better records, but not more influential ones."[36]

The fact that Pat Hare is really "the missing link between T-Bone Walker and Eric Clapton" notwithstanding, the sentiments are on the mark. This was the only Bobby Bland recording session with the legendary guitarist Pat Hare (not Mel Brown who would not join Bobby's band until 1973), who does, in fact, offer up a brilliant stinging solo on "Farther Up the Road," setting a very high standard for later covers by Freddie King and Eric Clapton.

At this point, Hare was the guitarist for Junior Parker's Blue Flames, the band that backed Junior and Bobby on the road. "Pat was actually Junior Parker's guitar player," Bobby noted. "He was with Junior during the time. But we did the session there in Houston. I don't think anybody else could have filled that guitar spot the way he did, because Joe [Scott] picked that particular guitar player."[37]

Born in Cherry Valley, Arkansas, on December 20, 1930, to sharecropper parents, Auburn "Pat" Hare gravitated to the Memphis blues scene at an early age, where he met and worked with Junior Parker in Howlin' Wolf's late-1940s band. Sam Phillips claimed Hare was his favorite guitarist and recruited this "new guitarist with the angry, spine-tingling tone" to play on James Cotton's debut session at Sun and also to record in May 1954 his own tragically prophetic "I'm Gonna Murder My Baby." Hare moved to Houston in 1954 to record for Duke and back up Bobby and Junior Parker on the road. He went on to Chicago, where he replaced Jimmy Rogers in Muddy Waters's Chicago band (circa 1958–63). With Hare's drinking and temperament causing problems, Waters fired him in 1963. Hare moved to Minneapolis to work with Waters's former harp man Mojo Buford, and in December 1963 fulfilled his first song's prophesy, shooting his girlfriend to death and then unloading on the policeman who responded to the crime, costing him life in prison, where he died of lung cancer in 1980.[38]

Continuing their never-ending quest for new talent, Bobby, Junior, and Joe Scott listened to a twenty-five-year-old Chicago guitarist, recently migrated from Oklahoma, who they believed possessed the seamless blend of blues and jazz playing that they had been seeking to replace Pat Hare. "Joe Scott heard him play," Bobby remembered, "so he thought he would fit me—which he did."[39] They hired Wayne Bennett on the spot, and he continued with Bobby, playing a major role in creating the new urban R&B sound over the next twenty years.[40]

Meanwhile, Don Robey was beginning to recognize the value of integration in the record industry. In February 1957 *Billboard* discontinued its "Rhythm-Blues Notes" column and replaced it with a column called "On the Beat." Writer Gary Kramer offered this rationale: "No abstract categories prevent the teenager today from buying records by Fats Domino, Elvis Presley, Bill Haley, Carl Perkins or Little Richard at one and the same time. The trade, therefore, must revise, and perhaps abandon, some of the old boundary lines."

So "the Big Beat" became the industry code word for crossover, and Robey leapt to take advantage of it by launching a new subsidiary label called Back Beat. Soon after its launch in August, three new releases were on the streets, featuring Doug and Josie, Tic and Toc, and Norman Fox and the Rob-Roys, two black guys and three white boys, one of whom, future composer-producer Charles Fox, wrote "Happy Days." Robey told *Billboard:* "The artists appearing on our new label are in most instances 'teenagers' in actual count or at heart. And as such, our new baby—'Back Beat'—is dedicated to the teenage market."[41]

Back Beat went on to record balladeer Joe Hinton ("Funny"), unsung soul great O. V. Wright ("Eight Men, Four Women"), blue-eyed soul man Roy Head ("Treat Her Right"), and Little Carl Carlton, whose version of "Everlasting Love" was a hit in the late seventies and who would later pen the hits "She's a Bad Mamma Jamma" and the Four Tops' "Baby I Need Your Loving."[42]

Not coincidentally perhaps, at about this time a Memphis brother and sister team, Jim Stewart (St-) and Estelle Axton (-ax), began recording local country and western artists in a relative's garage. The following year, Axton bought an Ampex tape recorder and they moved their operation, then called Satellite, to the nearby town of Brunswick. By 1960, they were back in Memphis, relocated to an abandoned theatre on McLemore Avenue, where they eventually became Stax and recorded with an integrated staff and musicians a true pantheon of soul greats, including Carla Thomas, the Mar-Keys, Booker T. and the MGs, Otis Redding, Eddie Floyd, Wilson Pickett, Johnnie Taylor, Sam and Dave, and Isaac Hayes.[43]

So, on the strength of their new hits, the Little Junior Parker/Bobby "Blue" Bland Blues Consolidated, as the revue was now being billed, tour continued to play the chitlin' circuit across the South, with the aid of a new road manager, John Green, a boyhood friend of Don Robey.[44] They played a big show at the Memorial Auditorium in Chattanooga, Tennessee, on August 8, 1957, with Little Richard, the 5 Royales, Big Maybelle, Jimmy Reed, and others. They avoided Little Rock in late September, where President Eisenhower on September 24 had ordered the 1,200-man 327th Airborne Battle Group of the U.S. Army's 101st Airborne Division from Fort Campbell to escort nine students who were attempting to integrate Little Rock Central High School, amidst angry white mobs and mounting violence in and around the school.

Bobby later recalled the period: "And then Junior had 'Next Time You See Me' and I came out with 'Further Up the Road,' '57. And then this is the first time we ever had a chance to really get on our own. Junior had some records. He was drawin' the crowd, you know, when I was working, if there was anybody there. He drew them. I didn't, at all, you know. So I didn't start drawing any people until around '58, is when I started really supporting Junior, you know. But from '55 all the way up, Junior did all the drawing. I was the guinea pig."[45]

On November 15, 1957, the revue stopped in Houston to rest a bit and record four new songs for Bobby that they had been rehearsing on the road. Backed at this session by the entire Bill Harvey Band, with Johnny Board added on sax and Clarence Hollimon returning on guitar, both prominently featured, the group cut Duke 182 with a followup to "Farther Up the Road" called "Bobby's Blues" on one side and a loping Texas blues, "Teach Me (How to Love You)," on the other. At the same session, they also recorded the jump blues, "Loan Me a Helping Hand," and the catchy, up-tempo shuffle, "You Got Me (Where You Want Me)," for Duke 185. The results churn with increasingly jazzier arrangements by Joe Scott and more punctuated, powerful vocals by Bobby. While there were no hits from this session, it demonstrated that "Farther Up the Road" was no fluke.

After the session, Bobby and the crew were back on the road again, returning home to Memphis, on December 6, 1957, to perform at WDIA's Goodwill Revue, the radio station's annual benefit for Memphis charities, where backstage at the Ellis Auditorium Junior and Bobby chatted with fellow

Memphian and blues admirer, Elvis Presley. "His appearance didn't cause the commotion that it had the year before," according to Elvis's biographer Peter Guralnick, "but he had his picture taken with Little Junior Parker (the originator of 'Mystery Train') and Bobby 'Blue' Bland, and he was quoted in the paper as saying that this music was 'the real thing . . . Right from the heart.' You couldn't beat it, he said, watching from the wings and smiling and swaying with the music. 'The audience shouted in time to the solid rhythm' reported the paper. 'Man,' grinned Elvis, 'what about that!'"[46]

Bobby remembers the night. "WDIA had a thing that they'd do every year called the Goodwill Revue for the homeless. I was traveling with Junior Parker during that time. Elvis would come down and always give us a nice booster, saying that he paid his dues with him. The gentleman in the picture along with Elvis and Junior and myself is Walter Bailey, who is my attorney now."[47]

Blues Consolidated continued touring through the end of 1957, with Junior's Blue Flames, whose leadership was now under Joe Scott, and occasionally with Big Mama Thornton. When the revue stopped in Nashville, they heard a twenty-two-year-old trumpet player named Melvin Jackson who had already cut his chops playing with Memphis Slim and Jody Williams. "Melvin came down and sat in with us and Joe [Scott] liked him. . . . He had a little raggedy horn, but he could really play it. That's the way it started . . ." Bobby recalled years later.[48]

"I played with Memphis Slim in 1955," Melvin Jackson remembers, "for about two or three weeks down in Florida. . . . He [Bobby Bland] came to Nashville and I was riding around and I heard that they was in town so I went by the club just to see the group. The trumpet player was leaving and they asked me would I sit in because I knew some of the guys in the group. I already knew their music because I had played with Gene Allison and we had a singer in that group named Earl Gaines and he was doing all of Bobby's stuff. So I already knew his stuff. Yeah, I was with Gene Allison also, for about a year and a half or two. I picked up the Bobby Bland songs because Earl Gaines was the opening act with Gene Allison. Yeah, I played with them [Bland's band] that night and I left with them the next day."[49]

Melvin Jackson would travel with, and later lead, Bobby's band for the next twenty years (except for a three year hiatus in 1968–71), one of the more enduring musical relationships on record.

Blues Consolidated: (standing) Little Junior Parker, Hamp Simmons, Jimmy Johnson, Eugene Ballow, Auburn "Pat" Hare; (kneeling) Bobby Bland and Joe "Papoose" Fritz, ca. 1958. Courtesy of Colin Escott.

6

Dreamer

1958–1960

Encouraged by the reception of the big band sound on "Farther Up the Road," Don Robey and Joe Scott bolstered Bobby's recording band with three trumpets (played by Scott and newcomers Melvin Jackson and Floyd Arceneaux), two tenor saxophones (played by Bobby Forte and Jimmy Beck), the usual Pluma Davis on trombone, Hamp Simmons on bass, Teddy Reynolds on piano, Sonny Freeman on drums, and, for the first time, Wayne Bennett on guitar. On January 9, 1958, this exceptional group of musicians entered the Houston studio to record four new songs. The first was a pretty ballad called "Last Night" which was backed by the classic "Little Boy Blue," both featuring Wayne Bennett's guitar. Next was an up-tempo "You Did Me Wrong," which should have been a hit, if not because of Bobby's maturing style, then because of Wayne Bennett's acrobatic guitar work, and the slow blues with a real big band bang, "I Lost Sight of the World," which someone inexplicably overdubbed with a flute for the single version (Duke 300), but not for the LP version (Duke LP 86).

It was at about this time that Bobby says he was really starting to create the sound that he liked. "I had this falsetto that I did for a long time, like the time when I did 'I Smell Trouble' and things. I was trying to be another B.B. King with it," he recalled.[1] "In fact, he put me on the right road. I was explaining to him some years back, I said, 'You know, B., I can sound just like you.' He said, 'That's very good, Bob. But you'll never get anything unless you get some kind of originality; the people identify you for who you are, not sounding like somebody.'"[2] The advice was not forgotten and was repeated one night years later when Bobby heard a young Tyrone Davis mimicking him. "Bobby said," according to Davis, "'Be you. Don't be me.'" That advice, said Davis, was "the best thing that ever happened to me."[3]

So, Bobby, adhering to B.B.'s counsel, started working on his own style. He explains: "It was '57 before I got a style of my own. Well, I was listening to Franklin a lot at the time—that's Reverend C. L. Franklin, Aretha's daddy— and my favorite at the time B.B. King, of course, that had the high falsetto. Well, actually I was listening to a whole lot of different things, whoever had the hottest record on the jukebox, really. See, I developed the softness by listening to different singers like Nat 'King' Cole or Perry Como or Tony Bennett. Man, they have a lot of feeling in their voices, they have a lot of what I call soul. I wouldn't say they would be able to sing blues, but they do a helluva job on ballads and such. But the thing is, I'd been listening to Reverend Franklin a lot—'The Eagle Stirreth His Nest'—and that's where I got my squall from. After I had lost the high falsetto. You see, I had to get some other kind of gimmick, you know, to be identified with. So I thought that was a good thing. And the first thing I tried it was in '56, I think it was, when I tried 'Little Boy Blue.' And I think it paid off."[4]

But it wasn't just a gimmick, the so-called "squall"—or the "chicken-bone sound," "what they call in London the 'love throat,'"[5] or more precisely a sharp, growlng-like clearing of the throat noise—it was also a unique pop blues style that Bobby was carefully crafting. He explains:

> Like, I try to do it in a ballad type say, where it won't be a strictly blues type, where they classify you as a blues singer and nothing else. But I don't want this. So I do a variety of things. But now basically what I have to rely on is blues, because this is what I know, and like, I grew up with this. And I educate myself through records and people that I think that has something to offer now. Like, take for instance, I've always admired Tony Bennett, Perry Como, Andy Williams. It's a thing that like, voice-wise that I listen to. Frank Sinatra was a thing like, they made, but didn't ever really kill me like, as a vocalist. Now he's a song stylist, more or less, I'd say. But he didn't have the feeling that I would say Tony Bennett or Andy Williams has, or Perry Como. So this is the thing that I based my blues on, and I have quite a few records of Tony, also Andy Williams and Perry Como that I listen to and learn from. How to breathe, how to say a note, to approach it and what have you, and I must say that I've learned quite a lot from Tony Bennett, which is an idol of mine that I really love, because he has perfect control, like voice, and I wish that I could really control. I have control to an extent, but I mean really to know how to bend a note. I can bend one better than him, at my thing. But like I'd like to know the classical way of doing a note, you know, and this he have. Very beautiful. I must say that, well, in my book, he's the best that I've heard. And Perry, which I love to listen to, you know, when the TV sign off. "Our Father." Have you heard this? Perry Como? It's a beautiful thing, and I like the way that he phrase words and how he attack things.[6]

"I liked Jimmy Witherspoon," Bobby continued. "Spoon was a little more upper crust for me. I liked that. I love to hear Otis Clay sing. Charles Brown was one of the people I took up with, because he had good stories. Back in his time you had to tell a story in a song. So if the lyrics hit me, I learn how to deliver the words in the right spot, where it means something. I basically sing to the ladies.[7] That's the best thing to kind of gear towards, because they're the special ones in everybody's life. When they make up their minds to go and do something, the men basically follow."[8]

So Bobby learned Jimmy Witherspoon's new jazz phrasing for the blues, singing the lyrics behind the beat rather than directly on it or next to it. As Joe Scott explained, "There's a strong-beat blues where the words are right on the beat, and then you can do it the way 'Spoon' does it, taking your time, pausing and then catching up with the band. As far as I know, 'Spoon' was the first to phrase that way."

Jimmy Witherspoon himself said it this way: "If I'm working with a band that doesn't know me I won't take liberties, because they're liable to think I messed up someplace—lost a chord or something. But as soon as I'm sure they know enough to hold on to the chords, I may wait a couple of measures or longer with some lines, to make my point."[9]

According to Dave Hoekstra, "But the one thing that never changes is Bland's behind-the-beat voice, which is the last living testimony to soul music. Bland is one of the few blues and soul singers who still sing across the mike, folding the tongue to create form and panache."

Bobby seldom analyzes his singing style to that degree, but he does admit that "E-flat is a good blues key, but I did most of my recordings in G and F. C doesn't treat me too good."[10]

"Didcha ever listen to Little Willie John?" Bobby asked. "I came from the younger generation, had that same delivery. We kind of added the St. Louis blues and W.C. Handy, or whatever."[11]

Always the student, however, Bobby also points to Nat "King" Cole as one of his favorite teachers, "I had a kind of learning process with Nat, because he's the only person that I've ever listened to that had perfect diction with a song, that you can hear every word. See, I kind of mumble some things because maybe I get off track, maybe I think I'm losing time with the music or whatever and jumble up the words—sometimes I say things a little too fast. But Nat was never like that. I got a lot of information from him about how to deliver a lyric. I met him twice before he passed. He was a delightful person to be around, to talk to. He loved the Dodgers and he loved to talk about baseball."[12]

"I work with whatever is available, whatever fits, whatever I can relate to," Bobby explained. "Then you take some of the things that happened, that disappointed you, that made you sad, something that puts you into the right mood for that lyric, and that's the way I do it.[13] I'm very funny recording, very moody. The scene has to be right. Like late at night and get in there and start feeling sorry for myself. Maybe remember some bad experience of disappointment."[14]

"He is not an intuitive singer," music critic Gary Giddins wrote about Bobby's singing style, "but rather a master of employing a cache of techniques for the optimum expression of a song's lyrics. His voice is unique, rimmed with a soft peach-fuzz, capable of gullying low like a cello, and ranging high with gargled *wanaaahhhs* and long melismatic moans. He's a screamer without being a shouter, in the Rushing-Turner sense, but he is always in control, never cracking into a desperate B.B. King yell. In this regard, he is really a pop singer working with a blues palette. He has superb time and knows where the drama in a song lies, when to climax and when to constrain himself. But he does not take overt chances because to do so might imply that his mastery of the tried and true is less than sufficient. . . . Bobby Blue Bland is a helluva singer."[15]

The resulting Bobby Bland sound, however, transcends these many influences and becomes more than the sum of its musical parts. Not exactly gospel, not traditional blues, not stylized ballads, but more of an amalgamative understanding of not just the lyrics, but of a deeper, visceral meaning that is coming from somewhere far inside the singer. In the end, the lyrics—often meaningful, but just as often banal—are not that important to the end product; it is, instead, the feeling that Bobby exudes from his own experiences, from too many cigarettes, late nights, liquor, and loves lost and found that listeners respond and become addicted to.

As respected jazz critic, J. B. Figi, in his first article for *Down Beat* in 1969, poetically quoted himself as his alter-ego pseudonym, novelist James Bey, "Bobby's voice is the lion which lies down with the lamb, a large sunwarmed brindle beast, tough but oh-so-gentle, smooth, muscle under suede, and plenty of male equipment. He's the only singer I have fully trusted since Lady Day. I guess his songs hang in the closet of all of us who came up a certain way in certain times."[16]

After this single 1958 recording session, the Blue Flames were back on the road again, returning long enough in February for Bobby to appear with Houston KCOH radio deejay Clifton "King Bee" Smith for a live broadcast.[17]

To take advantage of the burgeoning new LP record market and to cash in on Bobby's and Junior Parker's hits, Duke released, an LP, *Blues Consolidated*, in May 1958 with some of Junior's previously recorded songs on one side and Bobby's on the other, including "It's My Life, Baby," "I Smell Trouble," "Farther Up the Road," "Sometime Tomorrow," "You Got Me (Where You Want Me)," and "Loan Me a Helping Hand." The album was reissued in 1974 by ABC as *The Barefoot Rock and You Got Me.*

In July, Blues Consolidated headed to the West Coast and filled Los Angeles' famous R&B night club, the 5-4 Ballroom. For Labor Day weekend, Evelyn

Johnson booked the Revue, along with their old Beale Street buddy B.B. King, for a big R&B show at Houston's Civic Auditorium.[18]

"Little Boy Blue" was released at midyear and by October 6, 1958, was on *Billboard*'s R&B chart, going all the way to number 10 by Thanksgiving. "Bland laid into the gut-wrenching blues-soul hybrid with every ounce of vocal power at his disposal . . . ," Jeff Hannusch observed. "Especially riveting are its last 30 seconds, where Bland summons a pure sanctified fervor."[19] Asked once what song he really got "juiced" about playing, veteran bluesman Johnny Winter replied, "'Little Boy Blue' by Bobby Blue Bland is one of my favorites. I love that one."[20]

As popular as the tune was, it is no wonder that Bobby dropped it from his standard stage show a few years later, explaining, "It's too hard to do every night. You can't just stand up and do it at will. Because it takes a lot of effort to make it come out. I mean, like it supposed to."[21] Bobby's approach to a song is to work on it until he finds the definitive interpretation and then to sing it that way every time, until it becomes too difficult, and then he drops it from his live repertoire. A show every night takes its toll over the years, so there needs to be a certain conservation of energies if he is to continue.[22]

It is hard to believe with all this touring and recording that Bobby had much time for himself or anyone else, but somehow he met and fell in love with a pretty, young model named Grace Towles. They were married in November, and Bobby finally moved out of the Crystal Hotel and in with Grace in Houston.[23] Of course, Bobby really never moved in anywhere, traveling from hotel to hotel on the road most every night now. His career in music was taking off and he needed to be out promoting his hits and making more music. He asked Don Robey and Evelyn Johnson to send his royalty checks to Grace, and he lived on what little he made from live performances, enough to keep him in new clothes and jewelry and increasing amounts of alcohol to mellow out the endless stream of one-nighters.

So, soon after a brief honeymoon, it was back in the studio for a January 1959 session to cut Duke 303, with the usual studio band of Joe Scott on trumpet, Rayfield Devers on baritone sax, Johnny Board on alto and tenor sax, Clarence Hollimon on guitar, Hamp Simmons on bass, Teddy Reynolds on piano, and Sonny Freeman on drums. The two cuts they recorded were "I'm Not Ashamed," with Bobby's voice really upfront now, confidently leading the band, and "Wishing Well," which gives the band more of a workout, particularly Clarence Hollimon's swinging guitar. The record was released in April and by May "I'm Not Ashamed" was on the R&B chart, ultimately climbing to number 13.

This turned out to be the last session with Bobby for guitarist Clarence Holliman, who Bobby called not only "Injun" but also "one of the greatest guitarists in the world."[24] Born Milton Howard Clarence Hollimon in Houston on October 24, 1937, he dropped out of Wheatley High School in Houston's Fifth Ward to play full time with the Bill Harvey Orchestra. Sick of the road where he had been backing Big Mama Thornton and later Charles Brown since 1954, he continued to do session work for Duke/Peacock until 1962. In 1964, he temporarily moved to New York to work with Nancy Wilson and also played on Scepter recording sessions for Dionne Warwick and Chuck Jackson, among others. Upon his return to Houston the next year, he went back to work for Duke/Peacock and moonlighted with jazz bandleader and saxophonist Arnett Cobb, as well as working with Dan Wilkerson's Fifth Ward Express. He met and married Houston vocalist Carol Fran in 1983. Billed as Fran & Hollimon, they worked in Houston, touring throughout the world, and recording occasionally until shortly before his death on April 23, 2000.[25]

After the session the band hit the road again. Having just lost Sonny Freeman to B.B. King's band, they picked up a young drummer in Mobile, Alabama, named John "Jabo" Starks, who recalls the meeting: "Eventually, I played with a local group called the Castanets. We were *the* group in Mobile at the time. Bobby Bland and Junior Parker came through and heard us. They were traveling together with the same band and they had good records, so they were getting ready to go their separate ways. Junior Parker was going to take the band and Bobby Bland was looking for a new group, so he asked us. Nobody wanted to go but me! I said, 'Fine,' so they sent me a ticket to Houston and that's where it all started."[26]

On January 12, 1959, encouraged by the success of Duke as a successful black-owned record company, Tamla Records was founded by Berry Gordy in Detroit. Tamla would later become Motown Records, of course, and the leader in R&B pop music for the next two decades.[27]

By March 26, Bobby was back in the Houston studio, joined by Starks on drums, Wayne Bennett replacing Clarence Hollimon on guitar, Teddy Reynolds on piano, Hamp Simmons on bass, and Floyd McKissick on flute. The combo cut three songs that owed more than a little to the recent success of a twenty-eight-year-old gospel/blues/pop crooner named Sam Cooke. His "Everybody Likes to Cha Cha Cha" had just hit the charts and Bobby's "Is It Real" echoes its sentiments as well as its Latin dance beat. "That's Why" is a pretty ballad, and "Hold Me Tenderly" is a full-blown attempt at pop music, complete with flute, choir, and strings—the first time Bobby had recorded with them. He recalls, "I've always loved strings, but the type of stuff, the things that I was doing, singing, really didn't fit the strings. That's when I had to develop this other type of soft voice. I was really proud that it happened."[28]

"Oh man, it was beautiful, because all of those violins were so beautiful," Bobby added. "If you've never had the chance to perform with that, it's a big plus for you. Some of the things that I had heard the other people do with the strings and oboes and what have you, so I was very happy to get a chance to record with that kind of surroundings. It was something that I had been looking forward to. Joe [Scott] said I had to wait until I was ready."[29]

Shortly thereafter, on June 26, 1959, the entire band reunited in Houston for a very productive session. Joining the usual rhythm section were Joe Scott and Melvin Jackson on trumpet, Pluma Davis on trombone, Robert Skinner and L.A. Hill on tenor sax, Rayfield Devers on baritone sax, and Floyd McKissick again on flute. The session produced three killer hits. While the first song recorded, "Someday," never hit the charts, it is a classic Bobby Bland slow ballad that Bobby still occasionally sings. However, Duke coupled it with "Is It Real" (Duke 310) from the previous session and it reached number 28 on the R&B chart by the end of the year. Also hitting the chart by year's end was one of Bobby's biggest hits, the second to crossover to the pop charts and eventually going to number 2 on the R&B chart, "I'll Take Care of You," composed by pop singer Brook Benton. The third song, "Lead Me On," followed soon thereafter, breaking onto the chart in April 1960.

"I'll Take Care of You" is instantly recognizable by Teddy Reynolds's eerie overdubbed organ lead, which may be the first on a blues recording; at first listening, it sounds intrusive, but grows on you with each successive play. Bobby's voice is at its silky best, making you actually believe that he will, in fact, "take care of you."

"I would say that Clyde Otis [the first African American A&R executive with a major record label, Mercury, and Brook Benton songwriting collaborator] and Brook thought that I could do a real good job, especially Brook Benton," Bobby said. "Because I had met him on the road before. And he said, 'I've got a tune for you, Bob.' I said, 'Yeah, I'd love it!' That was one of my biggest tunes."[30]

"Lead Me On," written by Al Braggs, may be the ultimate Bobby Bland song that unloads just about everything Bobby and the band had to offer: flute, organ, strings, piano, choir, guitar, Bobby, everything melding perfectly together in one tight, billowing package—and, of course, opening with one of the most ominous couplets of all bluesdom:

> *You know how it feels*
> *You understand*
> *What it is to be a stranger*
> *In this unfriendly land*

The song can have a powerful effect, as evidenced by this florid tribute written by John Floyd for the Memphis *Flyer:* "Nearly 40 years after its release, Bobby 'Blue' Bland's 1960 single 'Lead Me On' remains one of the most frightening moments in the pantheon of human expression, a song of despair so bottom-less it can crumble even the most stable of emotional foundations. The thing is barely two minutes long, but by the time it's over, 'Lead Me On' has saturated your soul and psyche like a virus, leaving you shivering throughout the night, tormented by doubt, teased by blind hope, reaching for something you know damn well isn't there—or worse, reaching for something you actually *think* is there and coming up miserably, pathetically empty-handed. . . . 'Lead Me On' is as harrowing as the deepest, darkest blues, from Rabbit Brown's 'James Alley Blues' to Howlin' Wolf's 'Moanin' at Midnight,' from Blind Lemon Jefferson's 'See That My Grave is Kept Clean' to Robert Johnson's 'Hellhound On My Trail.'"[31]

These two songs, "I'll Take Care of You" and "Lead Me On," also represent the more expressive side of Bobby's increasingly rounded, mature male persona, taking the responsibility to care for someone on the one hand and needing to be cared for on the other. As Arnold Shaw once noted, Bobby's appeal had a lot to do with his "combination of helplessness and self-assurance."[32] They are also Bobby's favorites because, he says, "they're more of a spiritual to it. Because y'see, I picture a lot of things, y'know, how things really should be, and some notes that I sing on stage, I have to close my eyes because I can visualize, y'know, the word and the thought, and I put them together and it makes a beautiful picture."[33]

The sentiments in these two examples came from two different sources, how-ever. "I'll Take Care of You" was one of the few songs attributed to someone other than Don Robey or Deadric Malone. Brook Benton, a splendid crooner and talented songwriter from South Carolina, had hit it big earlier in the year with his own composition, "It's Just a Matter of Time," and continued to pro-duce hits throughout the 60s, with seven number 1 R&B hits, culminating with Tony Joe White's "Rainy Night in Georgia" in 1970. His suave, sophisticated style helped his songs cross over to the pop charts, and his composition credits also included hits by Nat "King" Cole ("Looking Back"), Clyde McPhatter ("A Lover's Question"), and Mavis Staples and himself ("Endlessly"). He died on April 9, 1988, at the age of fifty-six, from pneumonia while weakened by spinal meningitis.[34]

"Lead Me On" was attributed to one Deadric Malone, as were the vast majority of the Bobby Bland Duke recordings. Recordings prior to 1958 were attributed directly to Don Robey (and to David Mattis, under his pen name David James, while he was still with the company). Occasionally someone else would receive a credit on the label, most often Joseph Scott, who among the four—Robey, Mattis, Malone, and Scott—was the only one who actually deserved it. Robey would simply buy a song, often no more than a few words or a rhythm pattern, from songwriters who were desperate to make a quick buck. He would then turn it over to Joe Scott or another staff arranger to make into a real song, which he would then copyright for himself. It all went back, of course, to Robey's original all-encompassing business plan: discover the artist, record the artist, represent the artist, and copyright all the songs so the royalties would go to the company instead of the actual composer. Robey, as always, played by his own rules, and, while the practice was not unusual at the time, a songwriter, with a few exceptions, either conformed or did not work for Duke.

So, despite the fact that Robey could not play an instrument ("he only played the radio," Evelyn Johnson said), nor could he sing ("he had a tin ear"), nor read or write music ("are you kidding?"), all these songs were copyrighted directly to him or Deadric Malone, Robey's nom-de-copyright, made up from his middle name and his second wife's surname.[35] The pseudonym was invented to avoid criticism by actual songwriters, Robey told *Record World*: "'Well, he wants to be all of it. He wants to manufacture the records, maintain the artists and write the songs.' So I thought it was hurting a little bit and I stopped it; I wouldn't use Robey anymore." Gatemouth Brown was not fooled for a minute: "Deadric Malone was the fictitious name Robey used to claim authorship to things he didn't write. It was his way to get the royalties."

And royalties he got. By the end of his career, Robey/Malone had writer credit on more than 1,200 songs, according to the music licensing service BMI, "more songs than Holland-Dozier-Holland [Motown composers] and Harlan Howard [prolific country and western tunesmith] put together." And for each of these songs, Peacock/Duke paid the statutory mechanical rights fee of two cents per side for the rights to use the song on a record, or four cents per each record sold, which cost about seventy-nine cents at the time, to the copyright holder: Don Robey, in essence paying himself. In addition, he received quarterly checks from BMI for public performances, like radio and jukebox play, of each popular record.

"So far as buying of the songs," Evelyn Johnson said, "all of the people on our side [independent labels] of the business were doing it, but by the same token the big boys were doing it too. They were buying whole songs. This was just normal business."[36]

Robey would buy material from a variety of sources. Little Junior Parker remembers that his big hit, "Next Time You See Me," credited to Robey, was bought "from kids on the street in Houston. Do you know how much that song cost? $12.50."[37]

One of the Duke songwriters was a young performer who Bobby discovered in an after-hours club called the Golden Duck in Dallas around this time. Born in Dallas on May 23, 1938, Al "TNT" Braggs sang in the church choir and local gospel and doo-wop groups (the Five Notes, the Five Stars, the Five Masks) and taught himself how to play a variety of instruments. "By me playing at the after-hours places," Braggs recounted, "Bobby Bland would come by, him and B.B. and oh, I could sound just like Bobby, still can to this day. He'd come by and I'd sing all his stuff. So one night he told me. He said, 'How would you like to record?' And I said, 'Fine.' He said, 'Well, next time I come I'm going to bring Don Robey' to the after-hours place where I played, the Golden Duck, for Elmore Harrington. Sure enough four or five months later, Bobby used to come about six times a year. Well, the next time Bobby came in, he brought Robey in. Here I am. Don D. Robey. This man is a legend."³⁸ Robey started recording him for Peacock, and Braggs recorded twelve records for Peacock over an eleven-year period, with little success.³⁹ But some of the songs that he wrote for Bobby met with phenomenal success. According to Bobby, "Al wrote 'Lead Me On,' and 'Call on Me'—a gold record, and 'That's the Way Love Is.' He gave me the lines ahead of time when we were recording."⁴⁰

According to R&B historian Rob Bowman, John KaSandra really wrote "Ain't Nothing You Can Do"; former Amos Milburn guitarist Johnny Brown penned "Two Steps From the Blues"; and Joe Medwick (born Joseph Medwick Veasey) originated "Farther Up the Road" and "I Pity the Fool," among others.⁴¹ Evelyn Johnson remembers: "Joe Medwick would come and sit in the waiting room, and he might write five [songs]. And then he would go sell them to [Robey] for maybe five dollars a piece. Then [Robey] had people like Joe Scott and different musicians to write scores, and they were either paid scale for the job or they were salaried people."⁴²

Teddy Reynolds recalled working with Medwick on potential chart-busters. According to Reynolds, they would go to the studio and work all day. Medwick would hum a tune or a snatch of a tune and Reynolds would play it on the piano and either transcribe it or tape it. Medwick would then pitch them to Robey who, if he liked them, would pay $100 per song, considerably more than the five dollars that Johnson recalls, and Medwick would give $25 a song to Reynolds for his help. They both would then retire down the street to the Club Matinee to party away their earnings with other musicians well into the night.⁴³

Another of Medwick's collaborators was a nineteen-year-old Houston guitarist named Johnny Copeland who was just beginning his career in 1956. In a 1984 interview Copeland recalled how Bobby's first number 1 hit was written:

I didn't know nothing about writing at the time, so I get my friend Joe Medwick, and we sit down one night after hours. We started writing a song called "Further On Up the Road." We finished the song that night, and Joe went out to the studio the next day to submit the song to Mr. Robey because that was what Mr. Robey told me to do. I said, "You take it out there. I'm not going with you,"

because at the time I was married and I had little kids, and my wife was work-
ing during the daytime. I was home with the kids, and it was hard for me to
move around.

Well, when Joe got to the studio, Bobby was cutting an album, and they
needed one more song, and that was it. I'm not identified on the record because
Joe tied the song up with Don Robey, just as he did with every song. Joe sold Mr.
Robey maybe five hundred songs, ten, fifteen dollars apiece, and he cut maybe
five, but they were big hits. You understand what I'm saying.[44]

This arrangement worked profitably for Medwick until Robey found out
that the young writer was selling the same basic songs to two other record
producers. That ended that, and Medwick spent the subsequent years kicking
around the periphery of the business, cutting an occasional record and eventually reuniting with his old friend Grady Gaines as featured vocalist with the
Texas Upsetters band.

Still, there were apparently no hard feelings. "Don't you write nothing bad
about Don Robey," Medwick told the Houston *Chronicle* in 1990. "If you came
to him meaning business, he'd treat you like business. If you came to him wanting $30, he'd treat you like a $30 person. He got a bad name, but he was a man
with a soft heart."[45]

Bobby Bland expresses similar sentiments, "Shit, Robey didn't write none
of them. He got them from—well, there used to be a lot of writers who went
through there. No, he didn't steal them! They always got what they asked for.
It's not his fault that they didn't have time enough to wait."[46]

Bobby did, though. He had waited through three difficult years, recording
for three different labels with no hits and not much to show for it. He had
waited through more than two boring years in the Army with no more than
an honorable discharge and a bus ticket to Houston. And he had waited still
another two years, practicing, performing—persevering more than anything—
before finally recording a hit record. But now, it seemed, they were coming fast
and furious. Bobby had prevailed and his dream had finally come true. He was
at last a star.

On the strength on the number 1 hit "Farther Up the Road" in 1957, "Little
Boy Blue" in 1958, and three big hits in 1959, including the number 2 "I'll Take
Care of You," Bobby and the band stopped in Chicago on August 3, 1960, to
begin work on an album. Conventional wisdom at the time held that R&B fans
did not buy albums, but Bobby and Little Junior Parker's *Blues Consolidated*
LP had sold surprisingly well, as had a Duke compilation LP, *Like 'Er Hot*,
which contained Bobby's "Hold Me Tenderly" and "Farther Up the Road."
Don Robey wanted to try a solo album with Bobby, if Joe Scott could somehow
pull enough material together for it.

It was decided that the band would cut the album in two marathon sessions with nine new songs that Scott had worked up. Of the nine, seven were deemed polished enough to go on the album, three would become some of Bobby's biggest hits, and more than one would become true modern blues classics. Assembled for the sessions was the usual ensemble that, under Joe Scott's direction, was now jelling into a tight, well-rehearsed, bombastic, blues band: Scott and Melvin Jackson on trumpet, Pluma Davis on trombone, Robert Skinner and L. A. Hill on tenor sax, Rayfield Devers on baritone sax, Teddy Reynolds on piano, Wayne Bennett on guitar, Hamp Simmons on bass, and John "Jabo" Starks on drums.

"When we recorded *Two Steps From the Blues*," Jabo Starks recalled, "we did one side of the album in a few days, then we went out, stayed a week or two and came back and did the other side. A lot of times we'd go to Nashville. I think *Two Steps From the Blues* was recorded in Nashville."[47]

Well, actually in Chicago, but it was a long time ago. Why did they begin recording on the road rather than in Houston? Peter Guralnick asked Bobby, who answered: "'Well, it was the sound,' Bobby says at first, then thinks better of it. 'It was Robey, really. He was always mixing in, and he didn't know a damned thing about it. It really pissed me off, man.[48] Joe Scott would pick the places to record. He would check it out before we even did it. But [Chicago's] Universal Studio was one of the places I really liked. We did 'Stormy Monday' in Nashville, which was a good town to record in, period."[49]

The first session resulted in three songs that ultimately made it to the album. "Cry, Cry, Cry" went to number 9 on the R&B chart and stayed there for eighteen weeks. Dave Marsh selected it as another of his "1001 Greatest Singles Ever Made" and commented: "The vast, implacable sonorities of the records made by Bobby Bland, the most sophisticated of Southern bluesmen and most country of all soul singers, inspired a generation of white Southerners as they tried to imitate the inimitable. That meant trying to capture not only the preternatural dignity of Bland's singing but the resonances and angularities of Joe Scott's brilliant arrangements, which were both the site of Bland's sophistication and the key to his synthesis. 'Cry, Cry, Cry' ranks as a better example of Scott's work than of Bland's, since the real source of its ever-increasing excitement comes from the softly swinging support. Although Bland cuts loose for a quick, gospelly rant near the end, what's forever surprising here is the way the music reveals a tremendous amount of energy but keeps it contained. It's like a definition of bottled lightning."[50]

"I've Been Wrong So Long" displays why Bobby is renowned as the master of the blues ballad and why Wayne Bennett is the most articulate blues guitarist ever. "Two Steps From the Blues" extends Bennett's stature even further, without taking anything away from Bobby. Surprisingly, the song was never released as a single, although it became the title song for the album. Written by Houston guitarist Texas Johnny Brown, Joe Scott had recorded a demo of the tune at Shady's Playhouse in Houston's tough Third Ward and took it on the road to arrange. Brown explained:

> *When I started workin' with Bobby Bland and Junior Parker, then I started writin'. I rode up and down the highway with "Two Steps From the Blues" for about two years. I'd write it one way and I'd change it. I'd write it and I'd change it. I think I must have been in some kind of little conflict with my love life. I was tryin' to avoid sayin' it, you know. But if I avoided sayin' it then the song wouldn't be true. So I just said, "Hell, well, I'm just gonna tell the truth about it." I just backed up and told the truth about it. I brought it down and I gave it to Joe [Scott] and we listened to it. I just thought that one would be pretty fittin' tune for Bobby and Joe said, "Yeah. This is the one." So I played it out for him and he scored it. The only thing I played on was the demo. Wayne [Bennett] did the recording. What he did was what I put on the demo. See, when it was recorded, I was on the road with Junior Parker. But I was very happy with what he did. I loved it. He was a beautiful guitar player, man. Turned out to be the one too. That's the one Bobby got his gold record at. I was happy for him. . . . I got just a little money from "Two Steps From the Blues." Supposedly, sales wasn't up to where they should have been. . . . MCA's got those publishing rights now so I get mechanicals at least. I don't blame Duke Records. Don Robey was Don Robey and he did what he had to do.[51]*

Two other songs were recorded at this session but did not end up on the album: "Close To You," Bobby's first recorded attempt to achieve his childhood ambition of being a country and western singer, only here with a decidedly Joe Scott big band flare; and "How Does a Cheatin' Woman Feel," a dirgelike blues led by Wayne Bennett's guitar, like Teddy Reynolds's organ on "I'll Take Care of You," to which the tune was too similar to be included on the album.

On November 12, 1960, the album's second session was held in Chicago and resulted in a good cut of the standard Joe Primrose (a.k.a. Irving Mills) tune "St. James Infirmary," marked by a haunting Pluma Davis trombone solo and punctuated by the band's staccato horn section. They also recorded "I've Just Got to Forget You," one of Bobby's moodiest, saddest lost-love ballads. Both made it to the album, but "I've Just Got to Forget You" was seemingly forgotten and was not released on a single until it turned up on the flip side of the Don Davis produced "Keep On Loving Me (You'll See the Change)" in 1970, some ten years later.

"Don't Cry No More" was also recorded, released as a single, and went to number 2 on the R&B chart. It has to be one of everyone's favorite up-tempo, brassy Bobby Bland romps. A precursor to Bobby's next big hit, "Turn On Your Love Light," Jabo Starks's constant rhythm pounds incessantly right into Bobby's parting "Summer Time" cameo.

"I Pity the Fool" was also cut that day and went on to become Bobby's second number 1 R&B chart-topper; it is quintessential Bobby Bland. "Joe found that, really," Bobby recalled. "I can't think now who wrote that, but it was a good change. I always had some good writers after I got my first record out there, and writers started pinpointing on what would be good for Bobby Bland."[52] And no one did that better than Joe Medwick, who actually penned this popular hit.[53]

Blues historian and critic David Evans had this to say about "I Pity the Fool": "Bland begins this song singing calmly, stating that he pities the fool who loves a certain woman. Suddenly we learn that the fool is none other than the singer, as he bursts out screaming about the people who are standing around watching him make a fool of himself. Bland is the picture of utter humiliation in this frightening outburst, sounding like he is going to do harm to himself or somebody else. This is powerful soul blues at its emotional best. The 1960 performance is greatly enhanced by the arrangement of Joe Scott, featuring twin trumpets as part of a six-piece horn section. The relentless quarter-note beat is broken up by the jagged lead guitar lines of Wayne Bennett."[54]

Not bad for a day's work. Bobby's voice was maturing and gaining confidence, the band was coming together, and all were finally melding just the way Scott had envisaged. Bobby's Delta blues and gospel voice was somehow working with the more urban Texas Gulf Coast sound. "Bobby actually never did have that many musicians from Memphis," Hamp Simmons, Bobby's Houston-based bassist, observed, "because he came here when he was in the service in Austin, and he came to stay here. So he recruited most of his musicians from Houston. B.B. had quite a few from Memphis, but plenty of Texas guys too. . . . We all learned from each other."[55] The sound they created together was different, however: not exactly big band jazz, not really gospel, but certainly a new way of presenting the blues. As Count Basie once said, "Of course, there are a lot of ways you can treat the blues, but it will still be the blues."

At the heart of Bobby Bland's blues was Joseph Wade Scott, born December 2, 1924, in Texarkana, Arkansas.[56] He joined Bill Harvey's Orchestra as a trumpet player while the band was still in Memphis. When Don Robey moved Duke's recording operations to Houston in 1953, Harvey, Scott, and most of the rest of the band relocated to Houston to work for Robey. Scott was a trained musician who possessed a particularly good ear and talent for arranging. He joined the Johnny Ace Revue in 1953 and was with the band when Ace shot himself on December 25, 1954.

That was enough of the road for Scott, at least for a while, so he joined the Duke/Peacock session band and gradually assumed its leadership and arranging roles, as well as writing and revising songs ("Joe Scott did most of the writing," according to Bobby), assembling band members, and producing records—creating what would come to be known as "the Duke sound."[57]

"According to some insiders," Charles Keil wrote, "Bobby Bland is Joe Scott's creation."[58] When Peter Guralnick asked Bobby how important Scott was, Bobby looked at Guralnick incredulously and replied, "I would say he was everything."[59]

Ever generous, especially when it came to someone he respected, Bobby always had gushing words about Scott, giving credit where Bobby thought credit was due:

> *He was one of the best arrangers that has ever been through this time of life. He was more than an arranger—he was a teacher. I had the voice, but it took some-body to show me how to use it. He was a guy that was very, very serious about music. If I didn't catch on or do things quick enough for Joe, there were certain times that he didn't speak to me. That's just how serious he was.*
>
> *I liked the way he guided me, and applied things for me. He didn't allow me to forget nothing. Everything surrounded and fitted me. The wording and the approach, there was a lot of things that I was doing wrong, because I had the voice but not knowing what to do with it. He was a great lyric writer also, because a lot of things that were written by different people had to have some changes. And he was good at knowing what I could handle. Not no long drawn-out different lyrics, but short sentences and right to the point.*[60]

"Joe Scott guided me on how to approach a note," Bobby added, "and how you find the spots to enforce, the selling points in a song. The word has to be said exactly right. Joe Scott said, 'If you're going to get any kind of attention, you've got to let them know your feelings and have them feel it the way you do.' He said, 'Everybody has a problem just like you do, and if you conquer that particular thing in your singing, well then, it's all left up to the listener.'"[61]

In addition to teaching Bobby phrasing and timing, Scott also took care to select material he thought Bobby could handle, "either emotional, gut-wrench-ing slow ballads or mid-tempo workouts that kept building in intensity until they practically destroyed the audience."[62] As Bobby became more proficient, Scott widened the variety of styles and tempos, but there would invariably be harmonics and lyrics that Scott thought had hit potential. These were supplied by Scott, other band members, or independent songwriters/brokers (like Joe Medwick) who sold them to Don Robey.

"Joe Scott picked some good stories for me to tell," Bobby explained, "because he saw that I was a good story-teller if I had the lyrics. Not the long, drawn-out lyrics. Just make 'em short and to the point, and leave some opening for ad-libbing. A little time to play, see how you progress." Both Bobby and Joe also recognized the importance of appealing directly to the largest R&B record-buying populace, young black women.

Once Scott selected a song, he arranged it for each instrument in the band, taking into account Bobby's and the band's abilities, how he wanted to punch the lyrics to make the most dramatic impact, what current styles were selling, and, most importantly, how he envisioned or heard the song to be.[63]

Pianist Teddy Reynolds recalled: "That was the thrill of my life to be able to put these patterns that Joe Scott taught me behind Bobby Bland. Joe would put the sheet music, the chord structures, in front of me and tell me, 'Teddy, put your own feeling into these chords.' And I would play my own feeling, something from the heart. . . . Joe would engineer. He would tell the engineer what to bring up, what to bring down. He played trumpet, French horn, any brass. And he played a lot of piano, and that's where I got a lot of my knowledge at. Joe Scott."[64]

"We worked very hard in those days," Bobby remembers. "Sometimes we'd spend a month on a song before we got it down the way we wanted it. Joe would rework the songs so that I'd be comfortable with them. I'm at my best when I sing short phrases; I get tangled up in songs that are complicated."[65]

"If the lyrics were too long, Joe would put some in the bridge, or if there were three long verses, he would take the lines and make four or five short verses out of it," Bobby explained. "There would never be any long sentences. He believed in short turn-arounds, and that's because I basically did 12- and eight-bar blues. I still remember that in what I record today."[66]

Drummer Jabo Starks recalls the process: "They would set up a session and we'd spend a couple of days in Houston recording. Robey had his own studio, so time didn't mean anything to him, but Joe Scott had that stuff down before we got there. We went through a lot of it out there on the road. Sometimes it would take Joe a while and he'd sit up on the bus at night, or in the hotel and do the arrangement. When we played a gig, we'd go in earlier during the day and rehearse the things that we were going to record. By the time we got back to Houston to do the session, all we had to do was go in there, record it and leave it alone."[67]

Bassist Hamp Simmons remembers recording in other studios as well:

And then there were plenty of times that Joe Scott came out on the road with us—and would start writing and arranging for the band and everything. We got more sessions like that, and we stopped recording exclusively in Houston. We started also recording in Nashville and Chicago and Los Angeles—out there where we were making the rounds on the road. A lot of those songs, the actual recording came out of Chicago or Nashville—the ones that made the big, big, big money. But it was always the Houston musicians out there doing them. . . .

"I. J. [Gosey, bass player] and Johnny Brown [guitarist] and them would do some demos for Bobby [in Houston] and send them out to Bobby wherever we were on the road. . . . Joe Scott would bring those demos and tell us what he wanted. And wherever we were on the road at that particular time, we'd go into a studio and make the record. So whether it was in Houston or somewhere else, it was usually always Joe Scott calling the shots on our music.[68]

Both on the road and in the studio, a song was rehearsed repeatedly until Scott was satisfied with every nuance of Bobby's vocals and every detail of each instrument's performance. Charles Keil described the process in detail in his groundbreaking ethnomusicology study, *Urban Blues*, in 1966. Written as a master's degree thesis at the University of Chicago, *Urban Blues* was the first scholarly analysis of current rhythm and blues music, particularly its role in the African American community. Not only did Keil explain the focal role of the bluesman in urban black America, using B.B. King and Bobby Bland as prime examples, he also established for the first time contemporary R&B music criticism as something academically worthy. In the book Keil describes what happened when the rehearsals were complete and the recording began. Joe Scott would first record the band's rhythm and horn sections and then give Bobby the tape to practice the song's lyrics. Then Scott would record Bobby's vocal track on top of the band's tracks. In the studio, Scott, along with Al "TNT" Braggs, songwriter and Bobby's current opening act, and Dave Clark, Duke's promotion chief, would listen to the tape and then make suggestions to Bobby on how to do it differently on the next take. Thanks to multiple-track taping, Bobby could change a word, a phrase, or insert or delete something that did not sound quite right to the aggregation. Joe Scott, however, was the main director, whispering the next phrase in Bobby's ear, coaxing Bobby, phrase by painful phrase through the song, as Braggs, Clark, and the recording engineer listened in a glass-enclosed soundproof booth containing the long mixing board.

Keil witnessed a session at the plush Universal Studio in Chicago, in which Bobby had a hard time producing what Scott was looking for. On a song about a girl being like an angel that Keil described as "one more futile effort to launch Bobby into the lucrative teenage market," Bobby could not seem to get the phrasing right after multiple attempts. "I guess I'll have to try to stretch it out more," he told Scott. "Man, we're still goofing. I'm too damn hoarse." More throat clearing ensued. Bobby wandered around the studio, humming the tune to himself, and Scott suggested that they record the entire first verse and then work on it from there. Bobby sounded more confident on the next take, but Scott still cued him on every phrase. When they reached the song's bridge, still more problems were encountered. Bobby called for a halt. "I know what you want," he told Scott, "but I just ain't got it this morning." Scott finally called the session off and said they would try again in another few days.[69]

But when things were working, Joe Scott and Bobby Bland created an entirely new modern blues style that would dominate R&B for at least the next decade. It was marked by "sophisticated big-band arrangements, intricate instrumental voicings, and brass squalls to match Bobby's gargled vocal interpolations—dramatic orchestral flourishes in sharp contrast to the warmth, intimacy, and projected vulnerability of Bobby's singing voice."[70]

Like the tunes of the old Territory bands, most songs also called for some sort of solo instrumental response to the vocals, usually a T-Bone Walker–like guitar, or a tenor sax, or a Teddy Reynolds piano phrase. But it was the upfront horn counterpoint—never before heard on blues shuffles, ballads, and spirituals—that really set the sound apart. As Bobby says, "Well, you see, it was the brass that gave me a kind of identity, right from my first biggest record I ever had. That was Joe, because Joe liked the trumpets, you know, same as I have now."[71]

In the end, the sound was a masterly amalgamation of the two musicians' influences and infatuations, from gospel soul to down-home blues, from big band jazz to mellow crooners, from country and western to Texas shuffles.

"I wouldn't be out here today if it wasn't for Joe Scott," Bobby concludes.[72] "He was just a gift from God, Joe Scott."[73]

Al "TNT" Braggs, Don Robey, and Bobby Bland share a private joke in the early 1960s. Michael Ochs Archives/Getty Images.

Turn On Your Love Light

1961–1962

Don Robey was eager to release Bobby's first solo album. "Cry, Cry, Cry" was still on the R&B chart, having peaked at number 9, and "I Pity the Fool" was about to be released as a single. To take advantage of this momentum, Robey went to the vaults to complete the album, which had only seven new songs ready to go, choosing some of Bobby's past bestsellers: "I Don't Want No Woman" (1957), "Little Boy Blue" (1958), "I'm Not Ashamed" (1959), "I'll Take Care of You" (1959), and "Lead Me On" (1960). These selections of older songs mixed with the newer ones recorded a few months earlier proved to be a winner.

The album was released on January 1, 1961, and came to be regarded as one of the best blues albums ever recorded, as well as one of "the most successful blues album extant. . . ."[1] Music critic Stephen Thomas Erlewine reviewed it for the *All Music Guide*: "Without a doubt, *Two Steps From the Blues* is the definitive Bobby 'Blue' Bland album and one of the great records in electric blues and soul-blues. In fact, it's one of the key albums in modern blues, marking a turning point when juke joint blues were seamlessly blended with gospel and Southern soul, creating a distinctly Southern sound where all of these styles blended so thoroughly it was impossible to tell where one began and one ended. Given his Memphis background, Bobby 'Blue' Bland was perfectly suited for this kind of amalgam as envisioned by producer/arranger Joe Scott, who crafted these wailing horn arrangements that sounded as impassioned as Bland's full-throated, anguished vocals. . . . These are songs that blur the division between Ray Charles soul and Chess blues, opening the doors for numerous soul and blues sounds, from Muscle Shoals and Stax through the modern-day soul-bluesman. . . . [T]his remains an excellent, essential blues album on its own terms—one the greatest ever released."[2]

Even the album's cover received acclaim, here by Sean Elder: "The cover of Bland's 1961 album *Two Steps From the Blues* is a work of art, a Mondrian in black and blue. It's a color photograph of the singer standing in front of a one-story building at the bottom of, yes, two steps. His pants are gray, his shirt is black. His coat is thrown over his shoulder, Sinatra style, and dark glasses hide his eyes from the sunlight. The building that represents 'the blues' is paneled in squares of blue and white—you would think it was his hotel room except his name appears on one of the panels, as if he were perpetually playing there. (Talk about bringing your work home with you.) In fact, the only thing that isn't black or blue in the photo is Bobby Bland's brown skin."[3]

The exuberant liner notes by Dzondria LaIsac are also classic, providing a sparkling example of purple promotional prose at its braggadocious best: "It has been Bobby's job to show, in his own special way, that the blues is a many splendored thing—subtle, primitive, sometimes gutsy and harsh, yet a delicately beautiful art form . . . and he has done his job well! At the same time he has done something for the blues, something vibrantly warm and wonderful, creating a special acceptance-climate the world over for this great music form." LaIsac also wrote the liner notes for Johnny Ace's *Memorial Album*, and, according to Evelyn Johnson, "He was quite a brilliant person, a very learned man, a college man, and a writer. His [real] last name was Harper, and he worked for Peacock as a writer and may have done some of the accounts. He had the pseudonym when he came to work there."[4]

When asked what records he would take to a desert island, Robert Cray, the classic blues album artist heir apparent, answered: "Howlin' Wolf—something with 'Smokestack Lightning' on it. Johnnie Taylor, *Raw Blues*. O.V. Wright, *Nucleus of Soul*. Billie Holiday—something by Billie has to be there. Bobby 'Blue' Bland, *Two Steps From the Blues*."[5]

By this time, six of Bobby's singles had reached *Billboard's* R&B top 10. When "I Pity the Fool" became his second number 1 hit in February 1961 and the new album was selling well, Bobby decided it was finally time to break with Little Junior Parker and the Blues Consolidated Revue and light out on his own. As always, Bobby graciously gave Parker his due:

> *I wasn't makin' enough money in a sense, I'll put it like that. And I wanted to try. It wasn't Junior, because we're beautiful today, but I think I was in the frame of mind that I had something to offer to the public. And I caught hell, I'll tell you that, the first time out, like for about a year before I got a chance to get established, you know, so far as the people to know me as a single artist. And it really worked against me for a time being. But like Junior wouldn't raise me from the salary that I started out with. And I was doing all the driving and valeting, you know, settin' up the stage and what have you, and I didn't want but a $10 raise, actually. And I wasn't makin' but 35. I wanted $45. And Junior*

didn't agree to pay me, so after, well, I worked with him for eight years, actually at this price and so in '60 I decided that this tune "It's My Life Baby" did pretty good for me, and then "Further On Up the Road" kinda got me established where the public would know me. And so I decided to try it on my own, and from that, here I am. But I must say that Junior was very, very beautiful, and he taught me a hell of a lot about show business. And also Rosco Gordon, B.B. King, because I also, you know, I was drivin' for B. for a couple of years before I really got into the business.[6]

"I stayed with Junior a little better than eight years," Bobby recalls incorrectly; it was actually more like five years, but probably seemed like eight or even more. "That was the first person that ever took me out on the road. It was quite an experience because I never had been any place away from home for any length of time. We went different places, Louisiana, Mississippi, Georgia, Alabama, Texas, St. Louis, Chicago—that's about as far as we got until later on."[7]

The band's guitarist, Texas Johnny Brown, remembered their days on the road: "Mmmm-hmmm, I traveled with Bobby when Bobby and Junior was together as a team. It was kind of a revue show like. There was Bobby, Junior, Joe Hinton, sometimes Buddy Ace and sometimes Lavelle White. It was okay. Only time I had to deal with Bobby is when he came on stage. When he walked up to the mike to start singin'. I'd have to go up there with him. That's why I can say that I had a lot to do with formulating his style. The things I would bend into the strings, he would bend into his voice. Clarence Hollimon was out there with him too. Between the three of us, myself, Clarence and Wayne [Bennett], we kind of kept that flavor of things goin' for Bobby. Ladies' man, yeah, he was that kind. He was very popular. Bobby was Bobby. When you work with him, fine. After the gig is over, if you got anything to do go ahead on and do it. Once he was off the gig, he was closed up."

Closed up for the band maybe, but not for the ladies, for whom he apparently was open 24/7, sometimes booking as many as three extra hotel rooms, on three separate floors, each with a different woman, awaiting his arrival after the show. For Bobby, the road, with its nonstop travel, music, women, and whiskey was now a way of life. There was no turning back. As long as the hits kept coming, so did the royalties, the show bookings, and the high life. And for Bobby, the high life consisted of not much more than singing, drinking, and womanizing. Don Robey took care of the expenses, Joe Scott took care of the music, and John Green, his road manager, and increasingly Melvin Jackson, his gofer and confidant, took care of the rest.

"Just the opposite with Junior," Brown recalled.

*Junior was more a business-person like. He wanted to see that he kept the band
together, kept the band working. He'd check with people about their uniforms
and stuff. He kept the transportation together. He was a funny person, good for
tellin' jokes, havin' somethin' to laugh about but he took care of business.*

*Most likely we'd open up with a band segment. Two or three tunes. First we'd
bring Junior on. Then we'd ask someone to bring Bobby on. Keep that heat kind
of goin' all the time. One time we played a place in Birmingham called, heh
heh, O.J.'s Half Acre and I mean that place was packed. Hell, it was about a
block long. We came on with Joe Hinton. He got it stirred up, man. When Junior
came on and started doin' "Drivin' Wheel," oh God, it went on from there. By
the time Bobby got up there and opened his mouth to sing "Further On Up the
Road," the place was—POW! Man, tables was crashin'. People was runnin' and
goin' on, bustin' loose at it. People got so emotional over it, you know. They had
glass just all over the place.*[8]

Bobby eventually assumed a more subdued stage presence, but these early performances were anything but. As he did back in Chicago, he would
pull out all the physical stops to make an impression. Junior Wells, the great
Chicago harmonica player for Muddy Waters and Buddy Guy, grew up with
Little Junior Parker in West Memphis and would occasionally join the Blues
Consolidated tour. Wells remembered these wild shows with Parker and Bland
in his native Arkansas: "And I used to do a thing down there with Junior Parker,
me and Junior Parker and Bobby Blue Bland, when he got out of the service,
you know, he was thin then, had a real high-pitched voice. That's when Bobby
was smaller, he used to throw me on the floor and me and him used to do
Muddy's tune, "I'm a Man," and he'd be rollin' me over [his back] and all that.
We'd be dancin' around and then fall on your knees and all that stuff and then
Bobby'd grab me and pull me down there and we were rollin': oh-oh-oh-oh,
all that stuff. And then after he got to be a big old thing, 'Come on, let's do
'A Man,' Junior.' I said, 'Uh-uh, No, no.' He said, 'I'll mash your little ass to
death now.' [Laughs] I said, 'No, Lordy. That's not gonna work, brother.' We
was just clownin' around, man. People liked all that stuff when you was puttin'
on some kind of a show. We used to really put on some heckuva shows."[9]

Texas Johnny Brown concluded: "But after a while they both got pretty
hot and they separated Bobby and Junior. I took the band with Junior. Hamp
Simmons had the band with Bobby. Teddy [Reynolds] was with Bobby—
Wayne Bennett was too. I stayed out there until 1963."[10]

Little Junior Parker did not miss a beat when the Revue broke up, launching his own package show with Johnny Brown and other Houston musicians
and scoring two top 10 R&B hits in 1961: Roosevelt Sykes's "Driving Wheel"

and his own "In the Dark." After "Annie Get Your Yo-Yo" hit number 6 in the spring of 1962, Junior continued to score a series of minor hits throughout the decade. After ten years with Duke, Junior left to record for Mercury in 1967, and later for Blue Rock and Minit in 1969. Junior met jazz organist Jimmy McGriff at the Ann Arbor Blues Festival in 1970 and toured and recorded with him for United Artists, including a few single cuts—"Pretty Baby" and "You Don't Have to be Blind"—with Wayne Bennett on guitar, Robert Crowder on drums, and Phillip Upchurch on bass. His last hit, "Drownin' On Dry Land," was recorded for Capitol in 1971. Later that year, he recorded an impressive album for United Artists entitled *I Tell Stories Sad and True*, which included a song called "No One Knows (What Goes On When the Door Is Closed)," a thematic precursor to Charlie Rich's 1973 country and pop smash "Behind Closed Doors."[11]

Little Junior Parker, friend and mentor to Bobby Bland, classy big band blues stylist and leader, expressive songwriter and talented blues harpist, died of a brain tumor at St. Francis Hospital in Blue Island, Illinois, on November 18, 1971.[12] Two days before, as Parker's health continued to deteriorate rapidly, Bobby Bland, Howlin' Wolf, Muddy Waters, B.B. King, Jerry Butler, the Staple Singers, Otis Clay, Syl Johnson, Garland Green, and Little Milton entertained thousands of fans at a benefit performance at the Burning Spear night club in Chicago. They gave Junior's wife Jerri about $5,000 that night.[13]

Bobby summed up his time with Junior as "one of the greatest experiences I've had and it taught me a lot about out here and how to handle a group. I was a driver and all-around person. When I left Junior . . . it was one of the first mistakes I made. I thought I was pretty hip when I started to get more applause, but I didn't draw flies when I left Junior for six months."[14]

During his tenure with Junior, Bobby had indeed learned a lot. Now, no longer in Junior's shadow, Bobby acted the part of the experienced businessman and star and took the Blues Consolidated band, the Blue Flames, with him. "It just so happened that the fellows that were with us wanted to go with me," Bobby explained. "Me and the fellows kind of communicated a little better than with Junior 'cause we played together and what have you and Junior didn't drink, see?"[15] The fellows included what has come to be known as the classic Bobby "Blue" Bland Duke band: Joe Scott and Melvin Jackson on trumpet, Pluma Davis on trombone, L.A. Hill on tenor sax, Rayfield Devers on baritone sax, Teddy Reynolds on piano, Wayne Bennett on guitar, Hamp Simmons on bass, and John "Jabo" Starks on drums.

Bobby also picked up an opening act of his own: the young Dallas song-writer and performer whom he had introduced to Don Robey two years earlier, Al Braggs. "In 1961 Junior Parker and Bobby Bland were split up," Braggs said.

"When they split, the band went with Bobby, and they gave Junior another band. So they said, 'Who do you want, Junior?' and he says, 'Joe Hinton.' And Bobby says, 'Give me that kid out of Dallas.' So they called me, and I got to join Bobby in Indianapolis."[16]

Bobby was overjoyed to have Joe Scott continuing with him full-time. Why not stay in Houston and arrange and produce records, Peter Guralnick asked, instead of remaining on the road? "Why? Man, that's where the money was. You see, Bobby was a star."[17]

Bobby was almost as happy to see Melvin Jackson staying on. Jackson was only twenty-six years old at the time, but had been on tour since the age of six with his father, who led a musical revue that traveled the country performing. "I was born in Nashville, Tennessee in 1935," Jackson told an interviewer in 2008. "I picked up the trumpet when I was about seven or eight. I played trumpet for 40 years. My father was a musician. He had his own show. He was a show piano player—vaudeville. His name was Jerry Jackson. My father had his own band and so I got on the job training with his band and school, too. He had a touring band, like during the summer we did fairs and night clubs during the winter, across the South."[18] So Bobby not only gained a solid trumpet player, but also an experienced road master. "Yes, I grew up fast," Jackson told Peter Guralnick in 1975. "Very fast. I came through things that usually would stop a young cat. Like narcotics and shit. But my mind was strong enough to surpass all these things, even being in the environment. I credit my background with my always trying to be on top of things and hold my business mind together."[19]

Over the next few years Melvin watched Joe Scott carefully, helping him in any way he could to keep the road show together and moving on to the next town. He would also become Bobby's best friend and guardian, the one Bobby could always count on to solve a problem or buffer him from the constant annoyances of traveling nearly nonstop across the country night after night.

Pluma Davis, the band's trombonist from the beginning in 1955, was a graduate of Phillis Wheatley High School in Houston. He started out in Sammy Harris's band, which regularly played C. A. Dupree's Eldorado Ballroom; later, around 1952, he formed his own big band, playing with Big Joe Turner and other jazz and blues vocalists at the Eldorado. Davis joined the Peacock/Duke session group and eventually led the band, playing behind several Peacock/Duke artists, and also writing songs, including Gatemouth Brown's 1954 "Okie Dokie Stomp." Davis stayed with Bobby's band both on the road and in the studio until 1967, when he retired from the music business to become a cab driver in Houston. He died in September 1988.[20]

Tenor saxophonists came and went with the band. When Bobby took over the Blue Flames in early 1961, L. A. Hill and Robert Skinner were playing, but they were soon replaced by Jimmy Beck on tenor and Johnny Board on alto, with Bobby Forte on tenor joining later in the year.

Jimmy Beck, originally from Cleveland, continued with the band until 1967, when he left to play tenor sax for and lead the Earl Gaines Band. He continued in the music business, later recording "Pipe Dreams," among others, for Excello Records in Nashville, and as a producer and engineer.[21]

Johnny Board was born on December 8, 1919, in Chicago. He played in the Lionel Hampton, Sonny Stitt, and Count Basie bands before joining the original Bill Harvey Orchestra. Board played previously at Bobby's second Duke recording session in Memphis in 1952. He stayed with the band until 1967; on leaving the Bland band, he joined B.B. King's band and later worked with Donny Hathaway, Jimmy McGriff, Billy Stewart, Fontella Bass, and Quincy Jones. Johnny Board lived his final years playing in and around Chicago and died on December 15, 1989, in Oak Park, Illinois.[22]

Bobby Forte, a much heralded tenor saxophonist whose mother was a well-known gospel singer from San Francisco, stayed with the band until mid-1964, when he left to join B.B. King's band. Somewhere along the way the road became too much for him, and he suffered a mental breakdown. According to one of his fellow band members: "I been out here a few years now, man, and the chief problem, as I see it, is not to forget that it's not real out here. It's never-never land. If you start to think it's real, man, you're dead. That's what happened to Bobby Forte. He began to think it was real and then he went . . ."He then fluttered his lips with his fingers.[23]

Rayfield Devers, the baritone saxophonist, was with the band until the fall of 1963, when Charles Crawford took over. Devers then joined the Ike & Tina Turner Revue band, which became Sam & The Goodtimers after they left Ike. Relocated to Los Angeles, they became the house band at the California Club at Santa Barbara and Western, and later in the 1960s they played at another L.A. club called Soul'd Out. They were last heard of leaving to go on tour with the Monkees.[24]

Charles Crawford, Devers's replacement, was born in Memphis on February 18, 1931. He studied trumpet as a youngster and joined Buddy Wheeler's band in 1947, where he played until he was drafted on January 23, 1948. He served his time in the army playing clarinet and alto saxophone in the 137th Army Band, headquartered in Fort Dix, New Jersey. Upon returning to Memphis in 1956, he joined Phineas Newborn's famous band where he provided accompaniment for some of Satellite and Stax Records' earliest releases. In March 1961 Crawford joined Little Junior Parker's new band until Bobby lured him away to replace Rayfield Devers on baritone saxophone, while Bobby was playing the Regal Theater in Chicago.[25]

Hamp W. Simmons Jr., the band's longtime bassist, was another original member of the Bill Harvey Orchestra. Born on December 3, 1937, in Newton, Texas, Simmons moved with his mother to nearby Houston in 1947 when a fire destroyed their home in Newton. He played tuba and string bass at Harper Junior High School and Booker T. Washington High School. He also took private bass lessons from jazz player Carl Lott Sr. While still a teenager he joined a blues combo led by guitarist Joe Bell, where he met pianist Connie Mack Booker. As Simmons remembered in a 1998 interview: "[Booker] had been on the road, you know, so he knew B.B. [King]. He knew Bobby [Bland] and Junior [Parker] and everything. . . . And I come home one night, and Mama told me, she said, 'Connie Mack Booker says for you to come over to the Wheel Club and bring your bass.' So OK, I went over there. And when I got there, there Bobby and Junior were. . . . and Joe Fritz, Sonny Freeman, Jimmy Johnson—all that band they had then. They were performing and looking for musicians, particularly for a bass player. So I played with them that night. . . . And they asked me to leave that same night, to head out with them on a tour. . . . I tied that bass on top of the car, and we lit out for Big Springs, Texas." So from the earliest recordings in 1955 through 1967, Simmons was Bobby's bassist, both in the studio and on the road. "Whoo, man, I was on lots and lots of sessions with Bobby Bland," he said. "I can't name them all."

Traveling with Bobby and the big multi-star package revues, Simmons performed with Arthur Prysock, Aretha Franklin, Dionne Warwick, the Temptations, Sam Cooke, Jackie Wilson, and Little Willie John. "You'd do about thirty-five days together, night after night, playing behind all the featured singers," he explained. "Music took me all over the United States, but yeah man, I always got home broke." Simmons retired from the road in 1967, taking a full-time job in Houston with Chicago Bridge & Iron. He continued playing his bass in the evenings with local jazz and blues groups until he was diagnosed with throat cancer in February 1998. He died on December 2, 2000.[26]

Teddy Reynolds took over from Connie Mack Booker as the band's pianist in 1958. Born in Houston's Third Ward on July 12, 1931, Reynolds learned to play piano at his maternal grandmother's house where he was raised. His father, also named Theodore, played piano in so-called "bootleg houses" around Houston. Before dropping out of fifth grade at Blackshear Elementary School, his classmate Amos Milburn encouraged his piano playing. Later, when Milburn had become a star for Aladdin Records, Reynolds recalled seeing him drive through the old neighborhood in a new "torpedo Buick." That was it; Reynolds decided right then and there to pursue a career in music. He practiced and eventually excelled enough to land a job playing at Shady's Playhouse, where he met and played with the great Texas guitarists and vocalists at the time: Joe Hughes, Johnny Copeland, Johnny Watson, and Albert Collins.

In 1950 he recorded his first tune, providing the vocals for "Cry, Cry Baby" with Ed Wiley and His After Hours Band on the Sittin in With label. It became a number 3 R&B hit and the young musician became known thereafter around Houston as Teddy "Cry Cry" Reynolds. He recorded a few other numbers under his own name, but never hit the charts again. In 1958 he recorded for Mercury and played piano for Johnny Copeland's first recording, "Rock and Roll Lily," and Copeland in turn played guitar on several of Reynolds's Mercury cuts.

From 1958 until 1964 Reynolds played piano on the road and in the studio for Bobby Bland, as well as providing studio backup for other Duke/Peacock artists like Little Junior Parker, Joe Hinton, and Al "TNT" Braggs. When he left the band, he moved to California, where he recorded for the Crown label, as well as backing a variety of local acts. In late 1970, he moved back to Houston where he worked construction and oil-refinery jobs. In 1986 he tried music again, joining Grady Gaines's reunited Texas Upsetters. The group cut several albums for the Black Top label, with Reynolds supplying keyboards, vocals, and several compositions.

Perhaps Teddy's greatest claim to fame in the Houston area was his 1991 television commercial for Texas-based Blue Bell Ice Cream that ran for several years. He also continued to perform with a variety of Houston bands throughout the 1990s, including Johnny Brown's Quality Blues Band which recorded the 1998 CD entitled *Nothin' But the Truth*. In February 1997 Reynolds received an award from the Houston Blues Society. He continued working, lastly with the Phillip Walker band, until shortly before his death in Houston on October 1, 1998.[27]

John "Jabo" Starks, the band's drummer, joined the band in 1959, when Sonny Freeman left to join B.B. King's band. Hailing from Mobile, Alabama, Starks grew up idolizing drummers, like Shep Sheppard in Bill Doggett's band, at whom he peeked through a hole in the Club Harlem's back door. Jabo remembered the Bland band and how he became proficient in a 1995 interview with Jim Payne:

> *Wayne Bennett was on guitar and Bobby Forte played tenor sax. Bobby was just a natural player. He was out of the "holiness" church. That was the Joe Scott Orchestra—musically, that was the best band I played with.*
>
> *I was the youngest thing in the band and those guys taught me a lot—Joe Scott and Pluma Davis. Joe Scott, the trumpet player, was the bandleader, and*

Pluma Davis, the trombone player, arranged for the band, too. Pluma had his own band when I first met him. They taught me—"I don't care what you play, I don't care how you play, I don't care if you don't ever play fancy. I don't care if you don't ever play the greatest solos in the world, all I want you to do is remember this—play time. Play the time. Hold the time. You're the heartbeat. Once that time starts, you hold it right there. Whatever anybody else does, don't you go there. Make them come back to you."

I used to play with the metronome for at least six minutes straight. I'm not going to let you pull me and I'm not going with you. If you say the tempo is here, then it'll be here. When you finish what you're doing and get back, it'll be right here.

Joe Scott was in charge of the band and when we were in Houston we did a lot of recording. Joe was the head arranger for Don Robey at Duke/Peacock Records. From 1959 to 1965, I recorded everything Bobby Bland did. I also recorded "Driving Wheel" with Little Junior Parker and "Funny" by Joe Hinton, and lots of others.

Jabo left the band on January 2, 1966, to join James Brown's band, where he played—either as the sole drummer or in tandem with Clyde Stubblefield—on several of Brown's big hits: "The Payback," "Sex Machine," "Super Bad," among others. "James had heard me play after Bobby's band had gotten popular," Jabo said. "He would send different people from his organization to wherever we were working. Every time we would play the East Coast, there would be someone there saying, 'Mr. Brown wants you to join the group.' 'Well, I'm happy where I am,' I'd say." Finally, James offered enough money that Jabo just had to please the "Mr. Please, Please Man" and become his new drummer.

Starks finally quit the Brown band in 1975 to join the B.B. King band, where he played for several years. Recently, he teamed with Clyde Stubblefield to record an instructional video, as well as a CD as the Funkmasters. His and Stubblefield's drum tracks are some of the most sampled by today's rappers and hip-hoppers. Jabo Starks currently resides in Grayton Beach, Florida, where he performs regularly at the popular Picolo Restaurant and Red Bar.[28]

Unlike many other blues singers, Bobby Bland does not play guitar. However, he has been fortunate enough over the years to perform with some of the most highly regarded fretmen of his era: Matt (Guitar) Murphy, B.B. King, Roy Gaines, Clarence Hollimon, Pat Hare, Mel Brown, Johnny Jones, Freddy Robinson (Abu Talib), Jimmy Johnson, and (most famously and for the greatest length of time) Wayne Bennett.

Bennett was born in Sulphur, Oklahoma, on December 13, 1933. His father, Dewitt Bennett, was a chef on the Atchison, Topeka and Santa Fe Railways' elegant *El Capitan* line that ran between Chicago and Los Angeles. "I lived in Sulphur 'til I was six and then my parents moved to another small town in Oklahoma called Madill. My father was a great influence on me as far as getting an education," Bennett said. Part of that education was learning to play the guitar. When he was thirteen or fourteen his mother bought him a small Stella guitar, and he learned to play it by listening on the radio to country and western music and the big band jazz and R&B orchestras of T-Bone Walker, Louis Jordan, Lionel Hampton, and Joe and Jimmy Liggins.

By the end of the 1940s Bennett was in high school in Ardmore, at the secondary school closest to Madill. "I was able to train a little with a few musicians who played in a corner there," Wayne recalled. "And one night the Jimmy Liggins orchestra played in Ardmore. Their records were well known at the time. I went to see them, and they let me hang out with them. That's how I met Amos Milburn. One day he played in Fort Worth and needed a guitarist and he remembered me. But I was still in high school. The problem was if my mother would let me leave with an orchestra. She finally gave her permission with the condition that I would tour only during vacations and would go back to school in the fall, and that's what I did." His recording debut (at the age of seventeen, replacing Johnny Brown) was on Amos Milburn's "Bad Bad Whiskey," a number 1 hit for Aladdin Records in 1950. He continued touring and recording with Milburn and his fellow Texas musicians until 1954, when he moved to Chicago after a short stay with his uncle in Omaha.

"It was then that I met King Kolax and all the jazz musicians that played in the Chicago clubs at the time," Bennett remembered. "And it was then that I learned about harmony, with people like Junior Mance and Prentice McCarry, who were pianists for Kolax. He had Leon Hooper on drums and Cowboy Martin on bass. Kolax had a jazz quintet and he introduced me to different musicians like Johnny Griffin and Sun Ra. That's how I met Charlie Parker at the end of his career and Dexter Gordon. . . . I played at the Cotton Club when Johnny Griffin worked at the corner of Cottage Grove and 63rd Street. Yeah, I played in jazz groups in the city in the evenings at clubs, and I recorded blues with Otis Rush or Buddy Guy during the day. I met Willie Dixon who introduced me to all the Chicago blues musicians. . . . That was all good for me and that's how I began to be a part of the Cobra family and worked in the studio with Harold Burrage, Arbee Stidham, J. B. Lenoir, Otis Rush, Buddy Guy, Al Duncan, [Fred] Below, Lafayette Leake, Odie Payne. We all worked for Vee-Jay and Cobra. Cobra had its own studio on the west side on Roosevelt Road, a small studio with good sound. And I lived in Hyde Park between 1954 and 1984, except for a period of six months in 1966."

On the strength of their smash hit "Sincerely," Harvey Fuqua and the Moonglows hired Bennett to tour with them for a while and then he settled again in Chicago. There he played four nights a week at the Italian Club on the north side and did session work by day with most of the Chicago blues labels, backing Buddy Guy and Magic Sam on Artistic Records, Jimmy Reed on Vee-Jay, Fats Domino on Imperial, Otis Spann and Elmore James on Chief, among many other blues stars of the day. By the time Bobby, Junior Parker, and Joe Scott heard and hired him in 1957, Bennett was a highly skilled blues/jazz guitarist who could play elegantly in any style or speed required by Junior and Bobby's growing and varied repertoire.[29]

"Wayne worked eight years with me out on the road," Bobby explained. "We got together on a lot of things, like ideas, different phrases, and how to approach a note, and I must say that he taught me quite a bit, because it kinda grew me into a blues ballad thing. It wasn't really a harsh blues thing that we do. It's kinda mellow, and you can sit back and relax and listen to it."[30]

Johnny Jones, the great Gibson ES-345 guitarist who joined Bobby's band in the late 1970s, recalled the Bland guitar sound.

> *I had a chance to travel with Bobby Blue Bland from '76 through '79. Another one of my teachers was Wayne Bennett. He molded the sound of Bobby Blue Bland based on T-Bone [Walker]. To play for Bobby Blue Bland, you have to come off on a T-Bone mold. He don't want you bendin' no strings. He wants you to come straight off the boards like this. [Jones demonstrates with some cleanly-picked notes.] T-Bone came right straight off the board.*
>
> *Bendin' of the strings came on later with B.B. When I first got with Blue I had just a little bit too much of Lucille. He called me in one night to the back of the bus. He said "Dick"—we called each other Dick—"you got too much Lucille. Here take this tape." It had Mel Brown and Wayne Bennett on it. Any guitar player who plays with Bobby and pleases him got to come off the T-Bone mold.[31]*

Of course, T-Bone Walker did bend strings, just not to the extent that B.B. King did. What Bobby wanted from Jones and all his guitarists was a more jazz-oriented style of playing, like Walker, Bennett, and Brown, as compared to the more electrified note bending B.B. King brand of playing. As much as Bobby appreciated his friend King, he wanted his band to sound different, and he wanted his voice to be the star, not the band's guitar.

So there you have the classic Bobby "Blue" Bland–Duke/Peacock band, arguably the best big band blues ensemble ever assembled—the band that, with more or less the same musicians, would record some of the greatest blues hits ever recorded, craft one of the most dynamic stage shows in rhythm and blues, and create the platform of modern blues for black America in the second half of the twentieth century.

As Charles Keil pointed out in *Urban Blues*, this band seemed to confound the usual notion that blues musicians were normally malcontents who were either just drawing a check or biding their time until they got proficient enough to join a jazz band. This band instead seemed to be "a unit, not simply an accompanying group and they know it and show it at every performance."[32]

Again, credit for this exceptional unity needs to go to Joe Scott. Here was a bandleader who understood group dynamics before it was a popular term. He not only treated band members as key elements in creating a song, enabling them to participate with their own ideas, but also let them stretch their musical capabilities in solos and their interpretations of Scott's challenging charts. Above all, Scott was someone to be respected musically. Every band member knew that, if he kept sober and was on time, his life, though rigorous, was relatively secure and musically satisfying.

Bobby Bland was also a leader easy to follow. He deferred to Scott in almost all matters musical and was fair, calm, and evenhanded in dealing with all members of the group. Unlike other stars who were infamous for their inflated egos and hair-trigger tempers, particularly in dealing with band members, Bobby was firm but always the gentleman. The only disadvantage for a blues band member, besides the rigors of the road, was dependency on the star himself. As one musician declared, "If B.B. King were to retire tomorrow, or get killed in a car accident or something, we'd be nowhere, but like when Glenn Miller gets hisself killed in an airplane crash, the guys in the band go right along without him on his reputation, on his sound. But without B, we've had it."[33]

Still, there is not a popular musician alive then or now who would not be proud to list a stint playing with Bobby Bland on his résumé, which hundreds have. Since the beginning, the Bobby Bland band has always maintained a strong reputation for excellence and top musicianship.

Unfortunately, the band did not make the trip to Philadelphia with Bobby on March 29, 1961, when he became the first "blues singer" to appear on the popular *Dick Clark's American Bandstand* television program. He sang "I Pity the Fool," but, as was the practice on the show, he lip-synched the words. The white audience cheered him wildly.[34] "They had some kind of emergency came on and it didn't get a chance to air until later on," Bobby recalled. "But yeah, I was the first blues singer on Dick Clark's show."[35]

The band, however, was in full evidence on May 16 and 17, when they returned to the recording studio in Chicago to cut four new sides. The first was the Earl Hines and Billy Eckstine tune, "Jelly, Jelly, Jelly," which combines the big band sound of the original with Bobby's bluesy vocal, featuring some flowing piano work by Teddy Reynolds. The flip side was "Ain't That Lovin' You," a mellow, swinging song, punctuated by Scott's by-now patented blasting horns.

Not released until the next year, it peaked at number 9 on *Billboard*'s R&B chart in the spring of 1962. The next cut was "You're the One (That I Adore)," a country ballad, featuring Bobby's Tennessee twang and the band's rollicking rhythm section.

The final track for the session was country star Charlie Rich's "Who Will the Next Fool Be," which was recorded by Rich a few months before. With Joe Scott's arrangement it sounds more big band than country, but R&B fans took it to number 12 when it was released the next year. "I didn't think of it as country then," Bobby said. "The lyrics go either way."[36]

The Bland band continued to tour, returning to Memphis to appear at Sunbeam Mitchell's Club Handy on Sunday, July 16, 1961, to a sold-out show. While in Memphis, Bobby was chatting with his mother one afternoon after the lunch rush at the Sterling Grill and noticed an attractive young woman at the end of the counter. He overcame his shyness enough to strike up a conversation with her. He found out that her name was Willie Mae Martin, that she was just sixteen, that she was originally from Hernando, Mississippi, and that she wanted to become a nurse. Despite their age difference and Bobby's wife back in Houston, they made plans to see each other again when Bobby next returned to Memphis.

Bobby made his second appearance on *American Bandstand* on August 14, singing "Don't Cry No More," right before Satellite Records' Mar-Keys performed "Last Night," as the teen dancers twisted away to Satellite's first million-selling hit.

Back in the recording studio, this time in Nashville, on September 20, 1961, Bobby and the band recorded three songs: a jazzed up version of the Rodgers and Hart standard, "Blue Moon," a cash-in-on-the-twist-craze big band remake of "Farther Up the Road," called "Twistin' Up the Road," and a cover of the Harold Arlen–Johnny Mercer classic "Blues in the Night" that rivals Jimmie Lunceford's soigné 1941 version. A week later, they returned to the same studio with Skippy Brooks, a mainstay pianist at Nashville's Excello label, temporarily replacing Teddy Reynolds for the next two sessions, to cut two of Bobby's biggest hits: "Turn On Your Love Light" and "Stormy Monday Blues."

By the end of 1961 "Turn On Your Love Light" had reached number 2 on the R&B chart and an impressive number 28 on the pop chart. Written by Bobby's Duke/Peacock label mate and opening act Al "TNT" Braggs, the song has been covered by a multitude of bands from Them to the Rascals to the Grateful Dead, attaining the status of a true pop blues classic and the most recognizable song of Bobby's oeuvre.

The lyrics harkened back to the old Sunday School song, "This Little Light of Mine," and Jabo Starks recalled how he came up with the gospel-inspired drum beat for the tune:

We rehearsed "Turn On Your Love Light" in Dallas, Texas, at a steak house where we were playing. Bobby used to be real good friends with the owner. Joe Scott had this tune he wanted to record, but he didn't know what to do for the drums. He showed me Wayne Bennett's guitar pattern, and I thought of a pattern that I had already experimented with at home. It's out of the "holiness" church, that sanctified feel.

In the "holiness" churches they didn't have sets of drums, maybe just a snare drum or a bass drum, but they had tambourines, and they clapped. And the way they clapped, I just loved that feel. It's just a floating feel. They'd clap their rhythm against the songs they were doing—kind of a polyrhythm. One section of folk would be clapping one way, and the other section would be clapping another way, and then the tambourine would be going. I used to go to the "holiness" church when I was up in the country with my grandmother. I went almost every Sunday because I loved to hear the rhythms they were using. That's basically where a lot of it comes from for me. That sanctified rhythm influenced my playing.

So when I said that rhythm would fit that tune, Joe said, "I don't care what you play, as long as it works. Play what you want to play." I played it and then when it got to the middle part, he said, "Well, you got the solo." I said, "What?" I couldn't believe he was doing that. I said, "Well, I got a way I want to play that." He said, "Well, do it." When I started playing it, Bobby started singing and I said, "Well, okay!" And I just started the bell against what Bobby was doing. We went back to Houston [actually Nashville] and we cut that thing in two takes. That's the way that happened.[37]

Barney Quick named "Turn On Your Love Light" the Number 1 song on his "All-Time Top 100 R&B Tunes" at suite101.com: "This pivotal recording recalls the jump blues of r&b's infancy and anticipates the coming decade's soul sensibility, all the while crackling with gospel's thunderous fervor. . . . And, of course, there is Bland's vocal, ranging from a desperate whisper over a battery of urgent drums to the most sublime shouting ever captured on vinyl. This is r&b at its greasiest; the ultimate fish-fry music."[38]

"Stormy Monday Blues," also recorded at this session, reached number 5 on the R&B chart when it was released in the fall of 1962 and became the standard closer in Bobby's stage shows. Jabo Starks recalled the recording date: "T-Bone Walker's 'Stormy Monday Blues' was supposed to be a 'throwaway' tune. We had already finished the album, and Bobby said, 'Hey, man, I want to do that tune. Let's do that tune, just for me.' We said, 'Okay,' and we sat there and did it, just the rhythm section. I think it was two takes. Wayne Bennett, the guitar player, wanted to change something. Hamp Simmons out of Houston played an old Kay electric bass. He's one of my best friends. 'Stormy Monday Blues' turned out to be one of the biggest songs Bobby ever had."[39]

Wayne Bennett's big chords and sweeping bends on the track turned out to be a major influence on many guitarists, including Duane Allman's development of the Allman Brothers sound some years later. "See I was influenced by blues guitarists like T-Bone Walker and Pee Wee Crayton," Bennett said. "It all collaborated on that cut. I got a chance to know Duane. It was good to see those guys reaching forth and coming into the blues."[40]

"It was a favorite of mine for a long time," Bobby said of the song. "I was working with it to find out exactly what to do with it, because it was such a good job that T-Bone did, so you had to do something different. It's just like if you're doing a standard: If you can't enhance it, don't bother even doing it."[41] After T-Bone's and Bobby's success with the number, many others in the years to come tried to enhance it, most notably Benny Latimore, whose 1973 rendition went to number 27 (and, like Bobby, Latimore firmly stated that his version was nothing like its predecessors).[42]

In October 1961 Joe Scott and his Orchestra recorded "The King Bee" and "Pickin' Heavy" (Duke 1919)—their first and last attempts without Bobby, who remained the star of the show.[43] As a reward for such a productive year, *Cash Box* magazine named Bobby Bland the Rhythm and Blues Artist of the Year.[44]

On January 29, 1962, the band recorded in Los Angeles for the first time, and cut four sides. The first was entitled "Your Friends," a slow blues featuring Skippy Brooks on piano and a fine muted trumpet solo by Joe Scott. "You're Worth It All" is another mellow-voiced Bobby Bland love ballad, and "No Sweeter Girl" is a happy, up-tempo romp. The star song on the session turned out to be "Yield Not to Temptation," a spirited followup to "Turn On Your Love Light" that is the closest thing to gospel music Bobby had recorded thus far, replete with a choir, Bobby's patented squall, and a Bobby Forte squawking tenor sax solo. "It basically could be either one, R&B or spiritual," Bobby admitted.[45] The song reached number 10 on the R&B chart when it was released later that year.

By February 16 Bobby and the band were back on the East Coast for a one-week stand at Harlem's Apollo Theatre as a part of a big package show that also featured Ralph Cooper, the Corvairs, the Sensations, the Crystals, the Edsels, and Aretha Franklin's sister, Irma.

The band was back in Nashville on April 12 for its second, final, and most fruitful recording session of the year. The sound and the songs recorded at this session capture better than any other, except perhaps the "Love Light/ Stormy Monday" session, the experience of a live Bobby Bland stage show when Bobby was at the height of his career. Starting with "36-22-36," the announcer's spoken introduction employed at a live show is used to start the song after a grand horn fanfare: "Ladies and gentlemen, here's the man!" It builds to the grandest horn fanfare and the announcer's final proclamation: "The dynamic Bobby . . . Bobby Bland!" It comes dangerously close to being a novelty song in the Louis Jordan vein before Bobby and the band somehow modernize it enough to keep it from crossing the line.

The number 36 *Cash Box* hit "The Feeling is Gone" begins with the same buglelike horn flourish that was much later used to begin Bobby's 1998 *Live on Beale Street* album.[46] The Latin-inspired number 22 pop hit "Call on Me," Bobby's third number 1 R&B hit, was rumored to have sold over one million copies. "That's the Way Love Is," the final song cut at the session, and "Call on Me" remain mainstays of every Bobby Bland show. "Al Braggs wrote the lyrics. I think. 'Call On Me' was the one that he worked with for awhile. We did a lot of recording together. He was one of the best!" Bobby said. "He should have been like—during the time of Joe Tex and James Brown, they basically kind of copied from him. He started all that stuff,"[47] Bobby explained, referring to Braggs's dynamic stage performance.

Braggs remembers:

One time we were in Chicago, and I wrote my first song for Bobby. I'm a night person and I always carry around a little tape recorder to get down my ideas. Well, our rooms were next to each other, and I get this idea around three in the morning, and I call Bobby and wake him up. I told him I've got this wonderful tune. He said, "Who is this?"

"This is Al."

"Boy, go to bed and just call me in the morning."

"Oh, no, Blue. Just listen to it right now."

So I sung it, beating on the table, "Love and affection, a heart so true. I'm yours for the asking . . . When you need a good loving" . . . all that.

Bobby says, "Okay, call me in the morning."

The next day it wasn't any better. Bobby just did not like the song. He says, "I hated it, Al, and calling me at three o'clock in the morning didn't help it none." So I showed it to Robey, and he says, "How much do you want for it?" And I sold the song, which was named "Call On Me," for three hundred dollars. Well, Robey immediately decided to name Bobby's new album Call On Me. That was a hard lesson. I sold the song and that's all I got out of it. That was one of Bobby's biggest hits.[48]

"Most of the things I did with Bobby," Jabo Starks recounted, "Joe Scott gave me the freedom to do what I wanted. On one tune we recorded, I played nothing but mallets. I think it was 'That's the Way Love Is.' Bobby's band cut his records, so when you saw him in person, what you heard was exactly what was on the record. That was a groove. I enjoyed that."[49]

Later in 1962 Bobby's second album (and the first in stereo) *Here's the Man!!!* was released, containing most of the singles he had recorded since *Two Steps*

From the Blues, including the mega-hits "Turn On Your Love Light," "Who Will the Next Fool Be," and "Stormy Monday Blues." It reached number 53 on the *Billboard*'s Pop Albums chart. On October 23 Bobby returned to *American Bandstand* for his fourth appearance, this time to sing "Stormy Monday Blues."

Bobby Bland performing with the Joe Scott Orchestra at the Trianon Ballroom in Chicago, Illinois, on December 7, 1963. Copyright Ray Flerlage/Cache Agency.

8

Stormy Monday Blues

1963–1964

It's a Saturday night and a thousand black Kansas Citians are going out to play. The crowd begins to gather early, starting at around eight o'clock, even though they know the show will not begin for at least another couple of hours. Posters have been tacked to telephone poles throughout the African American neighborhoods east of Troost Avenue, the unofficial racial dividing line in the city. For the last week or so fifteen-second promos have been playing sporadically on KPRS, the city's most popular black radio station. Anticipation is high. Advance ticket sales have been strong. Bobby "Blue" Bland is one of the hottest acts in R&B right now and he is in town.

As show time approaches, the old converted Apollo Theatre at Linwood and Troost,[1] renamed the Town Hall Ballroom, takes on a buzzing, laughing, party atmosphere. Round tables are filling with drinking and talking fans dressed to kill in their Saturday night best—fashionable red, white, and black dresses, high-high heels, and recently coiffed hair abound. Men in stylish suits and spit-shined shoes, some with tilted homburgs, tack back and forth to the setup bar at the back of the large cavernous room. It is a BYOB affair tonight, but ice, paper cups, and mixers are for sale. As the room fills, the lines lengthen. Everyone seems to know everyone else. People stop to chat with others, cousins, friends, co-workers, neighbors. Kansas City is a big city, but the black community is still close. There is a lot of hugging and back slapping and black power handshaking and joking and just good old-fashioned carrying on. The house lights are up so everybody can see and be seen. Indistinguishable jazz music plays dimly in the background over the building's PA system.

Lines continue to lengthen at the setup bar on the main floor and at a smaller one upstairs in the cramped balcony. Someone has set up a Polaroid photography booth in the lobby with a phony blue-sky backdrop and some couples are waiting to be photographed for $2.00 a pop, so they will have a souvenir to remember years later of the night they saw Bobby Bland—how beautiful and handsome and young and happy they were! The restroom lines snake out into the hallway. Once inside, a joint is passed down the waiting line—more back slapping and handshaking.

The promoter will be happy tonight. By nine-thirty the place is packed; all the tables are filled on the main floor and in the balcony. Men stand against the walls, looking for single women. People are still table hopping, but as the band trickles onto the stage, they begin to settle a little. There is no stage curtain. The band members just mosey in from the wings, play with the sheet music on their music stands that say BOBBY BLAND AND JOE SCOTT ORCHESTRA and begin tuning. They come and go—just when you think they must be ready, they drift off stage again. It's after ten o'clock even though the posters and radio promos had promised a nine o'clock start.

Finally, at some unseen, secret signal, the band members, resplendent in black tuxedos, amble from the wings to their respective positions. Joe Scott arrives last with his shiny double-belled trumpet. He nods to Jabo Starks, who has settled in behind a large drum set, stage center rear, and Jabo pounds out a loud, solid, up-tempo rhythm. Joe raises his horn and the others follow; as the house lights dim, they blast out a big band number that grabs the audience's attention. They swing through several mid- and up-tempo jazz numbers that allow everyone to improvise a little and to show off their musical skills. Bobby Forte takes a wild, rollicking tenor sax solo that draws extended applause; Melvin Jackson solos on another number. The entire little set is designed to leave the audience saying to each other, "Man, these guys can really play. Not just the set R&B stuff, but real jazz." But no matter how much they show off, Joe Scott keeps them tight; there is no doubt that this band is one taut unit. The crowd applauds politely at extended solos and after each number. By the time the brief set is over, the house lights have been brought down, people have settled at their tables, and the Bobby "Blue" Bland Revue has begun.

Then an unseen announcer with a deep, clear voice proclaims, "Ladies and gentlemen, welcome to the Town Hall Ballroom and the Bobby 'Blue' Bland Revue. [Horn flourish] Introducing Mr. Al 'TNT' Braggs!" The band goes into Braggs's first number, as the warm-up singer literally slides onto center stage, where he does a 360 degree spin, like an ice-skater, grabs the microphone and begins wailing "Do You Love Me," his version of the recent Contours hit, wildly demonstrating each dance step mentioned in the lyrics, "Watch me now! I can mash potato, and I can do the twist, now tell me baby, mmm, do you like it like this?" From there, Braggs is everywhere, dancing, jiving, jumping, doing the splits—a cross between James Brown and Jackie Wilson, with an almost perfect imitation of "Baby Workout." He covers all the latest dance hits from "Twistin' the Night Away" to "Mashed Potato Time." He strips his tux jacket off and tosses his bow tie into the audience and works himself, if not the crowd, into a frenzy. The announcer shouts, "Al 'TNT' Braggs! Ladies and gentlemen. Let's hear it for Al 'TNT' Braggs!" as Braggs bounces off for the last time. The applause is more spirited this time. The people have not come to hear Al "TNT" Braggs, but they appreciate his talent and effusive effort.

The house lights are all but extinguished now; only the stage and safety lights are lit. The disembodied announcer voice returns after a grand horn fanfare by the band:

Ladies and gentlemen, here's the man!
[Another horn fanfare]
I mean the Man!
[Horn fanfare again]
The sensational!
[Another horn fanfare]
The incomparable!
[Horn fanfare once more]
The dynamic Bobby . . . Bobby Bland!
[Grand horn fanfare]

The band slides effortlessly from this rodomontade into the opening strains of "I Pity the Fool," Wayne Bennett cleanly pinching each note. A big, white-tuxedoed, freshly conked and manicured black man stomps a cigarette out in the wings and saunters onto the stage. A bright single spotlight picks him up about halfway to the microphone, beams flashing off his diamond rings and bejeweled wrist watch. He squints down at the screaming audience, shyly smiles, glances to the heavens for inspiration, pulls the microphone from its stand, idly fiddles with it, as if to insure the cord is still attached, and whispers in a low, hoarse voice, "It's time to get down to cases."

"That's right, Bobby!"

"Take your time, baby!" the audience responds.

There follows a nonstop medley of Bobby's hits, carefully paced to bring the audience up and then gently down a little. Some have compared it to a Baptist church service, particularly the call-and-response part of it, but it really is more like a slow love-making session than anything else. He gradually brings the audience, whose majority is female, screaming, up to the point of release and then, to extend the pleasure a little longer, he backs off, and then builds again, then eases off once more.

He ordinarily chooses a couple of pretty faces in the audience and directs his songs to them, songs about needing to be loved and wanting someone to love and take care of, with a couple of love lost and revenge tunes thrown in to break up the love litany. He strolls about the stage throughout the show, still playing with the microphone and flipping its cord about casually, but regularly coming back, on this night, to a lovely, young lady in a low-cut red dress sitting at a table near stage right. He sings to her on and off all evening, and finally, after the jacket and tie are doffed, he sits on the edge of the stage and croons "I'll Take Care of You" to her. It is just too much. She jumps up, pulls her chair up to Bobby's dangling feet, and suddenly climbs up, hikes up her dress, and straddles Bobby's lap. He doesn't know quite what to do, but she smiles adoringly and Bobby nods the two burly security men away. He finishes the song, laughs, kisses her on the cheek, gently eases her off his lap, stands, and continues the show.

He has four set shows that he uses, and he will select one of them on any given night, based on the venue, the audience's vibe, and how he feels. Despite fervid requests from the audience, he seldom deviates from the selected set once it has begun. That's because his stage shows have been as carefully crafted as his songs. Everything is planned and constructed to produce the desired effect. The tempo of the show is important: the ebb and flow love-making motion must be maintained, his biggest hits must be sung at some point, and the performance must build so no one becomes bored or inattentive. By the time Bobby comes on, the hour is inevitably late and the alcohol and drug consumption substantial. And since Bobby is not a show man in the style of Al Braggs or Little Richard—in fact, he pretty much stands flat-footed or strolls throughout—he must grab and hold the audience only with his voice and the drama of the performance.

But there is always so much of the "Little Boy Blue" affect in Bobby's performances that the ladies do want him to succeed, they want him to feel loved, and they shout their encouragement throughout every show, singing along with their favorite songs. They also recognize and understand that, despite the shy smiles, he is very serious about this and takes tremendous pride in producing a show that his fans will remember long after that souvenir photo has faded. These working people have, after all, shelled out a lot of cash for new clothes, hairdos, tickets, booze, babysitters, and, yes, souvenir photos, and many will be up in only a few hours to go to work or attend church. So Bobby has a responsibility, learned from his mentoring by B.B. King, Rosco Gordon, and Little Junior Parker, to make sure the band is selected carefully and well-rehearsed, that the show's structure provides the necessary energy, and that he leaves an impression that his fans will remember long after the lights have gone up.

The show always ends when the horn section abandons the rhythm section on stage and Wayne Bennett joins Bobby at center stage as "The Feeling is Gone" is cloned into "Stormy Monday Blues." At the "I kneel down 'n' pray" line, Bobby carefully removes a handkerchief from his pocket, spreads it on the

floor, and kneels in front of Bennett (as if he, Bennett, could personally send
Bobby's baby back home to him), wipes a bead of sweat from his forehead with
his index finger, and delivers, fittingly just a few scant hours before Sunday
school, the release the show has been building to for the last two hours:

Sunday I go to church
And I kneel down 'n' pray
. . . And this is what I say, baby [spoken]

Lord have mercy
Lord, have mercy on me.
You know I cried, Lord, have mercy [shouted]

Lord, have mercy on me [whispered]

You know I'm trying, trying to find my baby,
Won't somebody please send her home to me . . . Yeah [spoken]

Wayne Bennett then delivers another silky guitar solo, with Bobby and the
audience listening attentively until Bobby interrupts with his most fevered cry
of the night:

Well, I cried, Lord, have mercy!
Lord, have mercy on me [whispered]
I said I cried, Lord, have mercy
Lord, have mercy on me.

You know I'm trying, trying to find my baby.
Whoooa . . . send her home to me!

There is never an encore. The audience screams and applauds until Bobby has
left the stage, the band has stopped playing, and the house lights have come
up. The fans slowly, reluctantly, almost reverently, walk off into the dark Kansas
City night.

The band was now performing more than three hundred nights a year,
booked by Evelyn Johnson into larger and larger venues, sometimes in conjunction with big package tours that included, in addition to Bobby and Al Braggs,
Sam Cooke, Jackie Wilson, Little Willie John, among others. It had been
almost ten months since their last recording session. But finally, on February
7, 1963, the band stopped in Hollywood to record there for the first time.
All four cuts recorded that day sound a little slicker, with more sophisticated

arrangements than usual—owing perhaps to the glitzy Hollywood surroundings. Neither the brassy "Ain't It a Good Thing," Bobby's version of Marie Adams's 1952 Peacock hit "Honky Tonk," nor the pretty ballads "Cry Lover Cry" and "Queen For a Day" hit the charts.

The band sounded more comfortable when it entered the Nashville studio again on May 7–11, 1963, for sessions that produced some of the best popular blues ever recorded. Here is Bobby and the band at their height, accompanied by a silky string section and the Anita Kerr Singers, who were more accustomed to backing Music Row country crooners than squalling blues blasters like Bobby.

The Latin-inspired "Sometimes You Gotta Cry A Little" reached number 28, and the country-tinged "Dust Got in Daddy's Eyes" went to number 23, while the Ray Charles–influenced "I Can't Stop Singing" peaked at number 19 on the *Cash Box* R&B chart. But the non-hits are even better. "If I Hadn't Called You Back," "After It's Too Late," and "Today" must be near the top of every Bobby Bland fan's favorites, truly defining the soul blues style of which Bobby is king.

Not to mention the beautiful *Cash Box* number 5 hit, "Share Your Love With Me," which is songwriter Dan Penn's favorite song. According to Al Braggs, who wrote it, "Joe Scott went to Don Robey and said, 'Mr. Robey, we need to add strings.' And they did and the song 'Share Your Love' came out in 1963." Bobby says of the song, "I sing it pretty, then go into the preacher stuff at the end."[2]

Braggs continued: "One night we were playing the Regal Theater in Chicago and Aretha Franklin said she loved the song. She would stand in the wings and listen to Bobby sing 'Share Your Love.' And Aretha Franklin called me over and said, 'Can I record that record?' I thought she was kidding, and a year or two later she did it. And when it came out, it really took off. But I never received any royalties for the song. . . .

"Finally, I leave the company in 1969, and then I started working with Angus Wynne at his club called Soul City and with his company Showco. So after a while, they asked me about 'Share Your Love' and I told them that I never got any royalties. So they said they wanted to sue on my behalf, and won, but I didn't find out until I talked to Evelyn Johnson. They had to pay me all the back royalties,"[3] not only for Aretha's version, but ultimately also for covers by The Band, Freddy Fender, Phoebe Snow, and Kenny Rogers.

About the only thing that could top that gem is another Deadric Malone and Joe Scott–credited classic that was actually written by John KaSandra (born John W. Anderson), who later recorded for Stax's Respect label.[4] "Ain't Nothing You Can Do" went to number 3 on the *Cash Box* R&B chart, won *Music Business*'s R&B record of the year award, and became Bobby's biggest crossover hit (number 20). Marsh pays fitting tribute to the song in *The Heart of Rock & Soul:* "Unbelievable as it seems today, there was a time when real blues had a place on Top 40, not as recycled novelty music, but as the sound that spoke to and from the heart of a significant segment of the pop community. Bobby Bland was the last great blues singer, and this was pretty much his final shot as part of the pop mainstream. God knows, it's a magnificent send-off. Scott sets ranks of horns riffing like a syncopated locomotive. Bland sings the first few phrases of each verse with extreme delicacy, then begins shouting against flourishes from the brass. It's a marvelous, almost indescribably balanced performance."[5]

You can take issue with this being Bobby's swan song but not with this review, by Gavin Martin, of *The Best of Bobby Bland* CD in 1982: "For now, for the past two weeks 'Ain't Nothing You Can Do' has been declared *the* best song ever written. Listen to it pounding, searching, spurned—bound with shackles, wounded with pain and crashing on the shore in a shower of sobbing frustration. Maybe [Van] Morrison's version on *It's Too Late To Stop Now* [Morrison's 1974 live album] is better, but let's not split hairs. It goes—love is unbeatable, anguish is hell and frustration is the bridge worth burning, burning, burning. . . . 'Ain't Nothing You Can Do' is not embroidery around emotions, it is right there at the centre of the catharsis—it's why we're alive, why we should be more alive."[6] Bobby, succinct as ever, summed up his feelings this way: "Good lyric, all I can say about it."[7]

On the sales strength of Bobby's first two albums, Don Robey quickly gathered an assortment of available Bobby Bland singles and packaged them as *Call On Me*, which included the hit singles "That's the Way Love Is," "Call on Me," "The Feeling is Gone," and "Share Your Love With Me." It reached an impressive number 11 on the Pop Albums chart and prompted this comment from critic Hank Davis: "A near perfect collection of early '60s sides documents the man at his best."[8]

Meanwhile, Robey, never at a lack for new ventures, decided the gospel side of his business needed a fresh start and launched two more labels, Songbird and Sure-Shot to complement his established Peacock brand.

In August, Bobby and the band embarked on another package tour, appearing at the Memorial Auditorium in Chattanooga, Tennessee, on August 8 with Little Richard, Junior Parker, the 5 Royales, Wynonie Harris, Big Maybelle, Tab Smith, and Jimmy Reed. On September 14 Bobby began a new tour with big star Sam Cooke, Little Willie John, Baby Washington, Freddie Scott, and the white rock 'n' roll singer Dion. The next day in Nashville, they heard about the Sixteenth Street Baptist Church bombing in Birmingham, Alabama, in which four little girls had been needlessly killed—another grim reminder of the racial turmoil that broiled around them. "It hung like a shroud over the whole tour—the cops in Louisville who stopped the show because two white girls in front got up and started dancing, the teenage white boy in Charlotte, North Carolina, they chased up the aisle simply because he was having a good time," reported Peter Guralnick in his biography of Sam Cooke.

But the show must go on, and the performers at least enjoyed the fun and camaraderie of competing among themselves. J. W. Alexander, a close friend of Sam Cooke, tells a story about Bobby, Al Braggs, and Little Willie John deciding to team up one night and outdo Sam on stage. "They really planned to cut Sam up in the finale," J.W. said, which would be "Having a Party." They were doing a pretty good job of it, seemingly taking the song from Sam, when J.W. unexpectedly appeared from the wings and "you know, I could always dance, and a lot of the girls thought, 'This must be Sam's dad,' and I just brought the house down."

However, according to Guralnick, a teenage white girl who saw the show in Columbus, Ohio remembered "Little Willie John's childlike charm and the thrall she felt when Sam spotted her girl friend and her doing the twist in their fourth row seats. 'Sam pointed at us and said, 'Those girls are doing some twisting,' and we just went out of our minds. But when Bobby 'Blue' Bland did 'Stormy Monday,' and his guitarist, Wayne Bennett, played the liquid notes of the solo, 'I just slid down into my seat and felt like I was dying.'"[9]

"Bobby Blue Bland was sexy blues," according to Maurice Prince, owner of Maurice's Snack 'n' Chat restaurant in Los Angeles and a regular Bland concertgoer. "Men would flock to see B.B. but the women would flock around this guy because he would sing kind of quiet and come out with these sexy notes. He was softer than B.B.—you had to kinda listen and that got under your skin. When Bobby would sing something, it was more like he was talking directly to you."[10]

On November 20, 1963, *Billboard* discontinued its R&B singles chart and maintained only one singles chart, in the light of Motown's broad success and because of the perceived convergence of white and black music and the record-buying public's seemingly equal acceptance of both. (This practice continued only until January 30, 1965, when the charts were again separated into the Hot 100 and the Top 40 Hot Rhythm & Blues Singles, presumably because of the arrival of the Beatles and the British Invasion.)[11]

The next month, on December 14, in Nashville, Bobby recorded the LP version of Charles Brown's 1951 hit "Black Night." "Black night is falling / Oh, I hate to be alone"—perhaps an inadvertent summation of Bobby's life and career thus far: his cloistered childhood, securely safeguarded under his mother's wings in rural Tennessee; the brief mothering by Valerie Cannon at the Victory Grill in Austin while he was still in the Army; Evelyn Johnson's empathetic ear and tender tutoring when he was not at home with his wife Grace in Houston;

and, of course, a continuous stream of traveling and musical mentors, start-ing all the way back in Memphis with B.B. King, Rosco Gordon, and Junior Parker, through Bill Harvey, Joe Scott, and Melvin Jackson, and, inescapably, the adoring fans who were always all too eager to take care of Bobby, showering him with love, affection, and alcohol, and never, ever it seemed leaving him alone.

In January 1964, a tired Bobby and his band headed to the West Coast, where they played a few dates with Sam Cooke. On February 7 the Beatles ar-rived in the United States for the first time, setting off a near riot at New York's Kennedy Airport. Before taking off on their first American tour of twenty-five cities in thirty-two days, they appeared three consecutive Sunday nights on television's *Ed Sullivan Show*, triggering the start of the British invasion by the Rolling Stones, the Animals, the Kinks, the Dave Clark Five, Herman's Hermits, Freddy and the Dreamers, and many more.[12] By the end of 1964 British groups dominated the airwaves and record sales, and the year's Top 10 pop charts had the lowest percentage of records by black artists since 1950.[13]

In Miami Beach on February 25, twenty-two-year-old Cassius Clay defeated Sonny Liston to win the WBA/WBC heavyweight boxing titles. Two days later Bobby and the band were in Los Angeles to record the presto-penned John Green (Bobby's road manager)–Joseph Scott novelty tune "The Greatest." Bobby does a credible imitation of the champ on the cut, but thankfully the tune was not released until the 1994 Duke compilation *Turn On Your Love Light*, probably because Clay's album, *I Am the Greatest*, was released by Capitol Records the following month.

Another version of "Black Night" was also recorded, as well as the slow blues "Blind Man," reaching number 34 and 14, respectively on *Cash Box*'s Black Contemporary Singles chart. The bouncy "Steal Away," which should have been a hit but was not, was the final cut of the session. Otis Rush claimed that Bobby may have borrowed some of Rush's minor key singing style with "Blind Man." "Yeah, well that style, of minor things," Rush said, "that's what I said, minor keys. I guess he sorta picked that up from me."[14]

At about the same time, Little Milton released his version of "Blind Man." Milton Campbell Jr. was born on the Duncan Plantation in Sunflower County, Mississippi, on September 7, 1934. He saved his field earnings to buy a mail-order guitar when he was twelve and, after singing in his church, set out with Eddie Cusic's blues band to play throughout the South. He soon had his own band and began recording with Sun Records in 1953. Later he recorded for Meteor in Memphis, Bobbin in East St. Louis, and finally with Checker, the Chess subsidiary, in Chicago in 1961. Prior to "Blind Man," he had a hit with "So Mean To Me," that went to number 14 in 1962, and "What Kind of Love Is This," earlier in 1964 that peaked at number 39.

When asked in 1974 about "Blind Man" and his similarity to Bobby Bland, Little Milton responded:

Well, to be honest with you, this was Bobby Bland's heyday. He could do no wrong. Whatever he did, it was a smash. They thought he was invincible. Nobody but nobody could go into his thing. Well, I knew better than this. It wasn't my goal to go out to get Bobby Bland. My goal was to try to look out for Little Milton. But I heard the tune—they recorded it first—and I liked it. And it didn't do anything for them. They had it on an album. I thought it could be a smash, so I did it. But now in doing the tune, to maintain and preserve the values that the tune had in it, you had to do it just the way it was done—you had to stick to the basic melody. I decided I'd do that instead of trying to make it sound different—you could have lost the tune. I did put a little more guts into it and slowed it down some—gave it a little more meaningful beat. Fortunately, I guessed right and it came out as a hit for me.

Then you go into the thing of maybe a miscalculation on Duke Records' part. They covered it and didn't take the time to analyze what I had done to the tune. They just reached back into the album and pulled it out. When you compare the two records, ours was so much better put together than theirs, we just beat them out. Then some of the writers were saying I was a Bobby Bland imitator. But fortunately for me this helped me tremendously—it let people know who Little Milton was. Which brings us to the point: There's no publicity that's bad publicity. But for a good little while there, it used to bug me. Some of the local disc jockeys at that time would hit me with those kind of questions, "How does it feel to be sounding like Bobby Bland?" and all this kind of thing. Then finally "We're Gonna Make It" came out [in March 1965] and that helped me, got me away from that thing to some extent. But that's nothing strange because in the very beginning I was being branded as a B.B. King imitator, Fats Domino, some of the older guys, like Roy Brown. Yeah! You have to make up your mind and do what you really feel. If I put out a tune, it don't make me no difference who it sounds like, as long as I feel it. I do it me. If it sounds like somebody else, that's just too bad, tough.[15]

Although Bobby's and Little Milton's hits made the charts, by March 14, 1964, *Billboard* reported that sales of Beatles records were making up 60 percent of the entire singles market.

On March 20 Bobby and Joe Scott thought they had another hit ready, so they stopped in New Orleans to record "If You Could Read My Mind," one of the most polished, perfect blues ballads ever recorded by Bobby or anyone else. Dave Marsh: "Seekers of the Sinatra of the blues, you've reached your goal. The arrangement is a bathos of strings, flute, and airy female chorus, the lyric a preposterous confection that's wonderfully absurd from its very first line. But it's the way that Bland sings that first line that makes him a great singer, not just another saloon crooner. . . . And so it goes, a tour de force performance in which Bland never pushes, never strains and nevertheless leaves you feeling engulfed with a misery unmistakably *his*, the product of woes distinctly personal yet inseparable from all others."[16]

By April 22, 1964, the band was in Nashville for their final recording session of the year; Don Robey wanted another album on the shelves and they needed a few more songs. Nine were cut that day, two of which were *Cash Box* hits: "Ain't Doing Too Bad (Part 1)," went to number 4, and "Ain't No Telling" peaked at 20. Five made it to the album, highlighted by a classic midtempo Bobby Bland shouter, "I'm Gonna Cry," and the Lowell Fulson blues standard, "Reconsider Baby." One song, the driving Joe Scott instrumental "Soul Stretch," would end up on the *Soul of the Man* LP in 1966. Unfortunately, another one of Bobby's great blues ballads recorded at this session, "I Won't Forget," was not released until the 1994 compilation *Turn On Your Love Light*.

The resulting album, *Ain't Nothing You Can Do*, was rounded out with previously recorded hits, including "If I Hadn't Called You Back," "Steal Away," and "After It's Too Late." Despite its funky, cartoonish cover, the album is another classic to rival *Two Steps From the Blues*, showcasing Bobby and the band at their zenith. But it reached only number 119 on the Pop Albums chart. And soon after the album's release Bobby Forte, the band's brilliant tenor saxophonist, left to join B.B. King's band.[17]

Meanwhile, twenty-nine-year-old Sam Cooke, Bobby's friend and concert rival, was shot and killed in Los Angeles by a desk clerk at the seedy Hacienda Motel on December 11, 1964. The funeral on December 17 was conducted at the Mount Sinai Baptist Church in Los Angeles, where a crowd of 5,000 packed a 1,500-capacity sanctuary for an emotional, tear-filled service. Lou Rawls sang "Just a Closer Walk with Thee," with unrestrained emotion. Gospel singer Bessie Griffin became so overcome that she had to be carried out. Ray Charles, standing by Sam's open casket, asked the congregation what they wanted him to do. "Sing!" they responded. And he sat down at the piano and sang "Angels Keep Watching Over Me," which one observer characterized as "the greatest gospel rendition I ever heard in my entire life." According to *Ebony*, "women fainted; tears rolled down men's cheeks and onlookers shouted."[18] Arthur Lee Simpkins, a classically trained baritone and old Chicago friend of Sam's, sang "I've Done My Work." Bobby Bland temporarily suspended his tour to attend the service and fervently sung "I'm Coming Home Now Lord."[19] B.B. King was also in attendance and said, "We all went to the funeral and Bobby sang, and he did it so well. He left everybody with wet eyes."[20]

Bobby Bland surrounded by fans at the Trianon Ballroom in Chicago on December 7, 1963.
Copyright Ray Flerlage/Cache Agency.

Honky Tonk

1965–1968

Bobby and the band continued on the road after Sam Cooke's funeral. They were playing the Regal Theatre in Chicago in January 1965 when Cooke's "A Change Is Gonna Come" was posthumously released. Inspired by Bob Dylan's "Blowin' in the Wind," Cooke wrote the song "as if it had come to him in a dream,"[1] and it captured in one compact poetic package the sad, angry, hopeful place that almost every African American found himself at that moment in time:

I was born by the river in a little tent
Oh and just like the river I've been running ever since
It's been a long, a long time coming
But I know a change gonna come, oh yes it will

It's been too hard living but I'm afraid to die
'Cause I don't know what's up there beyond the sky
It's been a long, a long time coming
But I know a change gonna come, oh yes it will

I go to the movie and I go downtown
Somebody keep telling me don't hang around
It's been a long, a long time coming
But I know a change gonna come, oh yes it will

Then I go to my brother
And I say brother help me please
But he winds up knockin' me
Back down on my knees

There's been times that I thought I couldn't last for long
But now I think I'm able to carry on
It's been a long, a long time coming
But I know a change gonna come, oh yes it will

While in Chicago, on February 9 and 10 Bobby and the band recorded five new sides for their next album, *The Soul of the Man*. Two did not make it and were unreleased until the 1996 Duke compilation *That Did It!*: the Latin-tinged "Building a Fire with Rain" and "Angel Girl," the ballad that Bobby was having so much trouble with in *Urban Blues* and that Charles Keil had dismissed as "one more futile attempt to launch Bobby into the lucrative teen-age market."[2]

Also recorded were a swinging "Reach Right Out" and a remake of Little Willie John's 1956 hit "Fever." The highlight of the session was "Ain't Nobody's Business," Bobby, Joe Scott, and Wayne Bennett's version of the 1949 Jimmy Witherspoon smash hit. Bobby always said that the Arkansas-born blues/Territory band singer was one of his favorites and his rendition of this standard is a fitting tribute.

On March 21 Bobby and the band were back in Memphis to headline the opening of the new night club owned and operated by Bobby's old friend, Sunbeam Mitchell. The Club Paradise, at 645 E. Georgia Avenue, was billed as "the South's leading nite spot." Mitchell recognized early that Urban Renewal was coming to Beale Street, so he opened the 3,200-seat club far from Beale on Memphis's south side, to protect himself from the day the Club Handy, where Bobby, B.B., Junior, Rosco, and Bill Harvey had cut their musical teeth, would be claimed by the wrecking ball. The Paradise thrived through the years, booking not only Bobby but Little Milton, Sam & Dave, O. V. Wright, Funkadelic, the Delfonics, and many other R&B and jazz greats.

The club sported uniformed parking attendants under a covered entrance, private rooms for special parties, a large dining room, wall-to-wall carpeting and oak paneling, not to mention a dance floor for 250 partiers. Rudy Willing, director of Memphis's Alcohol Licensing Commission and familiar with every night club in Memphis, was duly impressed. "I haven't seen anything like it," he said. "Sunbeam went first class all the way. There isn't a club in Memphis which can seat as many, and it has so many different features and rooms it amazes you."[3]

Mitchell was an experienced and knowledgeable promoter. He booked and paid the bands generously, as well as the local white authorities as needed. He advertised on WDIA and posted Globe concert posters in beauty shop windows and on telephone poles throughout the black community. He hired his own security force and provided them with a guest list of local dignitaries to be pampered. He gallantly replaced items lost, stolen, or damaged in the club's coat check room, and, most importantly, he kept a low profile in the white community.

However, by the early 1980s, the club had lost its sheen and was operating in the red. "Back when we had segregation," Mitchell explained, "the only place a black entertainer could play before a mixed audience was at the Club Paradise. In those days we had Lou Rawls, Arthur Prysock, B.B. King, Ike and Tina Turner, Lavern Baker, Millie Jackson, folks like that. I would let them play at the Paradise and we would have packed houses—both black and white. Now we've got integration and they have all gone and left me. They are playing the big concert halls and I can't afford them anymore."[4]

So integration and changing musical tastes finally caught up with the "patron saint of Memphis musicians," and, after running Memphis nightclubs for forty years, Sunbeam Mitchell sold all of his holdings four years before his death in 1989.[5]

At about this time in 1965 Wayne Bennett, despite his satisfaction with the band's musical direction, was growing weary of the road and his treatment by Duke and decided to take a break and return to Chicago to do studio work and relax at home. "They made us promises a little after the break-up with Junior Parker in 1961," Bennett said. "We were made to believe that we would receive residuals for all our years of recording and performance, for becoming in reality one of the principal R&B orchestras of the time, up there with Ray Charles. We sold more records than Ray Charles, but he was with ABC and we were with Duke, which was a black company, so we did not harvest the true fruits of our success."[6]

Bennett was replaced by veteran Houston guitarist Joe "Guitar" Hughes. Born on September 29, 1937, in Houston's Fourth Ward, by the age of sixteen Hughes had purchased his first guitar with money earned as a dishwasher and formed a group called the Dukes of Rhythm that also featured Joe's neighbor, Johnny Copeland. The Dukes became so popular that they were hired in 1958 as the house band for Shady's Playhouse, Houston's most popular blues venue at the time. There, Joe and the band played for five years "seven nights a week and two times in the daytime [for Sunday and Monday matinees]," often backing headliners like Nappy Brown, Rosco Gordon, Lowell Fulson, and many others. In 1963 Hughes joined Little Richard's former band the Upsetters, which was led by Houston saxophonist Grady Gaines. The group toured with Fats Domino, Sam & Dave, and Gene Chandler in a revue-style show.[7]

Hughes and the rest of the band stopped in Detroit on April 28 to continue work on the next album. In addition to Hughes, the band was joined by Joe Hunter, Motown Records' first pianist, and Berry Gordy's first hire, who had backed early classic recordings by the Miracles ("Shop Around"), the Contours ("Do You Love Me"), Martha and the Vandellas ("Heat Wave"), and Marvin Gaye ("Pride and Joy"). Upon leaving Motown in 1963, Hunter worked as a freelance arranger and pianist for Jimmy Ruffin, Jimmy McCracklin, Junior Parker, among others. He published his autobiography, *Musicians, Motown and Myself*, in 1996, and won three Grammys with the Funk Brothers, Motown's house band memorialized in the 2002 documentary *Standing in the Shadows of Motown*. He toured widely with the reunited group until his death on February 2, 2007, at the age of 79.[8]

Not surprisingly, the arrangements worked out by Hunter and Joe Scott for this session have a decidedly Motown feel, with tighter rhythms, amplified drum tracks, and a more grandiose flare than the usual Duke brassiness. Since the band, beyond Hunter and Scott, was not identified on album liner notes or Duke internal records, some have surmised that Motown session musicians may have moonlighted on this and the next session.[9]

On "Let's Get Together" and "I Ain't Myself Anymore," both written by Darrel Andrews, a high school band director in Monroe, Louisiana,[10] Bobby cannot seem to harmonize with the female backup singers brought in for the session. Bobby previously had been successful with backup singers, but only when they were used to punctuate his voice. Here, they are used more to imitate the "girl group" sound coming out of Motown and Red Bird Records that was vastly popular at the time, and Bobby's voice is just too unique to fit in with the girls' tight harmonizing. There are some bright moments on Bobby's duet with Vi Campbell on "Dear Bobby (The Note)," and some very eloquent piano playing by Joe Hunter on "Sweet Lips of Joy," but overall it seemed that Bobby just could not get into the soulful Motown mood.

They tried again in a couple of days with three more songs. "Too Late For Tears" is a typical poor-Bobby sad ballad, again with a strong Motown drum beat and impinging girl group backup vocals. "Playgirl" is more up-tempo, but still in the same vein. The most successful effort from these two Detroit sessions is "These Hands (Small But Mighty)," which abandons the backup singers and lets Bobby more confidently do what he does best: let go on a big, bouncy, mid-tempo romp. The song quickly went to number 4 on the R&B chart.

As if reflecting the diverse sentiments of these two tunes, Bobby enjoyed the physical love that was always available to him on the road but also maintained a strong, old-fashioned romantic streak. The latter was a result of singing songs like these and watching melodramatic movie matinees as a teenager back in Memphis, but most of all bred by his instinctive sense that there had to be something better and more lasting than the one-night stands that by now were ruling both his personal and musical lives.

So even though he was discouraged by the dismal impact that his constant traveling had on his marriage to Grace Towles—whom, it seemed, he seldom saw anymore—Bobby was not bitter about love. And he was genuinely flattered when a pretty, eighteen-year-old education student at Wayne State University in Detroit, named Marty, who was interviewing him for the campus newspaper, showed more than a journalistic interest in him. Besides being good looking, she was smart and seemed intuitively to understand Bobby's unusual lifestyle and the pressures it placed upon him. He fell for her. And despite his wife Grace back in Houston, Bobby and Marty's age difference, and Bobby's continual touring, they somehow became a couple. Bobby entreated Evelyn Johnson to book him and the band into Detroit as often as possible.

On May 26, 1965, the Rolling Stones came to America to perform on ABC's popular television music show *Shindig*. They agreed to appear on the show, however, only if Bobby's old West Memphis buddy Howlin' Wolf appeared with them. So the Wolf sang "How Many More Years" with the Stones sitting worshipfully at his feet,[11] triggering the second cycle of the blues revival that had started a few years earlier when young folkies had rediscovered country blues. Now, with the help of the Rolling Stones and other blues-based British invaders, young people were finding out what happened to the blues when it left the Delta. The Chicago blues of Howlin' Wolf and Muddy Waters would be the first to be uncovered in this second cycle; could the more sophisticated styles of B.B. King and Bobby Bland be far behind?

Oblivious, Bobby and the band continued its never-ending odyssey of one-night stands, crisscrossing the country to continue cashing in on Bobby's expanding popularity. To smooth out the edges of the constant grind of the road, Bobby was becoming increasingly dependent on alcohol, often starting to drink before the shows in addition to after them. "You need a crutch on the road," Bobby said, "and J&B [scotch whiskey] was mine."[12]

So, it was good to take a brief break in New York City, on November 11, 1965, to record a song that his old friend Clyde Otis had written in collaboration with Belford Hendricks. Otis had helped Bobby get the Brook Benton song "I'll Take Care of You" in 1959, and Bobby was eager to have another song in the same vein by one of the hottest songwriting teams in the country. At this point, Otis was already a living legend in the business, having been the first black A&R director at a major label, Mercury, where he had produced thirty-three of Mercury's fifty-one chart hits in 1962, with stars like Brook Benton, Sarah Vaughn, Dinah Washington, and the Diamonds. He left Mercury and joined Liberty Records for a time, but he had recently launched the Clyde Otis Music Group to independently produce records like this one. To conduct the topnotch New York studio musicians, Otis brought in Broadway arranger George Butcher. The result was a patented Bobby Bland ballad, "I'm Too Far Gone (To Turn Around)," that is as crisp and clean as a blues ballad gets. Going to number 8 on the R&B chart, it was a fitting recording climax to a long, busy year for the increasingly popular star.

Bobby was on a roll now. The hits just kept on coming and Bobby was more in demand at larger and larger venues. There is an old adage in the entertainment industry that "you need to get it while you can." Popular tastes are so fickle and fleeting that all the popularity and adulation could end tomorrow; if you're hot today, better take full advantage of it now. Record as much as possible, perform every night, man the tour bus, and full speed ahead. Keep going until you can't go anymore. So Bobby pushed on, drinking more than ever and bragging that he could handle it, that he had never missed a show because of his drinking and never would.

And if the record stores were demanding more Bobby Bland, then you needed to deliver. So the band was back in Houston for still another recording session on January 14, 1966. Joining the usual personnel for this and the next session was Gil Caple, a songwriter and saxophonist who had written the Mar-Keys' 1961 hit "Last Night" and O. V. Wright's goofy flop "Monkey Dog."[13] Charles Crawford replaced Rayfield Devers on baritone sax and Clarence "Sleepy" Anderson (who had previously played on recordings by Dinah Washington and Gene Ammons) replaced Teddy Reynolds on keyboards. The only hit of the four songs cut that day was Gil Caple's "Good Time Charlie, Part 1," which went to number 6 on the R&B chart—a big, brassy number that owes more than a little to James Brown's recent hit "I Got You (I Feel Good)." The unremarkable "Sweet Loving" and "One Horse Town" made it to the *Touch of the Blues* album, and the penetrating, dirgelike blues "Deep in My Soul" turned up on the B-side of "You're All I Need," cut later that year.

A month later, on February 15, in Houston again, the same assemblage cut the sweet ballad "I Can't Stop" with a full female choir and "Back in the Same Old Bag," a rollicking rocker that let Bobby really wail. The latter reached number 13 on the R&B chart when it was released with the previously recorded "I Ain't Myself Anymore." With "I Can't Stop," they had enough new songs to complete the much anticipated album *The Soul of the Man*, which quickly went to number 17 on the Black Albums chart. The album contained all the recently recorded songs as well as a big, brassy Vernon Morrison instrumental, the aforementioned "Soul Stretch."

This session also marked the end of Jabo Starks's stint as the dynamic drummer for the band; after repeated entreaties from "the hardest working man in show business," he finally accepted a position in James Brown's band. He was replaced by Harold "Peanie" Potier Jr., who joined the band in Chicago on April 21, 1966, to cut four new songs by thirty-two-year-old singer/songwriter/producer Pearl Woods.

Woods was born Lily Pearl Woodward in St. Matthews, South Carolina. She moved to New York City in 1951 to live with her godmother in Harlem and work the summer before entering college. Instead, she spent most of her time at the Apollo Theatre catching the shows and singing in neighborhood street corner groups, where she met Doris Troy and Clyde McPhatter. She later wrote "Something's Got a Hold on Me" for Etta James and less well-known tunes for Ray Charles and Jackie Wilson, and recorded for several independent labels in the city, including one with a group called the Gems that included Doris Troy and four sides with Little Richard's Houston-based band, the Upsetters.

Earlier in 1966, she had met Don Robey at a record convention at the Waldorf-Astoria Hotel in New York City. "Dave Clark, who was Duke/Peacock's sales rep, introduced me to Robey," she explained, "who in turn offered me a job in radio promotion because Boo Frazier (Duke's East Coast promotion man) had left for another gig. So, I went out on the road promoting Duke/Peacock product to radio stations along the East Coast."

Regardless of Robey's reputation as a scoundrel, he was certainly not a sexist scoundrel, since he was fair enough not only to put a black woman in charge of a large part of his business, but also to hire a black woman to promote his company and to write songs for and produce records for his hottest property. (Less charitably and perhaps more likely, he just liked to have pretty black women around him.) Nonetheless, in the 1966 pop music world, women could sing and even write songs, but a black woman promoter or producer was unheard-of. But, as was usually the case, Robey's gamble paid off, since three of the four tunes cut in this session would become top 10 R&B hits and staples in the Bland repertoire.

Both "You're All I Need," which hit number 6 on the R&B chart, and "A Piece of Gold" use the "Ain't Nothing You Can Do" motif in creative new ways, with a big, bombastic band, including a glockenspiel on "You're All I Need," predating by several months what many regard as its first use on a pop record, J.J. Jackson's great hit "But It's Alright."

"Poverty," a typical Bobby Bland country blues, went to number 9. "That Did It!" is a loping mid-tempo wailer that takes Don Robey's advice to O. V. Wright to heart—"a good wet bottom, plenty of bass, and a nice loud shrill top"—that reached number 6 on the R&B chart with Pearl Woods's tongue-in-cheek lyrics: "You said you needed the money to pay the rent / But I saw you sittin' at the bar spending your last red cent / Woooo, that did it, baby!"

Unlike most other Duke songwriters, Woods possessed enough foresight to retain the royalty rights to this and all the songs she had written, and with her royalties and the money she saved promoting Duke/Peacock records, she and her husband Fred Johnson formed their own Pearl-Tone record label and Free Pea Music Publishing company in 1969. She later opened a record store, Soul Shack, on the Upper West Side of Manhattan, but in 1973 "we were saved by the Lord and made the commitment to serving God." Since then she and Fred have operated the Pearl Johnson Ministries in Florida. Happily, all of her recordings as a pop vocalist were released in 2004 on a CD by Night Train International, *Sippin' Sorrow (With a Spoon).*[14]

At about this time, Al "TNT" Braggs decided to set out on his own, and took Joe "Guitar" Hughes with him. Hughes stayed with Braggs until 1969 and then retired temporarily from the music business to stay at home and tend to his growing family of wife, seven daughters, and two sons. In 1985 his old friend Johnny Copeland talked Hughes into joining him for a concert in Utrecht, Holland. The audience reception was so favorable that the Dutch label Double Trouble offered him a contract that led to the album *Texas Guitar Master Craftsman*. Hughes later recorded albums for Black Top, Munich, and Blues Express, and toured frequently in Europe. He was also featured in two documentary films, *Battle of the Guitars*, produced by Alan Govenar, and *Third Ward Blues*, produced by Heather Korb. Joe Hughes continued to perform up until a few weeks before his death by heart attack on May 20, 2003.[15]

Braggs explained his departure from the Bland entourage this way: "I stayed with Bobby until 1965, 1966 and then went out on my own. He understood, but the company didn't like it. Bobby told me, 'If you don't make it, you can always come back to me.' But Don Robey, Evelyn Johnson, they didn't see it. So Evelyn says, 'If you're going to go out and die, I may as well go out and book you.' And she sent out a little flyer and she didn't think anything was going to happen, and I got three months of dates.

"Between 1959 and 1969 I had nine records released by Peacock. . . . Then I recorded about five or six that were never released. What hurt me so bad was that they took their time. If I got a release a year . . . the only ones that got good releases were Junior Parker and Bobby Bland."[16] Regardless, Bobby remained one of Braggs's biggest supporters. "He is one of the greatest entertainers I've ever known," Bobby said. "He was always exciting. We made a good team, like Bob Gibson and Sandy Koufax."[17]

Braggs continued to tour, playing juke joints and bars in and around Texas, forming the Forever Fabulous Chickenhawks Showband & All-Star Revue in 1980. He also produced lesser-known R&B acts like Little Joe Blue, Ernie Johnson, and R. L. Griffin. And he kept composing, hoping for hits, most notably penning Bobby's 1977 number 14 hit, "The Soul of a Man." He died of a stroke on December 4, 2003, at the age of 65.[18]

Incensed by the death of Malcolm X the previous year, Huey P. Newton and Bobby Seale formed the Black Panther Party in October, 1966, in Oakland, California, to fill the void in leadership in the African American community. The party rejected the peaceful moderation of Rev. Martin Luther King and espoused a doctrine of revolutionary armed resistance against white oppression.

Bobby Bland, however, paid little attention to this or any other political situation and never became directly involved in the civil rights movement or any other form of politics. Still sensitive about his illiteracy and lack of education, he knew he was not articulate enough to represent these or any other causes. Even at the pinnacle of his career, he remained to a large extent an insecure country boy. The only thing he had any self-confidence about was his singing, so he focused exclusively on that, often at the expense of his family and with little regard for the larger world around him. "I don't care for politics one way or the other," he admitted. "I've never been concerned about it. I stay away from it as far as I can. James Brown didn't like it [Bobby's processed hairdo], and he had a little talk with me at the Apollo. He said, 'Robert, when you gonna come on in? Be a brother?' I know what I am. Then B. got on me about it, so I changed from the process to an afro. Didn't want to. Wasn't my choice."[19]

In Chicago, Bobby and the band returned to the recording studio on November 30 and December 7, 1966, to record five new sides. The first was a funky tune called "Sad Feeling" that successfully includes one male singer and one female singer in addition to Bobby. The next was a quirky "Shoes" that sounds rhythmically, if not lyrically, close to Bobby Hebb's recent hit "Sunny."

"Driftin' Blues" is a remake of the 1946 Charles Brown blues standard, with Bobby and Wayne Bennett excelling. The song was the only one from these sessions to become a hit, rising to number 23. "Gettin' Used to the Blues" is a bouncy, up-tempo swinger, and "Road of Broken Hearted Men" is one more attempt at replicating "Turn On Your Love Light."

All in all, 1966 was another hectic and productive year for the rising star: fifteen new recordings, six of which reached the top 25 on the R&B chart, a new album, and, as usual, more than three hundred live shows. The question was how long could Bobby maintain this pace: a show every night, regular recording sessions, constant demands by friends and fans at every stop, an estranged wife back home in Houston, Willie Mae in Memphis, his new friend Marty anxiously awaiting his next gig in Detroit—with a soothing alcoholic haze hanging over everything like a shroud over a descending coffin.

Yet the session with Pearl Woods had gone so well that Don Robey decided to try Bobby with another up and coming young songwriter/producer, Willie Mitchell, who was working for Hi (which stood for Hit Instrumentals) Records in Memphis. At the same time, Mitchell was producing soul classics by Bobby's Duke/Back Beat labelmate, O. V. Wright—a highly unusual arrangement since Mitchell worked for a competitor, but then Robey was never one for conventionality. "Yeah, I produced for a lot of different people at that time," Mitchell recalled. "When Bobby came to record, we had just done 'Eight Men, Four Women,' with O. V. Wright, and Robey wanted more of the same with Bobby."

Willie Mitchell was born on January 3, 1928, in Ashland, Mississippi. He moved with his family to Memphis in 1930 and played trumpet in his high school band. When he went into the army in 1950, he learned how to arrange and score from pianist Onzie Horne, a Duke Ellington alumnus (and an early studio musician for Duke Records, where he played on one of Bobby's 1956 sessions). After Mitchell's discharge, he formed his own band that became quite popular in and around Memphis, even playing at private parties for Elvis Presley. "Between 1962 and 1967, my band played his parties every year," Mitchell recalled. "We were friends. He'd come around 1:00 a.m. and we'd play from two to six. One time he had Ann-Margret there and it was just a riot."

Hi Records signed Mitchell in 1959, and he and his band were soon producing hits. Later he became the leader of the label's house band and its resident arranger, a sort of Joe Scott equivalent, backing, arranging, and ultimately producing records for Hi artists like Al Green, Otis Clay, Syl Johnson, and Ann Peebles.

When Bobby arrived in Memphis on Valentine's Day 1967, Mitchell was ready with some Memphis's best studio musicians. Mitchell does not recall who all played on the session, but does remember that Reggie Young played guitar, Tommy Cogbill was on bass, apparently moonlighting from their regular gig at Chips Moman's American Sound Studio, and Mitchell himself played trumpet. "I remember too, sitting with Bobby at my desk, working out the lyrics. He couldn't read, you know, so I had to lay out the lyrics, line by line, so he could memorize them," he said. "But he was so easy to work with and such a talent."[20]

The first cut was the bragging "Lover with a Reputation"; next was the slow blues "Touch of the Blues," featuring some fine picking by Reggie Young, and the final side was a swinging "Set Me Free." "Touch of the Blues" reached number 30 on the R&B chart, and all of the cuts captured Mitchell's Hi sound of tight horn arrangements, sharp guitar work, and the Hi driving kick drum beat. "I had the greatest drummer in the world, Al Jackson, Jr., and we'd tune the drums to a piano," Mitchell said. "We'd say, 'Let's tune this thing down near C and get it where the harmonics would be the same.' That was one of our secrets."[21]

Mitchell was not quite satisfied, however. "I wanted to cut a record that would sell black and white," he said, "combine the two, you know, in a *pleasant* kind of music. With O. V. Wright and Bobby Bland, their style was too strong in one direction, it was too rough. I wanted to add more class to it. O. V.'s music was a little more laid back; Bobby's had a little more spark to it. But I was trying to get a combination of the two."[22]

He found it the next year when he heard a young man named Al Green in a club in Midland, Texas. By 1970 Willie Mitchell was vice-president of Hi and with Green turned out one hit after another, a collaboration that would continue fantastically through the 1970s and be re-inaugurated in 2003 with the album *I Can't Stop* and again in 2005 with *Everything's OK*. "Papa Willie," as he was affectionately called in his later years, continued to record artists such as Buddy

Guy, John Mayer, and Rod Stewart at his Royal Recording Studio at 1320 South Lauderdale in Memphis.[23] He could usually be found there, looking dapper, often surrounded by his grandchildren Lawrence and Archie, whom he adopted as sons, until he suffered cardiac arrest on December 19, 2009, which led to his death at Memphis's Methodist University Hospital on January 4, 2010.

"We had just gone past what was called race music and blues, which was looked down upon, to this R&B, this soul," recalled Al Bell, a former owner of Stax Records in Memphis and producer of Bobby Bland albums in the late seventies and early eighties. "We worked with each other so we could grow and improve our music, and Willie provided that kind of leadership. His handprint, thumbprint, footprint, heart print is all over Memphis music."[24]

After this recording session it was, of course, back to a show almost every night for Bobby and the band. Since the record royalties were so stingy from Don Robey, and Bobby did not write his own songs, the only way to support the life style of a big R&B star, what with jewelry, wardrobe, booze, cars, and cash, was to perform constantly. Of course, too, there was the "get it while you can" attitude that made Bobby push himself to the limit while his popularity was at its height.

But unlike the rock arena shows, the R&B acts of the time played much smaller venues, with audience capacities of anywhere from a few hundred to a few thousand, but rarely over three thousand even for a combined big package show. The limited ticket dollars had to be spread among a lot of people. Evelyn Johnson and Buffalo Booking, and subsequent agencies, received a cut, the club owner and local promoter got theirs, often a local radio station was paid to promote and emcee the show, and whatever was left went to Bobby and the band, and Bobby's band was comparatively large, with at least seven to ten pieces. So it was a living, but not a lush living, and a hard-fought one at that.

During these flush years, the band would be out for months at a time, playing every night. The venues varied, from hardly more than juke joints to relatively classy clubs, to big theaters, like the Apollo in New York, the Regal in Chicago, the Royal in Baltimore, and the Howard in Washington, primarily on the chitlin circuit but sometimes in integrated spots. Sheldon Harris lists a page full of Bland performance stops in his *Blues Who's Who*, many of them mainstays on the chitlin circuit for years: the 5-4 Ballroom in Los Angeles, Longhorn Ranch in Dallas, Palladium Ballroom in Houston, Groove Yard in Vancouver, Ruthie's Inn in Berkeley, the Back Door in San Diego, and on and on—"high-class joints, low-class joints, and even some honky-tonks."[25]

"We play all type of places," Bobby explains. "There are some times that you have to cater to the people that gave you the first start, and you don't think that the club is qualified for you after you get standard in the music world, but even though, you still have to play them. Because I feel that they entitled to this particular thing because we started out there, you know, and didn't no-body really know us. Cause there's a lot of people that wouldn't book us, you know, and like at this time they had a little thing going on. B.B. was with the company [Buffalo Booking Agency] durin' that time; in order to get B.B. you would have to book Junior Parker and myself. Can you dig this? The promoter would take a chance—well, he knew he wasn't gonna make anything off Junior and I, but he would book us ahead of B.B. B.B. would make up the slack that he had lost on Junior and myself."

Bobby remains grateful to promoters who helped him early on: "Dave Brown of New Orleans, George Barker and Mr. Sullivan out in California, and Boss Lewis out of Tampa, Florida."[26] These payback venues were mixed in with posher places, sometimes as far as 500, 600, or more miles apart.

"We both worked out of the same agency in Houston," B.B. King explained, "Evelyn Johnson's Buffalo Booking. And Evelyn was a smart lady, so if I had a hot hit, she would book us both on the strength of that, and if Bobby had a hot one, she would book on the strength of that. Rarely though were we on the same stage on the same night. When we were, Bobby'd always blow me and everybody else away. We knew it. We wouldn't even bother."[27]

"At Buffalo, Evelyn Johnson was in charge," King said, "and she would say, 'Tomorrow you gotta go just up the street, so be on time for the gig.' And like that would be 700 miles! And we used to complain among the band, we used to complain how we'd jump. When we got a job say, 300/400 miles, that was nothing. Man you name it, we played it, we played so many places."[28]

Not all promoters were appreciated, however. Gatemouth Brown tells a story of doing a show with B.B. King in Mississippi: "I remember one time we had about 3,500 people in the house and this guy didn't want to pay off nobody. Had a big .45 sittin' on the table and he didn't know I had a pistol in my pocket. So I pulled my pistol and I laid it right up above his head. I told B.B. to count his money out and count mine, too. And he did and I backed out the door with my gun, just like the wild west days. I hollered at my driver, I said 'Get this Pontiac rollin'!' He had the motor runnin', I got in that car and we burned rubber from there back to Texas."[29]

After every show the equipment had to be packed and loaded, initially in or on a station wagon, later onto a bus, and today in a trailer behind a mod-ern RV, and then there would be the drive to the next performance. Tired and sleepy, on dark, unfamiliar roads, accidents and mechanical breakdowns were not uncommon. Bobby has been fortunate never to have been involved in a serious accident, "but I've seen some though and had some narrow escapes. The baddest hours are at three 'til five, six in the morning. You get sleepy. I only nodded off once in my whole career of driving, from New Orleans to Mobile—had too much to drink. There again, not supposed to have the booze and drive, only hurting yourself."[30]

Others in the business have not been so lucky. From the beginning of automobile and air travel, blues artists have suffered from their constant rambling. On September 26, 1937, Bessie Smith was fatally injured in a car accident on Highway 61 between Memphis and Clarksdale, where she died in the town's African American hospital, now the Riverside Hotel. Buddy Holly, Ritchie Valens, and the Big Bopper, early rock stars, all died in an airplane accident on February 3, 1959. On April 29, 1967, J. B. Lenoir, the Chicago bluesman, originally from Monticello, Mississippi, died of a heart attack, related to a car accident three weeks earlier, at the age of forty. Later the same year, on December 10, Otis Redding, age twenty-six, his manager, the pilot, and four members of the Bar-Kays were killed when their chartered plane crashed into Lake Monona in Madison, Wisconsin. Texas guitarist Stevie Ray Vaughn died in a helicopter crash after a gig at the Alpine Valley Music Theater near East Troy, Wisconsin, on August 27, 1990. In the wee hours of the morning of April 19, 2001, Bobby Rush's tour bus crashed near Pensacola, Florida, resulting in the death of dancer Latisha Brown, the mother of two young children, and the serious injury of several other band members. Mack Laurin, the leader of Sir Charles Jones's band, died in a one-car accident, returning home from a Sir Charles show in Gadsden, Alabama, on May 16, 2006.[31]

But Bobby and other bluesmen continued to take these risks of the road even though the returns were modest. Evelyn Johnson claims that the only Buffalo Booking clients who made the agency any money were the ones who were not Duke/Peacock artists: "So far as Buffalo Agency's concerned, everybody owed me money but B.B. King and Ike Turner. . . . I sent as much out as came in. What happened was in the booking you get a deposit with a returned signed contract. It was supposed to have been 50 percent. That came in. However, I wound up giving back to [the performers] because they collected the balance on the spot. You see, it was always a breakdown in transportation, getting out of the hotel, and there were those who were users in the first place—they would get the money in order to keep from having it." She insists, however, that none of the money from Buffalo Booking went to Robey, but instead went "only to the artist."[32]

Upon arriving in any town, finding a suitable hotel could prove problematic, particularly in the years before integration. Sometimes the band resorted to sleeping in the station wagon or on the bus because no black hotels were available., Even finding something to eat could prove a challenge; restaurants were also segregated in the Jim Crow South. B.B. King's road manager and bus driver used the bus's 150-gallon gasoline tank as an incentive. They would pull into a gas station with a restaurant attached and say, "We need gas *and* food." But often they settled for sandwiches handed out the back of a kitchen.[33]

Then everything had to be unpacked again, the stage set up, instruments tuned, sound and light systems checked, and the usually cramped dressing room outfitted with wardrobes, food, and drink. With all the moving, something was always breaking, requiring simple or complex fixes. No PA system was the same, each claiming its own quirks and obstacles. Acoustics could be anywhere from perfect to dismal.

The performance itself rarely began before ten o'clock. Often there were two or even three shows a night—the first at around ten, the next at about midnight, and the last at two or three in the morning. The sun was sometimes coming up before the bus pulled out for the next town. In addition to the vagaries of a given venue, Bobby and the band never were sure what the audience would be like on any given night; but many fans were inebriated by the time Bobby came on. Jealousies and tempers often flared, and fights were not uncommon. One night at the converted former Municipal Airport in Kansas City, when Latimore had completed his set and Bobby was performing, Latimore remembers that a woman pulled a pistol from her purse and shot a rival right in front of the bandstand. The lights came up and Bobby and the band had to scurry from the stage and out the door as the police descended to sort things out.[34]

The travel, the problems, the routine were maddening and unrelenting. After packing up, driving all night, unloading, and setting up, there were rehearsals, sometimes recording sessions in the larger cities, interviews with local deejays and newspaper reporters, band member crises, entertaining local celebrities and friends before and after the show. And then again the next day, day after day after day.

But perhaps the most wearing was the loneliness and unreality of it all. It was not a normal life and certainly not one that a performer could endure for long without taking a break or relying on crutches like alcohol and drugs.

One of Bobby's band members described his feelings about life on the road on Valentine's Day:

Okay so it's well after 1 in the morning here in Tampa, FL. Not exactly having the greatest day or experience on this tour that I am a part of. No trucks hauling great gear, no surplus supply of tour busses. Then again it's like a blues tour. Most of the blues tours I have done, whether it be the B.B. King Blues Fest tour or other quote un-quote blues tours this is rather disappointing. 8 artists on the show and each set time is 20 minutes long. Take the money and flee type thing. I'm getting off track, I mainly am thinking about my woman at home and how much I would rather be with her taking her out romancing her, making my best attempt at singing to her with or without the strolling violinist. So I am extremely homesick more so now than usual with it being this type of holiday. . . . It's funny how there is this whole big misconception of what it's like on the road. . . . It's not all that fast paced. There are guys out here working trying to make dough doing what they know how to do to take care of their families back home. It's not always fun out here. . . .

For me, when I get the [message] from my agents informing me of my schedule two things go through my head. First, okay planning on certain amount of cash coming in. Second, and it's kind of a two parter. Well I gotta leave home and my woman to go out to make cash, and in that same breath anxiously plotting and scheming on how quickly I can get back home to her. In addition to missing my other half or blonder half, I miss the magic and chemistry taking place with my band-mates. What we do together as a unit to me is simply off the chain!! . . .

I miss home, my woman, (in her arms is home for me!!), my band and just not dealing with the day in day out living out of a suitcase and strange catering that happens. Don't get me wrong, I love playing the drums, love making music, entertaining the peoples, but I hate the price I pay. It's not that I have trust issues with my woman, or anything like that. It's more like a kid being told to go to bed by his parents and not wanting to go for fear they are going to miss out on something while they are asleep. So I am bored and alone in my room wishing I was home, yes both homes!!!!![35]

That's from Bobby's thirty-year-old son, Rodd Bland, who now plays drums in Bobby's touring band, written on Valentine's Day 2007. But it could have just as easily been written (not via blog, of course) by a band member of forty years earlier.

The Bobby Bland road band, by 1967, had been out on the road almost continuously for about six years, Bobby even longer. Many had already drifted away and been replaced: Sonny Freeman and Bobby Forte to B.B. King's band, Jabo Starks to James Brown's band, Wayne Bennett to do session work, and Al Braggs and Joe Hughes out on their own.

By this time Bobby was seriously dependent on alcohol. Joe Scott, who had been in touring bands, on and off, even before Bobby—with Gatemouth Brown, Johnny Ace, and Junior Parker—was sick to death of the travel and Robey's unfulfilled promises. Even Melvin Jackson, Bobby's closest friend and confidant, was fed up. So, if not so much as anything else but weariness and mutual consent, the original Bobby Bland touring band, what was left of it, broke up. Joe Scott and L. A. Hill returned to Houston to do session work. Melvin Jackson worked with Johnnie Taylor's band for a while and then quit the road altogether and enrolled in Cosmetology School in Houston. "Sure, I got my shit together," recalls Jackson. "When I left, I told him, you just call me when you're ready."[36] Charles Crawford returned to Memphis to marry singer Tina Bryant and work outside the music business; Johnny Board joined B.B. King's band; Johnny Beck went with Earl Gaines's group; and Hamp Simmons and Pluma Davis retired from the road altogether.

According to Peter Guralnick, Bobby viewed those years with the band with a "mixture of nostalgia and regret." He recalled with affection the music, the band members, and their camaraderie on the road and in the studio. He admitted that subsequent bands have never really matched the sound of Scott's and that he missed the fellowship and bonhomie that they shared. "We used to have a ball team then, too, man," Bobby remembered wistfully. "We played against the guys in the particular city, the musicians, you know. We'd get into Tennessee, Arkansas, Texas, in Florida we'd play against the policemen, because we knew them all. Yeah, we had gloves and everything, me and Joe Scott and all the fellows. Oh, we had a lot of fun back in those days. We had a real, real family then."[37]

The band, however, recorded enough new songs before breaking up to release a new album, *Touch of the Blues*, at the end of 1967 that reached number 38 on the Black Albums chart in 1968. "During his Duke tenure," wrote critic Ron Wynn, "Bobby 'Blue' Bland's rich, creamy voice was at its stark, dramatic peak. Like his other label releases, even when he got overly sentimental or just plain corny material, or the songs were overarranged, Bland's smashing leads made everything work."[38]

Don Robey also pulled together some of Bobby's bestsellers for the first *Best of Bobby Bland* album, which reached number 29 on the Black Albums chart, prompting these comments from British critic Gavin Martin: "Bland might not go to the top of the chart, but he goes straight to the centre of the heart . . . that's all that really matters. This is a catalogue from the past 20 years, and the distinguishing factors are: a big, bold yearning, heaving voice filled with passion, remorse and strength; all the things that matter, all the things that have ever mattered. The music is sharp, raw, gentle, light, deep, loving and vengeful—whatever is required, whenever required at the behest of stylish and persuasive arrangements."[39]

As 1968 began, Bobby was joined by a group of Duke studio musicians in Houston on January 20 to cut three new singles. All have a big, brassy Joe Scott sound, but they seem almost too professional in their stiff orchestral way. Nevertheless, Buddy Johnson's "Save Your Love For Me," which had been a hit for Nancy Wilson and Cannonball Adderley in 1962, went to number 16 on the R&B chart. The big band blues "Rockin' in the Same Old Boat," written by keyboardist Vernon Morrison and featuring Chicago guitarist Bobby King,[40] went to number 12, but Morrison's bouncy "Wouldn't You Rather Have Me" did not score.

That would be the extent of Bobby's recording output for the year. Upset by the breakup of the band, he drank more and more and began to wonder if his music career had run its course. "I was an alcoholic for eighteen years," he admitted to Peter Guralnick in 1975. "No, I mean I was an alcoholic, there's no ifs, ands, or buts about it. The reason I can say it is because I know it happened, and I'll tell you something true. There's nothing worser than a drunk. He's the sorriest ass on earth. As soon as I got in the car after the show I just let everything go. I'd be in the back of the limousine down on my knees going from one gig to the other. When I got to the hotel they just pack me out and I would sleep all day long. Then as soon as I woke up around six or seven I got the bottle right beside my bed, and I would start all over again. . . . I was drinking up to about three fifths a day, man."[41]

But what else besides singing, even with its concomitant hassles, could he do? He was basically a self-described "hick," uneducated and untrained and unprepared to do anything else. By now he was as much a slave to the road—of lookalike hotel rooms, room service meals, and 24/7 valet service—as he was to alcohol. "If I go any place," Bobby explained, "I wouldn't be able to enjoy myself, you know. Because it's always somebody will recognize you and you'll have to entertain them and answer questions or however. Truthfully I only go out on my good days, that I'm feeling good. . . . It makes you have different thoughts about it. Like is this the right thing for you, you know? Maybe this isn't the thing that you was supposed to be doing. You see, you have to be concerned about what you're doing. If you don't enjoy it, then really you're working against yourself. But then I say to myself, this is what you said you wanted to be all along—I never really thought of nothing else. So you just have to deal with it for what it is."[42]

"You know what it is day to day," Bobby said later. "A club here, different cities, different things that happen. . . . Sometimes you're in a place for 10 or 12 days, but mostly they're one-nighters. It wears you down. But you just get up and dust yourself off and get back into the race. I won't give it up until I can't do it anymore. . . . I've spent the biggest portion of my life on the road. It's not a good life, but it's my life."[43]

This life, constantly away from home and in an alcohol fog, would ultimately cost Bobby his first marriage to Grace Towles, who was left all but abandoned back in Houston. Soon after their divorce, Bobby moved to Detroit to marry and live with Marty, the Wayne State University student he had fallen in love with two years earlier. They started a family, and Bobby did his best to sustain it, despite the continuous traveling and attendant drinking.

So, with the band's dispersal, Bobby put together a rhythm section, figuring that was all most of the big rock bands traveled with anyway, and besides it would be less expensive and with fewer hassles. But the show suffered as a result, and he could not get accustomed to such an austere sound. "It's a must that you have your own tools," he soon realized. "I found that I was always looking for the horns. With just three or four pieces I didn't feel right. I didn't feel as if I was presenting myself, Bobby Bland."[44]

To keep Bobby out there while he worked through this difficult period, Don Robey hurriedly put together *The Best of Bobby Bland, Vol. 2*, made up of Bobby's lesser past hits, and released it in late 1968.

Unfortunately, the record-buying public was now more into Motown and Stax and sweet soul music than anything else. Gospel-inflected hits by Aretha Franklin, the Temptations, Smoky Robinson, James Brown, and Marvin Gaye not only were topping the charts, but they were also awakening a new generation of white kids to the joys of black music and its blues and R&B antecedents. So much so that Bobby's old Memphis mentor, B.B King, at the urging of new white bluesmen Mike Bloomfield and Elvin Bishop, was invited by rock promoter Bill Graham to play the heretofore white rock theater, Fillmore West, in San Francisco, where he was greeted by a standing ovation from the all-white audience. Later Graham booked him into the Fillmore East in New York City, where he was introduced by Mike Bloomfield as the greatest living blues guitarist and again received a standing ovation—before he even played a note. So, after the white public's discovery of country blues earlier in the decade, and later Chicago's electric blues, it finally was B.B.'s turn.

King also changed managers in 1968, replacing Lou Zito with Sidney A. Seidenberg, a New York show-business accountant who had been keeping B.B.'s books. Seidenberg was a real go-getter and soon was generating unprecedented PR for the veteran bluesman. B.B. was soon booked into Las Vegas and opened for the Rolling Stones on their 1969 tour. In 1970, "The Thrill Is Gone" was released and crossed over immediately to the pop charts. After twenty years on the chitlin circuit and almost fifty R&B hit records, B.B. found himself in demand on white college campuses, on European tours, on television shows like *Johnny Carson, Mike Douglas, David Frost, Merv Griffin*, and, yes, on October 8, 1970, even *Ed Sullivan*, and in high-class joints around the world. B.B. King had truly arrived.[45]

At about the same time, Evelyn Johnson had finally grown weary enough of the vagaries of the booking business that she dissolved the business and set her artists free to pursue other arrangements. Both B.B. and Bobby threw their lot with the Associated Booking Corporation in New York City, where they worked closely with Oscar Cohen to broaden their venue base to larger and whiter audiences.[46]

Meanwhile, Wayne Bennett, after having worked in 1965 and 1966 with his brother Jerry's jazz group in Des Moines, Iowa, returned to Chicago to join the Soul Crusaders, the house orchestra at the fabled Regal Theater on Chicago's south side. There the seventeen-piece group backed the most famous names in black music: Jackie Wilson, Aretha Franklin, Little Milton, Johnny Taylor, etc. Bennett was even there when eight-year-old Michael Jackson was discovered and signed to his first recording contract.

But Bennett was more proud of his work with Rev. Jesse Jackson as part of the official orchestra for Operation Breadbasket, one of the organizations founded by Jackson and the Southern Christian Leadership Conference (SCLC), then led by Martin Luther King Jr. Bennett explained: "Operation Breadbasket was the socio-economic branch of the SCLC. In collaboration with four other organizations, like CORE, Operation Breadbasket boycotted stores that did not sell products made by black firms, or who treated their employees differently because of the color of their skin, or even if they sold out-of-date items or items of poor quality. In the poor areas, where the people were white or black, they pressed for equal treatment for all. That's the problem in America. It says one thing, but does another. It's a great nation, but it has a way to go for justice to reign. Since we were the official orchestra for Operation Breadbasket, our job was to play at the rallies and meetings before King or other speakers came on. We would also accompany other performers like Roberta Flack, Mahalia Jackson, and Donny Hathaway."[47]

On March 29, 1968, Dr. Martin Luther King went to Memphis to support the black sanitation workers who had been on strike since March 12 for higher wages and equal treatment. A march in support of the strike was supposed to go from the Clayborn Temple AME Church down Beale to City Hall on Main Street, but some rowdy young men, not associated with the march, began smashing store windows on Beale Street, resulting in chaotic police intervention and reversal of the march.

On April 3 Dr. King returned to Memphis, but his plane was delayed by a bomb threat. When he finally arrived he addressed strike supporters at the Mason Temple, closing his speech with these words: "And then I got to Memphis. And some began to say the threats, or talk about the threats that were out. What would happen to me from some of our sick white brothers. Well, I don't know what will happen now. We've got some difficult days ahead. But it doesn't matter with me now. Because I've been to the mountaintop. And I don't mind. Like anybody, I would like to live a long life. Longevity has its place. But I'm not concerned about that now. I just want to do God's will. And He's allowed me to go up to the mountain. And I've looked over. And I've seen the promised land. I may not get there with you. But I want you to know tonight, that we, as a people, will get to the promised land. And I'm happy, tonight. I'm not worried about anything. I'm not fearing any man. Mine eyes have seen the glory of the coming of the Lord."

The next day, Wayne Bennett and the Operation Breadbasket orchestra arrived in Memphis from Chicago to perform at a rally with King. They were rehearsing in a room above the reception area of the Lorraine Motel when, at 6:01 p.m., a few doors away on the second floor balcony of the motel, Dr. King was shot and killed by James Earl Ray, an escaped convict, who confessed to (but later denied) being the assassin. Television news reports of the assassination, coming in the midst of the evening news, were incomplete, confusing, and inaccurate. A wave of riots spread quickly to more than sixty cities.

Five days later, on April 9, President Johnson declared a national day of mourning for the thirty-nine-year-old civil rights leader; 100,000 attended his funeral in Atlanta the same day. Two days later, President Johnson signed the Civil Rights Act of 1968, prohibiting discrimination in the sale, rental, and financing of housing. Shortly thereafter, the city of Memphis settled the strike, on favorable terms for the workers, but at a terrible cost to the nation.

Bobby Bland at Sunbeam Mitchell's Club Paradise in Memphis ca. 1970.
Copyright Ernest C. Withers Estate, courtesy Panopticon Gallery, Boston, MA.

Touch of the Blues

1969–1972

One high price Bobby paid for his band's breakup was the luxury of developing a new song within the relative isolation of the road with Joe and the guys and then going into the studio with the tune all but finished. Now the process took on a decidedly different turn, with new material being arduously worked out in the studio. But there were two characteristics that had stood Bobby in good stead throughout his career: determination and perseverance. And he called on them both again now, throwing himself full bore into working and making records.

His first 1969 recording session was on January 29 in Houston. Replacing Joe Scott as producer was the Texas trumpeter/songwriter/arranger Henry Boozier, who had worked with Gatemouth Brown on some of his earliest Peacock recordings, with Milt Jackson, the great jazz vibraphonist and his Modern Jazz Quartet, and most recently with B.B. King.[1] Don Robey also asked Oscar Perry to help with the session. Perry was "a deep-voiced singer and sweet-toned guitarist who [had] worked with Joe Scott not only as a collaborating songwriter but also later as a featured artist on Robey's Back Beat label. . . ."

"[Scott] showed me how to write for strings," Perry, now a producer and independent record label owner (TSOT and Perry Tone) in Houston, remembers. "When he had an arrangement and needed somebody to do a melody, he would come get me. We had a pretty close relationship."[2] Perry played this collaborative role for Boozier for this session, letting Wayne Bennett, who was now contenting himself with session work, provide the guitar lead and Harold "Peanie" Potier the drum beat. Boozier not only tightly arranged and played trumpet on the three cuts, but also wrote the slow, sad blues "Baby I'm On My Way," featuring Bennett's cool guitar, and the classic Bobby Bland blues ballad "Ask Me About Nothin' (But the Blues)," one of the prettiest in his repertoire, where you almost embarrassingly hear the singer's secret sorrow and resignation in each guttural, cigarette-inflected syllable, with Bennett's smooth counterpoint—one of Bobby's all-time best. Surely just as many fans bought Duke 449 for this song as they did for its number 9 flip side, "Chains of Love," recorded at the next session on February 28 in Chicago.

Don Robey, as usual, wanted a new album from Bobby, but since the band's breakup Joe Scott, Bobby, and the band had not had a chance to work on anything new on the road. So Scott and Robey came up with the idea of rearranging a number of modern blues standards that they thought would be good for Bobby. To help Scott with the marathon session, Robey hired arranger Jay Wellington, as well as an unlikely choice for a standards album, the maverick soul singer/songwriter/producer Andre Williams, who had written or sung a number of food-related novelty songs ("Bacon Fat," "Jail Bait," "Rib Tips," "Pig Snoots"), as well as the 1963 super hit for the Five Du-Tones, "Shake a Tail Feather."[3]

Bobby loved recording at the Universal Recording Studio in Chicago and Don Robey had arranged for several members of the old Bland band to work the session: Joe Scott (trumpet), Johnny Board (tenor sax), Wayne Bennett (guitar), and Peanie Potier (drums), joining session players Johnny Young (piano), Gerald Sims (guitar), Phil Upchurch (bass), and a full string section.

The first song they recorded was the Hoagy Carmichael–Stuart Gorrell classic "Georgia on My Mind." Bobby's lush version is slower than Ray Charles's 1960 hit, but if there were any doubt that Bobby could sing country this rendition extinguishes it. "We did two takes for 'Georgia,'" Bobby said. "If you're a blues singer, you have to think in terms of beauty. I had a chance to be around a girl named Georgia for about five years. Singin' this reminded me of some of those times—the happy times and the sad times too."[4]

Next came the Leslie Bricusse—Anthony Newley ballad "Who Can I Turn To." Originally written for the 1964 musical *The Roar of the Greasepaint—the Smell of the Crowd*, it was popularized by Tony Bennett the following year. Bobby loved Bennett. "Tony tells a story and puts real feeling in it," Bobby explained. "I love the way he sings. He inspired me to cut 'Who Can I Turn To.' I've always loved the softness—since Nat 'King' Cole. Joe Scott taught me how to reach the bridge, had trouble with it, but Joe said, 'It's just a half note.' We had about three takes to get it." Bobby's version, with Wayne Bennett's (no relation to Tony) fine guitar accompaniment, is a fitting tribute to the crooner who, when asked about Bobby's cover, sadly claimed never to have heard of Bobby Bland.[5]

They next recorded "Gotta Get to Know You," not a standard but a bombastic, pulsating romp penned by Andre Williams, replete with strident horns and female backup singers, that went to number 14 on the R&B chart.

Bobby's version of "Chains of Love," the 1951 number 2 R&B hit written for Big Joe Turner by Atlantic Records head Ahmet Ertegun under his pen

name Ahmet Nugetre (Ertegun backward—get it?–somewhat less subtle than
Deadric Malone), proved to be a hit again. As Chris Morris, senior writer for
Billboard, wrote in the liner notes to *Bobby Bland: Greatest Hits, Vol. One*:
"Bland's sensitive reading, dressed with a supple string arrangement, scored a
number 8 R&B hit in 1969. It proved again that, whether essaying material
crafted just for him or taking on somebody else's best, Bobby 'Blue' Bland was,
as he always will be, The Man."[6]

"Since I Fell for You" was composed in 1945 by Buddy Johnson for his sister, Ella Johnson. By the time Bobby recorded it, the song had been covered
by Stanley Turrentine in 1960, Vince Guaraldi in 1962, and Lenny Welch in
1963.[7] Bobby's version stands up well among these and demonstrates again his
mastery of the blues ballad form.

"Yum Yum Tree" is an up-tempo treat penned by Duke promoter Dave
Clark that shows that Bobby has now become vocally deft enough to handle
successfully rather complex, multirhythmic tunes like this one.

The final song recorded at this protracted session was another poor-Bobby
blues that lets Bobby really wail. "You Ought To Be Ashamed" was written
especially for Bobby by Clifton Smith, a popular deejay at Houston's KCOH
radio station, who was better known as King Bee and the emcee at the Club
Matinee's weekly amateur shows.[8]

"I was in a melancholy mood when we did these sessions in Chicago at
Universal Studio," Bobby recalled. "I have to get everything set up just right.
Alone in the studio with just the arranger and engineer. Late at night—around
midnight. I like night recording. You get a better feeling. I don't use headphones when I'm recording. Just a speaker in the corner to hear myself."[9]

Robey and Scott took all of these songs except "Yum Yum Tree" and added
four from previous sessions to create Bobby's new album, *Spotlighting the Man*.
The entire package represents an obvious attempt to reach a wider audience
outside the R&B community, but, while ultimately unsuccessful at accomplish-
ing that, it was well-received enough to reach number 24 on the Black Albums
chart and to prove that Bobby was now truly proficient at singing with his own
brand of soul and creativity in a variety of musical styles and motifs.

On the road, however, Bobby was still struggling with his pared-down
rhythm section. When his road manager since 1957, John Green, quit to move
to Los Angeles (to operate a limousine service eventually used by the *Tonight
Show* and other show-business clients),[10] Bobby stepped up his efforts to find
a full band. He finally heard about an established Tulsa band that might work.
The band was led by Ernie Fields Jr., who had been brought up playing saxophone in his father's traveling Territory band that combined big-band swing
and R&B in much the same way Duke did, scoring a big hit in 1959 covering
Glenn Miller's "In the Mood."[11]

The younger Fields therefore was accustomed not only to the sound Bobby was seeking but also to traveling extensively with a big band and all its baggage—physical as well as emotional. Fields played both tenor and alto saxophone as well as the flute. He and his trombonist, a twenty-five-year old New Orleanian named Alfred Thomas, could both arrange. Tommy Punkson on trumpet possessed a good solid tone. And Michael "Monk" Bruce, a white boy, added a rock touch with his guitar that Bobby thought could not hurt given the times. Bobby also persuaded Johnny Board to rejoin the band on tenor and alto sax. Board, a former Lionel Hampton band member, had backed Bobby off and on since 1957 and knew Joe Scott's charts by heart. And, fortunately, Harold "Peanie" Potier Jr., who had replaced Jabo Starks on drums three years earlier, agreed to stay on with the new band.

After some rehearsing the band sounded pretty good, Bobby thought. It was not the same as before, but a vast improvement over the rhythm section that he had been struggling with. Still booked nearly every night, Bobby again had a real band to work with, if not a perfect one.[12] "Ernie had a good rock-type sound, you know," Bobby explained, "but it wasn't right for me. It's kind of a different change for you to go back to this, like just plain maple syrup after you've had your taste of honey. Oh, it's a bitter pill to swallow, but like I say, you just have to learn to adjust and you learn to accept and make the best of what you have."[13]

In August *Billboard* changed the name of its chart from Hot Rhythm & Blues Singles to Best Selling Soul Singles, one more indication of the prevalence of that increasingly popular form.

On August 15–18, 1969, nearly 500,000 hippies and other, mostly white, young people descended on Max Yasgur's dairy farm in rural Bethel, New York, for the Woodstock Music and Art Fair. Featured at the four-day affair were some of the top pop acts of the day, among them the blues-influenced performers Richie Havens, Janis Joplin (who sang Big Mama Thornton's "Ball and Chain"), Sly & the Family Stone, Johnny Winter (Albert King's "Born Under a Bad Sign"), Joe Cocker, the Band, Ten Years After (Sonny Boy Williamson's "Good Morning Little School Girl"), former Little Richard guitarist Jimi Hendrix, the Paul Butterfield Blues Band (J. B. Lenoir's "Mama, Talk to Your Daughter"), Blood, Sweat & Tears, Canned Heat (Sam Cooke's "A Change Is Gonna Come"), Santana, and, of course, the Grateful Dead, closing their act as usual with Bobby Bland's "Turn On Your Love Light."

A few weeks later, and a year after B.B. King's initial appearance there, on September 5 and 6, 1969, B.B. King, Albert King, and Bobby Bland performed at the traditionally all-white Fillmore East in New York City. This led to several dates where the blues threesome would work together and to a growing number of shows for white audiences.

"Oh, yeah, we did something every year before Albert passed [in 1992]," Bobby recalled. "We would have at least a month, month and a half that we would travel and do the larger places, auditoriums and things of that nature. That was real fun, because B. and Albert were my two favorite people and I could learn each and every day from them. . . . [The energy] was hot, very hot. I think, speaking for B. and Albert and myself, we did a good job because we always tried to make it hot for the other fellow, not arrogant like or anything like that—just make one another work. You do your best, and it was a lot of fun. Being professionals, there was no jealousy of any sort there. It was just a matter of doing what you're supposed to do and give the public what they want."[14]

On October 10, in Chicago, Bobby and a studio band with strings recorded two songs arranged by Joe Scott and Jay Wellington. The first, "If Love Ruled the World," was a preachy soul ballad written by Joe Veasey, the only time the tunesmith better known as Joe Medwick was given writer credit on a Bobby Bland record; unfortunately for Medwick, it was one that never became a hit. The second song was a strange mid-tempo number (and top 10 hit) called "If You Got A Heart," with the sardonic refrain "it must be made of ice."

This was the last recording session with Bobby and Joe Scott, the man Bobby said "was everything." The two had been working together from the beginning back in Memphis and were as musically intertwined as any pair could be, as interdependent as Frank Sinatra and Nelson Riddle or Joe Williams and Count Basie. During the past decade the two had literally created modern blues, charting thirty-four R&B hit records, eighteen in the top 10, two chart-toppers, seven hit albums—and landing Bobby at number 5 (between the Temptations and Aretha Franklin) on Joel Whitburn's list of the Top 25 R&B Artists of the Decade, based on number of hits and chart positions.[15]

Taking the Territory band style out of Kansas City and Houston and mixing it with the 1950s Memphis band sounds of Bill Harvey and Pluma Davis, Joe Scott, with Bobby and their band, had developed an entirely new blues style that supplanted for black people the down-home country blues and electric Chicago blues now so popular with white audiences and created a sophisticated, urbane blues genre that reflected and spoke more directly to the tastes, self-image, and aspirations of the emerging postwar African American middle class.

Bobby, of course, continued with Don Robey and Duke, but Scott struck out on his own; as early as 1968 he did horn arrangements for the *Super Session* album by blues rockers Mike Bloomfield, Stephen Stills, and organist Al Kooper (later of Blood, Sweat, & Tears), and went on to arrange the *Half and Half* album by Frankie Valli and the Four Seasons in 1970. Al Kooper recruited him again in 1975 to write the horn arrangements for his album *Al's Big Deal/*

Unclaimed Freight. Stephen Stills used his horn arrangements for three of his albums in 1976–78, *Stills, Illegal Stills,* and *Thoroughfare Gap.*[16]

Trumpeter, bandleader, songwriter, teacher, and arranger extraordinaire Joseph Scott died of cirrhosis of the liver at the age of fifty-four, on March 6, 1979, in Culver City, California, where he had moved from Chicago about a year before. He is truly one of the unsung heroes of modern blues.[17] Coincidentally, Bobby and Joe's old Memphis mentor, Bill Harvey, died the same year at the age of 75, from complications due to diabetes and alcoholism.[18]

Regardless of Scott's departure, Bobby needed to keep going. His royalties from Don Robey were initially a ridiculously stingy one-half cent per record when the standard in the industry at the time was closer to two cents per side, depending on what was negotiated between the artist and the record company. To make ends meet in the style to which he had become accustomed, Bobby needed to continue making hit records *and* to tour. Since Robey had initially signed Bobby when he had not had a single successful record, Bobby felt some obligation to him. "I don't have any changes, like, in mind at all," Bobby told Jim O'Neal in 1971, "because I've been treated very, very nicely with the company, throughout say, 15 years that I've been with them. And I'm kinda satisfied where I am. I've had several offers, you know, but I can understand them wanting a blues singer on the label, but this was my first offer that really got me out of the gutter, was the Duke label. So I feel more or less partial to the company."[19]

And so far, Bobby was doing okay, doing what he liked and making some money. If he were to argue too forcefully about the royalties or threaten to move to another record company, Robey was a powerful enough man that Bobby's career could be seriously disrupted. So, in a sense, he was a slave to Robey. He had to continue with what was working, because he was not sure he could make it elsewhere or that Robey would not blackball him in some way. Now, however, without the old band and Joe Scott, his confidence was waning.

Bluesmen are unlike pop stars who sell millions of records to a broad audience; their audience is small by comparison, and a hit record rarely sells more than a hundred thousand copies. "You can book a Bobby 'Blue' Bland single," said R. T. Maier of *Popular Tunes*. "It may be a big hit or maybe not, but you can book that you're going to sell a good amount of it as soon as people find out it's out."[20] Enough hits and public appearances can soundly establish a singer's career so that each new record sells some copies and there is a steady demand for his shows.

Dave Clark, the first independent promotion man in the record industry, described how it worked at Duke: "Some of [the artists] didn't tend to be too smart; some of them were so smart they outsmarted themselves. Back in those days a guy would go out make him a record. First thing you know he wanted a Cadillac. Don Robey said, 'All right, I'll get you the Cadillac, but you got to pay me just like you pay the man.' And when royalty time came and you ain't made enough money out of the record to pay for your Cadillac [Robey would charge it against your account]. Guys would come get $4000 to $5000 at a time. You see all the artists wanted to be big shots. They all wanted big cars. They all wanted fine clothes and everything that went with it."

Unlike B.B. King, Gatemouth Brown, and a few other R&B stars of the time, most artists, including Bobby, let the record companies run their financial lives. "Peacock supported them," says Evelyn Johnson, "bought their clothes and their transportation and so forth and so on. In the contract, so far as the recording industry was concerned, all of this tended to be an advance against future royalties. . . . as a result of that the next thing you knew you were paying for the birth of the baby, and the girl, and the grandmother, and paying for the divorce and the whatever. I used to tease them all the time. I'd say, 'This is not a contract—this is an adoption paper.'"[21] Or, more accurately, modern-day papers of indenture.

Then, of course, there was the entire issue of the Buffalo Booking Agency. Bobby did not have a manager to negotiate his contracts and to guide his career. Basically, all he did, except sing, was done by Duke. Joe Scott, up until recently, provided the music; Evelyn Johnson, the performance bookings; and Don Robey, all the other necessities of life—the clothes, jewelry, limousine, valet, and a plentiful pocketful of money for whiskey and food—all advances against royalties.[22] "I feel like Jane Pittman, sitting on a porch in a rocking chair when I start talking about this kind of thing," Johnson said, "because it's so complicated and intermingled. You see, I operated in a conflict of interest."[23]

And when a major expense occurred, like replacing a tour bus, the company was there too. "Where's the money coming from, the record company?" Peter Guralnick asked Melvin Jackson when the bus broke down in Boston. "I don't know who it's coming from," answered Jackson, "but if somebody don't come up with something we just gonna sit down until they do. They'll come up with it."[24]

And while Bobby understood the position he was in, he felt powerless to do anything about it. Usually he tried to put the best face on it and keep going, but he sometimes became discouraged. "You know, I've been established as a blues singer for over twenty-five years," Bobby told Guralnick in 1975, "but I've never gotten paid. I don't know, over here it seems like they cater to an artist from over there much quicker than they would their own, and that pisses me off, man, that really pisses me off. You know, people talk to me about going over there to Europe, but nobody ever tell me nothing about the money they make over there. It's just publicity, I guess, but why they can't make me over here? That's a lot of bullshit, man, a whole lot of bullshit. It hurts, you know, to know your good years are gone and you haven't really been recognized. I mean, I don't want to be out here in my sixties. What the fuck can you do at sixty or seventy? That's what makes me angry. That's why I wish all this had happened when I was much younger, when I was thirty-five, say—cause I was really hollering then."[25]

"Old singers are like old baseball players," Bobby said in 2001, still touring at seventy-one, "none of us made a lot of money."[26]

Regardless of the cost, Bobby hated to compromise the act. So, now with a new band, he finally hired a replacement for John Green, his longtime road manager who had left the year before. Burnett Williams was an aspiring singer who would end up working faithfully and relentlessly for Bobby, doing whatever was needed or required to keep the show on the road. He also replaced Al Braggs as his opening act with Paulette Parker, a former Ikette in the Ike & Tina Turner Revue, who sang as pretty as she looked. "And I must say that she leave the stage just sizzlin' for the next act regardless to what it is, and I enjoy working with her," Bobby said. "And you can't get a better hotness, I'd say, on the stage, like, from the way that she leaves it, and it gives me a lot of inspiration."[27]

On Saturday, August 9, 1970, Bobby was near home in Detroit to headline the evening's performance at the second Ann Arbor Blues Festival. Also on the bill that night were Robert Pete Williams, Johnny Shines with Sunnyland Slim, Johnny Young, and Joe Turner with T-Bone Walker and Eddie "Cleanhead" Vinson. It was a great lineup and Bobby was thrilled to be on the same stage as T-Bone and so many of his heroes, not to mention to break through to the more lucrative, largely white festival circuit audience. Here was a chance not only to gain a fatter paycheck for a shorter than usual performance, but also to widen his audience beyond the segregated chitlin circuit crowd.[28]

Feeling better about his future, Bobby went to Muscle Shoals, Alabama, a few days later to record a couple of songs with producer Don Davis and a group of top FAME Studio musicians. The Muscle Shoals sound, strong rhythm and bass mixed with a distinct country feeling, was very big at the time. FAME stands for Florence Alabama Music Enterprise and was established by Tom Stafford in the 1950s above his father's drug store in Florence, Alabama—yes, the same Florence that spawned W. C. Handy and Sam Phillips. In 1960 Billy Sherrill and Rick Hall, two local musicians/songwriters, joined Stafford and began to record local musicians. After an argument in 1961, Rick Hall left the company, but retained the FAME name which he used to label his new studio in nearby Muscle Shoals.

After the studio's recording of Arthur Alexander's 1962 hit, "You Better Move On," and Jimmy Hughes's big 1964 hit, "Steal Away," Vee-Jay, Chess,

Dot, Dial, and other independent labels began requesting the studio's services, which included not only studio space and recording expertise but also production assistance, talented musicians, and creative songwriters such as Dan Penn and Lindon "Spooner" Oldham. In 1966 Atlantic Records producer Jerry Wexler recognized the special soul sound coming out of the FAME Studio and sent Wilson Pickett down to record his big hits, "Land of a Thousand Dances" and "Mustang Sally." As a result, Atlantic sent a continuous stream of artists, including Aretha Franklin, Arthur Conley, and Otis Redding (who was under contract to Stax, but distributed by Atlantic), to the studio, and the Muscle Shoals sound was soon in demand by everyone in the pop music business.[29]

Producer/songwriter Dan Penn was born Wallace David Pennington on November 16, 1941. He grew up next to a junkyard in Vernon, Alabama, and claimed he was crazy because of two things: second-year algebra and sniffing gasoline. Even though he was white, he fell in love with black music at an early age by listening to the radio. "I had three distinct personalities in those days," he remembers, "my own just got lost in the shuffle. When I wasn't Ray Charles or James Brown, I was Bobby 'Blue' Bland. There wasn't no such thing as Dan Penn then. It was 'Here comes Bobby "Blue" Penn.'"[30]

Throughout the 1960s, the studio was erratically run by volatile Rick Hall, "crazy" Dan Penn, "Sky High" Donnie Fritts, and cool-headed composer/pianist Spooner Oldham—and they often disagreed. "It seemed like Rick didn't believe in r&b during that time, after Arthur," Penn recalled. "I don't know why, something must have happened to him. He told me he didn't want any black people in there anymore. That's when I got him to listen to Bobby Bland, *Two Steps from the Blues.* After that we started seeing 'em pop up. Up to then I couldn't stick to no kind of music, either—it wasn't pop music, it was kind of watered-down Elvis, but it wasn't even that. We didn't know nothing until black people put us on the right road. I never would have learned nothing if I'd have stayed listening to white people all my life."[31]

By late 1966, having penned Percy Sledge's "It Tears Me Up," Aretha Franklin's "Do Right Woman," Clarence Carter's "Slippin' Around," Joe Simon's "Let's Do It Over," and James Carr's "Dark End of the Street," among many others, Penn and later Oldham were in Memphis working with Chips Moman to create many more hits at Moman's American Sound Studio.[32]

Backed by Jerry Wexler at Atlantic, the FAME rhythm section of Barry Beckett (keyboards), Roger Hawkins (drums), Jimmy Johnson (guitar), and David Hood (bass) left Rick Hall and FAME in March 1969 to start their own studio, the Muscle Shoals Sound Studio. There, everyone from the Rolling Stones and Rod Stewart to Paul Simon, Bob Seger, and Willie Nelson recorded over the next few years. In 1978 new facilities were built in nearby Sheffield, where the group launched their own record label, signing such artists as Delbert McClinton, Frankie Miller, and Levon Helm. These studios were sold to Malaco Records, Bobby Bland's current label, in 1985.[33]

Don Davis, a successful but controversial Stax producer and guitarist, was called on to produce Bobby's first Muscle Shoals session. Originally from Detroit, Davis had played on some of the early Motown sessions and co-owned Thelma Records with Berry Gordy's ex-wife and her mother, as well as producing and playing guitar for the Golden World, Wingate, and Revilot labels. He also owned his own Groovesville label, where he produced the number 9 J.J. Barnes hit, "Baby Please Come Back Home," in 1967. The following year he joined Stax and produced and played on Johnnie Taylor's "Who's Making Love" hit, which became Stax's biggest seller to that point. He produced seven successive Top Ten hits with Taylor, as well as hits by the Dramatics, the Dells, Little Milton, and others, before having a falling out with Stax's head Al Bell in 1973, and then joined CBS Records.[34]

Bobby and the FAME studio musicians first recorded Clifton Smith's "Keep On Lovin' Me (You'll See the Change)," a funky, modern dance number that went to number 20 on the *Billboard*'s soul chart. The other was a luscious cover of Detroiter Kenny Martin's 1958 hit by pianist Sonny Thompson, "I'm Sorry," which went to number 18.

Both were fine records, but that would be the extent of Bobby's recording for the year. Don Robey, however, was determined to keep Bobby out there and record sales healthy. So he released two new albums. The first was entitled *If Loving You Is Wrong*, which contained a curious selection of eight songs. Two of the tunes, "Ain't Nothing You Can Do" and "Call On Me," date back to 1963 and 1962, respectively. Four of the tracks—"City Woman," "Five Long Years," "If I Weren't a Gambler," and Stax's songwriting team of Homer Banks, Carl Hampton, and Raymond Jackson's "(If Loving You Is Wrong) I Don't Want to Be Right" (which predated Luther Ingram's smash hit version by about two years)—sound almost like demo cuts and are not listed in any Bland discographies as to recording dates, places, or personnel, nor do they show up on recording logs, compilations, or as singles, except "If Loving You Is Wrong," which was released as a single in a smoother, string-laden version in 1973.

And three of the tunes were to reappear in less funkier versions on Bobby's 1973 *His California Album*: "If Loving You Is Wrong," "This Time I'm Gone for Good," and "Up and Down World." The other 1970 LP was entitled *Introspective of the Early Years* and contained twenty-four of Bobby's prior hits on two LPs. Neither of the albums made it to the top album charts, and Bobby continued touring with Ernie Fields and his band as 1971 dawned.

They stopped in for a welcome five-day run, January 29–February 2, at the Burning Spear club in Chicago, where Bobby was interviewed after the Saturday night show by Jim O'Neal, founding editor along with his wife, Amy, of the new magazine *Living Blues*. The interview and the accompanying article about Bobby's stage show by Amy were featured in *Living Blues'* fourth issue a few weeks later. As they perused a recent *Living Blues* issue, this is how the interview ended:

> *They joked for a few minutes more, Paulette [Parker] discovered something else of interest in the magazine. "Somebody wrote this!" she exclaimed, and read some lyrics aloud: "I've been tryin' so hard to save my life, just to keep that preacher from my wife."*
>
> *"Yeah, that's right. Whoever wrote that is right," said Bland.*
>
> *"He will eat your chicken, he will eat your pie, he will eat your wife out on the sly," Paulette continued, and Bland added, "Sure will."*
>
> *"I went to my house about half past ten, looked on my bed where the preacher had been," she read.*
>
> *Bland grinned, "That's the fella would come up and eat them drumsticks and things on Sunday. He'll never come to my house, the preacher won't. Reverend Franklin showed me what they'd do. Reverence C. L. Franklin. The eagle stirs his nest. He the one told me about preachers."*
>
> *Ernie Fields cracked, "I know one in my neighborhood, run down the streets in his drawers."*
>
> *The dressing room was in hysterics. Everybody seemed tired, but everybody was happy. It was 3:30 a.m., and we decided it was time to leave. They still had another set to do, and two more the next night, and then they'd be off in the station wagon for somewhere else.*[35]

Only one recording session occurred during 1971, probably in Chicago, with Jay Wellington again arranging and producing. Three new songs were recorded: Vernon Morrison's "Shape Up or Ship Out," a mid-tempo Bobby-been-burnt wailer; a pretty, brassy ballad, "The Love That We Share (Is True)"; and the number 6 hit "Do What You Set Out to Do," a loping blues with strings that fit Bobby perfectly.

Later in the year, Michael "Monk" Bruce, the guitarist in the Ernie Fields band, decided that he had had enough of the road and returned to Tulsa, later working with Bob Seger and several Tulsa bands before contracting hepatitis during a Far East tour with Michael Jackson's sister, Rebbie. He was living with his wife, Cindy, in Bentonville, Arkansas, where he was waiting for a liver transplant, when he died on August 8, 2005, at the age of 58.[36]

Bobby picked up another guitarist on the road and continued touring. Then one night he was out partying with T-Bone Walker in Chicago, and their drinking got out of hand. "It was when him and T-Bone was together," Melvin Jackson recalled. "Last time they were really out together in Chicago, they both got extra sick. That's what really woke him up. Him and Bone."

"Yeah, Bone was my first idol," Bobby continued. "Maybe it was just seeing him fucked up the way he was. Then I met my wife [Marty], too. She was eighteen years old. She believed in me, and she helped me. She was the one got me to quit. Then she got a little drinking problem of her own, but we straightened that out. Now everything's fine."[37]

So Bobby quit drinking altogether and called Melvin Jackson, who closed up his cosmetology shop in Houston and rejoined Bobby and the new band on the road.

Shortly thereafter, in early 1972, Bobby returned to the recording studio to cut "I'm So Tired," produced by Eugene Dozier and Robert Evans, a driving bass- and drum-dominated tune that went to number 36 on the soul chart. Later that year, Bobby recorded his final two tracks with Duke Records, the fittingly titled "I Don't Want Another Mountain to Climb," a mid-tempo throwaway, and "That's All There Is (There Ain't No More)," a sad love lost ballad. And, as it would turn out, that's all there was for Duke.

On September 9, Bobby again headlined the Ann Arbor Blues Festival, sharing the stage with Little Sonny, Dr. John, and Pharoah Sanders. Atlantic Records recorded portions of the festival and included Bobby's live version of "Ain't That Loving You," with Malcolm Rebennack, better known as Dr. John, on guitar, Melvin Jackson back on trumpet, new band members Joseph Hardin, Jr. on trumpet and Charles Polk on drums, along with the rest of the Ernie Fields band.[38]

In a casual conversation a little later, Mick Jagger asked Mel Brown, a thirty-two-year old Los Angeles–based guitarist originally from Jackson, Mississippi, to introduce him to Bobby, who was on tour in Los Angeles at the time. When Mel called, Bobby turned the conversation around and asked Brown to join his band, and Mel took him up on the offer. Poor Mick never did get to meet Bobby.[39]

Mel Brown was just what Bobby was looking for to re-form his band with Melvin Jackson. Brown had played with Johnny Otis's band, had worked with Etta James, Nancy Wilson, and played on T-Bone Walker's *Funky Town* album, before cutting several of his own albums with ABC/Impulse/Bluesway. In addition, Brown played a hollow-bodied Gibson ES-175 guitar, a successor to the big Gibson ES5 played by T-Bone Walker and reminiscent of Wayne Bennett's Gibson Byrdland hollow-body.

"Bobby had split with Joe Scott, and Ernie Fields was his bandleader," recalled Brown. "The band was in disarray when I joined. When the group got to Los Angeles Bobby was looking to replace the guitar player that he picked up somewhere on the road. At the time there wasn't any harmony or good karma in the band. I tried to add something solid to what Bobby was doing because the band didn't have a very strong sound. . . . After a few months, Bobby fired the whole band except for me and Melvin Jackson. Bobby wanted us to put a new band together but there got to be a conflict between me and Melvin. Melvin thought he should be in charge because he came first. So Melvin took over as bandleader and I just backed off and played guitar."[40]

Bobby and Jackson continued to recruit other band members, and, by year's end, Bobby had a band that he was satisfied with. Jackson assumed the role of his mentor, Joe Scott. "Yeah, I always have thought of myself as his protégé," Jackson told Peter Guralnick. "I work with Bobby the same way. I'm a little different than Joe in that he didn't like to take care of business day to day. He had me do that. But I try to make things right for Bobby."

"Does Bobby need that?" Guralnick asked.

Eyes narrowing, Jackson replied, "Well, I think it speak for itself."[41]

Wayne Bennett and Bobby Bland performing somewhere on the chiltlin circuit, ca. 1975. Copyright D. Shigley, courtesy of the Blues Archives at the University of Mississippi.

Lead Me On

1973–1976

The touring band that Melvin Jackson, Mel Brown, and Bobby assembled included Jackson on trumpet, Brown on guitar, Leo Penn on bass, Charles Polk on drums, and Harold "Peanie" Potier, Jr., known as Bobby's personal drummer, Joseph Hardin Jr. on trumpet, Theodore Arthur on tenor sax, and the only two remaining members of Ernie Fields's original band: Al Thomas on trombone and Tommy Punkson on trumpet—a good swinging band, Bobby thought. Melvin Jackson was an experienced, capable leader who took care of business. Mel Brown was the next best thing to Wayne Bennett on guitar. The horn section, with three trumpets, a trombone, and a tenor sax, was tight. And the addition of another drummer gave the ensemble the relentless rhythm that it needed.

Ernie Fields Jr. wound up in Los Angeles, where he did session work for Marvin Gaye, Ray Charles, Aretha Franklin, Stevie Wonder, Natalie Cole, and Destiny's Child. He also toured with Fred Wesley's funk band and continues as one of L.A.'s top contractors, working on a variety of television shows, like the *Grammys*, *American Idol*, the *BET Awards*, and others.[1]

Meanwhile, Bobby and the band were hearing rumors about Don Robey and the Duke, Peacock, Back Beat, Songbird, Sure-Shot operation back in Houston. There were apparently some indications that the company was looking for a distribution deal that would expand its reach beyond the R&B world.[2] It was no secret to anyone that Stax's distribution agreement with Atlantic and Motown's own distribution network had eclipsed by far Duke's comparatively meager capabilities.

Robey himself was not getting any younger. Having started Peacock in 1949 when he was already more than forty-five years old, he was now nearing seventy and sometimes seemed more interested in hunting and raising thoroughbreds on his ranch near Crosby, Texas, than making records and promoting artists.

None of his college-educated children had an interest in the business, and it seemed to many that he had grown tired of the grind.[3]

The final determination came when the company lost a protracted legal battle that had been going on for 11 years with Chicago's Chess Records. Evelyn Johnson had warned him not to "defy those people in Al Capone town," but Robey was never one to back away from a fight. This one involved Peacock artists the Five Blind Boys and the Rev. Robert Ballinger, who Robey contended had been illegally signed by Chess. The courts disagreed, and Robey decided that he had had enough. He sold his entire company to ABC/Dunhill on May 23, 1973, for a reported one million dollars.[4]

In return, ABC/Dunhill received the copyrights to 2,700 songs, the contracts of about 100 artists, including approximately $250,000 worth of royalties that Robey had advanced, and some 2,000 unreleased masters. Robey was also to receive $25,000 per year to act as a consultant to ABC, scouting new artists and songs, and the free lease of a 1973 Cadillac for his personal use. After the sale Robey asked Evelyn Johnson to remain as his personal assistant, and she agreed.[5]

From 1952, when Bobby recorded his first song for Duke, "I.O.U. Blues," until the sale of the company in 1973, Bobby had been the label's most consistent revenue producer, almost single-handily at times insuring the business's positive cash flow and financial solvency. He had recorded nearly 150 songs during the period, 45 of which were hits, 22 of which were in the Top 10, and three of which were number 1 sellers. His songs had also appeared on a dozen Duke albums, and to most of his fans Bobby Bland and Duke Records were synonymous.

"When the company was bought out," Bobby said, "I knew there was going to be more doings, more publicity, promotion and a lot of different audiences and different rooms to play where I've wanted to play for a long time. It seems they're trying to pay me a little appreciation and I'm very happy it's happening."[6]

On the other hand, Bobby later admitted, "I kind of hated that change, but what could I say? Because it was new territory. I was basically used to a homelier type of surroundings, and it was difficult for me to get adjusted with new surroundings. But I must say that with ABC I met Steve Barri, and he was real down to earth and he wrote some good things. He had been studying Bobby Bland for a while. After I got in that mode with him and I started listening to the lyrics that he had, he had a lot of feeling for Joe Scott also. So it wasn't too hard."[7]

At first glance, Steve Barri was an unlikely choice to pair with Bobby. He was born Steven Barry Lipkin in Brooklyn, New York, on February 23, 1942.

After he and his family moved to Los Angeles when he was a teenager, Barri began writing songs and submitted them to the Screen Gems Music publishing company where Lou Adler, the company's head, hired him as a staff writer. When Adler left to launch Dunhill Records in 1964, he brought Barri and his songwriting partner, Phil Schlein (pen name: P.F. Sloan) along with him. They recorded one album of their own that same year as the Fabulous Baggys before writing their first big hit, Barry McGuire's ominous "Eve of Destruction." Two years later, upon Adler's departure, Barri, at age twenty-four, was named Vice President of A&R at Dunhill. There he helped to sign Steppenwolf, Three Dog Night, Steely Dan, Jimmy Buffett, and many more.

The company's success led to its purchase by ABC in 1967, when Barri was put in charge of the combined ABC/Dunhill A&R department. He went on to write and/or produce top hits for the Grass Roots, of which he was a founding member ("Where Were You When I Needed You"), The Turtles ("You Baby"), Johnny Rivers ("Secret Agent Man"), Tommy Roe ("Dizzy"), Mama Cass Elliott ("Make Your Own Kind of Music"), Herman's Hermits ("A Must To Avoid"), and the Four Tops ("Ain't No Woman Like the One I've Got").[8]

There was no doubt that Steve Barri at the age of thirty-one was a young pop producer phenom, and there was good reason for Bobby to compare him to Joe Scott. He was just as professional and meticulous as Scott, choosing just the right songs for the right artists, hiring topnotch musicians, carefully constructing rhythm, horn, string, and voice charts to create a production, not just a tune. Someone at Rhino Records once said that Steve Barri's productions made other records sound like demos.[9]

The question was, then: would the Barri touch result in over-production for a blues singer like Bobby Bland? If Barri were producing a more down-home singer like Muddy Waters or Jimmy Reed, the answer would have to be an emphatic *yes*. But Bobby and his fans were by now accustomed to the big-band, string-laden Joe Scott productions, and what Barri served up did not seem that much of a stretch beyond Scott's orchestral vision. After all, the sale to ABC was to provide not only a wider distribution network, but also a more pop sound that promised to broaden Bobby's appeal to a wider (i.e., whiter) audience.

"It was a gamble that we thought we'd take," Barri explained about the more elaborate productions. "Rather than go back to what he had recorded in the past, we wanted to do something different. That's why we called the first album *His California Album*, because we wanted to make people aware that it was a change."[10]

Barri tapped keyboardist Michael Omartian, who had recently completed a successful Four Tops album, to arrange and conduct the full orchestra of seasoned musicians, including Larry Carlton and Mel Brown on guitar, for Bobby's first Dunhill album. When they were all gathered at the ABC Recording Studios in Los Angeles on August 17, 1973, Barri was at first taken aback by Bland's unusual way of working. Bobby asked the new producer to sing the lyrics and then, while Bland was recording, to play the tape back in the left side of his headphones. This method went back to the Joe Scott days when Scott, and later other producers or songwriters, would prompt Bobby on each line of a new song.

"I felt like he was behind, on the back end of the beat all the time," Barri explained, "but that's what made him so great. A lot of that has to do with his [listening] to a line and singing it the way he wants to sing it."

As the session progressed, Bobby told Barri, "Just sing it, Steve. Just put it down. I'll take care of it. I'll make it right."

"And he always did," said Barri.[11]

Barri selected ten tunes for the inaugural LP. Two of them reached the soul singles chart. "This Time I'm Gone For Good" is a bitter blues written by Duke tunesmith Oscar Perry, and it went to number 5. And Bobby's supercharged version of St. Louis Jimmy Oden's driving 1941 hit "Goin' Down Slow," about a man's slow death from venereal disease, with a pulsating introduction borrowed from Percy Mayfield's 1963 hit "River's Invitation," rose to number 17. Bobby's soulful covers of Leon Russell's "Help Me Through the Day" and Gladys Knight & the Pips' "I've Got to Use My Imagination" provided some more modern tunes. The latter was written by Gerry Goffin (former husband of and lyricist with Carole King) and Barry Goldberg, who also wrote for the album "It's Not the Spotlight," which was covered two years later by Rod Stewart on his 1975 *Atlantic Crossing* album. *His California Album* ultimately went to number 3 on the Black Albums chart, the highest of any of Bobby's albums so far, where it stayed for nineteen weeks, but a disappointing number 136 on the Pop Albums chart.

A fair comparison of the old Duke production style and the new Dunhill approach can be made by listening to the three songs on this album which were previously recorded on the 1970 Duke *If Loving You Is Wrong* LP. Besides the title cut, the first Duke recordings of "This Time I'm Gone for Good" and "Up and Down World" all have a not surprisingly funkier, grittier, more appealing feel than the Barri/Dunhill versions. Nonetheless, *His California Album* does capture the Bobby Blue Bland sound, almost as certainly as adding the "Blue" back to his name for the first time in sixteen years reminds everyone that Bobby still remains the blues, pop production or not.

Despite his initial trepidation about moving to Dunhill, Bobby was pleased with this initial effort. "What made me so comfortable was Steve Barri," Bobby said. "I've never understood why a white boy would have such feeling. A lot of good things came out of that album, man, which was one of the greatest things I did on ABC."[12]

The respect was mutual, not only from Barri but also from the session musicians who looked up to the blues legend. The string players, who normally shunned pop music, usually hightailed it home after their work was done, but not at this session. "Even they would come into the booth to hear what the track would sound like because the guy [got to them]," Barri recalled.[13]

Meanwhile back in Memphis, Leroy Bland, Bobby's hard-working stepfather and namesake, died on November 8, 1973, at the age of fifty-six.[14]

On November 23, 1973, thinking of trying a live album soon, Steve Barri and ABC engineer Phil Kaye took portable recording equipment to the Whisky a Go Go club on the Sunset Strip in West Hollywood to record Bobby's show. The only released cut from the live session was an extended version of Oscar Perry's "This Time I'm Gone For Good," which didn't show up until 2001 on Bobby's *The Anthology* compilation album. At the time of this live session, Bobby's show band consisted of Mel Brown and Jim Carle on guitar, Tommy Ferguson and Joe Hardin on trumpet, multitalented Melvin Jackson and Theodore Arthur on saxophone, Al Thomas on trombone, Charles Green on bass, and Charles Polk on drums. And they sounded fine—the band and Bobby really working it out.

Bobby sang "This Time I'm Gone For Good" again and "Ain't No Love in the Heart of the City" on the popular television show *Soul Train* on December 8, appearing along with Ashford & Simpson.

Encouraged by their first album's reception, Bobby, Barri, and about the same group of L.A. studio musicians started work on March 18, 1974 on their next LP, to be entitled *Dreamer*. They chose five new Michael (born Harvey) Price and Dan Walsh compositions, along with two more by Duke writer and guitarist Oscar Perry, as well as William Bell's minor 1973 R&B hit, the bluesy "Lovin' on Borrowed Time." Price and Walsh were ABC/Dunhill writers who had penned five of the Grass Roots' charting hits and would continue composing for many other artists for many more years to come.

Three single hits came from the album. The brassy, Joe Scott–like "Yolanda," written by celebrated American Islam poet Daniel (Abdal-Hayy) Moore, went to number 21, and the Price/Walsh compositions, "I Wouldn't Treat a Dog (The Way You Treated Me)," a patented poor-Bobby mid-tempo swinger, reached number 3, while the aching love song "Ain't No Love in the Heart of the City" peaked at number 9.

"It was just a good lyric, and it was done in the right place, because it was overlooking Los Angeles," Bobby commented on "Ain't No Love." "You get a lot of inspiration from just looking down on all the lights. You see a city like that and there ain't no love, you know, so it kind of fit the situation."[15] The song has since been covered numerous times, most notably by the hard rock band Whitesnake in 1978 and by the rapper Jay-Z on the Kanye West–produced track of Jay-Z's 2001 album *The Blueprint*.[16] "Get this," Bobby remarked, "I didn't know a rapper could get into this particular thing. But when it worked out, it was a plus for me. Yeah, he did it justice."[17]

Oscar Perry's "St. James Infirmary"–inspired "The End of the Road" and the slow blues "Cold Day in Hell" are highlights, as are the defiant Price/Walsh song "I Ain't Gonna Be the First to Cry" and the swinging "Who's Foolin' Who." A mention also must be made of the album's cover, which is a kitschy reflection of mid-1970s Bobby and L.A. style: on the front, Bobby, with a neatly trimmed Afro and a pencil-thin mustache, sits unsmiling in a bright red, wide-lapelled suit, black and red patterned sports shirt wide open at the collar, jumbo diamond ring on his right hand and a burning cigarette in his left; on the inside left, Bobby on a yacht in a pink and purple psychedelic leisure suit, surrounded by two bikini-clad babes; and on the inside right, Bobby in denim, cocked cap included, smiling and sporting a middle-age, middle-class middle in his tight, bright blue T-shirt.

Album cover notwithstanding, it was a fine second effort at ABC; Bobby pleasantly proved that his voice was still full and mellow and that he could produce quality pop blues in new, slicker surroundings at the age of forty-four. *Dreamer* reached number 5 on the *Billboard's* Black Albums chart but only 172 on the Pop Album list. "[There were] a lot of good things on that album, man, which was one of the greatest things I did on ABC," Bobby boasted again.[18]

"All the cuts on this, his second ABC set, are priceless gems of controlled emotion," reported British critic Bob Fisher. "No matter how shallow the actual lyrical content may be, and on some songs it wouldn't cover your toes, Bobby imbues them with an involvement and interpretation that makes them seem the most important songs in his career. There aren't many singers around today on the popular front who give as much when interpreting other writers' material. . . . Apart from anything else though, the real star of *Dreamer* is the voice of Robert Calvin Bland, one of the greatest talents in America today, who's only just beginning to realize his true potential."[19]

Meanwhile, a new kind of music called disco was beginning to attract record buyers, with hit songs like The Hues Corporation's "Rock the Boat," the Blackbyrds' "Walking in Rhythm," Barry White's "Love's Theme," and Gloria Gaynor's "Never Can Say Goodbye."

For the time being, however, Bobby would stick to the blues, and even retreat a few years to join his old Memphis buddy B.B. King in recording some old blues standards together. "I had been wanting to do some things with B. for a long time," Bobby explained. "I studied his whole history of music, and

I did everything that he ever recorded. So I thought it would be good, because he's kind of familiar with me. I knew a little bit more about his music than he did mine, but I come to find out that he was pretty versed in what I was doing, too."[20]

"What I appreciated most was the opportunity to record a double-album date with Bobby Bland," B.B. King wrote in his autobiography. "I've already told you that Bobby's my man. We've been through the wars together, even had heartache with some of the same women and same IRS agents. I never thought I was in Bobby's category as a vocalist, but I always wanted to sing with him. When he was signed to ABC, the pieces fell into place. Because we knew each other so well, we didn't wanna plan anything formal. We cut the thing live in L.A. and made it up as we went along, singing a mess of blues, everything from 'Black Night' to 'Driving Wheel' to 'Goin' Down Slow.' It went down easy and mellow and, man, I loved it better than practically any album I'd ever made."

The double-disk album that they cut in late 1974 was entitled *B.B. King & Bobby Bland: Together for the First Time . . . Live*. Recorded at Western Recorders, Studio 1, in front of a live audience, and produced by Steve Barri, with a combined band of King and Bland band members, the thing, as B.B. said, was a mess. As the announcer on the album, Don Mack, said, "We didn't plan anything . . . we're just gonna go at it"—which they did, to create a rambling, shambling, inconsistent jam session that even ABC's crack engineer Phil Kaye couldn't salvage.

The critics, of course, unloaded, prompting King to note: "One critic for a national magazine [*Rolling Stone*] didn't agree. He rode me and Bobby hard. Said the album was a mess and called the music nothing. That bothered me. It's one thing if a critic says he doesn't like you, but another to call your music nothing, especially if he can't make music himself. I don't like arguing with critics, so I didn't. I waited. Waited to see the fans' reaction. Well, the fans loved it; *B.B. King and Bobby Bland . . . Together for the First Time . . . Live* went platinum. By then, I couldn't contain my emotions anymore, so I wrote the magazine, saying, 'Please let the critic who criticized my album criticize all my albums. With the success of my record with Bobby Bland, the man is bringing me luck.' Never heard back from the magazine. But I did hear from ABC, who said they wanted me and Bobby to cut another album, which we did a couple of years later. So much for critics."[21]

Bobby , however, was more embarrassed than anything by the effort. In a January 1975 interview, the Berkeley *Barb*'s Clark Peterson wrote: "Backstage [at Winterland in San Francisco] Bland toked a deep drag on a reefer, filling his lungs with more pressure than a tractor tire, and passed it over to me. His double live album with B.B. agreed upon as a turkey, the criticism is more of an inspiration than a faltering blow. 'The LP could have been much better,'

[Bobby said.] 'It was not really an experience. We're both pros and they don't think pros make mistakes. We had no rehearsals—it was off the top of our heads. But it was beautiful as a whole for me to work with B. The critics have their privilege. It's not the worst LP I've heard. If it wasn't for the critics I wouldn't be here today. That's their living. My critics, I love them. It was a big effort and chance to work with B. to open doors. It could have been more polished. The thoughts were from the 50's. I was a little uptight on it. But I'm very dedicated to my field. Actually, it wasn't good.'"[22]

As B.B. said, despite the critics, the album was a big hit, although hardly platinum, going to number 2 on the Live Black Albums chart and number 43 on the Live Pop Albums list. No one can argue with the good vibes readily apparent between B.B. and Bobby and among the musicians who include some of the best blues players of their generation, like trumpeters Melvin Jackson and Edward Rowe; drummers Sonny Freeman and Harold Potier; saxophonists Bobby Forte and Cato Walker; pianists Ron Levy and Teddy Reynolds; and guitarists B.B. King and Mel Brown.

As always, between recording sessions, Bobby and his band continued to tour, now with Burnett Williams, already bus driver and valet, promoted to Bobby's opening act. But with ABC's wider distribution and the recent blues resurgence, they were booked into larger venues and white festivals, like the International Blues Festival in Louisville, Kentucky, the Newport Jazz Festival in New York City, and the Toronto Blues Festival in Canada. On May 24, 1974, Bobby also appeared with Marvin Hamlisch, Olivia Newton-John, and Boz Scaggs on NBC-TV's *Midnight Special*, hosted that night by Richard Pryor, where Bobby sang "Ain't That Loving You" and "Gotta Get to Know You." He also got to get to know Scaggs, a young white rock vocalist, who became one of Bobby's most appreciative fans, recording many of Bobby's songs over the years. Later that year, on August 30, B.B. King hosted the *Midnight Special* and invited blues giants John Lee Hooker, Big Mama Thornton, Joe Williams, Jimmy Witherspoon, and Bobby Bland, who sang "Goin' Down Slow."

In the spring of 1975, Bobby and the band stopped for a weeklong engagement at the Sugar Shack in Boston. There, they were visited by a thirty-one-year-old Boston music writer named Peter Guralnick who, at the time, had published two books of short stories, a well-received collection of musician profiles entitled *Feel Like Going Home: Portraits in Blues, Country, and Rock 'n' Roll*, and music articles in several newspapers and periodicals. Already he was being hailed as a writer of unusual passion and enthusiasm who, at the same time, retained a keen sense of accuracy and understated objectivity. His piece on Bobby Bland proved no exception. It captured Bobby at a particularly key point in his midlife, after his career had peaked, with both an appreciation of his history and accomplishments and an empathetic understanding of the personal prices paid for his insulated vagabond way of life. Guralnick is perhaps at his best in providing a rare and insightful glimpse of Bobby's personal life.

Because this was an unusually long engagement in Boston, Bobby was joined on the trip by his young wife, Marty, and their six-year-old daughter Tahanee. Guralnick described Bobby's paternal and protective side, as he kidded with his daughter and prepared for the evening's performance, Tahanee bringing her father his shoes, combing his hair, and even passing a joint around to Bobby and Guralnick.

Guralnick also described how Melvin Jackson, Bobby's bandleader and righthand man, insulated the star and saw to his every need—"taking care of Bobby's business"—setting up interviews, seeing to the band, and shopping for a new bus, while Bobby and Marty, in their crowded, cluttered hotel room, tried to decide what to do about the flu that Tahanee was suffering from ever since arriving from Detroit. "It's different being an artist and a bandleader," Jackson explained. "For Bobby, I don't want him worrying about anything but the music. I want things to be just exactly right. After all, he's the one people come out to see. That's what's paying us, and I don't want nothing to bother him. When he go out there on stage, I want him in fine fettle. . . ."

Bobby continued his preparation for going to the club, deciding it was too late to call the hotel's doctor for Tahanee. Marty—"playful, girlish, her hair braided in pigtails that accentuate her fine West Indian features"—blow-dried Bobby's hair. He selected a shirt from a clothes rack, sprayed himself with cologne, and whispered to himself, "Damn, I ain't had a joint all day. That's bad business, bad business. You're not thinking, Bobby." He then rolled a couple of joints and beckoned Tahanee, "C'mere, baby." She proceeded to pass one of the joints to Guralnick, who passed it on to Marty, but Bobby intervened, explaining that his wife did not smoke. He would not let her go to clubs where he performs either, because "they're just joints."

Finally, decked out in denim and sunglasses he was ready to go. "Later, baby," he waved to his daughter. "Later," she said. "Right on," answered Bobby and kissed his wife good-bye.

As they descended to the hotel's lobby in the elevator, Guralnick asked Bobby if ever got tired of hanging around the hotel and not going out. Bobby shrugged and answered, "Well, you know, Boston's still Boston. Ain't nothing in the street I haven't seen, ain't nothing I'm gonna learn out on the street."

"When he hits the lobby," according to Guralnick, "he is altogether changed, bluff, alert, wary, speaking before he is spoken to, aware that everyone expects something of Bobby 'Blue' Bland."[23]

Bobby's marriage to Marty had been a struggle from the beginning. First his alcoholism, then her drinking, and then, as always, Bobby's constant rambling. There were some good times, of course, but in the end the strain became too much. Bobby loved her dearly and returned often enough to Detroit for Marty and him to have five children together. But, as before, Bobby's career demands and chronic absence took their toll, and, as Bobby became closer to his long-time friend Willie Mae, back in Memphis, Bobby and Marty sadly separated and eventually divorced.[24]

During his visit, Guralnick also witnessed some of the circumstances surrounding the firing of two band members, tenor sax man Theodore Arthur and drummer Charles Polk. He described the confrontation between Melvin Jackson and the tenor player in the club's dressing room, where, after stating a quiet ultimatum, Jackson stared the tenor player down. "What?" Jackson demanded. "I didn't say nothing," mumbled Arthur. Jackson smiled and said, "But you heard me." "Yeah, I heard you." "No more of that shit," said Jackson sternly, continuing his stare.

Later, Guralnick interviewed Burnett Williams, Bobby's opening act, valet, and bus driver. Burnett started out with Albert King, and he said that he appreciated Bobby for his patience, for his consideration, above all for his instruction. "I can go to him, and he can tell me anything as far as music is concerned—how to keep from getting hoarse, when I'm hitting wrong notes—and it usually come out the way he say. Because he *knows*, he's a master of music, he ain't been out here just five or ten years, he been out here a long time. As long as he's happy, I'm happy. He's the one that's got to be happy first."[25]

Having finally scored a new bus shortly thereafter, Bobby and the band headed out of Boston to do a concert at Temple University in Philadelphia. Then Bobby won an NAACP Image Award, which honors outstanding people of color in film, television, music, and literature.[26] By March 15 Bobby was back in Los Angeles, where he again appeared on *Soul Train*, this time with the Tavares, Lyn Collins, and Fred Wesley and Steam.

Don Robey suffered a heart attack on Monday, June 16, 1975, at his home in Houston. He was rushed to St. Luke's Hospital and pronounced dead at 12:35 a.m. He was seventy-one years old. Funeral services were conducted on June 19 at the Fifth Ward Baptist Church on Noble Street, and the former owner of the South's most successful independent record label was buried in the Paradise North Cemetery at 1040 West Montgomery Road.

He was survived by his wife, the former Murphy Louise Moore, whom he married in 1960, shortly after his divorce from longtime business partner Evelyn Johnson, whom he had married in 1953.[27] Don and Murphy Louise had three children and seven grandchildren together, and Robey in addition had four other children by previous marriages, none of them Evelyn Johnson's.[28]

Gatemouth Brown, Robey's first recording artist and the person for which Peacock Records was formed, said, "Robey was a cold man. He sold the company and cut music away from his life. Then one night awhile later, Evelyn told me, he was watching TV and got up, turned the set off, and dropped dead on the spot. I don't know how he had died, but he did. He turned the music off in his life."[29]

Despite his many detractors, Don Robey carved out a place in post–World War II popular music history. He was not the first black man to own a record company, but he was one of the most successful, paving the way for Berry Gordy at Motown, Sylvia Rhone at Elektra, and many more minority recording industry entrepreneurs to follow. Most independent labels, regardless of ownership, were short-lived and prone to financial failure, but Robey's Peacock, Duke, Songbird, Back Beat, and Sure-Shot operations survived for more than twenty years, enabling Robey to semi-retire in comfort and his children to be college educated.

While ethically suspect, no one can dismiss the fact that Don Robey discovered and launched the careers of some of his era's most important musicians, such as Gatemouth Brown, Little Junior Parker, Big Mama Thornton, The Original Five Blind Boys, O. V. Wright, and, of course, Bobby Bland.[30] At the peak of his tenure, in the 1950s and 60s, Robey had more than 100 artists and groups under contract and over the course of a single year used as many as 500 studio musicians and technicians.

"Robey gave every artist the benefit of the doubt starting out," Bobby said. "Robey was a regular businessman. It was the business that caused people to have all kinds of vibes about him. He was a hell of a man, and he was a help to a lot of black entertainers who would never have gotten a record label at all. Houston at that time was a blooming city."[31]

Bobby Bland, Joe Scott, and the rest of these entertainers, under contract to Robey, were instrumental in moving so-called "race" records from gospel, boogie woogie, and down-home blues to modern rhythm and blues and the birth of soul music in the 1960s. In this regard alone, he must be credited with being a true leader in American popular music history during his time.

At the same time, Robey was a product of Houston's wild-west, boom-bust, go-for-broke, Enronesque business environment, where no oilman was ever accused of being too polite. "He was a character out of *Guys and Dolls*," according to Walter Andrus, the audio engineer on many Little Junior Parker and Bobby Bland sessions. "You had to see him to believe him. He'd have a bunch of heavy guys around him all the time, carrying pistols and that kind of stuff, like a czar of the Negro underworld."[32]

Gatemouth Brown, in a more charitable mood, recalled, "People talk about the man and how rotten he was. Perhaps to some, but he treated me like I was his son. He was hard on me, but he taught me a lot about my way of life. He taught me how to dress, and he made me the best I could be at the time. Don was a good man."[33]

"Robey knew what tunes that would fit me," Bobby explained. "That's one thing you have to give him credit for. He had a good ear. No, there was no ill feeling whatsoever. A lot of artists wouldn't feel this way maybe, but I was always kind of partial to Robey and the Duke label, because they had faith in me, they thought I could really sing when no one else did.[34] He was a business man like anybody else. It just so happened that he was a black man and I think it didn't sit well with his own people or anybody else. But I don't have anything bad to say about him. He did some nice things also but you don't ever see that.[35] Anybody can say whatever they want about Robey, but he wasn't supposed to be your father; he gave you an opportunity. Robey was the biggest man in Texas, so you give thanks to the hand that feeds you."[36]

Despite Bobby's contention, there were many around the Duke offices who felt that Robey did in fact regard Bobby as his own son. Robey sent regular letters to Bobby while he was on the road. He dispensed advance monies to Bobby, his wife, or his mother whenever Bobby requested. And Robey sagely advised his most popular young artist, as in this letter: "As to your money, I hope you are spending it carefully. Your sales have been very good these past periods, as reflected in your royalty checks. But Bobby, this is a very unpredictable business. Invest your money so you will have something for the future. Be sure to call me when you get to Memphis and take care of yourself. . . ."[37]

Evelyn Johnson, whose intelligence, creativity, wit, and ingenuity had so much to do with Robey's success, was now out of work for the first time in twenty-four years. She soon took a position with a prominent Houston bank, then moved to New York for a few years. Later, she returned to Houston to work with a former Robey associate, Gaspar Puccio, who bought Robey's original pressing equipment when he sold pretty much everything else to ABC.

According to Gatemouth Brown, "Robey and his first wife had some beautiful kids . . . [then] Robey divorced her, gave her the house, paid 'em big money to stay out of his face. He educated his kids and all that. Then he started living with Evelyn. He promised to marry her, but he didn't [Evelyn says he did]. . . . He turned around and married another woman, had more kids by this woman, but he still had Evelyn to take care of the business. She was the brains. So when he died, everything went to his wife, beautiful home and everything. Evelyn got nothing. That was it."

But Johnson held no grudges nor regrets, at least not that she would admit publicly. "I prefer to forget the past and get on with my present life," she said. "It was just a business and music buffs pretty much know the story of Duke/Peacock already. . . . Half the time we didn't even know what we were doing. We just tried to do right and take care of business. The rest took care of itself."[38]

Evelyn Johnson died, at the age of eighty-five, on November 1, 2005, in Houston, Texas.

Robey's death freed Bobby to try some new ventures that Robey had discouraged. The first was something he had been wanting to do for a long time, an album of country and western music, his first love since way back in Rosemark. And it just so happened that ABC already had a good track record with the genre, with the likes of Donna Fargo, Barbara Mandrell, and the Oak Ridge Boys.

"I had an idea to record [a country album] before Ray Charles came out," Bobby recalled. "And when he came with his country 'n' western album [in 1962], there ain't nothing you can do about that. It just threw me off because the tunes he did, I had planned to do them. And he did such a hell of a job with them, so it took me a while before I could get something that I could bite down on."[39]

As it happened, ABC had a couple of experienced country music producers who were eager to work with a true blues legend on something new. Before joining ABC, Don Gant had worked at Acuff-Rose Music in Nashville as a songwriter and executive and had also produced records for Jimmy Buffett, Lefty Frizzell, and others. Ron Chancey had just finished working with the Oak Ridge Boys. They took Bobby to Nashville on August 5, 1975, to record with a studio full of country musicians. Horn tracks, arranged by Muscle Shoals Horns' Harrison Calloway Jr., were added later in Muscle Shoals. They cut nine songs that had been recent country hits by Conway Twitty ("You've Never Been This Far Before"), Johnny Paycheck ("Someone to Give My Love To"), and Roy Clark ("You're Gonna Love Yourself").

In addition, Bobby's version of Kenny O'Dell's "I'll Take It On Home" was the second song originally sung by Charlie Rich that hit the charts for Bobby, this one rising to number 41, not quite as high (number 12) as Rich's "Who Will the Next Fool Be" in 1962. The other hit (number 34) on the album was Bobby's brassy version of Buck Owens's and Merle Haggard's "Today I Started Loving You Again," a song Bobby still sings in concert. Bobby's cover of Tammy Wynette's "Too Far Gone" should have been a hit, with Bobby's passionate vocal performance invoking a sure tear in the beer from Billy Sherrill's resigned lyrics—"I guess I've been loving you too much, for too long . . ."

And there is a beautiful, pure rendition of Ronnie Milsap's 1973 hit "I Hate You" that was written by Leroy Daniels and none other than Dan Penn, another of Bobby's biggest fans. Penn recalls:

I found out that Bland did like country, because in the '70s, when he cut one of my songs, I got to meet him. I got to go down to the studio here in Nashville, where he was cutting a country album. Yeah. He cut my song "I Hate You." He just cut the fool out of it. He had a really great feel on it. I felt just great that I had a Bobby Bland cut, although it was late in the game, and it was sort of country—it was still Bobby Bland. He didn't really cut it country; he put a swing to it. I am [proud of that one], yes 'cause it's Bobby Bland. Some records you can count your money, and some records you can just count your blessings. He was just one of them people that you always admired so much. They used to call me Bobby "Blue" Penn back in the early '60's when I was with the Mark V and the Pallbearers. They did that in the South in a lot of places because I sang so much like Bland. And like all white guys doin' that, I thought I sounded just like him. And my wife Linda said that I did, and I am sure I didn't [laughing]. He was a big influence on white singers, I'll tell you that, and not only me. I think he had as much influence as Ray Charles, but Bobby Bland just took it one step further. Oh, man, he just kept going with that growl. He just put that growl on it, and it just floored all of us. . . .[40]

Deceptively entitled *Get On Down With Bobby Bland*, the album went to number 14 on the Black Albums chart and 154 on the Pop Albums chart. "We tried that, and they said it was a little too bluesy," Bobby mused about the LP. "I don't understand how Ray Charles did what he did and they didn't characterize that. But I guess it just wasn't really for me to do country and western, which I like. I've listened to it all my life."[41]

The problem with the album was not that it was "too bluesy," however. Bobby's voice is bluesy, of course, but his vocals sound great on these country tunes. The problem was that the album was so glitzy and overproduced that it lost much of any true country flavor that it might have had.

In the fall of 1975, Bobby and the band embarked on a Western tour, playing on September 20 at the 8th Annual Monterey Jazz Festival in California; October 8 at the Boarding House in San Francisco; and November 5, with B.B. King at the New Orleans Municipal Auditorium.

A little later, Burnett Williams, Bobby's loyal sidekick and opening act for the past few years, suddenly quit to join B.B. King's show,[42] but the move did not bother Bobby, who was already planning a second album with his old Memphis friend. Since the first B.B. King and Bobby Bland album had sold so well despite its critical lambasting, the ABC execs decided to cut another one, this time with a little more planning and production. There were even horn arrangements, by Johnny Pate, for the mixture of mostly studio musicians and some touring band members. Esmond Edwards, one of the first African American executives in the recording industry at Prestige Records and a respected photographer, produced the session, which was recorded live at the Coconut Grove in March 1976. The results are much more satisfying than the first effort and even produced one number 20 hit, a rollicking reprise of Louis Jordan's 1946 hit "Let the Good Times Roll."

On the strength of the album, entitled *Together Again . . . Live*, which reached number 9 on the Black Album chart and number 73 on the pop chart, Bobby and B.B. toured extensively together throughout the remainder of the year, hitting all the big festivals, like Newport, Kool Jazz, and the New Orleans Jazz & Heritage Festival, as well as some low-class joints and even some honky-tonks, as always.

On April 16, 1976, Bobby was booked into a new club in Austin, Texas, called Antone's. Opened on July 15, 1975, by twenty-five-year-old Clifford Antone, in what was once a furniture store at the corner of Sixth and Brazos across from the Driskell Hotel, Antone's was quickly becoming the preeminent blues showcase not only of Austin but also of the country. Antone himself had moved to Austin in 1969 from Port Arthur, where he was introduced to the blues by the African American men who worked in his father's liquor store. They took him to the Golden Triangle juke joints that dotted Highway 80, and later he ventured into the dingy blues clubs along the Sabine River bottoms—places like the Texas Pelican, the Sparkle Paradise, Big Oaks, and Lou Ann's. Antone was hooked. In Austin he had intended to study law at the University of Texas, but was arrested for trying to smuggle a bag of marijuana across the border at Laredo. The case was ultimately dismissed, but Antone dropped out of school and decided instead to pursue his real passion.[43]

"When I finally heard the Chicago blues, man, it was like I finally discovered what had been in my mind my whole life," he said. "We opened July 15, 1975, with Clifton Chenier. The second week we had Sunnyland Slim and Big Walter Horton. Sunnyland became the godfather of the club and got every blues guy in Chicago to call me. Then Hubert Sumlin came and lived with us for many years on and off. Sumlin and Luther Tucker taught a lot of Austin's young musicians about the blues. We had Texas blues artists like Gatemouth Brown, Johnny Copeland, Albert Collins. Acts like Ray Charles, James Brown, Bobby 'Blue' Bland, B.B. King, Sam and Dave. Country acts like George Jones, Willie Nelson, and Ray Price."[44]

The musicians just kept on coming, and Clifford Antone became one of their biggest benefactors. Like his elder counterpart in Memphis, Sunbeam Mitchell, Antone was the musician's best friend. He booked acts that did not draw and paid them a generous fee out of his own pocket. He booked them in for a week at a time so they would not have to travel so much. He bought guitars for those in need, kept up with the families of deceased bluesmen, even paid funeral expenses if need be. And, like Sunbeam, if someone down on his luck needed a place to stay, Antone helped him find a place in Austin and often paid for it as well. Like Bobby Bland, he was a big baseball fan, although more of a White Sox kind of guy than a Cubs man. He was also a charmer, like Bobby, and loved playing the host, offering up gushing introductions for his club's performers, and escorting single women safely to their cars late at night.[45]

Bobby's show on April 16 was, as usual, a big success. In addition to all the white college students, middle-aged African Americans showed up to welcome the star. Even Boz Scaggs, who Bobby had met a couple of years before on the set of the *Midnight Special* TV show, came to cheer on his hero. Unfortunately, no one told Antone's security force about their friendship, and, when Scaggs tried to visit Bobby backstage after the show, he was unceremoniously cold-cocked and dumped outside on Brazos Street.[46]

Later in 1976, B.B. King joined Bobby in Austin at Antone's for a memorable Independence Day show, which was marked by a lot of good cheer and not a single reported celebrity bashing.[47]

In addition to all the big blues stars like Bobby and B.B., Antone's also encouraged young local talent and other new acts, like the Fabulous Thunderbirds (who served as the club's house band before gaining national prominence), Angela Strehli, Lou Ann Barton, Stevie Ray Vaughn, and Sue Foley. But regardless of the big and new names and the club's growing, glowing reputation, the blues remained hardly lucrative, and Antone's original location closed in 1979, only to reemerge a few months later in a former rug dealership on Anderson Lane, a location that hosted James Brown but lasted only a few months. Antone's golden age started in 1981 when the club took over the old Shakey's Pizza Parlor at 2915 Guadalupe, where it remained until moving in 1997 to its present location at 213 W. Fifth.[48]

It was at the smoky Guadalupe digs that Bobby made one of his many regular appearances at Antone's and was asked one night to introduce a rising young performer who was catching Bobby's show after finishing his own gig elsewhere in Austin. Ed Ward of the Austin *Chronicle* tells the tale:

> *The best was yet to come: at one point in the show, Bobby stopped and announced, "We have a young gentleman in the audience, a very great performer, and I know he's already done his show this evening, but I was wondering if he'd like to come up here and do a number with me." What the . . . ? "Ladies and gentlemen, I'd like you to give a warm Austin welcome to Mister, uh, Izzy Bob!" Up pops Iggy [Pop].*
>
> *"You know 'St. James Infirmary,' right?" Bland asked, and Iggy nodded. The band went into the song, and as my jaw gaped open, Iggy did a credible job of trading lines with the blues great. I'd inched forward and was standing against a pillar, and at the song's end, Iggy jumped off the stage and ran up the aisle to where I was standing. "How'd you like that?" he asked with a grin. It was amazing, I said. "Hah! Just you watch. Ten years and I'm gonna be in Vegas, baby! And"—and here he jabbed my chest with his finger in each word—"I'm gonna be great!" Then he ran back to his companions.[49]*

Clifford Antone went on to establish a record store in Austin, as well as a successful record label, and, of course, continued to manage his famous club, despite constant financial problems, two more drug busts, and subsequent prison stints in 1984 and 2002, through it all having built an influential and lasting impact on Austin's and America's music scene that would extend well beyond his death from a heart attack on May 23, 2006, at the age of fifty-six.

The club continues to bear his name and is now owned by a board of directors headed by his sister, Susan Antone, and continues to book the best blues musicians of the day, including, of course, Bobby "Blue" Bland, who last appeared there with fellow Texan Barbara Lynn on November 8, 2009. Although born and raised in Tennessee, Bland spent nearly twenty years with Duke Records in Houston and considers himself an honorary Texan. "They treat me a lot better here, and they respect what I do a lot more," Bobby notes. "I'm more comfortable in Texas."[50]

By the end of 1976, Mel Brown had had enough of the road and settled in Nashville where he soon became much in demand as a session player. There he also joined fired drummer Charles Polk in country singer Tompall Glaser's short-lived Outlaw Band.[51] Later, like so many other legendary sidemen before him, Brown was to migrate to Austin and work for several years for Clifford Antone in Antone's all-star house band.

So with Mel gone, Bobby once again called Wayne Bennett, who had been working with Chicago's Operation Bread Basket, a musical and spiritual extension of the Southern Christian Leadership Conference. "I was involved with a unit of musicians, and we went places with people like Jesse Jackson, Sammy Davis Jr., Harry Belafonte and other people who were involved in the civil rights movement," Bennett said. "Things were taking place that had never taken place. Lunch counters were being integrated. Schools were being integrated. That was very important. I played at rallies and churches. We did a lot of gospel music to touch the minds and hearts of people. It brought overall togetherness." Bennett also worked with soul/jazz organist Jimmy McGriff during this period. "I lost my mother in 1971, and I had to get out of Chicago [to move to Texas] and get a little air," he said. "So I traveled with the Platters. And just before that I did Junior Parker's last album, *I Tell Stories Sad and True*. I just had to get Chicago out of my heart and out of my mind."[52] So the timing was right. After an absence of ten years, Bennett was beginning to miss the jazzy blues music that he had helped to create and was ready to rejoin Bobby and the band.

With Bobby's divorce from his second wife Marty, Willie Mae Martin, his friend in Memphis, became more of a force in his hectic life. About all that Marty saw of Bobby was the royalty checks that she regularly received, but ultimately not very much else. In the absence of strong figures like Don Robey, Evelyn Johnson, and Joe Scott, Bobby seemed to be drawn now to the firmer, more commanding countenance of Willie Mae who was beginning to assume the role of business manager that Bobby never heretofore had. So he spent more and more of what little spare time he had in Memphis, visiting his ailing mother and his friend and lover Willie Mae, who gave birth on November 22, 1976, to their son whom they named Roderick Cornelius.[53]

B.B. King and Bobby Bland performing at the London Blues Festival '82 at the Hammersmith Odeon Theatre in London on May 20, 1982. Copyright David Corio (www.davidcorio.com).

12

Gettin' Used to the Blues

1977–1984

In the spring of 1977, Steve Barri and Michael Omartian gathered a group of Los Angeles studio musicians, including strings and backup choir, at the ABC Recording Studios to record what would be their last Bobby Bland album, *Reflections in Blue*. The nine tracks were drawn from a wide variety of sources. "The Soul of a Man," which went to number 12 on the soul chart, was written by Bobby and his old opening act, Al "TNT" Braggs. "I'll Be Your Fool Once More," a pretty country ballad, came from the pen of country singer/songwriter Big Al Downing. "Sittin' on a Poor Man's Throne," which reached number 82 on the soul chart, was written by members of the Canadian pop group Copperpenny. There was also a very personal version of Eddie Boyd's 1952 chart-topper, "Five Long Years," and a resigned and resilient rendition of J.J. Cale's guitar-driven "I Got the Same Old Blues."

The year before, on June 12, 1976, a sad falling-out-of-love song by Bobby entitled "It Ain't the Real Thing," written by Michael Price and Dan Walsh, appeared on the *Billboard* soul chart, where it stayed for eleven weeks, peaking at number 12. It remains unclear exactly when it was recorded, but most discographers claim that it was cut at this session, nearly a year after it hit the chart as a single. While it did show up on this album, it was obviously recorded some time earlier, as was another tune on the album called "If I Weren't A Gambler," written by Oscar Perry, which was in fact recorded seven years earlier in 1970 for Bobby's *If Loving You Is Wrong* LP—the same recording is on two different albums. Apparently, *Reflections in Blue* was a bit short of material, so these two cuts were dredged from the vaults. Nonetheless, *Melody Maker* called it a "marvel" and it reached number 47 on the Black Albums chart.[1]

Steve Barri went on to work at Warner Brothers Records in 1979 as an A&R director and producer, where he produced a series of TV theme songs, among them themes for *S.W.A.T.*, *Welcome Back Kotter*, and *Happy Days*. By

1982 he was back working with his old Dunhill boss, Jay Lasker, who was now president of Motown Records, where Barri produced successful albums by the Commodores, Lionel Ritchie, and Rick James. Barri left Motown in 1986 and moved around from Capitol Records to Left Bank Management to JVC Records, and in 1998 to Gold Circle Entertainment, where he was named senior vice president of A&R in 2001.[2]

Later in 1977, Michael Omartian recorded an album of his own, with his wife, Stormie, entitled *Seasons of the Soul*, and continued to record several other albums with her, as well as producing LPs for others, including Michael Bolton, Whitney Houston, Rod Stewart, Trisha Yearwood, Clint Black, and others. He won three Grammy Awards in 1981 for his production of Christopher Cross's debut album, *Sailing*. And in 1985 Omartian, along with Quincy Jones, co-produced the USA for Africa super group's number 1 hit "We Are the World." In recent years he has produced several contemporary Christian music albums of his own music, as well as for others.[3]

On August 16, 1977, Elvis Presley died in the bathroom of his Graceland mansion in Memphis, from, according to the coroner's official report, "cardiac arrhythmia." He was forty-two years old. Meanwhile, Bobby continued to tour regularly with B.B. King, appearing on PBS's *Soundstage* television program, at Radio City Music Hall, at the Buffalo (NY) Theatre, as well as at many, many other clubs and arenas.[4]

In December 1977 the movie and soundtrack of *Saturday Night Fever* were released. The soundtrack by the Bee Gees quickly became the number 1 best-selling soundtrack of all time, and disco music moved into mainstream popularity. Record company executives jumped on the bandwagon and demanded disco-like songs from previously non-disco artists. So everyone—from Helen Reddy and Barry Manilow to Marvin Gaye and Diana Ross—was cutting disco-influenced records.

ABC called on two veteran record producers to push Bobby into the disco inferno. Al Bell was born Alvertis Isbell in Brinkley, Arkansas, in 1940, one of eight children. His family moved to North Little Rock in 1945. As a senior in high school, Al not only became student council president and president of the school's National Honor Society, but also a disc jockey on KOKY radio in Little Rock. He continued at KOKY throughout his years at Philander Smith College in Little Rock, where he received a degree in political science. After college, he moved to Huntsville, Alabama, to begin preparation for the ministry at Oakwood College, a historically black university operated by the Seventh-day Adventist Church. But in 1959 he dropped out to work in Midway, Georgia, with Dr. Martin Luther King's Southern Christian Leadership Conference (SCLC). After about a year, "I left Dr. King," Bell explained, "and went back into the music business because I was not about passive resistance. I was about economic development, economic empowerment."

In 1961 he landed a job as host of the 6:00 to 10:00 a.m. morning show at WLOK radio in Memphis. He fell in love with records coming out of Stax Records, as well as Bobby Bland's recordings, and began playing and promoting them on his show. Within a couple of years Bell found a higher-paying disc jockey job at WUST in Washington, D.C., where he continued to push Stax and Bland recordings. While in Washington he also began his own record label, De'voice and then Safice, producing records for Eddie Floyd and others. In the summer of 1965, Stax hired Bell to promote their records to disc jockeys and record stores throughout the country. He quickly became the *de facto* sales manager for Stax and then the company really took off. In October 1972 Bell, with a loan and distribution deal from CBS, bought out Stax's founder Jim Stewart, becoming, with Berry Gordy at Motown, an African American owner of one of the most successful record companies in America.[5] At that time, "I went to buy Duke/Peacock," Bell remembers, "just to get Bobby 'Blue' Bland and to get that enormous gospel catalog that they had, [but] ABC beat me to it."[6]

Despite producing huge hits by Isaac Hayes, Johnnie Taylor, Sam and Dave, Otis Redding, The Emotions, Albert King, and many more, in the mid-1970s Stax's financial practices came into question by the IRS and the company's bank, Union Planters National Bank in Memphis. The company was ultimately dissolved and Al Bell was indicted on September 8, 1975, along with bank officer Joseph Harwell, for conspiring to obtain more than $18 million in fraudulent loans. Bell was ultimately acquitted, but he was financially wiped out. Bell's wife, Lydia Isbell, had been forced to sell her jewelry to pay the lawyers defending her husband, and she, Al, and their two sons had to live in an unfinished basement in his father's house in Little Rock "so squalid that Al's children to this day have marks on their legs and arms from spider bites."[7] Bell told the *New York Times* years later, "I went from a man that owned a company whose masters were valued by Price Waterhouse at $67 million to a man that could scrape together 15 cents from time to time."[8]

But by January 1977 Bell was back in Washington, heading a new record label called the Independence Corporation of America (ICA), where he produced minor hits by Frank Lucas, Margie Evans, Vernon Garrett, and L. V. Johnson. That is where ABC found him in March 1978, when they were ready to start on a new Bobby Bland album. To assist Bell and do the arranging, ABC tapped producer and saxophonist Monk Higgins, who was born Milton Bland (no relation to Bobby) on October 17, 1936, in Menifee, Arkansas. Higgins began his musical career in Chicago, where he produced and arranged records for the One-Derful, St. Lawrence, and Chess labels, including singles by Muddy Waters, Junior Wells, and Etta James. On St. Lawrence he recorded several of his own instrumental songs, including the R&B single hits "Who Dun It" in 1966 and "Gotta Be Funky" in 1972. Higgins moved to Los Angeles in 1969 and arranged and produced for the United Artists/Imperial/Minit label complex.

There, he also recorded four of his own instrumental albums between 1972 and 1975.[9]

According to a music press story at the time: "Bell is suggesting that Bland be offered as 'more than just a blues singer.' It appears that the new look for Bland will feature lush strings and a sound not unlike disco. This move which [is being] initiated to improve Bland's appeal to young record buying audiences will please some and make others unhappy. Along with B.B. King, he was one of the few blues artists enjoying some exposure in the national media. And while he does not have his own new network show, Bland received a fair amount of attention in the major trade journals and enjoyed an unshakeable reputation as an important artist. But the name of the game is how much you can 'pull in' and your box office potential. If Bell's formula for Bland works without completely emasculating his music, the former Stax chief will have rendered another very important service to the recording world."[10]

They began their first session at the Filmway/Heider studio in Los Angeles on March 3, 1978, continued at the CBS Studios in Nashville, the P&S Recording Studio in Chicago, and finally the Sugar Hill Studios in Houston, apparently searching for just the right sound. It is debatable whether or not they found it. The resulting album, *Come Fly with Me*, has some very pleasant moments, notably some good songs, but the overall disco direction does not lead to a very satisfying destination. If Bobby's Steve Barri–produced albums were overproduced, this first Bell/Higgins attempt is over-the-top-produced, in the mode of mid-1970s disco dominance.

The bouncy title track, "Come Fly with Me," reached number 55 on the soul chart. "Night Games," written by guitarist Freddy Robinson (later known as Abu Talib), comes the closest to a real Bobby Bland number, owing primarily to Robinson's fine, bluesy guitar work. Robinson, after all, was an alumnus of the bands of Little Walter, Howlin' Wolf, Jerry Butler, and Ray Charles.[11] There is also a soulful rendition of Dinah Washington's "This Bitter Earth" that showcases Bobby's voice to good effect, and a lovely ballad "You Can Count On Me" by William Stuckey. The highlight of the album is keyboard player David Ervin's "Love to See You Smile," an infectious dance number that reached number 14 on the soul chart and still stands up well and will have to be a Bobby Bland fan's favorite disco song.

The album concludes with one of the few gospel songs recorded by Bobby, "Ain't God Something," and thankfully one of the only gospel songs ever recorded with a disco arrangement—GODisco, anyone? At any rate, the Margie Evans–arranged backup choir sounds beautiful. "I'd always wanted to sing," Bobby said, "but I had been singing spirituals because the background was a church background, basically. It wasn't that big a switchover, because the blues and spirituals have the same sort of phrasing, and you just sing 'baby' instead of 'My Lord.' I don't see anything wrong with singing the blues: I just don't put the two together. I'm just as much a believer today as I was before I knew anything about the blues. I serve The Lord in whatever I am doing, but I wouldn't put the two together. I believe in doing one thing at a time. I did a spiritual album [song] before the last one called 'Ain't God Something' and I can relate to that: He is something."[12] The album, which Bobby dedicated to his mother, and which included, despite Bobby's admonitions, both pop songs and the one gospel cut, went to number 31 on the Black Albums chart and number 185 on the Pop Albums chart. Bobby summed up his attempt at disco: "I could adjust. I wouldn't get too far out of pocket. The majority of the tunes I did, I kind of felt like told a story. They were a little weird, but I'll try anything once."[13]

Soon after these sessions, in June, Al Bell decided that Washington was too expensive and moved back to his hometown of Little Rock, Arkansas, where, between Bobby Bland recording sessions, he continued to produce a trickle of records for his independent ICA label.[14]

Bobby's touring continued unabated. On September 22, 1978, B.B. King and Bobby were booked into the Landmark Theater in downtown Syracuse, New York, on the very same night that Bob Dylan was playing at the War Memorial auditorium just four blocks down the street. By all accounts, white music fans left the Dylan concert disappointed and black blues fans left the packed Landmark elated.[15]

The touring band's membership continued its evolution. Stanley Abernathy, a thirty-one-year-old Chicago trumpeter, joined in 1978 and stayed on for the next thirteen years before moving to B.B. King's band in 1991.[16] When Tompall Glaser's Outlaw Band folded in Nashville, Bobby offered Mel Brown his old job back as guitarist with the band, despite the fact that Wayne Bennett was still serving in that position. Brown accepted, but soon found himself in an uncomfortable situation. "Wayne was a great musician," he recounted, "but he was hard to work with. Hard, hard, hard. He felt like because he was Wayne Bennett he deserved extra credit. When people would sit in with the band, like Roberta Flack, he'd overplay them and embarrass himself. He even overplayed Bobby a lot of times. Some nights Wayne wanted to play everybody's part in the band. The only way I fit in was by switching over to keyboards. We had a great group but Wayne wouldn't take a regular place like everybody else. He just overplayed his hand."[17]

Tom Hunter, the Texas guitarist and brother of veteran bluesman Long John Hunter, recalls meeting Bennett and Bobby on the road in Beaumont, Texas: "But by that time, my cap was set to play like Wayne Bennett. I met him when he was with Bobby Bland. They used to come to Beaumont at different clubs, and I always got a chance to hook up with him and shake his hand and talk with him. He was not a very outgoing type of guy. You'd talk to him for about a minute, then he was through with you. Now, I spent lots of time with Bobby Bland, talking to him, every time he came to Beaumont. In fact, Bobby Bland came to the Club Raven. And he was on his bus sleeping. The door was about half open, and I opened the door. His bodyguard told me, 'Shut that damn door!' But Bobby Bland said, 'That's okay; let him come on.' I was a kid. Man, I sat there and I talked to Bobby Bland for about twenty minutes. His music was really popular at that time; it's always been popular. And, man, I was just thrilled to death to be sitting there with him on the bus. He was real friendly. And every time he's come back to Beaumont—I wrote for about seven or eight years for the local newspaper, the Beaumont *Enterprise*, and each time he would come to Beaumont or Lake Charles, I'd always go backstage or meet him on the bus and talk with him. I don't think he would know me from anybody else, but I have experienced talking with him on several occasions."[18]

On January 12, 1979, the Bell/Higgins production team and Bobby returned to the Filmways/Heider Recording Studios in Hollywood to begin work on their second album together. They had only eight songs for the LP, and the title cut, "I Feel Good, I Feel Fine," did not even include a vocal track for Bobby, instead featuring the session's female backup group called the Sweet Spirit and crack trombonist George Bohannon. A Latin-inflected, Tyrone Davisesque "Tit for Tat" went to number 71 on the soul chart, but the rest of the tunes tanked (including an ill-advised remake of Nat "King" Cole's "Red Sails in the Sunset") except for one sweet gem: "Soon As the Weather Breaks." The "Stormy Monday"–influenced blues was written by Vee Pea (a pseudonym for Monk Higgins's wife Virginia Bland),[19] Bobby himself, and Margie Evans. Also a member of the Sweet Spirit backup vocal group, Evans was born Marjorie Ann Johnson on July 17, 1940, and had worked with the bands of Billy Ward, Ron Marshall, and Johnny Otis before cutting two charted hits, the last one in 1977 for Al Bell's ICA label, "Good Thing Queen—Part I."[20]

"Soon As the Weather Breaks," featuring a fine Freddy Robinson guitar solo, sounds a lot like pre-ABC Bobby at his best. It reached number 76 on the soul chart and is still included in Bobby's live shows. *I Feel Good, I Feel Fine*, with its cover photo of Bobby surrounded by three sensuous black beauties, peaked at number 34 on the Black Albums chart and 187 on the Pop Albums chart.

Three days later, on January 15, 1979, the Music Corporation of America (MCA) purchased ABC Records for a reported $20 million. Before long Bobby was expressing dissatisfaction with the new owners and starting to look around for a new label.[21]

Meanwhile, the constant touring continued, with Bobby and the band returning to Memphis on May 4, 1979, for a three-night stand at Sunbeam Mitchell's Club Paradise, where Bobby told a reporter, "I think it would be nice if I could go out and play when I want instead of having to do it 'cause I have to. But it's better than what I was doing. I didn't want to be parking cars."[22] So the band kept moving, playing the Civic Opera House in Chicago on June 2 with B.B. King and Albert King, then returning to Memphis, again with B.B. King, to play the sold out Memphis Auditorium on August 2, 1979. By now, according to newspaper reports, Bobby was playing "his saxophone with precision."[23] Melvin Jackson, the Bland band's longtime leader and trumpeter, had started playing around with a saxophone, teaching Bobby as he taught himself, and both by this time could play well enough to perform occasionally on the new instrument. On November 9 Bobby was again on the all-star blues bill with B.B., Tyrone Davis, Little Milton, Latimore, Bobby Rush, and Lynn White at the International Blues Festival in Jackson's Mississippi Coliseum. And by April 11, 1980, Bobby and the band were in New Orleans at Prout's Club Alhambra at 735 North Claiborne Avenue for a three-night stand.

Later in the year, Bobby was back in Los Angeles with Monk Higgins and Al Bell for another recording session, again with a full studio orchestra, but thankfully no backup singers on most cuts. Higgins's arrangements are as lush and suave as usual, but the material is better. Bobby, Vee Pea, and Margie Evans collaborated on a followup to the previous year's hit "Soon As the Weather Breaks"; "You'd Be a Millionaire" was the only single hit from the album, entitled *Sweet Vibrations*, and a minor one at that, peaking at a lowly number 92 on the soul chart, but still garnering a nomination for the Blues Foundation's Award for Blues Single of the Year (1981). The highlights of the disk are three Joe Scott songs that take Bobby back to his Duke roots, and a big, brassy prototypical Bobby Bland number, featuring Freddie Robinson on guitar, called "Just Because I Leave, That Don't Mean I'm Gone (Suspicious)" on the record label, but just "Suspicious" on the album's cover, written by Bobby's old Memphis buddy Rufus Thomas and Oriell Robberts, a pseudonym for an exotic dancer friend of Rufus.[24] A couple of other oddities were on the LP as well: Bobby does a credible job on the Harburg/Arlen standard "Over the Rainbow," and a reprise to Charles Brown's "Merry Christmas Baby" (called "New Merry Christmas Baby" on the label) is way overproduced, with too much orchestration and impinging backup singing to make it merry at all.

On November 8, 1980, Bobby was back with his new family in Memphis to perform at the Mid-South Coliseum for the International Blues Festival, where he and the new album received this review from Memphis *Commercial Appeal* reporter Walter Dawson: "Even in the midst of eight other performers, even though he came on near the end of the show when the audience had been drenched with blues of all shades—Bobby Bland stood out. It wasn't that his music was better, nor that his voice was any better than someone else's (although it was). It was just that his intensity was so unrelenting and so moving that it was almost impossible not to be drawn in. The man doesn't sing—he testifies. . . . His new album, *Sweet Vibrations* (MCA), has him in down-on-your-knees fervor that breaks like lightning."[25] The album, with Bobby's mug being replaced on the cover with a kneeling woman in her negligee, reached number 29 on the Black Albums chart.

Meanwhile, Bobby's continuing success did not go unnoticed by the Internal Revenue Service; on January 15, 1981, Revenue Officer Elaine K. Wagner placed a lien on Bobby's Memphis home on Benjestown Road. According to the "Notice of Federal Tax Lien Under Internal Revenue Laws," Bobby owed $23,858.03 for unpaid taxes in 1978.[26]

By Bobby's next album, in 1981, there was no doubt in which direction Monk Higgins and Al Bell were leading Bobby. Efforts at disco had not proved lucrative. A return to the blues didn't quite make it with Higgins's lush, sophisticated arrangements. So the next effort, to be entitled *Try Me, I'm Real*, was an attempt to put Bobby almost directly on the center stripe of the easy listening road. Recorded at the Wally Heider Recording Studio in Los Angeles and the Universal Recording Studio in Chicago, the album contained mostly sensuous love ballads which Bobby, of course, handled with aplomb. But the best cuts were two jazz standards: Bobby's versions of Dinah Washington's "What a Difference a Day Makes" and Erroll Garner's "I Cover the Waterfront" proved that Bobby could really sing jazz, particularly when accompanied by such classy musicians as Freddy Robinson and L. V. Johnson on guitar, Billy McCoy on electric piano, George Bohannon on trombone, Don Merrick on saxophone, and Bobby Bryant on trumpet. Why Bobby Bland never recorded a jazz album is a mystery; it could have been a smash.

Another touching number on the LP was another Bobby Bland–Margie Evans–Vee Pea tune entitled "A Song for You, My Son," inspired by Bobby's five-year-old son, Rodd, who was now beginning to occasionally perform alongside drummer Tony Coleman in Bobby's touring band.[27] The album went to number 52 on the Black Albums chart but contained no hit singles. And despite its middle of the road approach, the LP did not crossover onto the pop charts.

Nevertheless, there seemed to be some interest in Bobby percolating overseas. Ace Records in London had just been granted the rights to compile sixteen of Bobby's old Duke sides from 1952 through 1957 on an album called *Woke Up Screaming* (CH 41), and it was selling surprisingly well.[28] It was followed by a twenty-track compilation entitled *The Best of Bobby Bland: 1960–80*, on U.K. MCA in 1982, and the seventeen-cut *Foolin' with the Blues* on Charly in 1983.

Despite his recording of more popular songs, there remained no doubt about Bobby's blues credentials. In 1981 he was inducted, as a part of the second class, into the Blues Foundation's Hall of Fame, along with Roy Brown,

Blind Willie McTell, Professor Longhair, and Tampa Red, and also won the Foundation's Blues Vocalist of the Year award.[29]

At Chicago's Auditorium Theater on July 19, 1981, the National Academy of Blues's First Annual National Blues Awards ceremony was held. B.B. King was named King of the Blues, but Bobby came away the big winner, with trophies for Top Male Blues Singer, Blues Single of the Year ("You'd Be a Millionaire"), and Blues Album of the Year (*Sweet Vibrations*). In addition, Al Bell and Monk Higgins shared Producer of the Year honors for *Sweet Vibrations*, and Wayne Bennett won the title of Most Outstanding Blues Guitarist.[30]

Yet, despite all these accolades—and despite ABC's superior distribution network, huge promotional capabilities, and proven pop music producers—Bobby had barely cracked the white market. Although forty-two of Bobby's hits had crossed over onto the pop charts, none had made it higher than number 20 ("Ain't Nothing You Can Do"), and that was back in 1963 during the Duke heyday. And while it was also true that Bobby and B.B. King's *Together for the First Time . . . Live* album reached number 43 on the Live Pop Albums chart, only three others ever made it to the top 100 pop albums: *Here's The Man!!!* (#53) in 1962, *Call On Me* (#11) in 1963, and *Together Again . . . Live* (#73) in 1976.

The audiences for Bobby's live shows remained primarily black throughout the 1960s and early 1970s. His widest popularity was still in the Southern black belt—Georgia, Alabama, Tennessee, Mississippi, Louisiana, Arkansas, and Texas—and in cities with large black populations recently migrated from the South—Chicago, Detroit, and Cleveland. His records have never sold as well in Washington and Philadelphia, and he has never been effusively welcomed at Harlem's Apollo Theater—"The audiences there are such big critics," Bobby says, "they want more of the teenage thing."[31]

Beginning in the mid-1970s, however, Bobby started to play to larger white or mixed jazz clubs and white festivals, not only because of ABC's wider distribution, promotion, and production capabilities, but also because B.B. King had been discovered by white audiences and had introduced Bobby as another of his breed of bluesmen. Their two live albums and frequent joint shows provided openings to white venues that Bobby had never enjoyed before. "I think this new white audience is lovely," Bobby reported in 1975. "They really surprised me. I wondered at first how I was going to get over. I'm used to telling stories and I underestimated them listening to my songs. I found them altogether different. They meet me with a standing ovation and I've never had that before. Not that my people aren't less appreciative, but there's so much more that you have to do for them in order to deserve that. They make you work for what you get."[32]

The fact remains that when a sitting U.S. president can reminisce about a B.B. King–Bobby Bland show he once saw in Little Rock, as President Clinton did with B.B. King when King received Kennedy Center Honors in 1995, then Bobby has not been completely ignored by the white majority, even if the president was Bill Clinton, who has been referred to as "our first black president."[33]

Bobby Bland is still not a household name in white America, as perhaps, say, B.B. King is, but mention Bobbyblueband, as his name is properly pronounced by people of color, to one of those people and you will receive instant recognition, at least for those of a certain advancing age. So how does one account for this gross lack of recognition, let alone appreciation, for this much-praised vocalist and seminal figure in post–World War II American music?

Theories abound.

One of the obvious ones is that Bobby does not play an instrument, that is, if you do not consider the voice an instrument. Bobby's short-lived foray with playing the saxophone proved to be just that—short-lived. Black blues stars, this theory goes, require an instrument, most preferably a guitar, *a la* B.B. King, Buddy Guy, Albert King, Robert Cray, etc., to be accepted by a white audience. And one is hard put to name a black "stand-up" male blues singer with any substantial white following. For better or worse, white Americans, at least since the 1960s, have tended to associate the blues with the guitar, not with the horn-dominated sound of Bobby Bland.

Another theory holds that a black artist needs to be an exceptional showman to cross over, like Michael Jackson, James Brown, and Jackie Wilson. Certainly, Bobby's flat-footed, no-nonsense approach to performing will not earn him any points here, but anyone who has seen a Bobby Bland show, when Bobby was in his prime, will tell you he was just as exciting and charismatic in his suave, sultry way as his more energetic, athletic colleagues. "I can't concentrate on what I'm going to do if I move around a lot," Bobby explained. "I can't get my point across the way I'd like to hear it myself. If I'm pleased with it, I'm sure that somebody else will get something out of it."[34]

Others claim that Bobby's material is just too grown-up for youth-oriented record buyers, that his songs, sung in an older bluesy way, are about adult issues like love lost and found, two-timing, and other painful topics, instead of youthful pursuits like having fun and surfing and such. But Bobby refutes this. "When I crossed over in the '70s," he said, "I was surprised at how young my audience got, but I enjoy the young fans most of all. Young people who say they don't like the blues haven't listened to me or anyone else. They don't know where I'm coming from. If they listen, they like the blues."[35]

Others opine that Bobby was "too 'uptown' for white blues fans and too laid-back for white soul fans of the era."[36] B.B. King complained that young blacks found the blues too old-fashioned, representing a time and place they did not want to remember. He also pointed out that many white scholars were rediscovering the old down-home Delta bluesmen and viewed B.B.'s and Bobby's use of horns and a bigger sound as a corruption of the pure blues. B.B. did, however, give credit to Charles Keil, a white college professor who wrote *Urban Blues*, which celebrated the modern blues of B.B. and Bobby and contended that it was unfair and improper to label their style "impure."[37] But, while the book may have gained the pair a modicum of respect in the academic community, it is highly doubtful that it much affected the opinions of the young record-buying public.

Others claimed that Bobby offered "no point of identification for the largely narcissistic rock audience, and he is considered too unsophisticated by the jazz audience, which demands improvisatory risks and authenticity of technique."[38] There is certainly no doubt that Bland's broad repertoire can be confusing. Much of it is not blues in the formal sense, nor is it rock 'n' roll, jazz, or even soul.

All of these theories beg the question, however. They suggest that Bobby's style peculiarly fell through the cracks of the white record-buying public's fickle appreciation of what was good music, that if he would have just tweaked his approach in one direction or another he could have crossed over and expanded his audience into the white motherlode of popularity. But Bobby's music was, and remains, great music by anyone's standards, and, had certain circumstances been altered, he could have been at least as well known as B.B. King and arguably a much bigger star.

Bobby's greatest problem in this crossover dilemma was not his style or his brand of blues, but instead his lack of adequate promotion to the wider record-buying public. Of all of Don Robey's shortcomings, of which there were many, the most grievous, as far as Bobby's career was concerned, was his almost complete absence of promotional and distribution clout outside the black music community. Duke's salesmen in the fifties and sixties, notably Dave Clark and Irving Marcus, hawked Duke's wares almost exclusively to black record stores and black radio stations. When Bobby was at the height of his popularity in the 1960s, a white person, who may have accidentally heard a Bobby Bland record on a black radio station and liked it, would in most cities have to "cross the tracks" to find a black ghetto record store to buy a copy of it. And if he wanted to see Bobby perform, he would have to go to a chitlin circuit venue and be the only white face in attendance.

Had Bobby been a less cautious, less conservative, less loyal individual, he might have sought out another record company with a more expansive public relations and distribution network, or at least hired a manager as B.B. King and Elvis Presley had. But when he was off the stage he was still, at heart, a shy, suspicious country boy, insecure about his illiteracy, who was a virtual recluse except for a select group of female friends. As it was, Bobby's only promotion came from Don Robey's pitchmanship, Robey's salesmen, and Evelyn Johnson's booking efforts, all substantial and surprisingly effective considering their minority status in an isolated industry outpost like Houston, but nonetheless primarily limited to the black community. One can only surmise what heights Bobby's career might have attained had he been signed earlier on by a larger, more diverse company or represented from the beginning by a creative and energetic manager.

In addition, there was that important issue of timing. As in all of life, being in the right place at the right time can make all the difference. Certainly, had the popularity of the big band sound continued for a little longer, Bobby's big-band blues style would have been more appreciated. Had rock 'n' roll not taken off in a string band direction, Bobby's orchestral approach would have been more widely accepted. Had Bobby been signed to ABC or another major label twenty years earlier, when he might have appealed more widely to a younger audience, instead of at the age of forty-three, his career might have turned out differently. Oh, what could have been?

It was obvious, however, after a few years at ABC that the chance of a major crossover success was fading, and that what part pure and simple racism had to do with this was something Bobby had seriously considered. "They [those who control the recording/concert industry] only let one Black at a time get to the top," Bobby told an interviewer in 1977.

> *A Black man still has to do twice what the white man does [to be recognized in the business]. You got to turn flips or hang off the rafters.*
>
> *You're [singers] just a tool for them to auction off. You still have to know how to mind. [It's] politics or the mafia, whatever you want to call it. You can only peak so far. You can say what you please this week, but at next week's meeting they'll tell you what you said wrong. I'm the same one who went to the back door to get a sandwich. I make four or five hundred thousand a year, but that's what they allow. I know how to mind so I can keep breathing. This [singing] is what I like to do, so I try to stay healthy and keep doing what I like to do. You don't get enthused over $100,000, or whatever. You get accustomed to it. But you don't have your freedom with it. It's still controlled, even in the top brackets.[39]*

Bobby claimed that he was not bitter about it. "You can't really miss what you never had in a sense," he said. "I know there are some things that were unjust, that I should've been handled differently. But I thank God for the health and strength I've got. I'm happy to be 49 and still have a pretty good voice. I went to the woodshed and cried many times over things that I didn't think should've happened. But what can you do? It's spilled milk. So I just wipe it up and keep on steppin'."[40]

Bobby was more resigned than anything else. "I believe what is for you, you're gonna get," he said. "I have quite a bit of patience about certain things. If it's your time, it's your time. And if it's not your time, it's not going to happen."[41]

So Bobby and the band kept on steppin'—except for Mel Brown who decided to take a break from the road and left the band to move with his wife, Angel, to the country. "I left Bobby in 1982 and moved to the country in northeast Mississippi," Brown recalled. "I lived in a house trailer thirteen miles from the nearest telephone. I chilled and didn't play with anybody." That only lasted about a year, until Clifford Antone talked him into joining the house band at his famous club, Antone's, in Austin, Texas. There he backed blues luminaries like Buddy Guy, Junior Wells, Stevie Ray Vaughn, Snooky Pryor, James Cotton, and Clifton Chenier. In 1986, Albert Collins asked Brown to join his band, the Icebreakers, and Mel toured with Collins off and on, collaborating with him on Collins's *Cold Snap* album, and continuing to work at Antone's until 1989. Booked into a club called, of all names, the Pop-A-Gator, in Kitchener, Ontario, four days before Christmas in 1989, Brown ended up staying in Canada, where he worked the club circuit in southern Ontario with his band the Homewreckers, recording occasionally with them and his friend Snooky Pryor on the Electro-Fi label,[42] while perpetually perfecting his golf game, until his death from emphysema complications on March 20, 2009.[43]

With the release in Europe of the album *Woke Up Screaming* and the live albums with B.B. King, Bobby's popularity there was growing, enough so that he was invited, along with B.B. and John Lee Hooker, to perform at the London Blues Festival '82 on May 20–23 at the Hammersmith Odeon Theatre. Bobby had long held a fear of flying that had kept him from traveling to Europe thus far, but B.B. talked him into accepting the invitation, and they performed the concerts to sold-out houses.[44] Bobby overcame his flying phobia, but he received less than stellar reviews from the London press: "Bland was in Britain for the first time last week for the London Blues Festival, and there were moments in Hammersmith when he chose his notes with such sad precision that melancholy—sorrow as fate—seemed to take physical shape, to curl up through the seats silencing everyone. For most of the time, though, people talked and wandered to and from the bar. Bland was playing his traveling soul show to a guitar-struck rock audience, and without an emotional response. His style became a manner, his personal touches— the notes dragged from the back of his throat—eccentric."[45] Apparently "the squall" was just too much for the stuffy Brits.

In June 1982 *Billboard* changed its Hot Soul Singles chart to Hot Black Singles, signaling the declining popularity of soul music and the rising sales of something new called rap and hip-hop.

Back in Memphis, at the third annual Blues Music Awards show in the Peabody Hotel Ballroom, on November 16, 1982, Bobby was named the Blues Vocalist of the Year for the second consecutive year, Entertainer of the Year, and his *Woke Up Screaming* album on the English Ace label was named Vintage or Reissue Album of the Year in the foreign category. Bobby and his band closed the show before an appreciative crowd of blues musicians and fans. The awards program was sponsored by the Memphis-based Blues Foundation, a 400-member nonprofit organization dedicated to fostering and preserving blues music.[46]

Bobby and the band continued touring, as always; they played at Dallas Entertainment on November 19 and 20. On November 30 Bobby was back in Chicago at the Universal Recording Studio to finish another album that was begun earlier in the year in Los Angeles with Monk Higgins and Al Bell and a full studio orchestra, including George Bohannon on trombone, David Ervin on keyboards, Freddy Robinson on guitar, and the Sweet Spirit backup singers (Judith Jones, Sylvia Cox, and Yolanda Howard).

Perhaps the best of the Higgins/Bell Bobby Bland albums, *Here We Go Again* contains several fine moments, the best being one of Bobby's most touching ballads, "Never Let Me Go," written by Joe Scott, that surpasses Johnny Ace's original 1954 version and exemplifies what Bobby can do to a ballad surrounded by lush orchestration and expert musicians—truly a feat. Another stellar ballad is the Kentz/Mann jazz standard "Don't Go to Strangers," which Bobby sings with unusual feeling and style. The only hit on the album was "Recess in Heaven," another variation on "Stormy Monday" that went to number 40. There are also a couple of fine tunes by former Stax guitarist L. V. Johnson, "Country Love" and "Is This the Blues." The album, which reached number 22 on the Black Albums chart, concludes with a credible attempt at gospel, "We've Had a Good Time," by Monk Higgins.

"Gospel and inspirational [songs] came from my side of the aisle," Al Bell admitted, "and the standard songs came from Oscar Cohen's [Bobby's long-time booking agent] side of the aisle and in between we added Bobby 'Blue' Bland."[47]

On March 3, 1983, Bobby was finally married to Willie Mae Martin,[48] that pretty girl who he had met so many years ago at his mother's diner in Memphis, who had fulfilled her dream of becoming a nurse and who was the mother of his seven-year-old son Roderick, by now his *de facto* manager, and his faithful companion for lo these many years. The couple was married at the Union Valley Baptist Church in Memphis by the Rev. H. O. Kneeland Jr. The groom was fifty-three and the bride was thirty-eight, and they made their home in Germantown, a Memphis suburb.[49]

Not long after, on April 18, Bobby was back in the L.A. Recording Studio and later at the Ardent Recording Studio in Memphis to work on the next Higgins/Bell–produced album. As good as the previous album was, this one, entitled *Tell Mr. Bland*, is bad. It clearly demonstrates that by this time the Monk Higgins and Al Bell collaboration was running out of steam, material, and inspiration.

Three of the eight cuts were repeats of previous Bobby Bland recordings for Duke: "Ain't It a Good Thing" and "Queen for a Day," both from 1963, and "Fever" from 1965. And each new version pales in comparison to the earlier recording. "What Is It?" does not include Bobby at all, just the orchestra and the Sweet Spirit choir. And the one song that might have made the entire effort worthwhile, Bobby's version of Tommy Edwards's 1958 smash hit "It's All in the Game," written originally in 1912 by later U.S. Vice President Charles Dawes (under Calvin Coolidge) as "Melody in A Major," is a colossally overproduced disappointment.[50]

In 1983, in recognition of America's changing tastes in black music, *Billboard* changed the name of its Black Albums chart to Top R&B/Hip-Hop Albums. *Tell Mr. Bland* reached number 50 on the former and number 71 on the latter— hip-hop it was not!

On April 30 Bobby performed with Memphis Slim at the Smithsonian Institution in Washington, D.C., at a special program honoring fellow Memphian Nat D. Williams, WDIA's first black radio announcer, journalist, teacher, and original master of ceremonies at the Palace Theater's Amateur Night, where Bobby had competed as a young man some thirty-plus years before.[51] By the time of the concert Williams was nearing death, having suffered three strokes. His daughter Natoyen said that, just before his fourth and final stroke came on October 27, Williams still remembered the tune to "Beale Street Blues."[52]

On Saturday, September 3, in Long Beach, California, Bobby headlined the 1983 Long Beach Blues Festival, appearing with Clifton Chenier, Johnny Copeland, Willie Dixon, Albert King, and others. A recording was made of Bobby's performance that has surfaced on a number of CD imports: *Long Beach 1983* on England's Charly label in 1994 and again on the Netherlands's Blues Factory label in 2008, and as *Mercy Mercy Me* on England's Dressed to Kill label in 2000. The recording sounds pretty faithful for a live event at an outdoor venue, the athletic field at California State University in Long Beach. The band, featuring veterans Melvin Jackson on trumpet and Wayne Bennett on guitar, is in fine form and the energy level is high—a good place to hear some of Bobby's ABC/MCA tunes like "The Soul of a Man," "I Intend to

Take Your Place," "Soon As the Weather Breaks," "Today I Started Loving You Again," and "Recess in Heaven" without the studio overproduction, as well as some of the old standbys: "I'll Take Care of You," "Share Your Love with Me," "That's the Way Love Is," "Stormy Monday Blues," and "Farther Up the Road."

In early 1984 Bobby finally found someone to replace Mel Brown on keyboards. He hired Little Milton's Hammond B3 organ player, twenty-year-old Judge Kenneth "Lucky" Peterson. Peterson's grandfather had operated a juke joint in Alabama and his father, James, was a blues guitarist who owned a club called the Governor's Inn in Buffalo, New York. With his father's band, Lucky cut his first album when he was only five years old. It was produced by Willie Dixon and included a hit single entitled "1,2,3,4." With Dixon's help, the young prodigy appeared on the *Tonight Show, Ed Sullivan*, the *David Frost Show*, and *What's My Line* at the age of six. By the age of sixteen he was traveling with Little Milton's band, where he soon became the musical director.[53] On Sunday, June 3, Bobby, Lucky, and the rest of the band were in Memphis to play what was billed as a "Bobby 'Blue' Bland & Sunbeam Mitchell's Anniversary Celebration" at Mitchell's Club Paradise.

However, the changes in band personnel continued. Wayne Bennett decided to take another hiatus from the road after this latest stint of nine years. "And then in 1984, I left Bobby again," Bennett explained, "and I moved to New Orleans. Why? Because of the climate, and also my wife is originally from there. And on top of that, I've had a lot of friends there for many years."[54]

Later, Bobby was back in the L.A. Recording Studio and the Ardent Recording Studio in Memphis to start work on his next album, *You've Got Me Loving You*. This time Monk Higgins and Al Bell decided to do away with the strings; the Sweet Spirit backup singers are still heard on a few cuts, but for the most part it's Bobby's voice front and center. The resulting sound is much more satisfying than previous Higgins/Bell albums. Unfortunately, the quality of the material does not match the cleaner sound. All the tracks were written by Higgins and Bell, except for three, two of which are the LP's best songs: a pretty ballad entitled "Looking Back," by Clyde Otis and Brook Benton, recorded by Nat "King" Cole in 1958, and a mellow Christmas tune, "You Are My Christmas," by Renee Marks and Pete Cosey. The cover features a cute photo of Bobby with his eight-year-old son, Rodd, sitting on his lap. The album peaked at number 35 on the Top R&B/Hip-Hop Albums chart.

After the album was released, MCA released Bobby from his contract. For the first time in more than thirty years, Bobby Bland was not under a recording contract.

Milton Bland, a.k.a. Monk Higgins, left MCA shortly thereafter to launch his own recording company, Almon Productions. The City of Los Angeles awarded him a special commendation for his work with young entertainers in the industry. Milton Bland died at the age of fifty on July 3, 1986, leaving his wife, Virginia, a.k.a. Vee Pea, and three daughters, Joan, June, and Janesse.[55]

Al Bell continued with his ICA Productions in Little Rock. In 1988 Berry Gordy hired him as president of Motown Records, where he stayed briefly until Gordy sold the company to MCA and Boston Ventures for $61 million in June 1988. Bell then founded Bellmark Records in September 1989, hitting it big again with Duice's "Dazzey Duks" in 1992 and still again with the rap act Tag Team's "Whoomp (There It Is)" in 1993.[56] By 2009, at the age of sixty-nine, Bell was back in Memphis, reinventing himself once more as chairman of the Memphis Music Foundation, a nonprofit foundation formed to resuscitate the city's once great music industry.[57]

Despite not having a recording contract, Bobby continued to be much in demand for live performances, still playing more than 300 dates a year. On August 18 he was in New York City to play at the Beacon Theater with B.B. King and Millie Jackson, prompting this review by respected music critic Jon Pareles in the *New York Times:* "At the late show, Mr. Bland was the most consistently inspired performer. His voice sounds like it has been worn smooth by constant tribulation—it's a melancholic, liquid tenor almost an octave higher than his speaking voice. Using only a few notes, often poured quickly into the beginning of a line as if he doesn't expect to reach the next phrase, Mr. Bland sings like someone who's suffered so much bad luck already that he wouldn't think of giving up now."[58]

Bobby Bland at the London Blues Festival '82 at the Hammersmith Odeon Theater in London on May 22, 1982. Courtesy Sylvia Pitcher Photo Library.

13

Members Only

1985–1990

Tommy Couch Sr. grew up in Tuscumbia, Alabama, near Florence, the birthplace of W. C. Handy and Sam Phillips, and not far from Muscle Shoals, where Bobby Bland and other artists recorded so many southern soul-inflected hits during the sixties and early seventies. Couch went to college at the University of Mississippi, where he was elected social chairman of his fraternity, Pi Kappa Alpha, in 1961. That position required him to book bands for fraternity parties and dances, and he naturally selected bands that were popular in his hometown area: Jimmy Johnson's Del Rays, David Hood's the Mystics, and Dan Penn and the Pallbearers, among others. Following his graduation with a degree in pharmacology, Couch moved to Jackson, Mississippi, to become a pharmacist. But before long he was in the booking business again, forming Malaco Attractions with his brother-in-law Mitchell Malouf (Malouf + Couch = Malaco).

Gerald "Wolf" Stephenson, who in the fall of 1964 succeeded Couch as social chairman at Pi Kappa Alpha, soon joined the operation which promoted concerts in the area by the Dave Clark 5, Herman's Hermits, the Who, the Animals, and many others. Stephenson, born in 1943 and raised in rural Columbia, Mississippi, also studied pharmacology at Ole Miss, but found it a bit easier than his classmates, who did not have the benefit of a personal tutor in high school as Wolf had with his father who was an accomplished high school chemistry teacher. This advantage left plenty of time for Wolf to socialize and book rhythm and blues bands for all kinds of wild parties in and around Oxford.[1]

This entrepreneurial threesome began experimenting with some recordings in 1966 and, in 1967, opened a recording studio in a converted Pepsi warehouse at 3023 Northside Drive that remains Malaco's home to this day.[2] "We recorded everything in the world imaginable—country to symphonies to pop—and the only thing that really happened for us was black music," Couch recalled. "We are big fans of the music but we didn't really focus on rhythm and blues at first. I'd like to say we did but we just kind of did it by accident."[3]

Like Sam Phillips more than a decade before, they recorded anything they had to, to keep going—jingles, local bands, custom projects—and, like nearby Stax, they leased masters to other larger companies for distribution. Between 1968 and 1970, Capitol Records released six singles and the Grammy-nominated album *I Do Not Play No Rock 'n' Roll* by Mississippi Fred McDowell, all produced at Malaco. Other distribution deals were eventually forged with ABC, Mercury, and Bang.

In May 1970 veteran New Orleans arranger Wardell Quezergue, who owed local recording impresario Cosimo Matassa more than $70,000, offered to trade the services of some of his Big Easy artists for Malaco studio time and session musicians. Luckily for Malaco, now seriously starving for cash, the session resulted in two giant hits: King Floyd's "Groove Me," released on Malaco's Chimneyville label, and Jean Knight's "Mr. Big Stuff" on Stax.[4]

Atlantic Records, which helped distribute "Groove Me," soon sent the Pointer Sisters and James Carr, and Stax sent Rufus Thomas to Jackson to record at Malaco Studios. Even Paul Simon recorded part of his *There Goes Rhymin' Simon* album there in 1973. But by 1974 the momentum had stalled and cash flow was at an all-time low. "It was so slack we almost went out of business," admitted Couch, "[and] Malouf bailed out to sell real estate."[5]

Couch and Stephenson were still working as part-time pharmacists to make ends meet. Out of desperation, they scavenged the Malaco archives of rejected masters for something that might sell. With just enough money left to press and ship the record before Thanksgiving 1975, they released Dorothy Moore's "Misty Blue," originally recorded in 1973, which sold over two million copies worldwide, and was followed by thirteen more hits and five Grammy nominations for Moore by 1980.

By 1977 the company was also able to sign some quality songwriters, artists, and producers from the defunct Stax Records, including Eddie Floyd, Frederick Knight, the Fiestas, and David Porter.[6] In 1978 Stewart Madison, a fellow Ole Miss grad who had been heading a Shreveport, Louisiana, recording studio, came aboard to oversee the company's business affairs, enabling Couch to work more closely with artists and musicians and Stephenson to focus on the technical end of the studio.[7]

Meanwhile, disco was raging. Malaco's single incursion into the popular genre was providing the studio and session musicians, including Wayne Bennett on guitar, for Anita Ward's "Ring My Bell," which went to number one on both the pop and the R&B charts and sold more than ten million copies worldwide.

Re-enter Dave Clark, Bobby's old friend at Duke/Peacock who had been head of national promotion for seventeen years. Since leaving Duke/Peacock in 1971, Clark had taken over the reins of Stax's gospel label, Gospel Truth.[8] When Stax collapsed in 1975, Clark moved to Henry Stone's Miami-based disco label, TK Records, where KC and the Sunshine Band, Betty Wright, Foxy, Anita Ward, and others were producing big hits.

Frederick Knight produced Anita Ward's "Ring My Bell" for his own Juana label, which was distributed by TK. In addition to pushing "Ring My Bell" and other TK releases, Clark introduced a Malaco cut called "Get Up and Dance" by Freedom to New York's disco club scene in 1979. Beginning with Grandmaster Flash, the track became one of the most sampled records of all time.[9]

TK was sold to Roulette Records in 1980, and Malaco was first in line to gobble up the venerable Clark, at the ripe young age of seventy-five, to become its senior vice president of promotion. Clark wasted no time leveraging his respected ability to garner wide airplay and his solid credibility with artists. He recruited thirty-nine-year-old Texas bluesman Erzell "Z.Z." Hill for the Malaco roster, at a time when major record labels were all but ignoring anything associated with the blues.

"Dave was with Stax when we had 'Mr. Big Stuff' and with TK when we had 'Misty Blue' and promoted both those records," explained Couch. "Z.Z. Hill came here, I think because of Dave, and everybody after that came because of a combination of our success with Z.Z. and Dave."

"I thought Malaco had the ingredients," Clark recalled later. "The philosophy of the label is real down-to-earth black music but they just didn't have the promotion know-how. A lot of people couldn't even spell the name or know the label when I started working for them. That was one of my main jobs and one of the hardest—get people to know Malaco."

Z.Z. Hill's second Malaco album, *Down Home*, with its smash George Jackson title track, "Down Home Blues," took care of that. Selling more than 500,000 copies, it became one of the most successful blues albums ever released and proved, despite major labels' rejection, that the blues were still alive and kicking. "My first sign was from the record sales, not from radio," said Clark. "I was surprised because I had never had that kind of reaction on a heavy blues record before. The black record-buying public took it as it was, a song that relates to things that had happened to them. It was everyday life."[10]

"Z.Z. kept us all working," Bobby said. "Having 'Down Home Blues' be a hit really helped me and everybody else singing real R&B because it got people to pay attention to the music again."[11]

Hill was a big fan of Bobby's and told *Living Blues* in 1982: "And you know, I look at him now and he's doing the same show he did 20 years ago. He just stand there. He don't move. Just kinda wave his hands. Rear back, 'Whop!' You know? And he'll get over. I say 'Oh, wow, Bobby.' But I can't just stand there, man, I'll be across that stage. I said, 'Now here's a cat just stand there, man, and they love him to death. Here I am bustin' my butt off and I'm just *tryin'* to put on a good show.' Sometimes I get all down on my knees [laughs]. But a guy was tellin' me, he said, 'Man, you can turn 15 flips, 20 flips, if you don't have nothin' goin' for you record-wise to build up that name, you can *forget* it. Them folks don't *know* you.' I guess he's right 'cause Bobby have had a lot of hits. That's the difference. Once you get your name established, out there, and get it sold, you can work without a record. You get that image. They'll say, 'Well, Z.Z. Hill's in town.' 'Oh, I'm goin'!'"[12] Unfortunately, Hill died from complications resulting from a heart clot on April 27, 1984, before he had a chance to fully enjoy his growing fame.

However, the legacy he left was to become Malaco's main market niche, southern soul blues for an older black audience fed up with disco, rap, and hip-hop, who just wanted to hear some of that good ol' down-home blues. So Dave Clark and Malaco continued to serve it up, signing other R&B vets like Benny Latimore in 1981, Denise LaSalle in 1983, Little Milton Campbell and Johnnie Taylor in 1984, to work in Malaco's compact Jackson studio with Malaco's cozy house band, where overhead remained low enough that an album selling between 50,000 and 100,000 copies could make everyone some money.[13]

Clark headed a seven-person promotion department, including five field sales people who, with Clark's historical connections, could ensure wide airplay for a good record almost everywhere in the South and in most major cities with sizeable black populations. "They know they're [the artists] going to get a good radio shot here where at a major record company, they might get some kind of a shot," according to Malaco's business manager, Stewart Madison. "And the major record companies do not want these guys—they're not set up mentally or financially to sell 100,000 albums and be happy about it."[14]

When Dave Clark received the news in early 1985 that Bobby had been released from his contract with MCA, he was on the phone. "Dave Clark was with the Duke label for a long time," Bobby remembered. "Over the years, he got with Malaco, and he called me up when I was in between, from MCA. They didn't need another blues singer, they said, so they freed me from my contract. So Dave called me about a month later and said, 'I understand that you don't have a company.' I said, 'Well, not this year.' He said, 'Well, how would you like to come to Malaco?' I said, 'Well, I don't know.' He said, 'I'm with Malaco now.' When he said that, that was it, because Dave and I were real, real close. One of the best promotion men there ever was."[15]

According to Wolf Stephenson, Bobby trusted Clark enough that he immediately signed the contract that Malaco offered him. "He knew he had the clout to go to other places," Stephenson said. "I don't think he was at the point to where he felt like we were doing him a favor, by any means.[16] Bobby just wanted to get a record out, and he knew Dave would sell it, so it all worked out."[17]

Any self-respecting young teenager, black or white, growing up in the South in the 1960s knew about rhythm and blues in general and about Bobby "Blue" Bland in particular, at least knew of him. Tommy Couch and Wolf Stephenson were no exceptions, both claiming that Bobby's *Two Steps from the Blues* was one of the first albums they ever purchased.[18] They had been fans of his since college and felt honored to have signed such a music legend to their growing gaggle of veteran R&B stars.

Their familiarity with Bobby caused them to want to replicate the original soulful Bobby Bland/Joe Scott sounds coming out of Duke when they were young. So, for Bobby's first Malaco recording session on May 7, 1985, they spared no expense in rounding up some of the most talented R&B musicians at their disposal. It was like old-home week for Bobby. From their existing house band were Carson Whitsett on keyboards (former B3 organist for his older brother's Tim Whitsett & the Imperial Show Band, the first integrated band in Mississippi), Memphians James Robertson on drums and Ray Griffin on bass, and Shreveport native Dino Zimmerman on guitar; Muscle Shoals stalwarts guitarist Jimmy Johnson, trombonist Charles Rose, trumpeter Harrison Calloway, and tenor saxophonist Harvey Thompson; former Bar-Keys trumpeter Ben Cauley; superstar session saxophonist and flutist Jim Horn; not to mention veteran backup singers Jewel Bass, Thomisene Anderson, and George Soule; and a nine-piece string section to boot. The little Malaco studio in Jackson was packed. Like the Stax and Muscle Shoals studio bands, this one was interracial and truly gifted in producing the best southern soul sound around.

Larry Addison, a thirty-five-year-old Malaco staff writer and former keyboardist and vocalist for the Jackson R&B group Freedom, wrote "Members Only," the title song for this first Bland/Malaco album. Born in McComb, Mississippi, Addison moved with his family to Milwaukee when he was ten. There he became enthralled with the music of Ramsey Lewis and began studying piano. While in college at the University of Wisconsin, he returned to Mississippi for a family reunion and decided to stay. Moving in with his aunt in Hazlehurst, he received a music scholarship to Jackson State College, where he joined Freedom. But life on the road soon wore him down, and he applied for a job as a session player at Malaco. On his first gospel recording, "they threw me out," Addison remembered. "They said, 'When you learn how to play come back.'" Wolf Stephenson gave him a bunch of Malaco cassettes and told him to learn how to play with them, which he did during the day, while holding down a job at night playing background music at the ritzy University Club in downtown Jackson. Soon he was proficient enough in playing and writing R&B music and ballads that Malaco rehired him.[19]

"I told Larry that every good song needed a title that would immediately form a vision in the listener's mind, something simple, that brought an immediate note of recognition," Wolf Stephenson remembered. "Then you put that title/image right up front in the first line and build your hook around that. Larry said 'hmm, ok' and went off to write some songs. So he was going to his gig that night on the top floor of the Regions Bank and he got on the elevator to go up to the University Club, a private dining restaurant up there, and he sees the words 'Members Only' below the button in the elevator. He came in with the song the next day."[20] It was indeed an auspicious beginning, putting Bobby back on the *Billboard* R&B chart, at number 54, for the first time in almost three years.

Bobby said of the song, "I didn't think too much of it at first, because it was something different. I'd been used to doing different stories like 'I'll Take Care of You,' 'Stormy Monday,' or 'Share Your Love With Me,' something I could grasp right away. 'Members Only' kind of caught me off guard. After a few takes I got the story in my head. I tried thinking about clubs that you belong to, just members only can get in there, kind of upper crust. I have to surround myself with whatever the story is about and then I can tell my story better. That's when I can get into the tune really and be relaxed and not be uptight about how to say certain things because the story already has presented itself. There's no point in just singing to be singing. If you don't know what you're singing about, don't sing it. I don't!"[21]

The next track was a too-faithful rendition of Candi Staton's 1972 cover of Elvis Presley's "In the Ghetto," originally penned by Mac Davis. Then there's a slow blues by Vernon Davis entitled "I've Just Got to Know," featuring Rick Harvey's guitar, which Bobby still sings. Dave Clark even gets in on the act with a mid-tempo rouser, "Straight from the Shoulder," co-written with Tommy Tate, a southern soul singer and songwriter for the Stax, Verve, Atco, and Koko labels, who had now joined the Malaco writing team.[22]

"Can We Make Love Tonight," by Frank Johnson, is a pretty Bobby Bland ballad. George Jackson, another Malaco staff writer and former Goldwax, Hi, and FAME singer/songwriter (including Bob Seger's "Old Time Rock and Roll" and Z.Z. Hill's "Down Home Blues") adds two tunes, the discoesque "Sweet Surrender" and the Bobby ballad "Heart Open Up Again." There are also welcome covers of Geater Davis's 1970 hit "Sweet Woman's Love" and Little Willie John's 1956 "I Need Your Love So Bad."

In addition, re-recorded at this first Malaco session were two of Bobby's old 1960 classics: "Two Steps from the Blues" and "St. James Infirmary." Bobby did not want to record them again, because, he said, his voice had changed over the years, and the songs could not be improved, but Wolf Stephenson talked him into it, reasoning that they might as well make some money from the two classics, instead of it all going to MCA.[23] "Two Steps" is slowed down considerably from the original and suffers from the absence of Teddy Reynolds's overdubbed organ, and Bobby adds a couple of gratuitous squalls to the newer version of "St. James" not heard on the original. But here, a quarter of a century later, Bobby's voice sounds surprisingly the same, maybe a little more worn, but pleasantly so. The effort was "okay and fairly decent," according to Bobby, "but I didn't like it."[24] These two songs were not included on the *Members Only* album, but appeared on the 1987 compilation *First Class Blues*. Altogether a fine beginning at Malaco and a welcome return for Bobby to the more bluesy pre-ABC/MCA days.

Stewart Madison was pleased with the album's sales. "The first record we had on Bobby Bland hasn't gotten the first wisp of airplay in California and we sold 11,000 copies," he said. "Our distributor in Dallas maybe sold 17-18,000 copies and in New York, maybe 9-10,000 without airplay. If we make the right record with Bobby and got airplay in those places, he'll do a quarter of a million."[25]

Members Only was nominated for a 1985 Grammy Award in the Best Traditional Blues Recording category—ultimately won by B.B. King's *My Guitar Sings the Blues*. And on May 7, 2008, *Members Only* was inducted into the Blues Foundation's Blues Hall of Fame.

"Making good recordings is easy," Wolf Stephenson said of his formula, "as long as you have great writers, great musicians, and great vocalists like Bobby."[26] Bobby too was pleased with his new label. "Wolf Stephenson kind of does all the recording," Bobby said. "See, Wolf was a fan of mine when he was in college. So when I went to Malaco, he was very happy to work with me. That made things a lot better."[27]

"It's quiet there . . . very relaxing," Bobby said later. "You can really concentrate. Wolf Stephenson has a good ear for songs, and knows which ones are good for me. It's critical to find those songs."[28]

Clearly Bobby was glad to be out of the large, impersonal, cutthroat climate of the L.A. recording world and back in more comfortable country surroundings. "Malaco has a family atmosphere like Duke used to have," Bobby explained. "The people there know how to explain things to you; they show an interest in you as more than just a singer."[29] In fact, Bobby and Wolf Stephenson became close friends over the years. It was Wolf who replaced Joe Scott as Bobby's main musical mentor and advisor and cordially guided Bobby through the remaining years of his recording career. Paul LaMonica, Oscar Cohen's protégé in New York, oversaw Bobby's performance bookings, and Willie Mae took charge of everything else. As usual, Bobby had somehow arranged it so that all he had to do was be charming and sing—two things that by now he was a master of.

That summer, Malaco purchased the Muscle Shoals Sound Studios in Sheffield, Alabama, for just over a million dollars, as well as its publishing company, thereby ensuring a continuing residual revenue stream from such hits as "Old Time Rock and Roll," "Down Home Blues," "Starting All Over Again," and "Torn Between Two Lovers."[30]

Bobby and the touring band continued on the road with Denise LaSalle on January 4, 1986, at the Municipal Auditorium in Pensacola, Florida, and later with another big package show that toured the country and included Bobby, B.B. King, Albert King, and Stevie Ray Vaughn.

With the success of *Members Only*, Couch and Stephenson scheduled another pair of sessions in early 1986 at the Malaco Studios in Jackson and the newly acquired Muscle Shoals Sound Studios to work on Bobby's second Malaco album. Assembled for the sessions were the same musicians who worked on *Members Only*, but with the addition of guitarists Bernard Jenkins, Larry Byrom, a Huntsville, Alabama, native who had played with Steppenwolf and Tanya Tucker, another former Imperial Show Band member, Jerry Puckett, and Bobby's longtime road band guitarist, Wayne Bennett, who had decided to return to the band one more time;[31] as well as flutist Cybil Chessman; Muscle Shoals Horn Section co-founder, saxophonist Ronnie Eades; and legendary Memphis Horns trumpeter Wayne Jackson. Again there was a full string section, arranged along with the horns by Harrison Calloway, and a backup trio, with George Soule replaced by Catherine Henderson.

The resulting album, *After All*, contains several fine cuts, again all in the Bland/Scott/Duke vein, abandoning any further attempts at widening Bobby's audience and instead trying to tap into Bobby's original, now aging fan base and other lovers of big-band blues and southern soul music.

George Jackson again supplies a couple of satisfying tunes, "Second Hand Heart" and "I Hear You Thinkin'." The Malaco songwriting team of Sam Ray Mosley and Robert A. Johnson contribute the driving accusatory romp "Love Me or Leave Me" and the "Stormy Monday"–like "Sunday Morning Love." There is also a fine rewrite of Dinah Washington's 1948 hit "Walkin' and Talkin' (And Crying My Blues Away)"—this one by the ever-present Dave Clark, Tommy Tate, and Thomisene Anderson, called "Walkin' and Talkin' and Singin' the Blues"—and a credible cover of Jerry Butler's 1964 hit "I Stand Accused." The highlights of the album, however, are a pair of Larry Addison ballads, "Angel" and the album's title cut, which is one of Bobby's best ever. The album rose to number 65 on the Top R&B/Hip-Hop Albums chart.

In July 1986 Bobby led the list of nominees, with eight, at the 12th Annual Jackson [MS] Music Awards, garnering nominations for best recordings and Entertainer of the Year.[32]

Couch and Stephenson gathered approximately the same crew for Bobby's third Malaco album at the Malaco Recording Studio in mid-1987. The horn tracks, with Jim Horn returning on flute and alto and baritone saxophone, were cut separately at the Muscle Shoals Sound Studios. Muscle Shoals Rhythm Section legend Roger Hawkins joined James Robertson on drums. And Charlotte Chenault replaced Thomisene Anderson in the backup vocal trio.

The title of the album was *Blues You Can Use*, and it seems that most of the tracks are best used if you are breaking up with someone, as this seems to be the predominant theme of Cookie Palmer, Jerry Mannery, and Tommy Tate's mid-tempo "Get Your Money Where You Spend Your Time"; veteran Jackson tunesmith Cliff Thomas and Larry Addison's "Restless Feelin's"; Mosley and Johnson's bluesy "I've Got a Problem" and "Let's Part As Friends"; and George Jackson and Earl Forest's blues "For the Last Time." Jackson and Forest (yes, the original Beale Streeters' drummer of more than a quarter century ago in Memphis) also contributed the sweet ballad "Spending My Life with You," which is a welcome respite from all that parting stuff. The highlights of the album are Frank Johnson's (yet another sad breakup ballad) "There's No Easy Way to Say Goodbye" and Nashville R&B veteran Ted Jarrett's welcome up-tempo blues "24 Hours a Day."

Cookie Palmer remembers how the first tune came about. "Get your money where you spend your time" was a catch phrase used by one of Tommy Tate and Palmer's Jackson friends. "A lot of girls would come over to his house when they were going to college at Jackson State," Palmer laughed. "He helped them out and took care of them while they were going to school. A lot of times he'd see some of them about six months after they found their boy friend. They used to come back over there to see him when they done broke up. They asked him, 'James you didn't even call me for my birthday' and he started telling them that 'You need to get your money where you spend your time.' So we just took it from him and started writing it."[33]

With the Couch/Stephenson sound now growing a bit too familiar, the album went to only number 71 on the Top R&B/Hip-Hop Albums chart, but was nominated for a 1987 Grammy Award in the Contemporary Blues Recording category. Unfortunately, so was Robert Cray's *Strong Persuader*, one of the most popular blues albums ever recorded, which of course won the award.

"I've been through this before," Bobby said. "If I don't win, I'll keep trying. I didn't want to be classified as a blues singer. I do a variety: ballads, whatever. I'm mostly a smooth and melancholy kind of singer. The blues doesn't have to be gut bucket. We wanted to get the mellow side."[34] Perhaps serving as a consolation prize, Bobby's 1961 *Two Steps from the Blues* album was inducted in 1987 into the Blues Foundation's Hall of Fame in the category Classic of Blues Recordings—Albums.

Also in 1987, for Bobby's first release on compact disc, Malaco took the two 1960 classics rerecorded at the first Malaco session, "Two Steps From the Blues" and "St. James Infirmary" and added 14 other Malaco recordings to produce Bobby's first Malaco compilation album, entitled *First Class Blues*.

Not to be left out of Bobby's newfound success at Malaco, MCA took ten of the songs from the Bobby Bland/B.B. King live albums recorded in 1974 and 1976 and repackaged them in an album entitled *I Like to Live the Love*.

At about this time, keyboardist Lucky Peterson left Bobby's touring band to pursue a solo career in Dallas, Texas.[35] And, as Bobby's wife Willie Mae began to take an even more active role in managing Bobby's professional life, Melvin Jackson—after thirty loyal years—left the band to play saxophone (not trumpet) in B.B. King's band. "Well, I've known Mr. King for years—1,000 years, you know," Jackson told an interviewer.

> *I went and helped a friend of mine with a CD in L.A., named Buddy Ace. I helped produce his first album. This was around '86. I went to see B.B. He was in L.A. and I went to see him and the sax player was quitting and that's the way it happened. I was available so I told him I need that job, so he gave it to me. I said, "I've got to have this gig." I said, "It belongs to me," and he gave it to me.*
>
> *When I was leading Bobby's band, one of the tenor players wanted a tenor and I bought a tenor for him and when I bought it he didn't want it. So I said I'll just fool around with it and I'll teach myself something on it, but I wasn't really intending to play it. So I fooled around and I practiced a little bit and played it and the guys laughed at me. So when they did that I said, "Well, fuck it." I learned how to play the damn thing. By me being the bandleader, I could have on the job training. So I played trumpet and sax, yeah.*
>
> *No, B.B. didn't want me to play the trumpet because it might cause some confusion with the other trumpet player because I was pretty good. Of course, he asked me to play the saxophone. I knew the style of music because we had worked together off and on over this time. Like when he and Bobby did it together for the first time. I was the leader of Bobby's band at that time, too.*

Jackson continues to travel and play with King and is currently working on a CD of his own.[36]

Bobby had to hustle to replace Peterson and Jackson and regroup the band before his European tour scheduled for May 1988.

Bobby asked keyboardist Archie Turner, who toured with the band briefly in 1985, to return. Turner was born on January 25, 1946, in Detroit, Michigan. At the age of four he moved with his mother to Memphis where she met and later married Willie Mitchell, famed trumpeter, bandleader, and Hi Records head. While still in high school, Turner started a group called the Impalas with Leroy Hodges on bass, Teeny Hodges on guitar, Tommy Lee Williams on tenor sax, and his brother Horace on drums, which would later become the basis of the original house band that played on the Hi recordings of Al Green, Ann Peebles, Syl Johnson, and Otis Clay. Most recently, Turner had toured with Little Milton in 1986, and with Albert King until Bobby lured him away.

Bobby also called on another former band member to replace Melvin Jackson. Joseph Hardin was born on February 2, 1947, on a farm near Baton Rouge, Louisiana. He started playing trumpet at the age of twelve, listening to the bands of Bobby Bland, James Brown, Jerry Butler, Clifford Brown, and John Coltrane. From 1966 to 1968 he played in Bobby Powell's jazz band. From 1968 to 1970 he played in the 50th Army Band in Vietnam under the leadership of Ernie Hackett, the son of famous jazz trumpeter Bobby Hackett. After his tour of duty in Vietnam, Joe joined Bobby's touring band on September 9, 1972. He stayed with the band until 1984, when he joined Lee Charles Mitchell's band that did session work and played mostly in the Dallas, Texas, area. From 1985 until Bobby rehired him, he played in Johnnie Taylor's band. Joe is still with Bobby's band, still playing lead trumpet, now serving as its leader, and enthusiastically providing Bobby's introduction at every Bobby Bland performance.

In 1984 Bobby had lured Charles Crawford out of his almost twenty-year retirement from the music business to rejoin the band on baritone saxophone. Al Thomas, the only remaining member of the Ernie Fields band that Bobby had hired in 1969, was still playing trombone and arranging for the band. When Joe Hardin rejoined the band he brought along his Texas bandleader, Lee Charles Mitchell, to play alto and tenor saxophone. Born on January 24, 1952, in Birmingham, Alabama, Mitchell started out playing trombone, but switched to saxophone when he joined Laurence Webb's band. He later moved to Dallas, where he led his own band and worked as a session musician, recording behind Lynn Day, Sonny Buck, R. L. Griffin, and others. Ira Bassett, who was born on June 23, 1953, in Navasota, Texas, played second trumpet.

Reginald Richards, born on March 22, 1965, in Dallas, Texas, the son of a high school band director, was on bass. He remembered: "I started professionally when I was about 17. The first break, in terms of touring or working with a recording artist, would be January of '88. I received a call that Bobby Bland was going to need a bass player. I spent my first 13 years traveling with him. I wasn't familiar with all of his work, but I was familiar with some of it. I liked blues just as much as I liked funk and R&B. I knew enough to know that was a legitimate gig and at the time I had never toured. I was 22, so it was a serious crash course on the chitlin circuit. To spend that amount of time was a serious experience for me. New Year's Eve of '01 was my last date with him." Six months later, Richards received a call from James Bolden, B.B. King's band-leader, and he was off again with the King orchestra, with which he continues to tour worldwide to this day.[37]

And, finally, filling out the rhythm section were George Weaver on drums, and Wayne Bennett, who had been touring and recording with the Bobby Bland band off and on almost from the beginning in 1957, and now serving in his current stint as lead guitarist since 1986.

This band and Bobby played a week at Meridien in Paris to appreciative audiences every night.[38] Bobby was introduced to the French audience many years before when Disques Vogue licensed his and other Duke recordings for distribution throughout the country. Bobby's popularity even stretched to Japan, where Victor Records released *Bobby Bland—The Best of on Malaco*, a compilation of sixteen of Bobby's recent recordings.

When they returned to the States, Bobby was beckoned back into the recording studios—Malaco, Muscle Shoals, and Mack Emerman's Criteria Studios in Miami—with everything being remixed in Muscle Shoals. By this time recording technology had become so sophisticated that various parts of a song—for example, the rhythm section, the horn section, the string section, the backup vocals, and Bobby's vocals—could at one extreme, be recorded independently of one another and then remixed later to create the final product; or, at the other extreme, all could be recorded together in a single recording session with everyone playing at once and then remixed in various combinations to provide the emphasis where the producer thought it was needed; or, as was usually the case, somewhere in between.

"In Bobby's case, the usual method was to have Bobby record in the studio with the rhythm and horn sections, so there could be some interaction and collaboration," Wolf Stephenson, Malaco's chief engineer said. "Bobby would be cued by the writer or someone and the band would play with him. Usually we'd get it in two or three takes. Then we would lay the string and backup vocal tracks later and mix them with Bobby and the band's tracks."[39]

"Right off the bat there was a technical stumbling block that Bobby had never gotten used to," Stephenson continued. "That was recording with headphones. It's a difficult thing do if you've never tried it, because you don't recognize your own voice." Even though Steve Barri claimed that Bland had listened for cues and lyrics from the headphones back in the 1970s, apparently Bobby never really listened to himself. "He carries [his headphones] all the time now and he loves the way it sounds," Stephenson said. "He's gotten used to it and we just have a big time when we're recording. He's easy to work with, but he doesn't work with a whole lot of people. He's very particular about who he works with, and he's assertive, but not bullying, when you're trying to do something that just won't fit his vocal style."[40]

At any rate, maybe because of the change in surroundings at Criteria Studios, or because of the addition of the entire Muscle Shoals Rhythm section of David Hood (bass), Roger Hawkins (drums), and Mickey Buckins (percussion), or just because there was a lot of good new material, the tracks recorded for this *Midnight Run* album were the best since *Members Only*. The sound is funkier, less perfect, livelier than the usual Couch/Stephenson production.

Three of the album's songs, in fact, remain mainstays in Bobby's live performances: "You've Got to Hurt Before You Heal," a beautiful, sad Larry Addison ballad; "Take Off Your Shoes," another Bobby-been-burnt blues by backup singer Frederick Knight and Bettye Crutcher, with the snide refrain "If you're gonna' walk on my love, woman, the least you could do is take off your shoes"; and Bobby's fine rendition of Bill Withers's 1971 hit "Ain't No Sunshine When She's Gone," which Bobby leads as a loopy sing-along in his stage show, prompting the audience to do the "I know, I know, I know . . ." part over and over again.

"You've Got to Hurt Before You Heal" was written soon after Larry Addison's grandmother and favorite uncle had died. "I was looking at TV and *M*A*S*H* was on," Addison remembered. "They had brought somebody in that had been wounded and I guess it was meant in a joking manner but the dude said, 'Well, you know you've got to hurt before you heal.' I took that and something clicked. I thought about the grief I was going through. When you lose the ones you love, your heart goes through changes. You're gonna cry. I remembered the funeral. I didn't want folks to think it was a funeral song so I made it more of a love ballad."[41]

Wolf Stephenson remembers that Knight and Crutcher had first offered "Take Off Your Shoes" to B.B. King, who recorded it on his *King of Blues* album. "I went to the record store to check it out when it was released," Stephenson said, "and to my surprise 'Take Off Your Shoes' was not on the cassette of the album. It was only on the CD [in a re-mixed mix-up at that], but hardly anyone was buying CDs in 1989, so it was basically an entirely new song when we recorded it with Bobby later that year."[42]

The title song of *Midnight Run* was written by Tommy Tate and Cookie Palmer and took on a reggae sound. "Tommy Tate had to get me into that," Bobby admitted, "because it was a little different. It was good but it had quite a few changes in there and I'm not used to singing all them different changes. It was difficult for me to remember all the stuff after I did it. [The reggae groove] was for a person that doesn't sing straight like I do. Tommy Tate was good for doing that. That was his bag, he could really handle that. I did the best I could but not the best job that could have been done with the tune."[43]

In addition are another smooth Mosley/Johnson blues, "I'm Not Ashamed to Sing the Blues," and a spirited version of Mel and Tim's 1972 Stax hit written by Phillip Mitchell, "Starting All Over Again." "It really has a classic feel to it," Bobby said of the album when it was released the next year. "I hope it sells; there are some good young writers on it from down in Jackson, Mississippi. . . . After three or four years with Malaco things are jelling."[44] Indeed, *Midnight Run* went to number 26 on the R&B/Hip-Hop Albums chart and stayed on the chart for more than a year, resulting in a special achievement award from *Billboard* magazine.

By February 5, 1989, Bobby and his touring band played the Blue Note in New York City on August 18–21, 1988, prompting this opening night review by Jon Pareles in the *New York Times:* "A performance by Bobby (Blue) Bland, the great rhythm-and-blues singer . . . can be dizzying in its ironies. His songs hold the essence of desolation as he sketches misfortunes and betrayals in a voice that sounds as if it's been worn nearly threadbare through long suffering. . . . His voice is liquid and controlled, with a deep melancholy undertone, and his approach has been imitated by generations of soul singers, most recently Robert Cray. . . . when he's lingering over a line about heartache or loneliness, it's easy to believe that unimaginable pain lies just below the surface. . . . He's backed by a band whose sloppy horn section often drowns out the last lines of blues verses, and which seems to revel in corny arrangements. Yet that band also includes Wayne Bennett, the guitarist for some of Mr. Bland's classic 1950's recordings, who plays sustained blues lines and jazzy block chords with magnificent delicacy and suspense. The catharsis and corniness seem inseparable, as if shifting the balance could plunge both Mr. Bland and his audience into irrevocable despair."[45]

By February 5, 1989, Bobby and the band were in New Orleans for Mardi Gras, where they played the Benz Lounge on Louisiana Avenue and again brought down the house. On July 6 the "Malaco Records, Europe '89" entourage left Jackson for London, Paris, and Montreux, Switzerland. Joining Bobby and his band—without Ira Bassett, and with Stewart Melis replacing Lee Charles Mitchell and Charles Crawford on saxophone—were Malaco labelmates Denise LaSalle, Johnnie Taylor, and Mosley & Johnson, who were to be backed by the Muscle Shoals Horns and the Malaco Rhythm Section. It harkened back to the big Stax/Volt European tour of 1967. Malaco also brought along backup singers Thomisene Anderson and Jewel Bass, a host of roadies, and Bobby's tour manager Maurice DeLoach.

The traveling show arrived at Gatwick Airport in London, to be greeted by a press reception, and later a bus ride to central London. They had recovered enough from the long trip to open the tour on July 8 at the Hammersmith Odeon Theatre in London. Barney Hoskyns wrote this review for the [London] *Times*:

When Bobby Bland finally took the stage after a twenty-minute break, he was backed not by the Malaco band and the Muscle Shoals Horns but by his own eight-piece "orchestra," featuring none other than Wayne Bennett, his legendary guitarist from the Duke days. His slightly glazed, tottering appearance belied the innate majesty of his presence, and within a few numbers—a medley of "That's The Way Love Is"/"Ain't Nothin' You Can Do" and his first hit "Further Up The Road" [sic]—the audience was totally rapt. As with Sinatra, the voice is still there, if anything more richly resonant than ever. If he holds himself back for the occasional trademark squall, chewing diffidently through his words and flinching away from the mike, when he lets that gorgeous baritone sail, its beauty fair chills you to the bone. . . . At several points in the set he fixed his attention on one couple in the front row, gently serenading them with a smile that could have charmed the pants off a Mother Superior. It was all he needed to do: the great cracked authority of the voice said everything else. When he wound up the show with those exemplary gospel-blues classics "I'll Take Care Of You" and "Stormy Monday," the band barely whispering behind him, it was clear that thirty seven odd years have really taken no toll at all. For this is all Bobby "Blue" Bland does, is sing.[46]

They moved on to Paris on July 10, where they found their hotel rooms to be so cramped that part of the contingent moved over to the more spacious Warwick, not far from the historic, un-air-conditioned Olympia Theater, where that night they again had the standing-room-only audience standing on their seats by the time a sweat-drenched Johnnie Taylor closed the show. Afterward, the exhausted performers relaxed at Leroy Haynes's soul food restaurant in the 9th arrondissement. Chez Haynes was opened by an African American expatriate in 1949 and was continued by his wife Maria after his death in 1986. Not only was Louisiana-born Leroy a good soul food cook, but he also acted in several movies, wrestled professionally, and held a sociology degree from Atlanta University. A big, jocular man who welcomed film, jazz, and blues stars from around the world, as well as poor students and fellow expatriates, with a big smile, a bottomless glass of Beaujolais, and homestyle American meals, he was the true host of African Americana in Paris for almost forty years. So when Bobby and the Malaco crew landed there in the early morning hours of July 11, Maria was on hand to welcome them "home."

Next, after a day off for sightseeing or sleeping, the assemblage flew to Geneva and on by bus to Montreux, where they performed the following night, July 13, at the Casino de Festivals for what was billed as "A Night of Formidable Rhythm & Blues." On hand to capture the event on tape was Mountain Studios, which resulted in Bobby's sixth album for Malaco, the two-disc *Blues from the Montreux Jazz Festival—Bobby "Blue" Bland, Denise Lasalle, Johnnie Taylor, and Mosley & Johnson,* when it was released in 1991. Malaco selected just seven of Bobby's biggest hits for the album, but not in the order that he sang them, so his side seems a bit disjointed. Yet Bobby and the band do sound good and the listener gets a sense of what a Bobby Bland show was like at this time, not to mention how hot the rest of the Malaco crew could warm to once out of the structured confines of the Jackson and Muscle Shoals studios.

By the fall Bobby and the band were back in the States doing a West Coast swing, appearing with Theodis Ealey on September 8 in McCormack Hall at the Solano County Fairgrounds in Vallejo, California.

Meanwhile, back in Memphis, at 10:00 a.m. on November 3, 1989, the Internal Revenue Service auctioned off a 1965 Silver Eagle bus and a small television set that had been garnished from Bobby Bland to help pay Bobby's $294,464.78 federal tax bill. "That is the amount he owes for back taxes, personal income taxes, for six years," stated Don Boone, assistant public relations officer for the Nashville IRS district. Despite trusted accountants and lawyers, according to the IRS, Bobby had shorted tax payments for the years 1976, 1978, 1980, 1982, 1983, and 1984. "What we're trying to do is get the money back from him or his estate," Boone said. "The government filed a lien against him on May 31, 1988, in Shelby County."

According to newspaper reports, the bus looked as road weary as Bobby felt when he received the news. The tires were sagging, the batteries corroded, and the fake leopard-skin interior was ragged. "It's in dire need of renovation," said Kent Harwood, manager of Dick Diggons Body Works, where the bus was stored. The IRS did not disclose the amount the bus and TV sold for, but Boone said it was likely that the IRS would seek additional assets that it could attach to satisfy the tax bill.[47]

So, to add to the indignities of life on the road and the tiresomeness of being constantly in the spotlight, the ever-present IRS had to rear its ugly head again. Like so many other performers before him—B.B. King, Marvin Gaye, Jerry Lee Lewis, and Willie Nelson, to name a few of the most famous—Bobby had to face the grim, unforgiving hand of the U.S. tax man.

All too bruised by his own mistakes, Bobby later offered this worldly advice to Memphis promoter Julius Lewis: "Mr. Bland cautioned me not to ruin my taxes, avoid vices like drugs and alcohol, and never chase a lot of women."[48]

It remains confidential what served as replacement transportation after "Big Blue" was auctioned off or what kind of deal Bobby worked out with the IRS, but rest assured that the lawyers were well paid and touring continued uninterrupted, because, by whatever means, a few days later, on November 22,

Bobby and the band were in Chicago headlining a show with Millie Jackson and Bobby Rush at the New Regal Theater.[49]

Along with Bobby's bus, this was about the time when promoter extraordinaire Dave Clark finally came off the road, at age eighty. Clark for years had been telling radio station program directors in his distinctive squeaky voice that this current record was his last record promotion before he retired or died. For a while Malaco had hired a driver to haul Clark around to make these seemingly endless "last record" appeals, but by the end of 1989 it had become too much. For the next few years, Dave Clark, Bobby's longtime friend, columnist, songwriter, and venerated record promoter, was driven to the Malaco offices to see friends, hold court, and nod off, until his death on July 22, 1995.[50]

Despite being inducted into the Rock and Roll Hall of Fame on January 15, 1992, at the age of 61, Bobby Bland continued to sing the blues at more than 300 shows each year, like this one ca. 1991. Copyright Ebet Roberts/Cache Agency.

14

Walkin' & Talkin' & Singin' the Blues

1991–1992

Bobby's seventh album for Malaco, *Portrait of the Blues*, was recorded in early 1991 at the Muscles Shoals and Malaco Studios, and took the Malaco sound to its ultimate culmination. Here were all the great Muscle Shoals and Jackson rhythm section musicians—James Robertson and Roger Hawkins on drums; Clayton Ivey and Steve Nathan on keyboards; Duncan Cameron, Jimmy Johnson, Dino Zimmerman, and Jack Pearson on guitar; David Hood and Ray Griffin on bass; and Mickey Buckins on percussion. The horn tracks were arranged as usual by Harrison Calloway and recorded at the Muscle Shoals Sound Studios with Calloway and Mike Haynes on trumpet, Harvey Thompson on tenor saxophone, and Jim Horn on baritone, bass, and alto saxophone and flute. The full string section tracks were arranged by Mike Lewis and recorded at the Criteria Studios in Miami, Florida. The background vocal tracks, sung by Thomisene Anderson, Jewel Bass, and Dorothy "Misty Blue" Moore, were recorded in Jackson at the Malaco Studios. And Wolf Stephenson and Steve Melton remixed the entire ten song selection, written by Malaco house writers, back at the Muscle Shoals Sound Studios control board.

This aggregation represented pretty much the entire Malaco creative forces and the results, while certainly satisfying, are predictably the same as previous Bobby Bland Malaco productions: a big, full soul sound, but after six albums, almost too much of a good thing. "We do get a certain amount of criticism from people for everything sounding alike," Tommy Couch admitted. "Then we'll say we're gonna do something entirely different and release a record from somewhere and it will be the biggest flop of an eon. Nothing happens. We still have a lot of opportunities to do other things but we decline because we can really only do so many things well. You need to concentrate your abilities in one direction and that's what we do."[1]

There are no surprises on *Portrait of the Blues*. There is a fine country-flavored "Hurtin' Love" by George Jackson and Butch McGhee. Tommy Tate and Richard Kuebler add a pretty pair of ballads: the frequently covered "I Can Take You to Heaven Tonight" and the sad "When Hearts Grow Cold." John Ward and Tommy Polk provide a powerful Bobby workout with "The Last One to Know," and Ward and Sidney Bailey offering a catchy blues that Bobby still sings, "She's Puttin' Something in My Food."

The album went to number 50 on the Top R&B/Hip-Hop Albums chart with little fanfare.

Meanwhile, a record label little-known in the United States, the London-based Ace Records (not to be confused with the defunct Jackson, Mississippi–based 1950s label of the same name), released a CD, compiled by Ray Topping, of twenty-five of Bobby's earliest Duke hits, entitled *Bobby "Blue" Bland: The "3B" Blues Boy/The Blues Years: 1952–1959*. The British label (originally called Chiswick) was founded as a reissue house in 1975 by Ted Carroll and Roger Armstrong, the latter of whom compiled the follow-up twenty-six-song CD collection *Bobby Bland: The Voice/Duke Recordings 1959–69*.

Ace has become one of the largest and most important reissuers of blues and R&B records dating from the 1940s. In addition to licensing the rights from MCA for these two welcome Bobby Bland collections, over the years Ace has also acquired the rights to many other labels, including Fantasy, Stax, Specialty, Vanguard, and Modern,[2] where four of Bobby's earliest recordings for the Bihari Brothers in 1951 and 1952 are included on the 2000 Ace compilation *The Original Memphis Blues Brothers*, which also includes early recordings by Little Junior Parker, Earl Forest, Johnny Ace, B.B. King, Ike Turner, and Rosco Gordon.

Performers are eligible to be admitted to the Rock and Roll Hall of Fame twenty-five years after the release of their first recording, putting Bobby easily, with these early Modern cuts and the one Chess cut that predates them, in the first group of inductees in 1985. But he had to wait until the seventh group of inductees which was announced on November 21, 1991.

Bobby, of course, was on tour when he received the good news. Reached by telephone in Union City, New Jersey, where he was preparing for a two-night gig at Sweetwater's supper club on Manhattan's Upper West Side, Bobby told a *New York Times* reporter that he was honored to be included among such influential artists as Louis Armstrong, Ray Charles, and Little Richard. "I sure think that I've been in the business long enough to be chosen," he said. "I just wonder why they waited so long."

About his latest album *Portrait of the Blues*, Bobby said, "You kind of go along with the times, and they bring the music up to date. I don't use a whole lot of different synthesizers, that type of thing. My music is basically still the same."

At this point in his career, Bobby had slowed down from performing almost every night to about forty weeks a year, now joined during the summer by his fifteen-year-old son Roderick on drums.[3] "I have to keep the ham hocks on the table," Bobby said. "Everybody has to work; at least I do. You do a lot of work for a long period of years, but you're still playing the chitlin' circuit. I haven't gotten rich, is what I'm trying to say. But you have to keep working at whatever you believe in. Eventually it pays off, like going into the Hall of Fame."[4]

The actual induction ceremonies took place a couple of months later on January 15, 1992, at New York City's Waldorf-Astoria Hotel. This was well before the completion of the 150,000-square-foot glass tent and tower Hall of Fame building designed by I. M. Pei, which opened in Cleveland on September 2, 1995.

The other performer inductees that year, chosen by more than 500 music industry figures, were fellow Memphians Booker T. and the MGs, Johnny Cash, the Jimi Hendrix Experience, the Isley Brothers, Sam & Dave, and the Yardbirds, including Jeff Beck, Jimmy Page, and Eric Clapton (Clapton had covered Bobby's "Farther Up the Road" on his album *E.C. Was Here* in 1975). Nonperformer inductees were guitar innovator Leo Fender, songwriter Doc Pomus, and Bill Graham, who had given Bobby an early chance to cross over by booking him into Graham's Fillmore East back in 1969. Early influencers inducted were Elmore James and Professor Longhair.

The festive evening consisted of many speeches by famous presenters: Neil Young inducted Hendrix, U2's The Edge presented the award to the Yardbirds, Billy Joel did Sam & Dave, Little Richard stridently saluted the Isley Brothers, Robbie Robertson inducted James, Phil Spector presented Doc Pomus, Lyle Lovett did Cash, and, of course, the 1987 inductee B.B. King, Bobby's oldest musical friend, made the presentation speech for Bobby. "It's a thrill to be honored, just a pleasure," Bobby said. Referring to his Memphis days with B.B., Bobby joked, "There really wasn't much to do then."[5]

In part, Bobby's induction statement reads: "One of the premier rhythm & blues vocalists. . . . His hallmark was his supple, confidential soul-blues delivery. As a singer, Bland projected a grainy, down-to-earth quality, punctuated with guttural growls and snorts that would come to be known as the 'chicken-bone sound.' Yet his voice was simultaneously smooth as velvet, allowing Bland to bring audiences under his hypnotic spell as he walked a fine line between passionate expression and exquisite self-control. . . . To this day, Bland remains a fixture on the concert circuit, a hard-working professional who purveys a definitive union of Southern blues and soul."[6] Bobby's 1962 hit "Turn On Your Love Light" has also been named as one of the "500 Songs That Shaped Rock and Roll" by the Rock and Roll Hall of Fame.

The annual jam session after the ceremonies did not start until after midnight. Jeff Beck and Jimmy Page performed with Paul Shaffer's (*The Late Show with David Letterman*) band, augmented by keyboard player and vocalist Edgar Winter. Bobby had performed the night before and was scheduled again the next night, and begged off joining the band, saying his voice was "wore out. Paul Shaffer really tried to talk me into singing 'Turn On Your Love Light' that night, but I wasn't feeling well and we hadn't rehearsed. I just didn't feel comfortable, so I passed."[7]

A few days later, on January 24, 1992, Bobby Bland's birth father, Isaac J. Brooks, died quietly at the age of eighty, in the Hillhaven Health Care Center in Germantown, Tennessee, not far from Bobby's then current home. His death certificate listed him as a retired supermarket owner/manager and there is evidence to suggest that he also may have pastored the Phillips Christian Methodist Episcopal Church, an African American church located on Church Street in Huntsville, Alabama, from 1942 to 1951.[8] Bobby seldom spoke about his real father. He told Wolf Stephenson in 1998 that he only met his father twice, first when Bobby was eight years old, and later when he was twenty-four and in the military.[9] There is little doubt, however, that his absence brought Bobby and his mother unusually close during Bobby's early years and that Bobby's life-long dependence on a long line of strong parental figures somehow harkened back to this enduring, overshadowing void.

Of his father's death Bobby made no public mention; of his own induction to the Rock and Roll Hall of Fame, he admitted, "It's kind of surprising. I figured I'd get into the Rhythm & Blues Hall of Fame, but I'll take whatever I can get."[10] So it was not much of a surprise when later that year Bobby was named a Pioneer Award Honoree by the Rhythm & Blues Foundation, along with his old friend Rufus Thomas and nine others.

Encouraged by the sales of the two Ace compilations of Bobby's earliest hits, particularly in Europe, MCA issued the first of its three-set compendium of all of Bobby's Duke recordings. The 2-CD *I Pity the Fool/The Duke Recordings, Vol. 1* includes the first forty-four songs recorded by Bobby from 1952 through 1960 for Duke, showcasing Bobby's earliest hits as well as some previously unreleased material. Arranged in chronological order, it presents a great way to hear Bobby's vocal style mature and evolve, along with Joe Scott's progressively more sophisticated arrangements, during these early formative years of his career.

A little outfit called Home Cooking Records also got in on the act and in 1992 released a quirky throwaway album called *We Love You Bobby: A Tribute to Bobby Bland* that includes some covers of Bobby's songs by unknown artists like The Soul Masters and Big Roger Collins, as well as cuts by T-Bone Walker ("Farther On Up the Road") and Buddy Ace and Fenton Robinson of songs Bobby never recorded. Producer Roy C. Ames, a former Duke Records employee and chronicler, apparently had something in mind with this weird curiosity, but it's impossible to tell what, aside from a desire to cash in on Bobby's recent induction into the Rock and Roll Hall of Fame.

Soon after their European tour in 1989, Wayne Bennett came off the road for the last time, as heart problems became increasingly worrisome. He continued to work with New Orleans singer Johnny Adams, Texas guitarist Zuzu Bollin, and bluesman "Mighty" Sam McClain, with whom he had played on a live album recorded in Japan in the spring of 1988. Bennett continued to do session work in New Orleans with Champion Jack Dupree in 1990 and behind James Cotton and Jimmy McCracklin until just before he died at the age of fifty-eight of congestive heart failure on November 28, 1992,[11] a few days before he was scheduled to receive a heart transplant in Nashville. He was survived by his wife, Theresa, and twelve children.[12]

"I'm fortunate to have had two guitarists mainly, Wayne Bennett and Mel Brown," Bobby said, "who both have that mellow, hollow kind of sound and basically had somewhat the same idol. Which is T-Bone Walker. See, if they hear a lyric, they say, 'Well, Blue probably phrase it this way,' and they know how to stay out of my way and that's the most important part.[13] Wayne, I would say, plays guitar like a vocalist sings. Every note, every string bent means something. He gets something out of every note. Great feeling. Just gifted, I guess. Everything is right. He just plays the way a guitar player should play."[14]

By this time, for better or for worse, Bobby was again firmly ensconced with another primarily blues label, and, as such, was primarily labeled as a blues singer. Regardless of what Bobby actually sang—jazz, ballads, country, standards—the label would stick, be accepted, and ultimately bragged upon, as, for example, in Bobby's current stage introduction as "the world's greatest blues singer."

What this blues *is* exactly has been addressed in so many words and at so much length that it is well nigh impossible to believe anything really new about the subject can be summoned. It has been studied from its historical roots to its technical components to its ethereal aura, as in this description by eminent ethnomusicologist Dr. Willis James: "The blues in many respects is akin to religious song in its devoutness. It is one of the most devout musics to ever exist . . . one of the most believable musical utterances it is possible to find . . . based upon the cry, the genesis of song, the blues and the cry are almost one . . . all Negro music you listen to will have this feeling of the cry."[15]

What exactly Bobby Bland brought to the genre can also be argued about. He took his childhood love and his genuine feel for gospel music and country western music to a blues format that Louis Jordan, T-Bone Walker, and most directly Bill Harvey and Joe Scott urbanized with a big band jazz counterpoint.

In Bobby's sound, the listener finds a blues form and content, but not a traditional guitar and vocal country blues; a strong, single-note electric guitar lead, but not a Chicago style electric blues ensemble; a country twang and tears-in-your-beer lyric line, but not a country and western Nashville bar band; a gospel-inflected call and response delivery, but not a gospel solo, quartet, or choir production; a brassy jazz approach, but not a big-band jazz sound; a soulful, heartfelt delivery, but not a real down-on-your-knees soul singer rant. Something different, but not entirely different: the blues, but not just the blues.

In trying to explain all these blues labels, Bobby said: "I believe this is the basic thing that the colored man has, is spiritual and blues, which are two more or less combined. You might say 'baby' in the blues and then just turn with the same verse and say 'Lord.' You dig? There's just a different way of introducing or getting your point over. And I think this is our basic thing, spiritual and blues, that the colored man can say that he really own because nobody can do it but him. We've had people to try, and I must say that we had some very beautiful impressions of the blues. But I think that, speaking for B.B. King, Lowell Fulson, T-Bone Walker, Wynonie Harris, Jimmy Witherspoon, Big Joe Turner—well, we'll go back to Blind Lemon. Yeah, and Bessie Smith—this is where the blues really originated from."[16]

Asked about the blues as "delta music" and rhythm & blues as "city music," Bobby responded: "What they're trying to say is music like, I wasn't going to mention it, but, what they mean is Blues like you hear from Muddy Waters or John Lee Hooker or that type with the harmonica, you know, and so this is a little more modern. You know they got the Beale St. Blues, they got the Delta Blues, they got the Texas Blues. So you just put a label on it and it's the New Orleans Blues. It's all Blues."[17]

On the difference between blues and soul, Bobby commented: "Blues and soul . . . I don't see how you can define them. . . . I think they are just one and the same. They are about facing the facts and seeing that things are as they are. . . . if there is something that you can do about it, then you better try, and if it doesn't work out then you better just chalk it up to experience if it's not in your favor. That's what it's all about. I find myself weighin' things, because there's always two sides to everything, two different approaches or whatever. It's like havin' a good woman. You got to cherish her, you got to try and see things how she sees them, and feel what she feels. . . . I call that facin' facts.[18] I just sing what I feel. It's about life. You get hurt, you get happy. I don't know how to label that."[19]

Whatever the label, it is a sound that is heard today on the records from only a handful of independent labels, most notably Malaco and Memphis-based Ecko Records, and primarily in the Southeast and some larger black urban areas. The performers, for the most part, are younger than Bobby but beyond normal retirement age, artists like Marvin Sease, Willie Clayton, Bobby Rush, Mel Waiters, Shirley Brown, Denise LaSalle, Latimore, J. Blackfoot, and Barbara Carr, who have been tromping the chitlin circuit trail for years. There is a younger group of performers as well who surprisingly are breaking into the ever-declining southern soul/blues business—young entertainers like Sir Charles Jones, T. K. Soul, Floyd Taylor, Jeff Floyd, Sheba Potts-Wright, and O.B. Buchana.

"Blues is not lost to young players," according to Rodd Bland, "and we don't think of it anymore in terms of being 'slavery time' music. In fact, a young rapper named JayZ has sampled one of my father's tunes, 'Ain't No Love in the Heart of the City,' and kept his voice intact and recognizable within the body of the song. Yes, blues is moving back into the hands of young black artists and musicians like Ronnie Baker Brooks [son of Lonnie Brooks], Shemekia Copeland [daughter of Johnny Copeland], and Etta James' sons are proof positive that the real down home blues is being owned by the next generation. As young performers, we can not only play it technically, but we play it with the right blues feeling. The down home blues feels like it belongs to us, too. We're taking an active part in its vital expression."[20]

This phenomenon is relatively recent, however, and certainly not widespread. As rural black southerners migrated to the North during and after World War II, and as the civil rights movement spread and equal rights legislation finally prevailed, African Americans in large numbers slowly but steadily began to move into the middle and upper classes for the first time in American history. Since the blues was initially adopted by lower-class black Americans, this emerging African American middle class began to disassociate itself with anything it deemed lower class, including the blues, viewing it as "country" or "slave music" or just "too ethnic." Ed Cook at Chicago's WVON African American talk radio station gave his take on the diminishing interest of blacks in the blues: "Personally, I blame it on the so-called middle-class Negro who wanted to identify with white society so much that he thought that there was something to be ashamed of about the blues."[21]

Bobby put it this way: "Well it [blues] has had a pick-me-up. But it still hasn't had the world wide promotion that it should get because a lot of people pretend that they don't like certain things like blues. They play it behind closed doors, when they're at home. Blues has been kind of a downer for a lot of people. It's not the kind of thing that people want to identify with because it's kind of a sad story. Everybody has the blues but they don't want to admit that."[22]

Despite the enthusiasm for the blues by Bobby's son and some other young African Americans, Bobby concedes that the "blues is a downer to younger black people, mainly because our history carries a lot of guilt and disappoint-ment. Blues basically was done by being sad, being out in the country and not allowed to do certain things. So young black people, some of them don't want to look back on that era. They want to look ahead the way that Dr. King has brought them up to now. There's no looking back, we got to go forward. But the blues will always be here."[23]

Certainly for Bobby's fans who have remained loyal through the years—overwhelmingly African American and predominantly over fifty now, and mostly in the Southeast and the inner cities of the industrial North. As this generation grows older, it is difficult to predict what will become of this brand of blues. The obvious answer is that it will die along with its fans, but history suggests otherwise; as in the past, the sound is likely to evolve and mutate with the musical tastes of the time. There's no doubt that this younger genera-tion of blues artists have, with mixed results, added synthesizers, hip-hop, and modern rock and jazz elements to their acts. Small chitlin circuit clubs and holiday blues festivals featuring the remaining soul/blues performers continue to be well-attended by older black folk and their record sales sufficient enough to sustain the handful of labels still recording them. Of course, Bobby Bland is still out there with them—mixing mostly chitlin circuit dates with posher white jazz/blues venues and festivals of all kinds of blues for audiences of all shades of colors—now the elder statesman of the genre that he has presided over for more than half a century.

Regardless of the audience, the message of Bobby Bland and the blues re-mains at the heart of its lingering appeal. This common, cathartic recognition of feelings of hurt, heartbreak, and frustration, within a blues phrase, somehow helps us deal with these maladies in a way that affects some sort of closure. "The blues has feeling and meaning to it," Bobby explains. "The lyrics are living. They're experiences that you sing about and people respond because they've had the same experiences. If a song doesn't have anything to say, if it doesn't tell a story, I don't mess with it."[24]

"A song's got to have a story," Bobby reiterates. "Everybody just sitting down listening to a beat isn't enough, and I'm not knocking rock and roll, but you can just push that so long. So I think blues and spirituals are the only true messages people will relate to. . . . I think blues is here to stay and there will always be some kind of blues."[25]

"Well, it's about life," Bobby continued. "Some of the things that I sing about actually happened to me. Maybe you have a girlfriend and you lose her. It's not a good feeling, not if you care for her. Blues is based on feeling, what happens in life. I see things on TV, people that don't have anything to eat, starving. That's the blues. You think of those type of things to change the mood when you're singing. If I have a lyric that has anything pertaining to sadness, I just go back and think of whatever happened or how I felt at certain different times. It helps me to say things better and have more meaning to them. You can't be happy and sing the blues as far as I'm concerned. Maybe some people can, but it's news to me if they do."[26]

"Bland's music is the gospel of bad news," according to noted critic Nelson George, "the tales of choices made and the consequences of those decisions. Where most contemporary black pop concerns itself with receiving sex and/or love, the blues dealt with the next morning and day after that, often with great humor—though Bland's voice and arrangements make one feel a deep blue cloud is always hovering about, even when he's laughing. . . . Which for me sums up Bland's music, the bittersweet reality of the blues, and its often forgotten power to purge the listener of personal demons."[27]

As Bobby says, "People have particular songs that make them reminisce about when they were doing such and such and sometimes it puts them back together. Well, I think the blues does this."[28] *Puts them back together.*

Despite triple bypass heart surgery in 1995, Bobby Bland continued to tour, performing more than 100 shows a year like this one at the Beale Street Music Festival, in Memphis on May 8, 1999. Copyright Ebet Roberts/Cache Agency.

15

Years of Tears to Go

1993–1999

Dan Penn, the white Alabama songwriter who had started writing songs, including Bobby Bland's "I Hate You," in Muscle Shoals many years before, in early 1993 was putting the finishing touches on his first solo album with Sire Records, entitled *Do Right Man*. When it came time to take the photograph for the album's cover, Penn insisted on one pose: him on the steps of the Muscle Shoals Sound Studio, where Bobby was now doing most of his recording for Malaco, wearing sunglasses and with a jacket thrown over his shoulder, just as Bobby had posed for *Two Steps from the Blues* more than thirty years before.[1] Unfortunately, the folks at Sire did not see fit to use this photo, but Penn had made his point: for him there was no one higher in pop music echelons than Bobby "Blue" Bland, Penn's once and always hero.

Bobby and the band continued touring, stopping in Clarksdale, Mississippi, on July 3 to headline the River City Music Festival at the Expo Center Fairgrounds. Also appearing were Earl Gaines and Microwave Dave and the Nukes, among others. Soon after, Bobby himself was back in the Muscle Shoals Sound Studios working on his eighth LP for Malaco. *Years of Tears* does away with the strings and reverts to a simple Muscle Shoals blues sound that features all of the Studio's great rhythm and horn players, as well as backup singers Thomisene Anderson, Jewel Bass, Valerie Kashimura, and Frederick Knight.

Knight was born in Bessemer, Alabama, on August 15, 1944. He attended J. S. Abrams High School there and played in several bands, as well as singing in the school's chorus. He excelled enough to earn a music scholarship to Alabama A&M University in Huntsville, where W. C. Handy had once served as band director many years before; upon graduation, Knight moved to New York City to seek his fortune in the music business. Things in New York did not work out, so he returned to Alabama and continued singing in local clubs in and around Birmingham. Later, he sent a demo tape to Elijah Walker at Stax and was hired. His first release for Stax, "I've Been Lonely for So Long," became a number 8 R&B hit in 1972. In 1975 he scored again with "I Betcha Didn't Know That" on Stax subsidiary Truth Records. When Stax and its subsidiaries folded later that year Knight moved to Juana Records, where he wrote and produced Anita Ward's smash hit "Ring My Bell" in 1979, as well as his own 1981 hit "The Old Songs," which was covered by Barry Manilow and became a number 15 pop hit later that year. Knight continued to write songs and produce records for Juana, as well as its distributor, TK Records, until TK was acquired by Roulette Records in 1980. Shortly thereafter, he joined the Malaco staff to write songs and produce records.[2]

Three of the tunes on *Years of Tears* were written and produced by Knight: "I Just Tripped on a Piece of Your Broken Heart," "Sweet Lady Love," and "There's a Stranger in My House," which was written after Knight heard a Ronnie Milsap song with the same title. "When I heard it I thought it should be something else," Knight said. "He was talking about an influence from outside; another guy interfering with their relationship. That's what his story idea was. But when I heard it, I immediately said, 'No, the stranger needs to be *her!* That's the way I went with it. [Malaco] had zeroed in on a formula with Bobby of just being basic blues. You don't want to try to get too slick, you try to keep it within the comfort zone of Bobby. That's primarily what I tried to do on that particular track, just give him a basic groove that he could lock in on with a good sing-along melody."[3]

The album has a decidedly looser, more swinging feel than previous Malaco efforts, partly because of Knight's songs, but also because of the incomparable chemistry among the veteran Muscle Shoals musicians, prominently featuring Clayton Ivey on keyboards and Jimmy Johnson on guitar. Other highlights include Larry Addison's title track, "Years of Tears to Go," a sad "St. James Infirmary"–like poor man's anthem; George Jackson and George Soule's mid-tempo "Hurtin' Time Again"; and Jimmy Land's swinging "Love of Mine." Jimmy Land was better known as Buddy Ace and had toured with Bobby and Junior Parker forty or so years before. He died on Christmas Eve, 1994, and his stirring tribute album, *From Me to You Bobby Bland*, was released posthumously the following year.[4]

Although *Years of Tears* only reached number 80 on the Top R&B/Hip-Hop Albums chart, the listener somehow gets the feeling that Bobby and the band were having a real good time making this fine, fun, funky production. For their efforts, Bobby won both the Blues Foundation's 14th Annual (1993) and 15th Annual (1994) Blues Music Awards' Soul/Blues Artist of the Year awards, as well as *Years of Tears* receiving the Soul/Blues Album of the Year award for 1994.

Bobby was also honored in 1994 at the *Celebrate the Soul of America Music Awards*, where a medley of his songs was sung by R&B star Gerald Levert as Bobby listened proudly.[5]

Despite the fact that Bobby took a hiatus from recording in 1994 and 1995, there continued to be several "new" Bobby Bland albums released during the period. British label Charly released *Long Beach 1983*, a live recording of a portion of Bobby's performance at the Long Beach Blues Festival on September 3, 1983. And a tiny upstart label in Soho, New York, called Monad Records, released another live album entitled *Bobby "Blue" Bland: Really the Blues*. Monad did not last long, and it remains unknown where and when the CD was recorded. Judging by the audience background sounds, it was probably recorded in a small club somewhere, perhaps in New York City. The song selection and arrangements, ranging from 1959's "I'll Take Care of You" to 1973's "This Time I'm Gone for Good" suggest that the performance took place during the mid-1970s. Bobby's voice retains the range and smoothness of these years. How Monad got around contract issues with MCA and Malaco (if, in fact, it did) is another unanswered question, but the bootlegged result is a kick to listen to, offering a good sense of what a live Bobby Bland performance was like during the period.[6]

MCA also released the second two-CD set, *Turn On Your Love Light: The Duke Recordings Vol. 2*, of its complete Bobby Bland Duke recordings compendium. It includes fifty songs Bobby recorded from 1960 through 1964, a few of which were previously unreleased—great years for Bobby and great tunes.

While the recording schedule abated, the touring schedule did not. Bobby and the band, along with Johnny Adams, played the Cimarron Strip Ballroom in Port Allen, Louisiana, on February 4, 1995. By June they were in Seattle. While on stage, Bobby felt twinges in his back and shoulders. After the show, he called Willie Mae in Memphis and described the pain. As a nurse, Willie Mae recognized the symptoms. She caught the next plane to Seattle and brought Bobby back home. The next day in Memphis, Bobby underwent triple bypass heart surgery.[7]

A few months later he was back on the road, health problems undetectable.[8] "I went back a little sooner than they expected," the resilient bluesman reported. "It was supposed to be six months, and I went within four and a half."[9]

Willie Mae did insist that Bobby quit smoking and cut his touring schedule back to only about 20 weeks a year, and she put him on a strict diet of vegetables and broiled fish and chicken. His son Rodd was assigned to keep an eye on him, in addition to his drummer duties, and Willie Mae herself began accompanying him on the road, particularly on blues cruises and other inviting gigs.[10]

The following year, 1996, brought the final two-CD collection of Bobby's Duke recordings, *That Did It! The Duke Recordings, Vol. 3*, fifty-four songs in all, recorded from 1965 through 1972. Though it does not include as many classics as the previous two Duke collections, there are plenty of gems here, some long-unavailable, that make the modest investment well worth the money.

On March 1, 1996, Bobby and band played a double bill with Clarence Carter at the Bell Auditorium in Augusta, Georgia. On April 10 Bobby was back in Memphis to witness the placement of his honorary Walk of Fame brass "note," proclaiming him "Boss of the Blues," on the sidewalk in front of the Orpheum Theater on Beale Street, behind which he had parked cars at Bender's Garage almost fifty years before. Later that day, a few blocks down Beale Street at the New Daisy Theater, Bobby was reportedly "moved to tears" when he was presented by the Memphis chapter of the National Academy of Recording Arts and Sciences with its highest honor, the Governor's Award. He was joined by his friends Johnnie Taylor, Rufus Thomas, Bobby Rush, and B.B. King.

The following evening Bobby fronted his own nine-piece band at the New Daisy to film his first DVD, "*Live" from Beale Street*, which was released the next year, and the accompanying album, "*Live" On Beale Street*, which was released in 1998.[11] Bobby's band by this time consisted of Carson Whitsett on keyboards, Ray Neal on guitar, Reggie Richards on bass, Rodd Bland and George Weaver on drums, Joe Hardin and Stan Abernathy on trumpet, Al Thomas on trombone, and Morris Atchison on tenor saxophone.

Sean Elder offered this review of the film: "Slow and stately in a three-piece white suit, sporting a diamond pinkie ring as big as the Ritz, Bland appears unbowed by four decades of hard living. Some of the higher notes have been replaced by a pained whisper, and he takes a stool almost immediately, handing his bow tie to his valet (a job he once performed for King and Junior Parker). . . . It's a good set, tight but not by-the-numbers, though Bland never looks completely at ease. Maybe it's the cameras, catching his every move; maybe it's the floral arrangements at the front of the stage that create a barrier between him and his fans. Whatever it is, his eyes betray a certain wariness as he sings the funeral 'St. James Infirmary' for the millionth time. That's a song about seeing your lover dying—the ultimate break-up—but Bobby 'Blue' Bland keeps right on living."[12]

The DVD and CD provide a glimpse at what Bobby's stage show was like during this period—amazingly high energy and good fun. Bobby sings seventeen songs in an hour, some from the old days ("I Pity the Fool" and "Farther Up the Road"), some from the new ("Double Trouble/She's Puttin' Something in My Food" and "Love of Mine") and lots in between ("Members Only" and "Sunday Morning Love"). Old friends Johnnie Taylor and Bobby Rush join Bobby onstage to help out with "Stormy Monday," and everyone seems to enjoy the show, prompting a female fan to scream at one point, "We love you, Bobby 'Blue' Bland."

"We love you too, sweetheart," Bobby answers, "we love you too."[13]

Soon after, Bobby was back in the Muscle Shoals Sound Studios again to work on his ninth Malaco LP, to be called *Sad Street*. Assembled was the usual

Malaco crew, augmented by a string section again arranged by Mike Lewis and recorded at the After Hours Studio in Miami, Florida.

Most of the songs are mid-tempo Bobby romps written by the veteran Malaco songwriting team of Robert A. Johnson and Sam Mosley. Bobby also tries a remake of Billie Holiday's "God Bless the Child That's Got His Own" and a cover of Rod Stewart's 1976 hit, "Tonight's The Night,"—both ill-advised but pleasant enough. The highlight of the album is George Jackson's title song, which prompted this laudatory review by John Floyd: "'Sad Street,' though, is a marvel—utterly contemporary, politically charged like the finest call-to-arms soul of the '70s, yet steeped in the legacy of Bland's definitive work. . . . 'The street used to be filled with love, all you hear about now is blood,' he groans, singing that last word like he's knee-deep in it, with ominous horns and eerie wah-wah guitar underpinning his sorrow and rage. It's a bone-chilling commentary. . . . It's a different kind of sorrow and rage, though, for a man who's spent the last four decades essaying the pains and perils of romance and misery. But as 'Sad Street' fades, with Bland facing the realization that he has to call that bleak, blood-soaked place home, the song takes its place next to the sad, desperate likes of 'Lead Me On,' driving home the fact that, emotionally or otherwise, Bobby Bland has never lived anywhere else."[14]

George Jackson, who wrote the song, as well as more than 500 others for everyone from James Brown ("It's Too Funky in Here") to Bob Seger ("Old Time Rock and Roll") to Wilson Pickett ("A Man and a Half") to Z.Z. Hill ("Down Home Blues") to the Osmonds ("One Bad Apple"), and many voices in between, was born in Greenville, Mississippi in 1936. While still a teenager, he met Ike Turner at a concert and introduced himself. Turner took him to New Orleans to record at Cosimo Matassa's studio. In 1963 Turner's Prann label released Jackson singing "Won't Nobody Cha-Cha With Me." Nobody bought the record either, and Jackson headed to Memphis, where he was rejected by Stax Records, but met Louis Williams who formed a vocal group with Jackson called the Ovations. The group recorded in Memphis for Goldwax Records, where they scored a number 22 hit in 1965 with a song entitled "It's So Wonderful to Be in Love." While at Goldwax, George also penned songs for labelmates Spencer Wiggins, Willie Walker, and James Carr.

In addition, Jackson worked for awhile with Willie Mitchell at Hi Records in Memphis, cutting a record called "So Good to Me" in 1967. Then he recorded as Bart Jackson for Decca, releasing "Wonderful Dream" in 1968.

At the suggestion of producer Billy Sherrill, George moved to Muscle Shoals's FAME Studio, where many of the Goldwax singles were recorded. There he worked as a staff writer, penning hits for Candi Staton ("Just a Prisoner") and Clarence Carter ("Too Weak to Fight"), who were married to each other for a time. When MGM sent the Osmonds to Muscle Shoals to record, Jackson offered them a song he had originally written for the Jackson 5. "One Bad Apple" became a number 1 pop hit for the Osmonds in 1971. George returned to Memphis in 1972 to cut "Aretha, Sing One for Me" and "Let Them Know You Care" in 1973 for Willie Mitchell's Hi Records.[15]

Jackson then moved back to Muscle Shoals, again to write for the Muscle Shoals Sound Studios. While there, he also sent demo tapes to Malaco. "He'd sent us a demo," Wolf Stephenson remembers, "that was horrible, but the idea was fantastic. We'd have to call him on the phone to see what the words were. You couldn't understand the words and the song might be nine minutes long. He'd just go for days. But, he came up with some great stuff. He was drunk as a dog when he wrote all that stuff."[16]

Stephenson heard a demo of "Down Home Blues" and "Cheatin' in the Next Room" in Muscle Shoals. He liked them so much that he brought them back to Jackson for his partner Tommy Couch to hear. "He didn't think too much of them at first," Stephenson recalled. "Then we were looking for a couple of tunes to fill out Z.Z. Hill's second album and I remembered we still had those two songs sitting on a shelf somewhere. I found them and played them again for Tommy. He says, 'Wow, where did you get these?' I said they're George Jackson songs and I played them for you last year. He says, 'No way. I've never heard these songs. They're great.'"

Based on the success in 1982 of that second Z.Z. Hill album, *Down Home*, and especially those two songs, Stephenson phoned Jackson, who had moved back to Memphis, and said, "George, what do you have goin' there in Memphis? Why don't you move to Jackson? George says, 'Well, okay.' I told him to stay right where he was and I'd send someone to get him. At the time, George was living on beer. He'd wake up in the morning and start drinking beer and writing songs and wouldn't eat or do anything else. He was down to about 90 pounds when we brought him to Jackson. I told the driver not to stop at any place that sold beer or we would surely lose George. Well, George made it to Jackson and finally dried out and has been our main house songwriter since, making more money [from all his writing royalties] than any of us."[17]

Jackson continued singing as well, releasing an album entitled *Sweet Down Home Delta Blues* on the Amblin' label in 1985 and *Heart to Heart Collect* on Hep Me Records in 1991.[18] "I'm still writing for Malaco," Jackson writes on his MySpace page, "and make my way over there almost every day. It's a good life!"[19]

Sad Street went to number 11 on the Top Blues Albums chart and was nominated for a Grammy for Best Contemporary Blues Album, but Bobby lost again, this time to Keb' Mo's *Just Like You*. However, on February 26, 1997, the National Academy of Recording Arts and Sciences honored Bobby with its coveted Lifetime Achievement Award, recognizing lifelong artistic contributions to the recording industry. Also receiving the award at that year's ceremony were Frank Zappa, the Everly Brothers, Judy Garland, Stephane Grappelli, Buddy Holly, Charles Mingus, and Oscar Peterson.[20] "I guess it's that time, you know," Bobby said. "I really feel good about it. It's way overdue, so I guess better late than never. I really was very impressed and very happy about it. It's been a long waiting period, but yet still it's here, and I'm proud of it."[21]

Two months later, on May 1, in Memphis, Bobby was again named the Soul/ Blues Male Artist of the Year by the Blues Foundation at its 18th Annual W. C. Handy Awards Ceremony.

In the spirit of Don Robey, to take advantage of the publicity surrounding these recent awards, MCA rushed to the record stores a new compilation of ten of Bobby's old Duke recordings entitled *Soul Legend*. The next two years also brought four more compilations. The first was entitled *Just One More Step*; released in 1998 by 601 Music, a division of Malaco, it contained ten Malaco favorites on one disc. Not to be outdone, MCA released later that year two more single-disc compilations of Bobby's popular Duke and ABC/Dunhill recordings: *Bobby Bland, Greatest Hits Vol. One/The Duke Recordings*, with sixteen hits recorded from 1957 through 1969; and *Bobby Bland, Greatest Hits Vol. Two/ The ABC-Dunhill/MCA Recordings*, with sixteen later hits recorded from 1973 through 1982. And, if that were not enough of Bobby, in 1999 MCA followed with *Blues & Ballads*, a welcome compilation of sixteen of Bobby's best slower tunes.

The year 1998 also finally brought the release of the *Live on Beale Street* album that was recorded along with the DVD at the New Daisy Theater in Memphis in 1996. It went to number 8 on the Top Blues Albums chart.

Later in 1998 Bobby was back in the Malaco Recording Studio in Jackson to begin work on his eleventh Malaco album, *Memphis Monday Morning*. The personnel changed slightly, with Bob Johnson joining Clayton Ivey on keyboards; Sam Mosley, Will McFarlane, and Butch Bonner on guitar; Willie James Hatter joining David Hood on bass; Jim Williamson and Steve Patrick on trumpet and flugelhorn; and Doug Moffet and Tom Malone joining Harvey Thompson on saxophone and flute. Joe Hardin, Bobby's road bandleader, also wrote and played trumpet on two cuts, the jaunty mid-tempo romp "My Baby Is the Only One" and the sexy ballad "I Hate Missin' You."

There are several other delights on this definitive Bobby Bland production, like Billy Ray Charles's "There's a Rat in My House," which prompted this tribute by Nicky Baxter: "On 'There's a Rat in My House,' Bland suspects his woman is stepping out on him. His voice quivering with pent-up resentment, the singer details a litany of complaints: 'You know, my icebox is empty every time I come home from work/Somebody's been eating my food . . . and loving my woman for dessert.' By the time he's done, Bland is slowly inching toward acceptance of a hard fact, the repressed pain in his voice turning into steely resolve."[22]

The title track, "Memphis Monday Morning," by George Jackson, Raymond Nelson, and Dennis Nelson perfectly evokes both the moody blues of "Stormy Monday," this time with a mellow flugelhorn solo by Steve Patrick, and the romantic city from whence the Bobby Bland sound emerged some forty years before. Bobby's driving cover of Z.Z. Top's "Lookin' for Some Tush" was actually recorded back in 1985 at Bobby's first Malaco session and no doubt left unreleased because it did not fit the more bluesy corner into which Malaco was determined to paint Bobby. But it is amazingly effective, making one wonder what would have happened if Bobby had ridden down a more raucous rock 'n' roll road.

Three other cuts are worthy of mention, not only because they capture the patented Bobby Bland sound, but also because they are fine examples of the best of the veteran Malaco songwriting team of Robert A. Johnson and Sam Mosley. "I'm Bobby B" is the type of fun, up-tempo romp that you can almost hear Bobby smiling through. "The Truth Will Set You Free" is a gorgeous Bobby Bland minor-key ballad that features Bobby's impassioned voice at its mature best. And finally "I'm Glad" is the type of jazzy, building, mid-tempo workout that Bobby is known for.

Both Johnson and Mosley were born and raised in New Albany, Mississippi, where they formed Sam and Bob and the Soul Men when they were just teenagers. Later they called themselves Mojoba, and finally Mosley and Johnson. After recording a few unsuccessful singles with Hi Records and Polydor, Willie Mitchell at Hi suggested that they try to complete their new album, *Rock Me*, at Malaco. Tommy Couch agreed and signed the duo to a recording and publishing contract that resulted in innumerable album cuts of their songs by most of the Malaco artists.[23]

Unfortunately, before Bobby's *Memphis Monday Morning* hit the shelves in 1999, Robert A. Johnson died while performing with his longtime songwriting partner Sam Mosley, and the Mosley & Johnson Band on August 21, 1998. Johnson's final writing efforts resulted in an album that harkens back to vintage Bobby Bland, one of his best Malaco albums since the debut *Members Only*. Johnson and Mosley's songs seem to have propelled Bobby and the band into a warmer, more expansive mood, working together with genuine caring, chemistry, and creativity. It just sounds good, worthy of replay after replay. It went to number 12 on the Top Blues Albums chart and was nominated for the 2000 Grammy Award for Best Traditional Blues Album, losing out this time to B.B. King's *Blues on the Bayou*.

On November 9, 1998, Bobby received the Blues Foundation's Lifetime Achievement Award. Before the ceremony at Dan Aykroyd's House of Blues in

Los Angeles, Bobby and his guests had to wait outside while the management found passes for them.[24] Once inside, Bobby was presented the award by one his biggest fans, rocker Boz Scaggs, who earlier that year had released an R&B tribute album, *Come On Home*, that included Scaggs's interpretations of fourteen classic R&B songs by his favorite artists. The only artist to merit a pair of covers was, of course, Bobby Bland: "Ask Me 'Bout Nothin' (But the Blues)" and "Don't Cry No More."[25]

"He means everything to me," Scaggs said. "He's been in some ways a hidden gem and in other ways an enormous talent and influence on everybody. You want so much for the world at large and the new generation of people to hear Bobby's work. Bobby's voice is incomparable. There is no other."[26]

Bobby and the band appeared twice on the television show *Austin City Limits* in 1999, first on January 31 and again on May 1, with a young Susan Tedeschi. After the first show, Bobby said, "I thought it was pretty good. I made one, two, or three mistakes. I almost forgot a lyric and that does happen, but other than that I think everybody was wonderful and did everything they could to make the show go on tonight. I appreciate being here on *Austin City Limits* because it was good. . . . They [the audience] seemed like they were having a good time and that is what we are out here for—to have fun. I was wondering, when I was up there, who won the Super Bowl?"[27]

Bobby and the band were in Memphis on May 8, 1999, headlining Saturday's shows at the Beale Street Music Festival. Resplendent in a white linen suit, Bobby was comfortable and in good spirits as he introduced one of his oldest Memphis friends, as well as one of his youngest. Bobby asked Rufus Thomas to join him at center stage, just as Rufus had beckoned Bobby to the same spot at the Palace Theater on Amateur Nights some fifty years prior. Rufus, fashionable as always in red Bermuda shorts and knee-high leather boots, hobbled to Bobby's side with the aid of a cane, as the audience thundered its appreciation for two of Memphis's all-time favorite musical sons. Later in the show, the only person in town who could have possibly upstaged them both joined Bobby onstage: cute three-year-old Kayla, Bobby's granddaughter, Rodd's daughter, even more elegant than the aging hipsters in her perfect white party dress. Bobby doted on her, of course, and sweetly serenaded her with Larry Addison's beautiful "Angel," as she giggled and blushed—a touching and memorable moment in Memphis music history.

By the end of the twentieth century, Bobby Bland, now nearing seventy, had become an artist of monumental musical stature, having recorded more than 500 songs and thirty original albums primarily for three record labels: Duke, ABC-Dunhill/MCA, and Malaco. Forty-two of his singles had become pop hits and 63 had reached the R&B charts; three were number 1 R&B hits; 27 were Top 10 R&B hits; and 51 were Top 40 hits. Of his original albums, nearly all were R&B hits, four were nominated for Grammys, and four received Blues Foundation awards.

Bobby is ranked number 14 on Joel Whitburn's list of Top 100 R&B Artists, 1942–2004, based on number of hits and their *Billboard* chart ranking positions. Whitburn also ranks Bobby as number 5 on his list of Top 25 Artists in the 1960s, 11 in his list of artists with the Most Charted R&B Hits (63), 12 on his list of artists with the Most Top 40 Hits (51), 15 on his list of artists with the Most Top Ten Hits (27), and 13 on his list of artists with the Most Crossover Hits (42).[28]

Bobby was inducted into the Blues Foundation's Hall of Fame in 1981, became a member of the Rock and Roll Hall of Fame in 1992, was recipient of Lifetime Achievement Awards from both the National Academy of Recording Arts and Sciences (Grammy Awards) in 1997 and the Blues Foundation in 1998, recipient of the Pioneer Award by the Rhythm & Blues Foundation in 1992, and with his Soul/Blues Male Artist of the Year award for 1999 from the Blues Foundation, he became the unprecedented winner of the award for the seventh time.

And, of course, he continued to entertain audiences with his stage performances, still numbering more than 100 each year.

Bobby Bland pays tribute to his old partner, Little Junior Parker, at the 15th Annual Sunflower River Blues and Gospel Festival in Clarksdale, Mississippi, on August 9, 2002. Copyright Gene Tomko.

Funny How Time Slips Away

2000–2007

Bobby and the band joined Van Morrison, another longtime Bobby Bland fan, in Birmingham, England, on March 14, 2000, to begin another UK tour. Their first performance, at the Birmingham Academy, was followed by shows in Cardiff on March 16, Manchester on March 17, Glasgow on March 18, Brighton on March 19, concluding on March 21 and 22 with performances at London's Royal Albert Hall. There Bobby sailed through a few of his hits, "I Pity the Fool," "That's the Way Love Is," "Everyday I Have the Blues," "Ain't No Sunshine," and "If You're Gonna Walk on My Love," before giving way to Morrison with these words to the audience, "Don't forget who I am. When you hear the name again, say 'Oh yeah, I caught him once. He's that blues singer.'"[1]

Bobby later joined Morrison for duets on "Ain't Nothing You Can Do" and "Tupelo Honey," and, according to the *Evening Standard* in an article called "The Van Has Been Overtaken," "If this was Morrison's show, he allowed Bland to steal it."[2]

Prompted by the publicity and success of the tour, England's Dressed To Kill label rereleased the live recording of Bobby's 1983 Long Beach Blues Festival performance, for some inexplicable reason renamed *Mercy Mercy Me*, and, as noted earlier, Ace Records released a compilation called *The Original Memphis Blues Brothers*, which contains four of Bobby's earliest recordings for Modern.

Meanwhile, at the dawn of a new century, MCA was in the midst of issuing a group of "best" albums by some of its historically hottest acts, called appropriately the Millennium Collections, including CDs by the Temptations, Marvin Gaye, the Four Tops, Rod Stewart, James Brown, and others, including, of course, *The Best of Bobby Bland—The Millennium Collection*, with twelve of Bobby's biggest hits.

The new century also brought the deaths of many of Bobby's old friends and associates. On July 21, 2000, David James Mattis died at the age of eighty-five in Wheeling, West Virginia. Soon after signing Bobby to his first record contract with Mattis's fledgling Duke label in 1952, Mattis sold the company to Don Robey in 1953 and moved back into radio broadcasting for good, working with several stations before his retirement in 1980.[3]

By August 19, Bobby and the band were in cooler climes, playing the 15th Annual Portsmouth Blues Festival in New Hampshire, where Bobby was presented with a Life-Time Achievement Award from the Blues Bank Collective, sponsor of the event.[4]

On September 23, 2000, Bobby was back in Memphis to be honored with the 2000 Blues Ball Pyramid Award. Performing at the benefit tribute were Jerry Lee Lewis, Isaac Hayes, Carla Thomas, Rufus Thomas, and Little Jimmy King.[5] Later, on November 26, Bobby and the band performed at a Sunday night early show at the New Era in Nashville.

The one person who had encouraged Bobby's singing from the beginning, when Bobby was a boy back in the cotton fields, who had taken him to Memphis at the age of fifteen to provide him with more opportunity, who had encouraged and supported him throughout his life and career, the one and only constant, Mary Lee Bland, Bobby's mother, died in Memphis, on January 2, 2001, at the age of eighty-nine.[6]

After his mother's funeral and burial at Memorial Park in Memphis, Bobby, drained and bereaved, took some time off from touring and recording, not returning to the recording studios for nearly two years. MCA, however, filled the gap with *The Anthology*, an excellent two-disc collection of 50 of Bobby's best Duke, Dunhill/ABC, and MCA tracks, in chronological order, including a previously unreleased eight-minute 1973 live recording of "This Time I'm Gone for Good." What is missing are his earliest recordings for Chess and Modern and his later recordings for Malaco, of which only "Members Only" was a charting hit single. If the previous three-volume, six-disc, complete compilation by MCA is too much of a good thing, then this collection is about right. If not, Universal-MCA Music, MCA's United Kingdom distributor, also released in 2001 a single-disc, twenty-two-song collection called *Ask Me 'Bout Nothing (But the Blues)*, that provides a bit more selective sampling.

To compound the emotional toil of Bobby's mother's death, Bobby's wife, Willie Mae, underwent surgery a few months later in April. However, by May, she was well enough to join Bobby, Rodd, and the rest of the band on the Tom Joyner Fantastic Voyage Cruise 2001. Other performers on the cruise included Al Jarreau, Isaac Hayes, who borrowed Malaco drummer James Robertson for his band, and Boyz II Men. The comedian Sinbad was also on board and asked Bobby for some advice on learning how to play the guitar. Bobby, who had given up the saxophone years before and never played the guitar, encouraged him to start off learning jazz and blues style guitar playing. "Do that," Bobby advised, "and everything else will come into its own, young man."[7]

Later that year, Bobby and the band joined the 10th Annual B.B. King Blues Festival that toured for several months throughout the United States. By Labor Day weekend, Bobby was again headlining the second night of the Long Beach Music Festival, then in its twenty-second iteration. On the bill with Bobby that night were soul blues greats Little Milton, Shuggie Otis (Johnny's guitar-slinging son), Denise LaSalle, Percy Sledge, and Solomon Burke.[8]

If there was one other special person, besides his mother and B.B. King, who had encouraged Bobby from the start and continued as a friend throughout the years, it was Memphis music legend Rufus Thomas. After helping to launch the careers of Bobby, B.B. King, Rosco Gordon, and many other Memphis musicians as host of the Palace Theater's Amateur Show and later as a deejay at radio station WDIA, Thomas pursued his own singing career with Sam Phillips's Sun label. There he cut "Bear Cat," a follow-up to Big Mama Thornton's "Hound Dog," which gave Sun its first hit—as well as a plagiarism lawsuit from Don Robey, which Robey won. In 1960 Thomas recorded "Cause I Love You" with his seventeen-year-old daughter Carla for the new Satellite label, its first successful record. Satellite, of course, soon became Stax, and Thomas led the label with a string of doggone good novelty hits, including "The Dog" and "Walking the Dog" in 1963, "Can Your Monkey Do the Dog" and "Somebody Stole My Dog" in 1964, "Do the Funky Chicken" in 1970, "(Do the) Push and Pull Part I," number 1 in 1970, "The Breakdown" in 1971, and "Do the Funky Penguin" in 1971–72. At Stax's Wattstax concert in 1972, Thomas performed in his trademark outfit of high-heeled boots and flashy Bermuda shorts. By now in his 50s, he was billed as "the world's oldest teenager."

After Stax folded in 1975, Rufus discontinued recording for awhile, but became a fixture on Beale Street, emceeing local shows and holding court up and down the street he loved. In the late 1980s, Rufus returned to WDIA, where for fifteen years he co-hosted the radio station's Saturday morning blues program with J. Michael Davis. Thomas also did some recording in the 1980s, including the bluesy 1988 Alligator LP, *That Woman Is Poison*. Later, a stretch of Hernando Street in Memphis was renamed Rufus Thomas Boulevard, and the city gave Thomas his own parking space, which he used frequently until his death on December 15, 2001.[9]

Bobby and the band continued touring throughout 2002 and 2003. Among their shows: Montego Bay in February 2002; at the 5th Annual Air Jamaica Jazz & Blues Festival, along with Harry Belafonte, Babyface, Yolanda Adams, Bebe Winans, and others; at a little chitlin circuit venue, the Elks Lodge in Huntsville, Alabama, with the Dazz Band, on March 10; throughout the United States again with the traveling B.B. King Blues Festival; in Clarksdale, Mississippi, on August 9 at the outdoor Sunflower River Blues and Gospel Festival, with Clarksdale natives Big Jack Johnson and O. B. Buchana, in a special tribute to another Clarksdalian and Bobby's old friend Little Junior Parker; and in Brooklyn, New York, on January 18, 2003, at the Brooklyn Academy of Music, where he received this review from the *New York Times*'s Jon Pareles: "Bobby Blue Bland is a connoisseur of quiet heartache and smoldering fury. His set at the Brooklyn Academy of Music on Saturday night was like one long sad song, changing in the particulars of rhythm and melody but retelling an eternal story: he loved her, she did him wrong, and maybe someday she'll regret it. . . . Mr. Bland stayed on the imploring side of the blues, singing in the highest, gentlest, most disconsolate part of his range. 'I wouldn't treat a dog the way you treated me,' he sang. Every now and then he'd break through his velvety phrases with a harsh growl. Now the growl has receded to an occasional ratchety punctuation, and his voice as smooth as a stone polished by a rushing river."[10]

That fall Bobby was back in the Muscle Shoals and Malaco studios to record his twelfth and final Malaco album, *Blues at Midnight*. The usual Malaco/Muscle Shoals band was on hand, without strings but with a crack eight-piece horn section, to cut eleven new songs. The best are a final pair from Johnson and Mosley, a slow blues entitled "You Hit the Nail on the Head" and an up-tempo jump tune called "Baby What's Wrong with You," both patented Bobby Bland; and another fine trio by Larry Addison, the "Stormy Monday"–like "My Sunday's Comin' Soon," a strong ballad, "The Only Thing Missing Is You," and a reprise to "Sad Street" called "Ghetto Nights," in which Bobby sings "I lived on the outside of Memphis, a little town called Millington, Tennessee, and then we moved to the city . . . ," referring to the little town listed on Bobby's birth certificate, near rural Rosemark where he grew up.

"Bobby's my man," Addison said. "Bobby would always say 'Man, what you got for me?' He'd just be waiting around for me to bring him a song. He didn't care if it was a hit or not. Bobby liked good songs. You can't write a whole lot of words for Bobby [whereas] Milton can take words and just run them back to back. Bobby, you have to get straight to the point and you have to have some meaning in what you're saying and you only have a limited time to do that. That's hard. Once I laid a song for Bobby, Bobby'd sing it just like I did. Every song I ever brought to Bobby, he would sing it just like on the demo and that would make me the happiest man in the world. The way I felt the song should go, he would interpret it just like that."

Larry Addison and Bobby Bland were for almost twenty years the ultimate ballad-producing team at Malaco. Bobby loved Larry's songs just as much as Larry loved Bobby's crooning of them. "I would think in that flavor," Bobby summed up modestly. "I call myself being a kind of balladeer. I wasn't as good as Nat Cole but those were my thoughts. That's what made me do the blues different from the average blues singer. I thought in terms of being kind of like a ballad singer."[11] Larry Addison continues to write songs and can be heard singing them most evenings at the piano in the upscale bar of the Char Restaurant in Jackson, Mississippi.

Two other interesting inclusions on *Blues at Midnight* were Bobby's tribute to some of his favorite artists: to Louis Armstrong on "What a Wonderful World," which Bobby handles handily, and to some of the pioneering bluesmen on Joe Shamwell, A. D. Prestage, and Walter Godbold's "I'm a Blues Man," which celebrates not just the song's original singer, Z.Z. Hill, but also the swaggering profession to which Bobby had dedicated his life:

> *Oh Lord, listen to me*
> *Little story here*
> *I was raised up on Jimmy Reed*
> *Cornbread, collard greens, and black-eyed peas*
> *I took my first bath in Muddy Waters*
> *And, all you mothers, you better watch out for your daughters*
> *'Cause I'm a bluesman . . .*
>
> *Listen, said I'm an original, one of a kind*
> *I don't do nothing but what's on my mind*
> *Ain't got no bossman houndin' me*
> *I'm out here on the road, huh*
> *And I'm totally free*
> *'Cause I'm a bluesman . . .*
>
> *I'm a manchild in the promised land*
> *Plenty good lovin', I'm gonna get all I can*
> *Don't need no mojo, uh-uh, to see me through*
> *'Cause I got a jones, Lord, that'll conquer you*
> *'Cause I'm a bluesman . . .*

In addition to the song's macho lyrics and Muddy Waters's "I'm a Man" melody, there is some fancy slide guitar work by Reggie Young, Jimmy Johnson, Larry Byrom, Will McFarlane, and/or Sam Mosley. Thirty-eight-year-old Tommy Couch Jr. produced this cut, his first for Bobby since joining the company in the mid-1980s, after booking fraternity dances like his father and earning a marketing degree at Ole Miss. At Malaco, Couch Jr. started the subsidiary Waldoxy Records to produce alternative rock and white blues bands, but ultimately drifted back to the more gritty black blues with records by McKinley Mitchell, Joe Poonanny, Bobby Rush, Artie "Blues Boy" White, and others. Other currently popular Malaco blues artists are Vick Allen, David Brinston,

Shirley Brown, Willie Clayton, Theodis Ealey, Denise LaSalle, Latimore, Carl Sims, Peggy Scott-Adams, Marvin Sease, and Mel Waiters.

Meanwhile, Malaco continued to grow its popular gospel section, garnering several awards each year. It also launched Freedom Records to produce records by contemporary Christian artists, as well as Malaco Jazz Records to reissue a series of vintage live European recordings by Duke Ellington, Count Basie, Louis Armstrong, Dizzy Gillespie, Lionel Hampton, Cannonball Adderley, Thelonious Monk, and others. And the company's new "urban contemporary" label, J-Town, even scored a Top 40 R&B single in 1997 with Tonya's "I've Been Having an Affair."[12]

Soon after its release on January 21, 2003, *Blues at Midnight* went to number 4 on the Top Blues Albums. "I'm just a storyteller," Bobby explained about the album, "and I've always depended on getting good material to sing. Since the Duke days, you know, the songs that have come my way haven't always been the best. But this time I got some great stories from guys like George Jackson, Joe Shamwell, and Larry Addison that I could really feel. That's important. I think it worked out pretty good. I'd go in with the rhythm section and we'd usually get everything down in one or two takes. I prefer doing my vocals in one take, but sometimes you need to try again. If it ever gets past four takes I'd just leave that tune alone and come back to it another day. Otherwise, you just end up getting frustrated."[13]

On June 30, 2003, Sam Phillips—the man who in the 1950s had first recorded Bobby, B.B. King, Howlin' Wolf, Ike Turner, James Cotton, Rufus Thomas, Rosco Gordon, Little Milton, not to mention Elvis Presley, Carl Perkins, Jerry Lee Lewis, Charlie Rich, Johnny Cash, and Roy Orbison—died of respiratory failure at the age of eighty in his adopted town of Memphis, Tennessee, only one day before his original Sun Studio was designated a National Historic Landmark. One by one, all of these famous blues, rock 'n' roll, and rockabilly artists had left Phillips and Sun.[14]

And eventually too Phillips himself lost interest in making music and left the record business altogether, selling Sun to Shelby Singleton in 1969. "I thank myself for having the good judgment to get out of the business rather than trying to compete against certain economic blocs that I just could not control," Phillips explained.[15]

Sam Phillips was to become one of the first investors in Memphis-based Holiday Inn, owned several radio stations, and lived a wealthy but modest life in Memphis. He was inducted as part of the first group into the Rock and Roll Hall of Fame in 1986, as well as into the Rockabilly Hall of Fame, the Alabama Music Hall of Fame (1987), the Blues Hall of Fame (1998), and the Country Music Hall of Fame (2001). He is interred in the Memorial Park Cemetery in Memphis, where Bobby's mother lies.[16]

Bobby and the band continued on the road. They were at Gilly's in Dayton, Ohio, on July 20, 2003, for a one-night stand. Leroy "Sugarfoot" Bonner, a founding member of Dayton's famous funk band the Ohio Players, was on hand and commented, "Bobby 'Blue' Bland is one of the reasons I play music. Bland came out on stage one time when I was a child, and for the first time in my life I heard 17 horns. When you hear a horn, that's fine. When you hear that many horns—Whoa! He had a bass, a drummer and 17 horns. I was gone. I couldn't even play music, but I immediately wanted to be a musician. It was the most incredible thing—it was like Gabriel was playing for me."[17] Well, probably not that many horns, but you can bet it sounded like it.

Even on holidays, the road work continued, with Bobby and Denise LaSalle playing the Annual Thanksgiving Breakfast Dance, BYOB at 10:00 a.m., on November 27 at the Kansas National Guard Armory in Kansas City, Kansas. The year 2003 was also touted as "The Year of the Blues," and Bobby was booked into the exclusive Sabre Room in Chicago on December 26 to help celebrate the year's culmination. Tickets were $50, $75, and $100 for each of two shows. Also on the bill were Floyd Taylor, Stan Mosley, JoJo Murray, and Howard Scott. The show's local promoter was legendary WVON-AM disc jockey Pervis Spann, who joined the station (owned by Leonard and Phil Chess, the men who released Bobby's first record) at its conception in 1963. Known then as the "Voice of the Negro," the station is now called the "Voice of the Nation." Spann told the Chicago *Sun-Times:* "I'm on the air five hours a night, six nights a week (Saturday through Thursday starting at midnight). I have played over a million records, but Bland is a standard bearer. I can always build my show up with a Bobby Bland song. No live human being in America has played more Bobby Bland music than I have."

"Spann was the man," Bobby recalled. "He played everybody—blues, soul, rhythm and blues—he kept me hot for a lot of years around Chicago. He had a radio station [WXSS-AM] in Memphis that gave competition to the stations around here."

"I am the first black American that built a 50,000-watt radio station on United States soil," Spann said proudly. "And I built it in Memphis. It was like having twin boys. This was in the 1980s. I could listen to my station in Memphis riding up and down the Dan Ryan Expressway. Then I'd ride all over [his native] Mississippi listening to my station. Made me feel good. That's the reason, Bobby Bland, I didn't have no girlfriends."

To which Bobby replied, "I won't bother with that. I'm married."[18]

On April 29, 2004, Bobby and the band were in New Orleans, where they shared a bill with fellow Memphian Al Green at the Saenger Theatre on Rampart Street. They were in Philadelphia, not a big blues town, on October 8, to open the Eighth Annual Greater Philadelphia Blues Festival, prompting this review in the Philadelphia *Tribune:* "After a few brief words from Blues Fest founder Blaine Stoddard, the Bobby 'Blue' Bland Band took the stage. Although all the veteran musicians were supremely talented, it was immediately evident that Rod Bland, the headliner's son, was the backbone of the ensemble. A skilled and flamboyant drummer, the younger Bland kept time like a metronome, and has a style that blends many colors and nuances. After a dynamic instrumental introduction, Bobby 'Blue' Bland, a 1992 inductee into the Rock and Roll Hall of Fame, took the stage and was met with a standing ovation."[19]

On to the North Fork Theater at Westbury, New York, for a twin bill with B.B. King, where Bobby cited recent laser eye surgery as the reason "why I'm sitting down like you. If you're not sure when you're standing, it's best to be cool."[20]

Bobby's popularity also continued in England, where, on November 20, 2004, the Universal Music Group, released a new compilation of twenty-seven of Bobby's old hits entitled *The Best of Bobby Bland*, which it rereleased in 2008.

After inspiring Don Robey to launch Peacock Records in 1949 and later Evelyn Johnson's Buffalo Booking Agency, Clarence "Gatemouth" Brown recorded a few hits for the new label before leaving it to work independently in 1960. He worked awhile in the mid-1960s as leader of the band, featuring pianist Skippy Brooks, on the R&B television program *The Beat!!!* Always an iconoclast, he recorded a few country songs, moved to New Mexico, and worked as a deputy sheriff.

Brown made a musical comeback in 1971, when he was rediscovered by European audiences. By the late 1970s he had moved to New Orleans, where he worked with his manager and producer, Jim Bateman, resulting in the album *Blackjack* for the Seattle-based Music is Medicine label. Throughout the 1980s, Brown recorded for Rounder Records, winning the 1982 Grammy for Best Traditional Blues album for *Alright Again!* The recipient of numerous awards, Brown continued throughout the 1990s to tour widely and record on several labels.

Hurricane Katrina destroyed Brown's home in Slidell, Louisiana, on August 29, 2005, forcing him to relocate to his niece's home in Orange, Texas, where he died of heart disease and complications from lung cancer and emphysema on September 10, 2005, at the age of eighty-one.[21]

As more and more popular blues artists passed away—including Malaco mainstays Johnnie Taylor on May 31, 2000, and Little Milton Campbell on August 4, 2005—the market for blues recordings continued its decline. And it did not help that the illegal downloading and sharing of digital music had pretty much devastated the commercial recording industry that Malaco had entered almost forty years before. So it was no surprise then that, in 2005, the company reluctantly decided to sell its Muscle Shoals Sound Studios in Sheffield, Alabama.[22]

Still very much alive, however, and still singing the blues and preparing to celebrate his eightieth birthday on September 16, 2005, B.B. King released his album appropriately entitled *80* on September 13. It is a fine collection of blues standards that B.B. sings with an impressive list of famous singers, including John Mayer, Eric Clapton, Howard Tate, Daryl Hall, Billy Gibbons, Gloria Estefan, Elton John, Roger Daltrey, Van Morrison, Sheryl Crow, and, of course, B.B.'s favorite blues singer, Bobby Bland, on a touching version of Willie Nelson's "Funny How Time Slips Away."

"Bobby did a great job on that one," B.B. said. "Man can sing anything. He's always been my favorite blues singer. I never really considered myself a singer, especially compared to Bobby."[23]

On November 22 Bobby was recognized at a jazz concert as the 2005 recipient of the Distinguished Achievement in the Creative and Performing Arts Award, given by the College of Communication and Fine Arts at the University of Memphis. The award has been given annually since 1979 in memory of Elvis Presley to a living Mid-South artist whose work has resulted in national and international recognition and influence. Previous recipients include Isaac Hayes, Dixie Carter, Rufus Thomas, Chet Atkins, Carroll Cloar, B.B. King, Al Green, and Booker T. Jones of Booker T. and the MGs.[24]

Bobby, as always, was not resting on this or any other of his growing library of laurels. Instead, he was out on the road working as usual. On the afternoon of August 5, 2006, his big, brown RV pulled into a dusty hay field called Sportsman Park in rural Harvest, Alabama, which looked eerily like Rosemark, Tennessee seventy years before. And it was hot. The modest crowd of country folks waiting to hear him were scrunched together to the right of the makeshift stage in the stingy shade of a scrub oak grove, fanning themselves with souvenir fans and sipping the cold drinks they had hauled from their cars and pickup trucks in huge plastic picnic coolers. Sheba Potts-Wright, with guest guitarist Stacy Mitchhart, started the show, next would be Bobby, followed by Latimore, and finally Bobby Rush. Each set would go about thirty or forty minutes. Bobby and his band could drive over from Memphis in about four hours, do their thing, and be back home before bedtime.

A few local friends and dignitaries were permitted entrance to Bobby's air-conditioned RV, each for only a brief audience, re-emerging rather quickly with a green bottle of Heineken beer. When their time came, Bobby's band set up expeditiously, with what appeared to be a pickup horn section, excepting Joe Hardin on trumpet, who, as usual, introduced Bobby as "the world's greatest blues singer," after an obligatory warm-up number. Bobby, in a beige pajama-style leisure suit, was helped up the stairs to the stage and deposited on his chrome stool, where he commenced to fiddle with the microphone, smiling shyly, as the older crowd in all forms of matching shirt and shorts ensembles and funky sun hats emerged from the shade to pay tribute in front of the stage. It was so hot that Bobby broke a sweat even before he launched into a nonstop medley of some of his biggest hits—"That's the Way Love Is," "I Pity the Fool," "I'll Take Care of You," "St. James Infirmary," "Members Only," "Share Your Love With Me," "Ain't No Sunshine"—which there was, in fact, in abundance as the crowd sang along.

The band, dressed in black, struggled to appear cool and together as Bobby, ever the trouper, pressed on to "Stormy Monday" to end his all-too-brief set. Before Latimore took the stage, Bobby's RV was creeping, beeping backward out of its space, heading back to Memphis and bed, presumably with cash in hand.

On June 19, 2007, Van Morrison's *The Best of Van Morrison Volume 3* was released with a duet of Morrison and Bobby singing "Tupelo Honey," recorded on the tour they had done together in 2000.

Bobby's old record label, MCA, acquired Geffen Records in 1990. In 2007, as part of its *Definitive Collections* series, which included compilations by Chuck Berry, Etta James, John Lee Hooker, and Muddy Waters, Geffen paid tribute to Bobby with its *Bobby "Blue" Bland: The Definitive Collection* CD. The album includes twenty-two of Bobby's biggest pre-Malaco hits, from 1957's "I Smell Trouble" to 1976's live duet with B.B. King, "Let the Good Times Roll"—perhaps not definitive, but a representative enough sampling from this period.

Bobby suffered severe chest pains on Tuesday, June 26. Willie Mae rushed him to the hospital where he was diagnosed with congestive heart failure.[25] The doctors treated him and ran extensive tests. Bobby was scheduled to perform on Friday of that week in conjunction with a celebration of Black Music Month, at Chicago's Harold Washington Cultural Center, built across the street from the former Regal Theatre at which Bobby had often performed before it was demolished in 1973.

"He was expected in town on Wednesday to relax before the show," former alderman Dorothy Tillman told a reporter. "Bobby is a dear friend of mine and I call him the Master of the Blues. I am asking fans in Chicago to pray for his speedy recovery, and from 2 to 6 p.m. on Friday, we are asking people to come by to sign a get-well card. There will be a concert, but with special guest artists paying tribute to Bobby."[26]

God must have heard their prayers, because Bobby was miraculously recovered and back on the road by August 7, where he appeared at the posh Dakota Jazz Club in Minneapolis, Minnesota, where tickets were going for $50 a pop.

During the show, Bobby would cough occasionally during a song and have to stop, at one point telling the audience, "I got to do it again—that shit pisses me off." But overall he seemed in good spirits. After a swig of fruit juice, he confessed that "this used to be the Johnny Walker Red Label," and when he asked a younger woman near the stage if she had a boyfriend and she answered that she was waiting for a man with money, Bobby retorted, "Well, you're not gonna find it up here on this stage."[27]

Ernest C. Withers, the young man who was in the first group of black policemen in Memphis in 1948 and who later became one of the country's most acclaimed photographers, particularly of civil rights movement figures, Negro League baseball players, and jazz and blues artists, the latter collected in his book, *The Memphis Blues Again*, died on October 15, 2007, at the age of eighty-five at the Memphis Veterans Medical Center, from complications of a stroke he suffered a month earlier.[28]

One of the performers that Ernest Withers photographed back in Memphis, in addition to Bobby Bland, was a young prodigy named Ike Turner. After Turner recorded for Sam Phillips on "Rocket 88" and other songs and took Bobby Bland to Modern Records for his second recording session in 1952, he moved to East St. Louis, Illinois, in 1954, where his band, the Kings of Rhythm, became a favorite around the St. Louis area. In 1958, he met a teenage singer from Nutbush, Tennessee, named Anna Mae Bullock. Before long, the Ike & Tina Turner Revue, booked by Evelyn Johnson at the Buffalo Booking Agency, became the hottest, sexiest act on the chitlin circuit. In 1966 Phil Spector produced their smash single "River Deep, Mountain High," which catapulted them to international fame.

Ike Turner, whose father was beaten to his eventual death by a gang of white thugs when Ike was just a child, was a temperamental star with an addictive personality that led to alcohol and cocaine dependency and ultimately to his divorce from Tina in 1975. Afterward, both his life and career spiraled downward. Tina's account of years of domestic violence, infidelity, and drug use in her 1986 autobiography, *I, Tina*, and the 1993 movie based on it, *What's Love Got to Do With It*, made Ike a public villain, even though he said it was overstated.

Turner was in jail on narcotic charges in 1991 when he and Tina were inducted into the Rock and Roll Hall of Fame. Tina accepted for them both. In addition to writing his autobiography, *Takin' Back My Name: The Confessions of Ike Turner*, he rerecorded "Rocket 88" for his 2001 album *Here and Now* and returned to touring. In 2006 he recorded a new album, *Risin' with the Blues*, which won the Grammy that year as Best Traditional Blues Album. He even began visiting schools to warn students about the perils of drug abuse.

So it was a shame when whatever demons that tormented him throughout his wild, tumultuous, but musically influential life conquered him for good when he succumbed to an accidental overdose of cocaine on December 12, 2007, at his home in San Marcos, California, a San Diego suburb, at the age of seventy-six.[29]

Bobby Bland and Mick Hucknall of Simply Red chat about Hucknall's album, *Hucknall: Tribute to Bobby,* in Memphis in November 2007. Copyright AndyFallon.co.uk

Farther Up the Road

2008–

For Bobby, the line from his first hit in 1957, "Farther Up the Road"—
"You got to reap just what you sow, that old saying is true"—was becoming a reality. But instead of "Like you mistreat someone, someone's gonna
mistreat you," what Bobby had sowed over the years was lots of love and hap-
piness, and, now, in his final years, he was reaping the reciprocal love and appreciation from his fans, family, and friends for all his efforts.

At the 4th Annual Dallas Blues Festival on February 9, 2008, Nancy Johnson,
of Corsicana, Texas, joined Bobby onstage after his show to present him with
a custom designed "Master of the Blues" Trophy that she had been working
on for the past two years. According to Johnson, the trophy's concept, with a
45 rpm record on top, was centered on Bobby's initial number 1 hit "Farther
Up the Road." Bobby apparently was pleased, inviting Johnson and her guests
backstage for photos and reminiscences with his wife, Willie Mae, who was
celebrating her sixty-third birthday that night.[1]

A few nights later, on February 15, Bobby and the band were back near
Memphis for the 7th Annual Blues Bash at Sam's Town Casino's River Palace
Entertainment Center. Bobby headlined the show that also included Shirley
Brown, who recorded Stax/Truth's last big hit, "Woman to Woman," in 1974;
J. Blackfoot, who, as John Colbert, fronted Stax's popular Soul Children; and
old friend Bobby Rush.[2]

"The deepest friendship in the music is probably Bobby Bland," Rush said.
"We don't talk to each other on an everyday basis, but there's a deep, embed-
ded friendship with Bobby and I. Bobby has taught me about style and staying power. You may hear Muddy Waters' name mentioned more on the blues
circuit, but Bobby Bland is the biggest artist by far. He probably sold as many
records as B.B. King.

"I think the advice he gave me was the way he carried himself in the music business. And I listened and watched how he got over with nothing to go on. Because the time he was coming on was earlier than me, and he had nothing to go on. Bobby 'Blue' Bland didn't tell me anything, but I could see what he was about, and that's very neat."[3]

If there were not already enough Bobby Bland record compilations, Germany's Digimode Entertainment released a collection of twenty of his earliest recordings, many seldom reissued, as a part of a series called *Brothers of Soul: Early Years Collection.* Other artists in the series include the Drifters, Fats Domino, James Brown, Johnny "Guitar" Watson, Ray Charles, Jackie Wilson, and Sam Cooke.

The consistency of Bobby's live shows in these later years suffered considerably, as did the makeup of his touring band. Much of the problem had to do with the way that blues music was now being presented. The chitlin circuit venues where a performer like Bobby would provide an entire evening's entertainment, doing two or three longs sets in one evening, were largely replaced with blues festival–like venues, like those in Dallas and Tunica, where from four to ten acts did quick twenty- to forty-minute sets back to back. While the money was good for such a short performance, there was no time to develop a show and work the audience in the way that Bobby had mastered. As a result, these mini-shows were not very satisfying for either Bobby or the audience. The audience did get to hear Bobby's major hits, of course, but in a perfunctory medley, while Bobby barely got a chance to warm up his vocal cords or his audience. Band members were no happier, since they had little chance to solo or learn new material; so they tended to come and go. Even Joe Hardin, Bobby's longtime bandleader and booster, looked bored at times, putting the band through the exact show they had perfected and repeated night after night after night—after a while, with little need for Joe's direction at all.

Bobby finally got sick of it and, at the urging of his son Rodd, the band's drummer, bravely decided to reconstitute the band in the fashion of the old show bands of yore. So he asked Joe Hardin, the trumpeter who had helped reorganize the band after Bobby had fired Ernie Fields and his band in 1972, to recruit new players for this new iteration of the Joe Hardin Orchestra. It did not take Joe long to locate several seasoned veterans of the blues band scene to play with the one blues legend, besides B.B. King, who still had a vision of a big, brassy, full-bore blues band and not a synthesized imitation. In addition to a solid rhythm section of guitar, bass, and drums anchored by Rodd, Joe rounded up a full horn section of himself on trumpet, with a tenor saxophonist, an alto saxophonist, and a trombonist, to ensure that "St. James Infirmary" would now include the obligatory trombone solo at the bridge. The only instrument missing was a B3 organ—but maybe that would be added soon.

This new band could now not only play the festival-type shows with a fuller, more professional sound, but could also develop a more complete repertoire of Bobby Bland material to present in ninety-minute single-band sets. This was a gutsy thing to do for a septuagenarian performer with a fan base easing into old age, but was necessary if Bobby were to continue to perform. First, because his voice was no longer what it was, he needed the band to fill in the gaps and to make his show more appealing. Also, he needed the more accomplished players to attract and retain other band members in a creative ensemble. But, most importantly, he needed the better band to satisfy his own musical ear of what was right for him; for if he were going to continue touring, he wanted what he was presenting to sound right, since that was the only way he could be happy.

And happy he was at his first extended show on February 17, 2008, at the Crossroads Music Hall, a recently renovated club in downtown Huntsville, Alabama, that ordinarily featured alternative rock and pop bands for the twenty-something set. Bobby's booking agent was looking for a gig on the way home from Atlanta to Memphis where the band could practice its extended show, after doing several weeks of festival shows, with the likes of Bobby Rush, Shirley Brown, J. Blackfoot, Willie Clayton, and Mel Waiters, throughout the South. And the Crossroads management had recently drawn decent older crowds for shows by New Orleans stalwarts the Dirty Dozen Brass Band and the Radiators, so it seemed a plausible fit.

The crowd that began gathering about an hour before show time was unusual in several respects. First, it was integrated, about 50 percent black and 50 percent white. In the South, even in 2008, night clubs, like churches, were mostly segregated—voluntarily so, to be sure, but segregated nonetheless. The Crossroads was ordinarily white, depending on the band, but a place that blacks felt welcomed, particularly with the normally younger clientele. Usually Bobby played in Huntsville's chitlin circuit venues, like the African American Elks Lodge on Pulaski Pike, but it had been closed for a few years now because of never-remedied electrical violations. There, only a few white faces were evident at Bobby's shows. But here at the Crossroads, black people felt comfortable enough to cross the color line, especially to see Bobby Bland, maybe for the last time, and a surprising number of white fans felt comfortable enough to leap the age line and go out to a kids' club who would not have breached the color line to go to a black club. And there were even some kids, who trusted the Crossroads' booking policies enough to give Bobby a try, even if they had never heard him, or who just needed some place to go on a Sunday night before a President's Day holiday. At any rate, it was likely the first time in Huntsville history that such a diverse crowd had gathered to hear a musical performance, particularly a southern soul/blues musical performance.

Live music venues for young people generally have very limited seating; the clientele is expected to mingle and dance all night. So the few booths and tables that lined the walls of the Crossroads were full of older people, who preferred to alight by 7:30 p.m., a half hour before the announced show time of 8:00. John Coltrane played on the sound system as the crowd filled the room and mingled pleasantly. Who would have thought that there were so many Bobby Bland fans of all ages and colors on a Sunday night in a family-friendly town like Huntsville? It felt genial—even before the black-clad band sauntered on stage at around 9:00 to begin tuning up.

Joe Hardin finally gave drummer Rodd Bland his cue and the band broke into an upbeat brassy number reminiscent of the early touring days of Blues Consolidated fifty years ago. The floor in front of the bandstand quickly filled as the band moved into a medley of first bars of Bobby's hits. Then Joe Hardin leaned into the microphone and announced a long litany of Bobby Bland hits that would soon be played, concluding with "the world's greatest blues singer, Bobby Blue Bland." From the back of stage center a curtain was parted and a large brown man in a light brown casual suit appeared, supported by an even larger brown man in blue denims, who led the star to his stool at center stage between the horn section at his right and the rhythm section at his left. Bobby fiddled with the microphone for a few seconds, eyed the cheering crowd, smiled, and launched into "Call on Me," which morphed into "That's the Way Love Is" and on to "Farther Up the Road," "I Pity the Fool," "Ain't Nothing You Can Do" . . .

Bobby spotted a pretty girl in front of the stage and began to flirt. "You here alone, baby?" Later, to her companion: "You better watch her, man, the way she movin'. I think she got something on her mind." Then into "Stormy Monday"—not at the end of the show, as was the custom, but in the middle. "I'll Take Care of You" to "St. James Infirmary" to "Ain't No Sunshine," with the usual audience singalong. Then "I Wouldn't Treat a Dog," "Soon as the Weather Breaks," "Members Only" with another singalong, and concluding with a lovely "I Love to See You Smile." Bobby was smiling, joking with the audience throughout, obviously having a good time, and now slowly exited the stage with the help of his denim-clad bodyguard.

The audience stood for several minutes, cheering, astonished by what they had just witnessed—a completely revamped Bobby Bland show just two weeks after his seventy-eighth birthday. There were no new songs, but the song selection from his wide repertoire mixed the big hits with some lesser-known songs not heard in concert in years, to complete what sounded like a fresh new show.

The audience shook its collective head in wonder, laughing, pleased, satisfied. On the way out, one fan remarked to local blues singer Microwave Dave

Gallaher, another big Bobby Bland fan, who had in fact dedicated his 2000 album *Wouldn't Lay My Guitar Down* to Bobby, "Man, I bet you wish that you could be able to sing like that at seventy-eight." To which Dave replied, "I wish I could sing like that now."

Outside, another fan found the band's drummer, Rodd Bland, leaning against a parking meter, smoking a cigarette, waiting for the oversized RV to be loaded by the crew. "Great show," the fan complimented. "Who came up with the playlist?"

"We've been working on that for a while," the younger Bland answered. "After doing all those twenty-minute package shows, with only the big hits, we wanted to do something different, so we searched around for some songs Dad hadn't sung for a while but still stood up. It was our promoter's [Paul LaMonica] idea to end with 'I Love to See You Smile.' He really likes the song, so we did it for him one night. And it went over so well, we just left it in there at the end."[4]

The young fan kiddingly admonished Rodd about not responding to her MySpace message to him. He laughed, embarrassed, and apologized profusely, leading her back inside the club to the bandstand, where he retrieved a pair of used drumsticks and presented them to her apologetically.

Then it was back to Memphis for a few days rest before heading for the next gig in Cleveland and other points north. Bobby now does fewer than 100 shows a year, spacing them so he does not have to fly much and can get back home more often. If the show is in a particularly pleasant destination, his wife, Willie Mae, joins him and Rodd for sort of a family vacation time.

Even though the voice is understandably not as strong as it once was, it is still beautiful and "as smooth as melted chocolate," as one fan remarked. Bobby is again enjoying the band and the audience adulation and interaction. And he has no plans to stop now.

"Well, you know what?" he said. "Actually I wouldn't know anything to do but what I love and what I get paid for—not that I should, but I do get paid. I don't think you can try to change anything that's something you love doing and if you can get a little piece of change for it you should enjoy it. And, you know, the thing of it is that the public is greatest out here because they're the ones that keep you here and without them you wouldn't be anything anyway.[5] So I'd like to stay healthy and sing until I just can't.[6] My wife's involved in a lot of clubs and charities, but I don't go outside. I don't have hobbies. And I don't play golf."[7]

"Sometimes," he concluded with some satisfaction, "I feel like the last of the Mohicans."[8]

Bobby has indeed somehow survived, some might say even thrived, throughout more than half a century in the fickle, hard-tumble world of popular music.

From the Jim Crow cotton fields of west Tennessee to the most upscale jazz clubs of Chicago, New York, and Los Angeles, and, also, of course, to the shabby chitlin circuit stages of the rural South, he has persevered. From the last of the big-band jazz and crooner era, through rock 'n' roll, disco, hip-hop, and rap, Bobby has endured. In a career that started with 78 rpm shellac records, to 45 rpm singles, 33 1/3 rpm long-playing albums, to plastic compact discs, and finally to the digital downloads of today, Bobby's career has spanned them all. Constantly on the road, still playing mostly one-night stands across the country in all manner of "high-class joints, low-class joints, and even some honky-tonks," Bobby has kept going. Even the physical vicissitudes of aging— chronic diabetes, hypertension, triple bypass heart surgery, Lasik eye surgery, congestive heart failure, pneumonia—have not deterred him.

Despite an eighteen-year bout with alcoholism, three marriages, at least six children, assorted grandchildren, and innumerable affairs of the road, Bobby remains today a happily married family man who enjoys his wife, children, and grandchildren. He relishes the awards that continue to come his way, of course, but he has never gotten rich in the process, instead living a comfortable but modest upper-middle-class life in suburban Memphis.

The shy boy who grew up as a lonely only child in rural Tennessee, who learned to sing the blues by listening to the jukebox in his mother's diner and to his friends on Beale Street, who gained a bit of much-needed swagger in the U.S. Army, who later signed a record contract and worked for a notorious Texas hustler who matched him with one of the best R&B writers and arrangers of his time, who went on to R&B stardom and constant entertaining: like many postwar African American men, Bobby Bland somehow overcame the hardships and the many obstacles—economical, social, and racial—and endured, survived, and prevailed.

On May 7, 2008, at the Tunica RiverPark in Tunica, Mississippi, the Blues Foundation honored Bobby again by inducting his album *Members Only* into the Blues Hall of Fame. There was talk about an upcoming project with Boz Scaggs, a new Malaco album, another "best of" collection, and gigs scheduled soon at the House of Blues in New Orleans, B.B. King's Blues Club & Grille in New York City, the Ridgefield Playhouse in Ridgefield, Connecticut, the Birchmere in Alexandria, Virginia . . .

On June 3, 2008, forty-six-year-old Barack Obama, the son of a black Kenyan father and a white Kansan mother, claimed the Democratic presidential nomination in a victory speech before thousands of supporters in St. Paul, Minnesota. "Let us begin the work together," he exhorted. "Let us unite in common effort to chart a new course for America. . . . Tonight, I can stand before you and say that I will be the Democratic nominee for president of the United States."[9]

Bobby was, of course, enthused about the possibility of a black president, but he seemed almost as excited about the news that Mick Hucknall, the vocalist for the British rock band Simply Red, was planning to release his first solo album on June 30, to be entitled *Hucknall: Tribute to Bobby.*

"Yeah, this guy is a hell of a singer," Bobby exclaimed after listening to a preview copy of the CD. "I listened to it and didn't want to believe it. I know some of the tunes I do are hard and for somebody to cross over they have to really study them. He did songs like 'I'll Take Care of You,' 'That's the Way Love Is,' 'Cry, Cry, Cry.' This guy did a beautiful job."[10]

The album, when it appeared, was indeed a good one, as Bobby had predicted. "He doesn't do typical blues," Hucknall said. "His music has this sophistication to it, a jazz tinge. There's also the darkness of his lyrics—Bobby sings with a really twisted pain and sorrow. He's one of those vocalists who influenced my singing style long before I became a slave to pop success."

The album begins with a jazzy, almost hiphop version of "Farther Up the Road" and continues through a pulsating "Ain't That Lovin' You," then on to a pretty version of "I'm Too Far Gone (to Turn Around)" and rollicking, driving covers of Dave Clark and Pearl Woods's "Poverty" and Daniel Moore's "Yolanda." Increasing the tempo and production of "Stormy Monday Blues" does not really work (although Bobby liked the new interpretation), but Hucknall's more faithful takes on "I Wouldn't Treat a Dog (the Way You Treated Me)" and "I'll Take Care of You" prove how timeless these tunes really are. Hucknall's jazzy, countrified treatment of "Chains of Love" is not that successful, but on the final three cuts of the album, he really lets go: an angry "I Pity the Fool," a building "Cry, Cry, Cry," and finally an exceptionally well-crooned "Lead Me On."

The arrangements, by Hucknall and Andy Wright, as well as Hucknall's phrasing, are predictably and satisfyingly updated, of course, but still manage to capture the spirit, if not the exact horn-pulsing, soul-saturated sound of the originals. Hucknall's voice is certainly no match for Bobby's, but he does not at all seem intimidated by the legendary originator of these classic R&B hits, as he opens up and really wails on most of them.

"What I tried to do with these songs is get them across to people who don't know Bobby's work," Hucknall explained. "With the production, we tried not to forget that this is the twenty-first century, so it would be pointless to rerecord the original horn arrangements and productions. It was important to put a contemporary slant on it, but keep that traditional R&B sound."

"What you did with the arrangements, I like 'em," Bobby complimented Hucknall. "'Stormy Monday'—I never dreamed it like that. It's a big twist, but you've got the flavor there. Now I might do it like that! One note you didn't bend, you just sung it straight through. The first time I hear anybody do my material, usually they try to do it like me, but you changed everything, which I really liked."

Bobby was obviously happy with and flattered by the effort. The album's accompanying seventeen-minute documentary DVD, by Paul Spencer, provides a moving moment as Bobby and his protégé chat in the corner of a kitschy suite at the Peabody Hotel in Memphis. Bobby holds court as the wise old veteran, disarmingly charming and gracefully generous, as the two discuss recording techniques and production. There are also a couple of reverent cameos by an ageless B.B. King who compliments Bobby on his "voice as soft as silk," and an aging Van Morrison who quips glumly that Bobby is "just an individual stylist, you know, the phrasing and the way he interprets a song—I can't really describe it in words."[11]

Bobby, palpably pleased with the project, praised Hucknall's respectful tribute. "You've got a smooth voice," he told him. "Either [you've] gone through the ghetto, or slept in there. It's the way you feel in here," Bobby said, tapping his heart. "Somebody's hurt you, or you've been through some bad times. That's what my whole life is about—being misused and abused."[12]

A little more than one year after President Obama's inauguration, on January 27, 2010, Bobby Bland celebrated his 80th birthday at Sam's Town Casino Arena in Tunica, Mississippi, while President Obama delivered his first State of the Union Address at the U.S. Capitol in Washington, D.C. In the Delta, sitting proudly at the table of honor with family and friends and at times visibly moved, Bland was serenaded and heralded by an all-star cast of southern soul greats, including J. Blackfoot, Shirley Brown, Harvey Watkins, Jr. and the Canton Spirituals, Clarence Carter, Millie Jackson, B.B. King, Latimore, Bobby Rush, and Floyd Taylor. The venerable bluesman was scheduled to depart in a few days on still another tour, this time covering 15 cities in 55 days. Copyright Patricia Kuhn.

Epilogue

Soon after the release of Mick Hucknall's tribute album, in early July 2008, Bobby began having trouble breathing. His breath became so labored that Willie Mae had no choice but to rush him to the hospital again. The doctors diagnosed the problem as pneumonia, exacerbated by Bobby's chronic diabetes and hypertension. It took a few days for the medical staff to stabilize the situation, but thanks to Willie Mae's nursing background and patient persistence and Bobby's unrivalled resilience, the bluesman was soon on the mend, and, after a brief stay in a rehabilitation unit, able to return home by July 29.

Wolf Stephenson called him the next day to wish him well. "How you doing?" he asked. "Better? Good. Ready for me to send in the dancing girls? Not yet. Well, let me know. You're sounding better. Give Miss Willie my best and thank her for taking a switch to those doctors. Okay, chief, take care of yourself. I'll check on you later."[1]

By August 4 Bobby was talking about going back to work again,[2] and by August 8, when Latimore visited him on his way to the annual Sunflower River Blues and Gospel Festival in Clarksdale, Bobby was rehearsing the band for a show the next night, only a few minutes from his home, at the DeSoto Civic Center in Southaven, Mississippi, where he would headline the annual Tri-State Blues Festival, with his old friends Willie Clayton, Bobby Rush, J. Blackfoot, Theodis Ealey, and relative newcomers Floyd Taylor (Johnnie's son), Sir Charles Jones, and Sheba Potts-Wright.[3]

On August 19 Bobby and the band were out of the Delta and in Alexandria, Virginia, to perform the show at the Birchmere that had been postponed because of Bobby's health problems. According to the *Washington Post*, "When he arrived at the club . . . he looked frail and fatigued as he moved, with the help of an aide, to a seat at center stage." But apparently once the performance began, it didn't take long for Bobby to warm to the crowd. When a fan shouted, "Turn up the heat, Bob," Bobby smiled slyly and answered, "I can't heat up anymore." And then went on to "sustain a slow burn onstage," proving once again that his "soulfulness remains undiminished."[4] Two days later the band was in New York City to perform at B.B. King's Blues Club and Grill, "lending some authenticity to this Times Square club," according to the *New Yorker.*[5] They were booked next into the Freddie King Blues Fest, with Hubert Sumlin and the Wanda King Blues Band, at the Grenada Theater in Dallas on August 31.

And when the new $14.2 million B.B. King Museum and Delta Interpretative Center opened in Indianola, Mississippi, on September 13, Bobby and Willie Mae made the trip down from Memphis. Bobby even joined B.B., Robert Cray, Keb' Mo', and Kenny Wayne Shepherd on stage to sing a bit. "He came down for that," B.B. King said. "I had invited him, but he didn't tell me he was coming. I looked up at this black tie affair and there he was. I was so surprised and happy. Any time we meet, we have this special camaraderie. He's such a great artist and just a very good person."[6]

Then, on November 4, 2008, Barack Hussein Obama was elected the forty-fourth president of the United States, as the country where Bobby Bland and so many others had fought their way out of racial segregation and rural poverty chose its first African American chief executive. Soon after "Sweet Home Chicago" blared over an exuberant crowd of tens of thousands in Chicago's Grant Park, Obama began his emotional victory speech with these words: "If there is anyone out there who still doubts that America is a place where all things are possible, who still wonders if the dream of our fathers is still alive in our time, who still questions the power of our democracy, tonight is your answer."

Amid the throng stood a graying Jesse Jackson, the leader of Chicago's Operation Breadbasket, where Bobby Bland's longtime guitarist Wayne Bennett had volunteered some forty years before. As Jackson listened to Obama echo the words of Sam Cooke, like others there and throughout America, tears of joy streamed down his face. "It's been a long time coming," the new President-elect preached, "but tonight, because of what we did on this day, in this election, at this defining moment, change has come to America."

Awards

Billboard
Special Achievement Award	*Midnight Run*	1989

Beale Street Walk of Fame
Honor "Note"	1996

Blues Foundation
Blues Vocalist of the Year		1981
Hall of Fame		1981
Blues Vocalist of the Year		1982
Entertainer of the Year		1982
Re-issue Album of the Year (Foreign)	*Woke Up Screaming*	1982
Classic of Blues Recordings—Albums	*Two Steps from the Blues*	1987
Soul/Blues Male Artist of the Year		1993
Soul/Blues Album of the Year	*Years of Tears*	1994
Soul/Blues Male Artist of the Year		1994
Soul/Blues Male Artist of the Year		1997
Lifetime Achievement Award		1998
Soul/Blues Male Artist of the Year		1999
Classic of Blues Recordings—Albums	*Members Only*	2008

Cash Box
Rhythm and Blues Artist of the Year	1961

Celebrate the Soul of America Music Awards

Honoree	1994

College of Communication and Fine Arts University of Memphis

Distinguished Achievement in the Creative & Performing Arts Award	2005

Grammys (National Academy of Recording Arts and Sciences)

Best Traditional Blues Album Nominee	*Members Only*	1985
Best Contemporary Blues Album Nominee	*Blues You Can Use*	1987
Best Contemporary Blues Album Nominee	*Sad Street*	1996
Memphis Chapter's Governor's Award		1996
Lifetime Achievement Award		1997
Best Traditional Blues Award Nominee	*Memphis Monday Morning*	2000

NAACP

NAACP Image Award	1975

National Academy of Blues

Top Male Blues Singer		1981
Blues Single of the Year	"You'd Be a Millionaire"	1981
Blues Album of the Year	*Sweet Vibrations*	1981

Rhythm & Blues Foundation

Pioneer Award	1992

Rock and Roll Hall of Fame

Inductee		1992
"500 Songs That Shaped Rock and Roll"	*Turn On Your Love Light*	

Selected Discography

With over 500 songs and 30 original albums to his recording credit, it is challenging to select only a few of Bobby Bland's best albums. But, in the interest of space, here is a list of essential titles that will delight any Bobby Bland fan and bedazzle anyone not already familiar with his large and varied oeuvre. Arranged loosely in chronological order, these selections provide a solid sampling of Bland's vocal development and progressively powerful prowess from the beginning of his career until the present. For those with a deeper interest, a complete session discography of Bland's 75 recording sessions—including dates, locations, personnel, song selection, chart positions, and awards, along with a complete album number index—may be found at www.soulofthemaп.com.

Modern Years

The Original Memphis Blues Brothers   Ace LP CH26   Ace CDCHD 265
    This introductory collection includes four of Bobby's first early recordings with Modern Records in Memphis, as well as cuts recorded during the same period in the early 1950s by Little Junior Parker, Earl Forest, Johnny Ace, B.B. King, Ike Turner, and Rosco Gordon.

Duke Years

Two Steps from the Blues   Duke LP74   MCAD-27036
    Modern blues doesn't get much better than this. Bobby's first solo album lays all his burgeoning young talent right out there on the line with classic Joe Scott arrangements of some of the best blues songs ever recorded: "Cry, Cry, Cry," "Lead Me On," "I Pity the Fool," "Little Boy Blue," "I'll Take Care of You," and seven others. A true classic.

Ain't Nothing You Can Do   Duke LP78   ABC/Duke DLPX-78
  Released three years after *Two Steps from the Blues*, Bobby's third album captures the bluesman at his height with showstoppers like the title cut as well as "Steal Away," "If You Could Read My Mind," "Black Night," and eight other gems. An overlooked masterpiece of modern blues.

The Soul of the Man   Duke LP79
  Here are Bobby and Joe Scott at their zenith, with Bobby showing off his ability to sing in a variety of styles and tempos and Scott providing the precise gritty horn counterpart that made the pair an indispensable team. From the up-tempo blues of "Reach Right Out" to the covers of Jimmy Witherspoon's standard "Ain't Nobody's Business If You Do" and Little Willie John's steamy "Fever," there's soul aplenty and a mighty groove to move.

The Best of Bobby Bland   Duke LP84   ABC/Duke DLPX-84   MCA 31219
  The first of many Bobby Bland compilations and arguably the best, certainly for the Man's early megahits like "I Smell Trouble, "Turn On Your Love Light," "Call on Me," "Farther Up the Road," and "Stormy Monday." Put this baby on and enjoy sixties R&B at its funkiest.

I Pity the Fool/The Duke Recordings, Vol. 1   MCAD2-10665
Turn On Your Love Light/The Duke Recordings, Vol. 2   MCAD2-10957
That Did It!/The Duke Recordings, Vol. 3   MCAD2-11444
  These three compilations, each containing two CDs, consist of all available recordings by Bobby while he was with Duke Records, 1952–72, in chronological order. Of the 148 songs presented, the listener will find all of the bluesman's big hits, as well as his clunkers, and everything in between, a few of which were unreleased or unavailable on albums or CDs until this complete collection was released in 1992–95.

ABC-Dunhill/MCA Years

His California Album   Dunhill 50163   MCA 10349
  This is Bobby's first and best album with arranger Steve Barri and conductor Michael Omartian and proved beyond a shadow of a Duke that, at age forty-three, the Man could still holler with the best of them. Includes big pop blues arrangements of hits "This Time I'm Gone for Good" and "Goin' Down Slow," as well as eight others.

Get On Down with Bobby Bland/Reflections in Blue   BGOCD449
  This duo-album CD contains two of Bobby's best efforts with ABC. While

Bland always claimed that country and western music was his first love, *Get On Down* is his only country and western effort—a bit brassy, but still down-home enough to satisfy both blues and country fans. *Reflections in Blue* stands alone as a classic of blues pop with the hits "The Soul of a Man," "Sittin' on a Poor Man's Throne," and the original of "It Ain't the Real Thing."

The Anthology   MCA 088 112 596-2
This two-disc compilation contains fifty of Bobby's best songs from his Duke and ABC-Dunhill/MCA recordings, dating from 1952 ("Lovin' Blues") through 1982 ("Recess in Heaven"). If there is one essential collection that best represents the Man's talents during these years, this is it.

Malaco Years

Members Only   Malaco LP7429
Malaco Records was an established soul company well before Bobby joined it in 1985 to record this smash album. Producers Wolf Stephenson and Tommy Couch pulled out all the Malaco stops—songwriting, musicians, and production—to put together this fine debut LP.

First Class Blues   Malaco MAL-5000-CD
This was Bobby's first CD, and it contains selections from his first three Malaco albums, as well as remakes of "Two Steps from the Blues" and "St. James Infirmary," which demonstrate conclusively that Bland had not lost his formidable vocal power over the years.

Years of Tears   Malaco LP7469
Bobby's eighth album with Malaco is one of his best, thanks to a pared down production, strong backup by veteran Muscle Shoals musicians (minus strings), and terrific tunes by Malaco writers George Jackson ("Hole in the Wall," "Hurtin' Time Again"), Frederick Knight ("There's a Stranger in my House," "I Just Tripped on a Piece of Your Broken Heart," "Sweet Lady Love"), and Larry Addison on the title track.

Blues at Midnight   Malaco MCD7512
Bobby's last album is a fine tribute to his long and distinguished career and shows the Man can still wail when he needs to. Highlights include "Where Do I Go From Here," "You Hit the Nail Right on the Head," and "I'm a Blues Man." Proof positive that Bobby's blues at whatever time of day or night is timeless and vibrant.

Notes

Opening Quotes

Maddix, Jacquie, "Interview: Bobby 'Blue' Bland," *Blues On Stage*, Minneapolis, KFAI Radio, October 1, 2002, at www.mnblues.com/review/2002/bobbybluebland-intv-11-02-jm.html.

Baldwin, James, "Last of the Great Masters," review of *The World of Earl Hines* by Stanley Dance, *New York Times Book Review*, October 16, 1977.

Byrd, Bobby, *White Panties, Dead Friends & Other Bits & Pieces of Love*, El Paso, TX, Cinco Puntos Press, 2006, 15.

Introduction

1. King, B.B., with David Ritz, *Blues All Around Me: The Autobiography of B.B. King*, New York, Avon Books, 1996, 134.

2. Summers, Lynn S., and Bob Scheir, "Living Blues Interview: Little Milton," *Living Blues* 18, Autumn 1974, 20.

3. Whitburn, Joel, *The Billboard Book of Top 40 R&B and Hip-Hop Hits*, New York, Billboard Books, 2006, 783.

4. Worsham, Doris, "The Saga of Bobby Bland," Oakland *Tribune*, March 8, 1975, 12-E.

5. Figi, J. B., "Time for Bobby Bland," *Down Beat*, August 7, 1969, 16.

6. Back, Les, "Bobby Bland's Influential Voice," *Oxford American* 27/28, 1999, 84–85.

Chapter 1

1. Cohn, David L., "Sing No Blues for Memphis," *New York Times*, September 4, 1955, 14, 66.

2. Stephenson, Wolf, Liner notes for *Blues at Midnight*, Jackson, MS, Malaco Records, 1998, 2.

3. *Ibid.*, 3.

4. Robertson, Rebecca L., *City on the Bluff: History and Heritage of Memphis*, Memphis, St. Luke's Press, 1987, 39.

5. Cohn, 14, 66.

6. Sigafoos, Robert A., *Cotton Row to Beale Street: A Business History of Memphis*, Memphis, Memphis State University Press, 1979, 137.

7. Sigafoos, 182.

8. Cantor, Louis, *Wheelin' on Beale: How WDIA-Memphis Became the Nation's First All-Black Radio Station and Created the Sound That Changed America*, New York, Pharos Books, 1992, 7.

9. *Ibid.*, 8.

10. *Polk's Memphis (Shelby County, Tenn.) City Directory* 1945, 1946, 1948, 1950, 1955, 1960, 1961, 1967.

11. Lee, George W., *Beale Street: Where the Blues Began*, New York, Robert O. Ballou, 1934, 13–14.

12. McKee, Margaret, and Fred Chisenhall, *Beale Black & Blue: Life and Music on Black America's Main Street*, Baton Rouge, Louisiana State University Press, 1981, 15.

13. Webb, Arthur, "Bobby Blue Bland," *Downtowner Magazine*, August 1997, 33.

14. Merrill, Hugh, *The Blues Route*, New York, William Morrow, 1990, 62–63.

15. King, 133–34.

16. Cantor, 1.

17. Leadbitter, Mike, *Delta Country Blues*, Bexhill-on-Sea (UK), Blues Unlimited, 1968, 33.

18. Webb, 33.

19. Merrill, 61–62.

20. Gordon, Robert, "Bobby 'Blue' Bland: Love Throat of the Blues," in Guralnick, Peter, Robert Santelli, Holly George-Warren, and Christopher John Farley, *Martin Scorsese Presents the Blues: A Musical Journey*, New York, HarperCollins, 2003, 147.

21. Cantor, 12.

22. Klibanoff, Hank, "Ernest C. Withers: The Eye on the Prize," *New York Times Magazine*, December 30, 2007, 44–45.

23. Kain, John F., "Postwar Metropolitan Development: Housing Preferences and Auto Ownership," *American Economic Review* 57, no. 2, May 1967, 223.

24. Stephenson, 3.

25. *Ibid.*, 2.

26. O'Neal, Jim, "Bobby Bland! Backstage," *Living Blues* 4, Winter 1970–71, 13.

27. Cantor, 37.

28. Palmer, Robert, *Deep Blues*, New York, Penguin Books, 1982, 229.

29. Cohn, 66.

30. Connell, Mary Ann Strong, *The Peabody Hotel*, Thesis, Oxford, University of Mississippi, 1959, 91.

31. Cheseborough, Steve, *Blues Traveling: The Holy Sites of Delta Blues*, Jackson, University Press of Mississippi, 2001, 24–33.

32. Palmer, *Deep Blues*, 207.

33. *Ibid.*, 229.

34. Davis, Francis, *The History of the Blues*, New York, Hyperion, 1995, 175–98.

35. Keil, Charles, *Urban Blues*, Chicago, University of Chicago Press, 1966, 61–66.

36. Worley, William S., *Beale Street: Crossroads of America's Music*, Lenexa, Kansas, Addax, 1998, 21.

37. Keil, 61–66.

38. Bailey, Joe, "The Texas Shuffle: Lone Star Underpinnings of the Kansas City Jazz Sound," *Journal of Texas Music History* 6, no. 1, 2006, 3–19.

39. Brisbin, John Anthony, "Jay McShann: I Always Thought Blues and Jazz Went Together," *Living Blues* 149, January-February 2000, 19.

40. King, 68.

41. Palmer, *Deep Blues*, 64.

42. George, Nelson, *The Death of Rhythm & Blues*, New York, Pantheon, 1988, 20.

43. Evans, David, *The NPR Curious Listener's Guide to Blues*, New York, Penguin, 2005, 40–41.

Chapter 2

1. Wexler, Jerry, and David Ritz, *Rhythm and the Blues: A Life in American Music*, New York, Alfred A. Knopf, 1993, 62.

2. Tosches, Nick, *Unsung Heroes of Rock 'n' Roll*, New York, Charles Scribner's Sons, 1984, 133.

3. Keil, 66.

4. Shaw, Arnold, *Honkers and Shouters: The Golden Years of Rhythm and Blues*, New York, Macmillan, 1978, 225.

5. King, B.B. interview with author, Von Braun Concert Hall, Huntsville, AL, September 21, 2008.

6. King, 135.

7. Salem, James M., *The Late, Great Johnny Ace and the Transition from R&B to Rock 'n' Roll*, Urbana, University of Illinois Press, 29–30.

8. Davis, Hank, "Living Blues Interview: Roscoe Gordon," *Living Blues* 49, Winter 1981, 13.

9. Gordon, *Martin Scorsese Presents the Blues*, 146.

10. McKee and Chisenhall, 66.

11. Cantor, 37.

12. McKee and Chisenhall, 66–67.

13. Guralnick, Peter, *Lost Highway: Journeys and Arrivals of American Musicians*, New York, Perennial, 1989, 60–61.

14. Hannusch, Jeff, "Bobby 'Blue' Bland: Storied Blues Singer Anything but Bland," *Goldmine*, October 31, 2003, 14–18.

15. Aykroyd, Dan, and Ben Manilla, *Elwood's Blues: Interviews with the Blues Legends & Stars*, San Francisco, Backbeat, 2004, 10–11.

16. O'Neal, Jim, "Bobby Bland! Backstage," 14.

17. Lofgren, Tommy, "Bobby Blue Bland: Ain't Doing Too Bad," *Jefferson* 27, 1974, 9.

18. Lauterbach, Preston, "Chitlin' Circuit," *Memphis: The City Magazine*, August 6, 2005, 3.

19. King, 133–34.

20. Mitchell Hotel business card, from the Beale Street Collection of the Memphis/Shelby County Room of the Memphis/Shelby County Public Library and Information Center.

21. Goldman, Albert, *Elvis*, New York, McGraw-Hill, 1981, 104.

22. *All Day and All Night: Memories from Beale Street Musicians*, documentary film produced by Judy Peiser, Southern Folklore Center] 1990.

23. Burk, Bill E., "'Sunbeam' Mitchell Is Puzzled at 75," Memphis *Press-Scimitar*, November 5, 1981, A5.

24. King interview.

25. Sawyer, Charles, *The Arrival of B.B. King*, Garden City, NY, Doubleday, 1980, 71.

26. King interview.

27. King, 138.

28. Webb, 32.

29. McKee and Chisenhall, 248.

30. Gordon, *Martin Scorsese Presents the Blues*, 146.

31. Palmer, *Deep Blues*, 228.

32. King interview.

33. Sawyer, 55–63.

34. Cantor, 78–79.

35. Sawyer, 63.

36. "Moohah" [A. C. Williams], "What's Happening in the Big M," *Tri-State Defender*, November 24, 1951, 10.

37. King interview.

38. Sawyer, 63–64.

39. King interview.

40. Sawyer, 63–64.

41. Grendysa, Pete, "The Making of Rhythm & Blues," *Collecting Magazine*, 1985.

42. Dolby, Ray, "Some Musings on Progress in Audio: A Quest for Better Sound at Affordable Prices," Heyser Memorial Lecture, AES 112th Convention, M.O.C.-Center, Munchen, Germany, May 11, 2005.

43. Eliot, Marc, *Rockonomics: The Money Behind the Music*, New York, Franklin Watts, 1989, 38.

44. Evans, 39.

45. Shaw, throughout.

46. *Ibid.*, 194–95.

47. *Ibid.*, 202.

48. Sawyer, 64–65.

49. Whitburn, 317. During this period, there were three main weekly recording industry publications that featured charts that ranked a song's popularity: *Billboard* (1894–), *Cash Box* (1942–96), and *Music Vendor*, which changed its name to *Record World* in 1964 (1946–82). Each used slightly different methods of ranking a song at various times—usually, but not always, including jukebox popularity, record sales, and radio airplay. The names of the charts also varied through the years, but *Billboard* and *Cash Box* maintained separate charts for popular music songs in urban, primarily African American venues, except from November 30, 1963, to January 23, 1965, during which time *Billboard* included R&B music with other types of popular music in a single chart, presumably because of the wide popularity of Motown records. All references to a chart number are therefore to *Billboard*'s African American chart, regardless of its name (Rhythm & Blues, R&B, Soul, Black, Hip-Hop), because the *Billboard* charts are best documented, except for the period when *Billboard* did not publish a separate R&B chart, for which period the *Cash Box* Black Contemporary Singles Chart is cited.

50. King interview.

51. Shaw, 204.

52 Guralnick, *Lost Highway*, 75.

53. Mohair Slim, "The Rosco Gordon Story," at www.bluejuice.org.au/rosco_story. html, 2.

54. Gordon, *Martin Scorsese Presents the Blues*, 146–47.

55. "Sam Phillips' Sun Records," at www.history-of-rock.com/sam_phillips_sun_re-cords.Htm, 1.

56. Palmer, *Deep Blues*, 218–19.

57. *Ibid.*, 220–23.

58. Escott, Colin, with Martin Hawkins, *Good Rockin' Tonight: Sun Records and the Birth of Rock 'n' Roll*, New York, St. Martin's, 1991, 13–24.

59. Whitburn, 221.

60. *Ibid.*

61. Davis, Hank, "Living Blues Interview: Roscoe Gordon," 12.

62. Mohair Slim, "The Rosco Gordon Story," 1–2.

63. Mohair Slim, "Rosco Gordon Interview," at www.bluejuice.org.au/rosco_intrview. html, May, 2001, 8.

64. Escott, 26–27.

65. Hoskyns, Barney, and James Maycock, "'Rocket 88' and the Birth of Rock & Roll," *Mojo*, February 2002.

66. Whitburn, 221.

67. Mohair Slim, "Rosco Gordon Interview," 7–8.

68. *Ibid.*, 3–8.

69. "Rosco Gordon," Wikipedia.

70. Gordon, *Martin Scorsese Presents the Blues*, 147.

71. King, 134–35.

72. King interview.

73. Point, Michael, "Murphy, Matt 'Guitar,'" in Komara, Edward, ed., *Encyclopedia of the Blues*, New York, Routledge, 2006, 711–12.

74. Santelli, Robert, *The Big Book of Blues: A Biographical Encyclopedia*, New York, Penguin, 1993, 322–23.

75. Gart, Galen, and Roy C. Ames, *Duke/Peacock Records: An Illustrated History with Discography*, Milford, NH, Big Nickel, 1990, 27.

76. *Bobby 'Blue' Bland: Long Beach 1983*, Liner notes, Lelystad, Holland, Blues Factory, 2.

77. Dahl, Bill, "Bobby 'Blue' Bland: Soulful Seduction," *Blues Revue* 88, June/July 2004, 12.

78. Evans, 104.

79. Guralnick, *Lost Highway*, 76.

Chapter 3

1. Tennessee Department of Health Office of Vital Records: *Verification of Birth Facts for Robert Calvin Bland*, September 17, 2007; Tennessee Department of Health, *Certificate of Death for Mary Bland*, January 12, 2001; Tennessee Department of Health, *Certificate of*

Death for Isaac J. Brooks, January 24, 1992; State of Tennessee Marriage License, County of Shelby, *I. J. Brooks and Mary Lee Smith*, September 26, 1929.

2. *1930 United States Federal Census* [online database], Ancestry.com.

3. Rowe, Mike, *Chicago Blues: The City and the Music*, New York, DaCapo, 1981, 26.

4. McKee and Chisenhall, 74.

5. Miller, Kelly, Memphis *World*, September 18, 1931.

6. Rowe, 26.

7. Biles, Roger, *Memphis in the Great Depression*, Knoxville, University of Tennessee Press, 1986, 92, 107.

8. Stephenson, 1.

9. Rutkoff, Peter, and Will Scott, "Preaching the Blues: The Mississippi Delta of Muddy Waters," *Kenyon Review*, New Series, vol. XXVII, no. 2, Spring 2005, 6.

10. Guralnick, *Lost Highway*, 74.

11. Webb, 30.

12. Stephenson, 1.

13. *1920 United States Federal Census* [online database], Ancestry.com. "Marriage Record, Tipton County, Tennessee, Leroy Bland and Mary Lee Smith, October 26, 1936," *Tennessee State Marriages, 1765-2002* [online database], Ancestry.com.

14. Stephenson, 1.

15. Spitzer, Nick, "Bobby 'Blue' Bland Interview," 2003 audio interview at www.yearoftheblues.org/features.asp?type=4&id=%7B024252EB-DB9.

16. Standifer, Jim, Bobby Blue Bland interview for African American Music Collection, at www.umich.edu/~afroammu/standifer/bland.html.

17. Rutkoff and Scott, 6.

18. Guralnick, *Lost Highway*, 74.

19. Stephenson, 1–2.

20. Osteen, Faye Ellis, *Millington, The First Hundred Years*, Southhaven, MS, King's Press, 2002, 142–43.

21. Aykroyd and Manilla, 9.

22. Rutkoff and Scott, 7.

23. Dahl, Bill, liner notes for *Bobby "Blue" Bland: The Definitive Collection*, Geffen Records, 2007, 1.

24. Dahl, Bill, liner notes for *Bobby "Blue" Bland: The Anthology*, MCA Records, 2001, 2.

25. Wisor, Donna Rae, "Bobby Bland: It's All 'Biscuits' and Gravy, Baby," *Beaumont Journal*, October 25, 2006, 1.

26. West, Hollie, "Records," *Rolling Stone*, May 31, 1969, 35.

27. Stephenson, 2.

28. Aykroyd and Manilla, 13.

29. Guralnick, *Lost Highway*, 74

30. Gordon, Robert, "Bobby 'Blue' Bland," *Rolling Stone*, May 28, 1998, 13.

31. Dawson, Walter, "Bobby 'Blue' Bland Keeps On Steppin'," Memphis *Commercial Appeal*, April 29, 1979, 3.

32. Worsham, Doris, 12-E.

33. McClusky, Dan, audio interview with Bobby Bland, broadcast on Tom Mazzolini's *Blues by the Bay*, KPFA, San Francisco, February 17 and 24, 2007, at kpfa.org/archives/index.php?arch=19033.

34. Robson, Britt, "True Blue," Minneapolis *Star Tribune*, August 5, 2007.

35. Stephenson, 1–2.

36. Komara, Edward, "Blues," in Komara, 119.

37. McKee and Chisenhall, 85.

38. Guralnick, *Lost Highway,"* 74.

39. Webb, 31.

40. McKee and Chisenhall, 249.

Chapter 4

1. Salem, 35.

2. *Ibid.*, 41.

3. Cantor, 184.

4. Moonoogian, George, and Meeden, Roger, "Duke Records: The Early Years. An Interview with David J. Mattis," *Whiskey, Women, and . . .* 14, June 1984.

5. Gart and Ames, 27–32.

6. Salem, 55.

7. Sawyer, 134.

8. Salem, 43.

9. Gart and Ames, 32–33.

10. Marion, J. C., "I Smell Trouble: Bobby 'Blue' Bland," *JammUpp* 24, 2002.

11. Dawson, 3.

12. Kreiser, Christine M., "Don Robey and Duke—Peacock Records," Year of the Blues 2003 web site www.yearoftheblues.org/features.

13. Gart and Ames, 5.

14. Salem, 47–55.

15. Wasserzieher, Bill, "The Lion in Winter: Clarence 'Gatemouth' Brown," *Blues Revue*, January 2002.

16. Salem, 54–57.

17. Shaw, 479–80.

18. Vera, Billy, liner notes for *Junior's Blues*, MCA Records, 1992, 3.

19. Govenar, Alan, *Living Texas Blues*, Dallas Museum of Art, 1985, 57.

20. Shaw, 479–80.

21. Salem, 68–69.

22. Gart and Ames, 32–33.

23. Salem, 78.

24. McKee and Chisenhall, 249.

25. Bad Dog Blues, "'Beale Streeter' Forest Dies," Rochester, NY, WITR, August 2003, www.baddogblues.com/archives/8.03/news.htm.

26. Morthland, John, "Royal Blue," *Texas Monthly* 5, no. 8, August 1997, 58–60.

27. Gart and Ames, 35.

28. Paul, Mike, "Don Robey," obituary, *Living Blues* 23, September-October 1975, 5.

29. Moonoogian and Meeden.

30. Salem, 69–70.

31. Davis, Hank, "Living Blues Interview: Roscoe Gordon," 15–16.

32. Gart and Ames, 62.

33. Salem, 69–70.

34. "Korean War," Wikipedia.

35. U.S. Department of Defense, "United States of America Korean War Commemoration," www.korea.50.army.mil/history/factsheets/afroamer.shtml.

36. Schoenherr, Neil, "Korean War Had Major Impact on Race Relations in the United States," *Washington University in St. Louis News & Information*, July 25, 2003.

37. Gart and Ames, 80.

38. Guralnick, *Lost Highway*, 75.

39. Morthland, 58–60.

40. Moonoogian and Meeden.

41. Salem, 107.

42. Shaw, 482–87.

43. Vera, 3.

44. Shaw, 488.

45. Gart and Ames, 60.

46. Wood, Roger, *Down in Houston: Bayou City Blues*, Austin, University of Texas Press, 2003, 187–88, 200.

47. Sawyer, 134–40; Salem, 128–30; Gart and Ames, 72–73.

Chapter 5

1. Guralnick, *Lost Highway*, 75.

2. Webb, 33.

3. Hannusch, "Bobby 'Blue' Bland," 14.

4. Govenar, Alan, *The Early Years of Rhythm & Blues: Focus on Houston*, Houston, Rice University Press, 1990, 16.

5. Snyder, Mike, "With Its Rich History, Fourth Ward Is Strong in Symbolism," Houston *Chronicle*, January 9, 2000, A-24.

6. Govenar, *The Early Years of Rhythm & Blues*, 3.

7. Minutaglio, Bill, "Texas Claims Its Rightful Rank in History of Blues," *Corpus Christi Caller Times*, undated article in the Bobby Bland file at the University of Mississippi's Blue Archives.

8. Associated Booking Corp., "Bio: Bobby Bland," 3.

9. Wood, *Down in Houston*, 159–60.

10. Gart and Ames, 94.

11. Topping, Ray, Liner notes for *Bobby 'Blue' Bland: The "3B" Blues Boy*, London, Ace Records, 1990, 5.

12. "Roy Gaines—The Legendary Blues Guitarist and Musician," www.roygaines.com.

13. Vera, 4.

14. Marion, "I Smell Trouble," 2.

15. O'Neal, Jim, "Bobby Bland! Backstage," 17–18.

16. Shurman, Dick, Jim O'Neal, and Amy O'Neal, "Living Blues Interview: Otis Rush," *Living Blues* 28, July-August 1976, 17.

17. Gart and Ames, 81.

18. McClusky.

19. Hoskyns, Barney, "Rock's Backpages Audio Interview with Bobby Bland," July 8, 1989, www.rocksbackpages.com.

20. Wood, *Down in Houston*, 197.

21. Govenar, Alan, "Evelyn Johnson," *Living Blues* 83, November-December 1988, 31.

22. Aykroyd and Manilla, 240.

23. Salem, 57–58.

24. *Ibid.*, 126–27.

25. Morthland, 58–60.

26. Wood, *Down in Houston*, 205.

27. George, *The Death of Rhythm & Blues*, 17–18.

28. Marion, J. C., "Mystery Train: Little Junior Parker," *JammUpp* 24, 2002.

29. Stapleton-Corcoran, Erin, "Clark, Dave," in Komara, 210.

30. Guralnick, *Lost Highway*, 77.

31. Marion, "I Smell Trouble."

32. Gart and Ames, 82.

33. Hannusch, "Bobby 'Blue' Bland," 15.

34. Rooster, "Rooster Pickin's," *Blues Access* 41, Spring 2000, 2.

35. Hannusch, "Bobby 'Blue' Bland," 16.

36. Marsh, Dave, *The Heart of Rock & Soul: The 1001 Greatest Singles Ever Made*, New York, New American Library, 232.

37. Hannusch, "Bobby 'Blue' Bland," 17.

38. Komara, 402–3.

39. Hannusch, "Bobby 'Blue' Bland," 17.

40. Santelli, 28–29.

41. Gart and Ames, 99–100.

42. Hogan, Ed, "Deadric Malone: Biography," *All Music Guide*, shopping.yahoo.com/p:Deadric%20Malone:1927158802:page=biography.

43. Larkin, Colin, *The Virgin Encyclopedia of R&B and Soul*, London, Virgin Books, 1998, 314–15.

44. Wood, *Down in Houston*, 79, 192.

45. O'Neal, "Bobby Bland! Backstage," 15.

46. Guralnick, Peter, *Last Train to Memphis: The Rise of Elvis Presley*, Boston, Little, Brown, 1994, 442.

47. Aykroyd and Manilla, 11.

48. Worsham, 12-E.

49. Camarigg, Mark, "All the King's Men," *Living Blues* 200, April 2009, 14.

Chapter 6

1. Dahl, liner notes for *Bobby "Blue" Bland: The Anthology*, 5.

2. Gordon, *Martin Scorsese Presents the Blues*, 147.

3. Sisario, Ben, "Tyrone Davis, Singer of Soul Songs Tinged with the Blues, 66," *New York Times*, February 14, 2005.

4. Guralnick, *Lost Highway*, 77.

5. Aykroyd and Manilla, 12.

6. O'Neal, "Bobby Bland! Backstage," 15.

7. Hoekstra, Dave, "True 'Blue' WVON's Pervis Spann and Legendary Bobby Bland Make Beautiful Music," Chicago *Sun-Times*, December 23, 2003.

8. Hannusch, "Bobby 'Blue' Bland," 18.

9. Keil, 62.

10. Lisle, Andria, "The Soul of a Man," *Mojo* 175, June 2008, 69.

11. Hoekstra, Dave, "New Regal Picks 'Blue' Bland for 2 Holiday Shows," Chicago *Sun-Times*, November 22, 1989.

12. Aykroyd and Manilla, 13–14.

13. Blau, Robert, "Travelin' Man Bobby 'Blue' Bland Hits Road 40 Weeks A Year To Sell His Brand Of Soul," Chicago *Tribune*, March 27, 1986, TEMPO Section.

14. Dawson, 3.

15. Giddins, Gary, "Bobby Blue Bland Meets the White Folks," *Village Voice*, September 1, 1975, 100–1.

16. Figi, 16.

17. Marion, "I Smell Trouble."

18. *Ibid.*

19. Hannusch, "Bobby 'Blue' Bland," 16.

20. Aykroyd and Manilla, 240.

21. Guralnick, *Lost Highway*, 77.

22. Guralnick, "Farther Up the Road," *Real Paper*, April 30, 1975.

23. Marion, "I Smell Trouble."

24. O'Neal, "Bobby Bland! Backstage," 14.

25. Point, Michael, "Hollimon, Clarence," in Komara, 450.

26. Payne, Jim, *Give the Drummers Some!*, Katanoh, NY, Face the Music, 1996.

27. Hannusch, "Bobby 'Blue' Bland," 17.

28. Dahl, liner notes for *Bobby "Blue" Bland: The Anthology*, 6.

29. Hannusch, "Bobby 'Blue' Bland," 16.

30. *Ibid.*

31. Floyd, John, "Black Nights," Memphis *Flyer*, May 10, 1999.

32. Hoskyns, Barney, "Two Steps from the Blues: The Gospel According to Bobby 'Blue' Bland," in *From a Whisper to a Scream*, London, Fontana, 1991.

33. Haralambos, Michael, *Right On: From Blues to Soul in Black America*, New York, Drake, 1975, 133.

34. Larkin, 26.

35. Salem, 197.

36. *Ibid.*, 64–65, 196–98.

37. Gillett, Charlie, "Junior Parker: Junior's Last Stand," *Creem*, January 1972.

38. Govenar, Alan, "Al 'TNT' Braggs," *Living Blues* 83, November-December 1988, 32.

39. Gart and Ames, 120.

40. McCluskey.

41. Gart and Ames, 107.

42. Salem, 197.

43. Gart and Ames, 107.

44. Govenar, Alan, *Texas Blues: The Rise of a Contemporary Sound*, College Station, Texas A&M University Press, 2008, 312.

45. Gart and Ames, 107.

46. Guralnick, *Lost Highway*, 79–80.

47. Payne.

48. Guralnick, *Lost Highway*, 81.

49. Hannusch, "Bobby 'Blue' Bland," 17.

50. Marsh, 402.

51. Brisbin, John Anthony, "Texas Johnny Brown: I Just Want to Do It All Well," *Living Blues* 167, March-May 2003, 43, 51–52.

52. Hannusch, "Bobby 'Blue' Bland," 16.

53. Gart and Ames, 115.

54. Evans, 176–77.

55. Wood, *Down in Houston*, 203.

56. Sinclair, John, "Scott, Joe," in Komara, 866–67.

57. Guralnick, *Lost Highway*, 79.

58. Keil, 115.

59. Guralnick, *Lost Highway*, 78.

60. Dahl, liner notes for *Bobby "Blue" Bland: The Anthology*, 5.

61. Gordon, *Martin Scorsese Presents the Blues*, 147.

62. Gart and Ames, 115.

63. Dahl, "Bobby 'Blue' Bland: Soulful Seduction," 13.

64. Govenar, Alan, *Meeting the Blues*, Dallas, Taylor Publishing Company, 1988, 108–10.

65. "Bobby Bland: Here's the Man," *Goldmine*, January 16, 1987, 78.

66. Hoekstra, "New Regal Picks 'Blue' Bland for 2 Holiday Shows."

67. Payne.

68. Wood, *Down in Houston*, 212.

69. Keil, 90–92.

70. Guralnick, *Lost Highway*, 81.

71. *Ibid.*

72. "Bobby Bland: Here's the Man," 78.

73. Dahl, *Bobby Bland: The Definitive Collection*, 2.

Chapter 7

1. Murray, Charles Shaar, *Blues on CD: The Essential Guide*, London, Kyle Cathie, 1993, 228.

2. Erlewine, Stephen Thomas, "Bobby 'Blue' Bland," in Bogdanov, Vladimir, Chris Woodstra, and Stephen Thomas Erlewine, eds., *All Music Guide to the Blues*, 3rd ed., San Francisco, Backbeat, 2003, 47.

3. Elder, Sean, "Brilliant Careers: Bobby 'Blue' Bland," at cobrand.salon.com/people/bc/2000/03/14/bland/.

4. Salem, 235.

5. Bandyke, Martin, "Modern Blues Guitarist Goes Live," *Kansas City Star*, March 16, 2008, F3.

6. O'Neal, "Bobby Bland! Backstage," 16.

7. Aykroyd and Manilla, 11.

8. Brisbin, "Texas Johnny Brown," 51–52.

9. O'Neal, Jim, "Junior Wells," *Living Blues* 119, February 1995, 12–13.

10. Brisbin, "Texas Johnny Brown," 51–52.

11. Shaw, 487–88.

12. Vera, 1.

13. Spann, Purvis, and Jim O'Neal, "Junior Parker," obituary, *Living Blues* 7, Winter 1971–72, 6–7.

14. Worsham, 12-E.

15. Dawson, 3.

16. Govenar, "Al 'TNT' Braggs," 33.

17. Guralnick, *Lost Highway*, 82.

18. Camarigg, 14.

19. Guralnick, *Lost Highway*, 70.

20. Gart and Ames, 84.

21. "Jimmy Beck," All Music Guide, www.allgame.com/cg/amg.dll?p=amg&sql=11:acf oxqr51dje-T4.

22. "Johnny Board," All Music Guide, www.allgame.com/cg/amg.dll?p=amg&sql=11:h cfwxqy51dae-T4.

23. Sawyer, 16.

24. "Early Sixties in Hollywood," www.hollywoodhangover.com/early_sixties_in_hol lywood.htm.

25. Mohr, Kurt, "Les Hommes de Bobby Bland," *Soul Bag* 115, 1989.

26. Wood, Roger, "Hamp W. Simmons, Jr.," obituary, *Living Blues* 156, March-April 2001, 100–101.

27. Wood, Roger, "Teddy Reynolds," *The Handbook of Texas Online*, www.tsha.utexas .edu/handbook/online/articles/RR/fre67.html.

28. Payne.

29. Danchin, Sebastian, "The Many Sides of Wayne Bennett," *Soul Bag* 115, 1989.

30. O'Neal, "Bobby Bland! Backstage," 14.

31. "Gibson Guitar Hero Video: Johnny Jones on Bobby Blue Bland—The Bend of the String," www.//blip.tv/file/495532.

32. Keil, 117.

33. *Ibid.*, 116–17.

34. Armstrong, Roger, liner notes for *Bobby Bland: The Voice*, London, Ace Records, 1991, 4.

35. Maddix.

36. Hannusch, "Bobby 'Blue' Bland," 17.

37. Payne.

38. Quick, Barney, "The All-Time Top 100 R&B Tunes—Part 1: The Top Ten," suite101.com, March 3, 2001, www.suite101.com/article.cfm/r&b_history/62034.

39. Payne.

40. Hoekstra, Dave, "Revues Bring Distinct Styles of Music to Town," Chicago *Sun-Times*, March 23, 1990.

41. Hannusch, "Bobby 'Blue' Bland," 17.

42. Latimore, Benny, author interview, Sunflower Blues and Gospel Festival, Clarksdale, MS, August 8, 2008.

43. Gart and Ames.

44. Govenar, *The Early Years of Rhythm & Blues*, 8.

45. Hannusch, "Bobby 'Blue' Bland," 17.

46. Albert, George, and Frank Hoffman, *The Cash Box Black Contemporary Singles Charts, 1960–1984*, Metuchen, NJ, Scarecrow Press, 1986, 32–34.

47. Hannusch, "Bobby 'Blue' Bland," 17.

48. Govenar, "Al 'TNT' Braggs," 33.

49. Payne.

Chapter 8

1. "Kansas City's Classic Theatres," at members.aol.com/screenviews/theatres.html.

2. Haralambos, 33.

3. Govenar, "Al 'TNT' Braggs," 33.

4. Gart and Ames, 115.

5. Marsh, 59.

6. Martin, Gavin, "Bobby Bland: The Best Of (MCA)," *NME*, June 5, 1982.

7. Davis, Hank, "Bobby 'Blue' Bland," in Bogdanov, 47.

8. Hannusch, "Bobby 'Blue' Bland," 17.

9. Guralnick, Peter, *Dream Boogie: The Triumph of Sam Cooke*, New York, Little Brown, 2005, 521–23.

10. Snowden, Don, liner notes for *Bobby Bland: I Pity The Fool, The Duke Recordings, Vol. 1*, MCA Records, 1992, 4–7.

11. Whitburn, viii–x.

12. Leopold, Todd, "When the Beatles Hit America," Cable News Network, 2007, at cnn.com.

13. Palmer, Robert, *Rock & Roll*, 43.

14. Shurman, O'Neal, and O'Neal, 17.

15. Summers and Scheir, 20.

16. Marsh, 608.

17. Daguerre, Pierre, and Kurt Mohr, "Bobby Bland Discography," *Soul Bag* 115, 1989, 11.

18. Robinson, Louie, "The Tragic Death of Sam Cooke," *Ebony* 20, February 1965, 93.

19. Hillinger, Charles, "Thousands Attend Rites for Singer Sam Cooke," Los Angeles *Times*, December 20, 1964, EB.

20. King interview.

Chapter 9

1. Guralnick, *Dream Boogie*, 512, 540–41.

2. Keil, 91.

3. Johnson, Robert, "Good Evening!" Memphis *Press-Scimitar*, March 18, 1965.

4. Burk.

5. Lauterbach.

6. Danchin.

7. Wood, Roger, "Joe 'Guitar' Hughes," obituary, *Living Blues* 169, September-October 2003, 115–16.

8. Zugna, Daniel, *FortiFi@ Public Journal*, February 8, 2007, journals.aol.com/kingbing1/FortiFi/entries/2007/02/08/motown-pianist-joe-hunter-die.

9. Morris, Chris, liner notes for *Bobby Bland: Greatest Hits, Vol. One*, MCA Records, 1998, 7.

10. "Darrel Andrews: Spider Soul," cdbaby.com/cd/darrel3.

11. Bogdanov, 258.

12. McClusky.

13. "Gil Caple," discography, www.discogs.com/artist/Gil+Caple.

14. Goins, Kevin L., liner notes for *Sippin' Sorrow (With a Spoon)*, New York, Night Train International, 2004, 4–12.

15. Johnson, Greg, "Joe 'Guitar' Hughes," Cascade Blues Association, *BluesNotes*, November, 2003.

16. Govenar, "Al 'TNT' Braggs," 33.

17. McClusky.

18. Bad Dog Blues, "Al 'TNT' Braggs Dies," WITR Radio, Rochester, NY, January 2004, www.baddogblues.com/archives/1.04/news.htm.

19. McClusky.

20. Mitchell, Willie, author interview, Royal Recording Studio, Memphis, TN, August 8, 2008.

21. Kubernik, Harvey, "Tell 'Em Willie Boy Was Here," *Mojo*, undated article in the Willie Mitchell file at the University of Mississippi's Blues Archives.

22. Guralnick, Peter, *Sweet Soul Music: Rhythm and Blues and Southern Dream of Freedom*, New York, Harper & Row, 1986, 302.

23. Lumb, Lisa, "Turn Up That Noise," Memphis *Flyer*, November 22, 1999.

24. Sisario, Ben, "Willie Mitchell, Soul Music Producer, Dies at 81," *New York Times*, January 6, 2010.

25. Harris, Sheldon, *Blues Who's Who*, New York, Da Capo, 1981, 51.

26. O'Neal, "Bobby Bland! Backstage," 15.

27. King interview.

28. Broven, John, *Rhythm & Blues in New Orleans*, Gretna, LA, Pelican Publishing Company, 1988, 100.

29. Gart and Ames, 24.

30. McClusky.

31. Lauterbach.

32. Salem, 127.

33. Sawyer, 73.

34. Latimore Interview.

35. Bland, Rodd, "My Funny Valentine's Day??" February 14, 2007, at http://blog.myspace.com/index.cfm?fuseaction=blog.view&friendID=112843785&blogI...

36. Guralnick, *Lost Highway*, 84.

37. Guralnick, *Lost Highway*, 85.

38. Wynn, Ron, "Bobby 'Blue' Bland," in Bogdanov, 47-48.

39. Martin, Gavin, "Bobby Bland: The Best Of (MCA)."

40. Shurman, Dick, Liner notes for *That Did It! The Duke Recordings, Vol. 3*, Universal City, CA, MCA Records, 1996, 7.

41. Guralnick, *Lost Highway*, 83.

42. Guralnick, *Lost Highway*, 88.

43. Blau.

44. Guralnick, *Lost Highway*, 84.

45. Sawyer, 106-117.

46. Sawyer, 187.

47. Danchin.

Chapter 10

1. "Henry Boozier: Credits," music.msn.com/artist?artist=16113848&menu=credits&ip p=10.

2. Wood, *Down in Houston*, 215.

3. "Andre Williams," Wikipedia.

4. McClusky.

5. McClusky.

6. Morris, 7.

7. "Since I Fell for You," Wikipedia.

8. Wood, *Down in Houston*, 161.

9. McClusky.

10. Wood, *Down in Houston*, 79, 296.

11. Chadbourne, Eugene, "Ernie Fields, Jr. On Fathers," *All Music Guide*, www.found ersacademy.org/Gallery_EFJ/ABOUT%20EFJ.html.

12. O'Neal, Amy, "Bobby Bland! Onstage," *Living Blues* 4, Winter 1970–71, 10–11.

13. Guralnick, *Lost Highway*, 84.

14. Aykroyd and Manilla, 12.

15. Whitburn, 783.

16. "Joe Scott," All Music Guide, wc03.allmusic.com/cg/amg.dll?p=amg&sql=11:f9fpxq rkldoe-T4.

17. "Joe Scott," obituary, *Living Blues* 43, Summer 1979, 48.

18. King interview.

19. O'Neal, "Bobby Bland! Backstage," 16.

20. Dawson, 3.

21. Salem, 60–61.

22. Keil, 85.

23. Salem, 126.

24. Guralnick, *Lost Highway*, 90.

25. *Ibid.*, 87–88.

26. Williams, Mark, "Blues Worth the Drive—R&B Legend Bland Plays Houston Tonight," *The Bulletin*, July 13, 2001.

27. O'Neal, "Bobby Bland! Backstage," 16.

28. "History: The Lineups," *The Ann Arbor Blues & Jazz Festival*, at a2.blues.jazzfest. org/history/lineup.html.

29. Tschmuck, Peter, *Creativity and Innovation in the Music Industry*, New York, Springer, 2006, 129.

30. Guralnick, *Sweet Soul Music*, 188.

31. *Ibid.*, 198–99.

32. Larkin, 259.

33. "Muscle Shoals Sound Studio," Wikipedia.

34. Bowman, Rob, *Soulsville, U.S.A.: The Story of Stax Records*, New York, Schirmer, 1997, 161, 301, 352.

35. O'Neal, "Bobby Bland! Backstage," 18.

36. "Mike 'Monk' Bruce," *Tulsa Area Music Archives*, 2005, www.preservemusic.org/tributes.htm.

37. Guralnick, *Lost Highway*, 84-85.

38. "History: The Lineups."

39. "Mel Brown: Artist Bios," *Electro-Fi*, www.electrofi.com/melbrown_bio.htm.

40. Hannusch, Jeff, "Mel Brown," *Living Blues* 154, November-December 2000, 34–38.

41. Guralnick, *Lost Highway*, 85.

Chapter 11

1. Brown, Ryan, "Band Leader & Male Lead Vocals: Ryan Brown," www.k2band.com/singer-band.html.

2. "Blues," unattributed article in the Bobby Bland file at the University of Mississippi's Blues Archives.

3. Gart and Ames, 127.

4. Salem, 185.

5. Gart and Ames, 127–28.

6. Worsham, 12-E.

7. Hannusch, "Bobby 'Blue' Bland," 8.

8. "Steve Barri: Biography," *Golden Grass—The Grass Roots Fan Page*, at home.att.net/~souldeep69/biosbarri.html.

9. *Ibid.*

10. Streissguth, Mike, "From Memphis to Malaco: Bobby 'Blue' Bland Turns on Your Lovelight," *Goldmine* 391, July 21, 1995, 34.

11. Streissguth, 34.

12. Dahl, liner notes for *Bobby Bland: Greatest Hits Vol. Two*, MCA Records, 1998, 7.

13. Streissguth, 34.

14. Leatherwood, Tom, Shelby County Register of Deeds: Death Records 1949–2005.

15. Hannusch, "Bobby 'Blue' Bland," 9.

16. "Ain't No Love In the Heart of the City," Wikipedia.

17. Welch, Chris, "Legendary Blues Man Has No Plans To Slow Down," Huntsville *Times*, February 14, 2008, GO.7.

18. Hannusch, "Bobby 'Blue' Bland," 9.

19. Fisher, Bob, "Bobby Bland: Dreamer," *NME*, November, 1974.

20. Dahl, "Bobby 'Blue' Bland: Soulful Seduction," 14.

21. King, 263–64.

22. Peterson, Clark, "B.B. King, Bobbie Blue Bland Knock 'em at Winterland," Berkeley *Barb*, January 17–23, 1975.

23. Guralnick, *Lost Highway*, 69–73.

24. Worsham, 12-E.

25. Guralnick, *Lost Highway*, 72, 90.

26. Streissguth, 36.

27. Salem, 186.
28. Gart and Ames, 127.
29. Govenar, *Meeting the Blues*, 107.
30. Gart and Ames, 3.
31. Govenar, *The Early Years of Rhythm and Blues*, 8–9.
32. Salem, 186.
33. Wasserzieher.
34. Guralnick, *Lost Highway*, 82.
35. Klanac, Bob, "Bobby Blue Bland," Klanac Industries, klanac.blogspot.com/2006/09/bobby-blue-bland.html.
36. Morthland, 58–59.
37. Gart and Ames, 94.
38. Gart and Ames, 128.
39. Streissguth, 36.
40. Back, 85.
41. Hannusch, "Bobby 'Blue' Bland," 9.
42. Guralnick, *Lost Highway*, 91.
43. Govenar, *Texas Blues*, 488.
44. Davis, John T., "A Farewell to the Man Behind the Blues," XL Music, www.austin360.com/music/content/music/stories/xl/2006/05/2.
45. Morthland, John, "Everybody Comes to Antone's," eMusic Spotlight, www.emusic.com/features/spotlight/292_200606.html.
46. Patoski, Joe Nick, "Okie Dokie Stomp," Austin *Chronicle*, May 26, 2006, Music Section.
47. Gray, Christopher, "Blues for Clifford," Austin *Chronicle*, May 26, 2006, Music Section.
48. "Antone: The Man Who Gave Austin the Blues," www.austin360.com/news/content/music/stories/2006/05/28antone.html.
49. Ward, Ed, "Buried Alive in the Blues," Austin *Chronicle*, May 25, 2006, Music Section.
50. Morthland, "Royal Blue."
51. Hannusch, "Mel Brown," 38.
52. Hoekstra, Dave, "Revues Bring Distinct Styles to Town."
53. Tennessee Department of Health Office of Vital Records, "Verification of Birth Facts for Roderick Cornelius Bland," May 7, 2008.

Chapter 12

1. "Vinyl Statistics: Bobby Bland," press release from ABC Records.
2. Steve Barri: Biography."
3. "Michael Omartian," Wikipedia.
4. Harris, 51.
5. Bowman, *Soulsville, U.S.A*, 80–84, 277.
6. Streissguth, 36.
7. Bowman, *Soulsville, U.S.A.*, 383.

8. Sontag, Deborah, "Out of Exile, Back in Soulville," *New York Times*, August 16, 2009, AR-21.

9. Larkin, 152.

10. Hobson, Charles, "Following the Stars," *Black Stars*, May 1978, 56.

11. Larkin, 283.

12. Murray, *Blues on CD*, 2.

13. Streissguth, 38.

14. Bowman, *Soulsville, U.S.A.*, 381.

15. Brisbin, John, "B.B. and Bobby vs. Dylan," *Living Blues* 41, November-December 1978, 27.

16. Camarigg, 17–18.

17. Hannusch, "Mel Brown," 38.

18. Govenar, *Texas Blues*, 387.

19. Bogdanov, 145.

20. Whitburn, 170.

21. Guralnick, *Lost Highway*, 91.

22. Dawson, 3.

23. Collier, Aldore, "B.B. and Bobby Bland—Royal Blues," Memphis *Press-Scimitar*, August 3, 1979.

24. "Stax Records 50th," at stax50.com/blog/2007/12/.

25. Dawson, 3.

26. Leatherwood, Tom, Shelby County Register of Deeds: Instr # S20152, "Notice of Federal Tax Lien Under Internal Revenue Laws," January 15, 1981.

27. Bland, Rodd, "Bobby Blue Bland Gigs," at blog.myspace.com/index.cfm?fuseaction=blog.view&friendID=112843785&blogId=282194248.

28. Topping, 3.

29. "Blues Foundation 1981 Hall of Fame Inductees," www.blues.org/halloffame/inductees.php4?YearId=24.

30. "The National Academy of Blues Awards," *Living Blues* 5, Summer 1981, 23–24.

31. West, 35.

32. Worsham, 12-E.

33. King, 284.

34. Hannusch, "Bobby 'Blue' Bland," 18.

35. Prudhomme, Chester, "Bobby 'Blue' Bland," *DISCoveries*, December 1989, 30.

36. Gart and Ames, 116.

37. King, 213, 230–31.

38. Giddins, Gary, 101.

39. Long, Ron, "Bobby Bland, Top Blues Singer, Says 'You've Still Got To Mind,'" *Jet*, October 20, 1977.

40. Dawson, 3.

41. Guralnick, *Lost Highway*, 87.

42. Hannusch, "Mel Brown," 38–39.

43. "Mel Brown," obituary, *Living Blues* 201, June 2009, 73–74.

44. *Bobby 'Blue' Bland: Long Beach 1983*, liner notes, 6.

45. Frith, Simon, "All That Glitters," *Sunday Times*, May 30, 1982.

46. Clayton, Rose, "Third Annual Ceremony: Bland Wins Three Blues Awards," *Billboard*, vol. 94, no. 49, December 11, 1982, 54.

47. Streissguth, 38.

48. Tennessee Department of Health Office of Vital Records, "Verification of Marriage Facts for Robert Calvin Bland and Willie Mae Martin," December 7, 2007.

49. "Bobby Bland Takes Bride," *Jet*, September 5, 1983, 13.

50. Whitburn, 132.

51. Office of Public Affairs, Smithsonian Institution, "B.B. King, Bobby Blue Bland and Memphis Slim Star in April 29–May 1 Smithsonian Program Celebrating the Memphis Blues," news release, December 17, 1982, 1.

52. Patterson, Dale R., "Radio's Jackie Robinson: Nat D. Williams," *Rock Radio Scrapbook*, rockradioscrapbook.ca/natd.html.

53. O, Don, "Lucky Dallas: Lucky Peterson Interview 3/19/98," www.geocities.com/bluesdfw/lucky.htm.

54. Danchin.

55. "Milton Bland, 50, Music Producer," obituary, Chicago *Sun-Times*, July 13, 1986.

56. Bowman, *Soulsville, U.S.A.*, 381.

57. Sontag, AR-1.

58. Pareles, Jon, "Concert: Country and Blues," *New York Times*, August 20, 1984.

Chapter 13

1. Stephenson, Gerald "Wolf," author interview, Malaco Records, Jackson, MS, July 30, 2008.

2. Barretta, Scott, "The Jackson Blues," *Living Blues* 173, March-June 2004, 55.

3. Snowden, Don, "Malaco: Rhythm & Business," Los Angeles *Times*, May 9, 1987.

4. Bowman, Rob, "The Malaco Story," www.malaco.com/story.php.

5. Snowden, "Malaco."

6. Bowman, "The Malaco Story."

7. Snowden, "Malaco."

8. Bowman, *Soulsville, U.S.A.*, 254–56.

9. Bowman, "The Malaco Story."

10. Snowden, "Malaco."

11. Point, Michael, "Hill, Z.Z.," in Komara, 431–32.

12. O'Neal, Jim, "Living Blues Interview: Z.Z. Hill," *Living Blues* 53, Summer/Autumn 1982, 20.

13. Bowman, "The Malaco Story."

14. Snowden, "Malaco."

15. Dahl, "Bobby 'Blue' Bland: Soulful Seduction," 14.

16. Streissguth, 38.

17. Stephenson interview.

18. Hoskyns, Barney, "Malaco: Soul's Retirement Home," London *Times*, July 10, 1989.

19. Bowman, Rob, *Malaco Records: The Last Soul Company*, Jackson, MS, Malaco Records, 1999, 70–71.

20. Stephenson interview.

21. Bowman, *Malaco Records: The Last Soul Company*, 77.

22. "Tommy Tate," Wikipedia.

23. Stephenson interview.

24. Streissguth, 38.

25. Snowden, "Malaco."

26. Stephenson interview.

27. Hannusch, "Bobby 'Blue' Bland," 17.

28. Williams.

29. Manheim, James M., "Blue Bland," www.answers.com/topic/blue-bland.

30. Bowman, "The Malaco Story."

31. Danchin.

32. Myers, Leslie R., "Bland Leads Jackson Music Awards Slate With 8 Nominations," Jackson *Clarion-Ledger*, July 11, 1986, D1.

33. Bowman, *Malaco Records: The Last Soul Company*, 78.

34. Scruggs, Afi-Odelia, "Elegant Bobby Bland Wears A New Style," Jackson *Clarion-Ledger*, undated article in the Bobby Bland file at the University of Mississippi's Blues Archives.

35. O, Don.

36. Camarigg, 14–15.

37. *Ibid.*, 16–17.

38. Mohr.

39. Stephenson interview.

40. Streissguth, 40.

41. Bowman, *Malaco Records: The Last Soul Company*, 86.

42. Stephenson interview.

43. Bowman, *Malaco Records: The Last Soul Company*, 87.

44. Prudhomme, 30.

45. Pareles, Jon, "Review/Blues: Despair Dotted by Smiles," *New York Times*, August 19, 1988.

46. Hoskyns, "Malaco: Soul's Retirement Home."

47. Downing, Stanley, "Bland's Tour Bus to Be Sold Friday," Memphis *Commercial Appeal*, November 1, 1989, B1, B3.

48. Lewis, Julius, "Birthday Wishes From Julius Lewis," Memphis, TN, Heritage Entertainment, *Bobby "Blue" Bland Official Program*, 2010, 4.

49. Hoekstra, "New Regal Picks 'Blue' Bland for 2 Holiday Shows."

50. Bowman, "The Malaco Story."

Chapter 14

1. Snowden, "Malaco."

2. Rye, Howard, "Ace (United Kingdom)," in Komara, 5.

3. Nager, Larry, "Rock Honors Surprise Bland," Memphis *Commercial Appeal*, January 15, 1992, C3.

4. Schoemer, Karen, "Bobby (Blue) Bland, Honored At Last," *New York Times*, November 22, 1991, C1.

5. Harrington, Richard, "The Guitar Stars: Hall of Fame Inducts Yardbirds, Hendrix, Fender," Washington *Post*, January 16, 1992.

6. "Bobby 'Blue' Bland," Rock and Roll Hall of Fame + Museum, www.rockhall.com/inductee/bobby-blue-bland.

7. Williams.

8. Tennessee Department of Health, "Certificate of Death for Isaac J. Brooks," January 24, 1992.

9. Stephenson, 1.

10. Nager, C1.

11. Point, Michael, "Bennett, Wayne T.," in Komara, 73–74.

12. Hoekstra, Dave, "Bluesman Bennett Dies Waiting for Transplant," Chicago *Sun-Times*, December 2, 1992.

13. Guralnick, *Lost Highway*, 81.

14. McClusky.

15. Hendricks, Jon, "Responding to the Blues," unattributed article in the Bobby Bland file at the University of Mississippi's Blues Archives.

16. O'Neal, "Bobby Bland! Backstage," 17.

17. Webb.

18. Murray, Charles Shaar, "Talkin' Blues: John Lee Hooker/B.B. King/Bobby 'Blue' Bland," *NME*, June 5, 1982.

19. Ellis, Bill, "The Golden Voice of the Blues," Memphis *Commercial Appeal*, May 21, 1997, G5.

20. Maddix.

21. Haralambos, 61.

22. Klanac.

23. Aykroyd and Manilla, 13.

24. Long.

25. Worsham, 12-E.

26. Ackroyd and Manilla, 13.

27. George, Nelson, "Bobby 'Blue' Bland: Storm Warnings," unattributed article in the Bobby Bland file at the University of Mississippi's Blues Archives.

28. Haralambos, 60.

Chapter 15

1. Hoekstra, Dave, "Bland Through the Years," Chicago *Sun-Times*, December 26, 2003.

2. Concord Music Group, "About Frederick Knight," www.concordmusicgroup.com/artists/Frederick-Knight/.

3. Bowman, *Malaco Records: The Last Soul Company*, 87–88.

4. Point, Michael, "Ace, Buddy," in Komara, 5.

5. Holsey, Steve, "Bobby 'Blue' Bland, One Night Only," *Michigan Chronicle*, July 5, 1994.

6. Rosenberg, Merri, "Making Records Far From the Urban Beat," *New York Times*, February 4, 1996.

7. Morthland, 60.

8. Shurman, 8.

9. Dahl, Bill, "Relaxed Blues Master Bobby 'Blue' Bland Continues to be the Man," Chicago *Tribune*, November 15, 1996, Friday-59.

10. Morthland, 60.

11. Hoffman, Larry, "Bobby Bland Honored in Memphis," *Living Blues* 128, July-August 1996, 10.

12. Elder.

13. Hoffman, 10.

14. Floyd.

15. Kelly, Red, "George Jackson—My Desires Are Getting The Best Of Me (Fame 1457)," *The B Side*, December 6, 2006, at redkelly.blogspot.com/2006/12/george-jackson-my-desires-are-getting.html.

16. Bowman, *Malaco Records: The Last Soul Company*, 70.

17. Stephenson interview.

18. Bogdanov, 271.

19. Jackson, George, profile www.myspace.com/ legendarygeorgejackson.

20. "Pop/Sneak Peek: Zappa, Bland Honored For Musical Contributions," Los Angeles *Daily News*, January 3, 1997.

21. Booth, Phillip, "Time Is Right For Bobby Bland," Sarasota *Herald Tribune*, September 26, 1997, 11.

22. Baxter, Nicky, "Bland Man's Blues," San Jose *Metro*, March 18–24, 1999.

23. Bowman, *Malaco Records: The Last Soul Company*, 81–82.

24. Elder.

25. Reagoso, Joe, liner notes for *Bobby Bland: Blues & Ballads*, MCA Records, 1999, 5.

26. Ellis, Bill, "The Golden Voice of the Blues," Memphis *Commercial Appeal*, May 21, 1997, G5.

27. "Bobby 'Blue' Bland," interviews at www.pbs.org/klru/austin/interviews/bbland interview.html.

28. Whitburn, 773–85.

Chapter 16

1. Martin, Gavin, "Arts: The Main Event—None More Blue—Van Morrison/Bobby 'Blue' Bland, Royal Albert Hall, London," the *Independent*, March 23, 2000.

2. Bell, Max, "The Van Has Been Overtaken," *Evening Standard*, March 22, 2000.

3. Eagle, Robert, "Duke," in Komara, 287.

4. Chase, Alan, "The Blues Will Be Smokin' in Portsmouth This Weekend," archive .seacoastonline.com/calendar/2000/8_17coverstory.htm.

5. "Gibson Memphis to Host Blues Ball Gala Saturday Night," press release, September 21, 2000.

6. Tennessee Department of Health, "Certificate of Death for Mary Bland," January 12, 2001.

7. Bland, Rodd, "Sailing the Seas with Rod Bland and Some Friends," at www.drum sontheweb.com/DOTWpages/ArtistForumpages/centerfoldpages/centerfold.

8. "Long Beach Boasts Big Blues Bash On Labor Day Weekend," Los Angeles *Sentinel*, August 29, 2001.

9. Barretta, Scott, "Rufus Thomas," obituary, *Living Blues* 163, May-June 2002, 86.

10. Pareles, Jon, "Blues Review: A Wounded Man, Still Singing That Sad Old Song at 72," *New York Times*, January 23, 2003.

11. Bowman, *Malaco Records: The Last Soul Company*, 85–86.

12. Bowman, "The Malaco Story."

13. Perlich, Tim, "Bland At His Best: Soul-Blues Icon Roars Back . . . Again," *Now Toronto*, January 16, 2003.

14. Guralnick, *Lost Highway*, 335.

15. *Ibid.*, 337.

16. "Sam Phillips," Wikipedia.

17. Thrasher, Don, "Bobby Bland Is Here To Stay," Dayton *Daily News*, July 19, 2003.

18. Hoekstra, Dave, "True 'Blue' WVON's Pervis Spann and Legendary Bobby Bland Make Beautiful Music," Chicago *Sun-Times*, December 23, 2003.

19. Roberts, Kimberly C., "Bland Brings Down the House at Blues Fest," Philadelphia *Tribune*, October 12, 2004.

20. Graham, Bonnie D., "Concert Review: B.B. King with Bobby 'Blue' Bland," *Improper Magazine*, May 2005.

21. Wood, Roger, "Clarence 'Gatemouth' Brown," obituary, *Living Blues* 181, November-December 2005, 86.

22. Stephenson interview.

23. King interview.

24. Bladon, Patty, "Bobby 'Blue' Bland to Receive Distinguished Achievement Award," University of Memphis press release, November 3, 2005.

25. Bland, "Bobby Blue Bland Gigs."

26. Foster, Stella, "We're All Blue," Chicago *Sun-Times*, June 28, 2007.

27. Lang, Joe, "Rock and Roll Hall of Fame Week at Dakota Club on 8/7/07," *How Was the Show*, August 22, 2007.

28. "Other Deaths: Ernest Withers," obituary, *Living Blues* 194, February 2008, 75.

29. Whiteis, David, "Ike Turner," obituary, *Living Blues* 195, April 2008.

Chapter 17

1. Fullylove, Kaye, "Bobby Bland Proclaimed Master of the Blues," www.theboogiere port.net/jboogiemasononline/id73.html.

2. Jordan, Mark, "Casino Scene: Doobies Leader Says Modern Lineup Rocks Out Better Than Ever," Memphis *Commercial Appeal*, February 15, 2008.

3. Tipaldi, Art, *Children of the Blues*, San Francisco, Backbeat, 2002, 90.

4. Bland, Roderick, author interview, Crossroads Music Hall, Huntsville, AL, February 17, 2008.

5. Webb, 33.

6. Klanac.

7. Williams.

8. Morthland, 60.

9. Raum, Tom, "Obama Proclaims Himself the Democratic Nominee," Associated Press, June 3, 2008.

10. Welch, GO.7.

11. Spencer, Paul, *Simply Blue*, DVD, documentary recorded in Memphis, Tennessee, in November 2007 and included as part of the album *Hucknall: Tribute to Bobby*.

12. Lisle, Andria, liner notes for *Hucknall: Tribute to Bobby*, simplyred.com ltd., 2008.

Epilogue

1. Stephenson interview.

2. Hardin, Joseph, Jr., telephone interview, August 4, 2008.

3. Latimore interview.

4. Joyce, Mike, "Bobby 'Blue' Bland's Soulful Sound," Washington *Post*, August 21, 2008, C12.

5. "Night Life: Rock and Pop," *The New Yorker*, August 25, 2008, 9.

6. King interview.

Sources Cited

"Ain't No Love in the Heart of the City," *Wikipedia*.

Albert, George, and Frank Hoffman. *The Cash Box Black Contemporary Singles Charts, 1960–1984*. Metuchen, NJ: Scarecrow Press, 1986.

All Day and All Night: Memories from Beale Street Musicians. Documentary film produced by Judy Peiser. 30 minutes. Southern Folklore Center, 1990. Videocassette.

Ancestry.com. *1920 United States Federal Census* [online database]. Provo, UT: Generations Network, 2005.

————. *1930 United States Federal Census* [online database]. Provo, UT: Generations Network, 2002.

————. "Marriage Record, Tipton County, Tennessee, Leroy Bland and Mary Lee Smith, October 26, 1936." *Tennessee State Marriages, 1765–2002* [online database]. Provo, UT: Generations Network, 2007.

"Andre Williams." *Wikipedia*.

"Antone: The Man Who Gave Austin the Blues." www.austin360.com/news/content/music/stories/2006/05/28antone.html.

Armstrong, Roger. Liner notes for *Bobby Bland: The Voice*. London: Ace Records, 1991.

Associated Booking. "Bio: Bobby Bland."

Aykroyd, Dan, and Ben Manilla. *Elwood's Blues: Interviews with the Blues Legends & Stars*. San Francisco: Backbeat, 2004.

Back, Les. "Bobby Bland's Influential Voice." *Oxford American* 27/28, 1999.

Bad Dog Blues. "Al 'TNT' Braggs Dies." WITR Radio, Rochester, NY. January 2004. www.baddogblues.com/archives/8.03/news.htm.

————. "'Beale Streeter' Forest Dies." August 2003. www.baddogblues.com/archives/8.03/news.htm.

Bailey, Joe. "The Texas Shuffle: Lone Star Underpinnings of the Kansas City Jazz Sound." *Journal of Texas Music History* vol. 6, no. 1, 2006.

Baldwin, James. "Last of the Great Masters," review of *The World of Earl Hines* by Stanley Dance. *New York Times Book Review*, October 16, 1977.

Bandyke, Martin. "Modern Blues Guitarist Goes Live." Kansas City *Star*, March 16, 2008.

Barretta, Scott. "The Jackson Blues." *Living Blues* 173, March–June 2004.

"Rufus Thomas." Obituary, *Living Blues* 163, May–June 2002.

Baxter, Nicky. "Bland Man's Blues." San Jose *Metro*, March 18–24, 1999.

Bell, Max. "The Van Has Been Overtaken." *Evening Standard*, March 22, 2000.

Biles, Roger. *Memphis in the Great Depression.* Knoxville: University of Tennessee Press, 1986.

Bladon, Patty. "Bobby 'Blue' Bland to Receive Distinguished Achievement Award." University of Memphis press release, November 3, 2005.

Bland, Rodd. "Bobby Blue Bland Gigs." blog.myspace.com/index.cfm?fuseaction=blog .view&friendID=112843785&blogI d=282194248.

———. "My Funny Valentine's Day??" February 14, 2007, blog.myspace.com/index .cfm?fuseaction=blog.view&friendID=112843785&blogId=282194248.

———. "Sailing the Seas with Rod Bland and Some Friends." www.drumsontheweb .com/DOTWpages/ArtistForumpages/centerfoldpages/centerfold.

Blau, Robert. "Travelin' Man Bobby 'Blue' Bland Hits Road 40 Weeks A Year to Sell His Brand of Soul." Chicago *Tribune*, March 27, 1986, TEMPO Section.

"Blues." Unattributed article in the Bobby Bland file at the University of Mississippi's Blues Archives.

"Blues Foundation 1981 Hall of Fame Inductees." www.blues.org/halloffame/inductees .php4?YearId=24.

"Bobby Bland: Here's the Man." *Goldmine*, January 16, 1987.

"Bobby Bland Takes Bride." *Jet*, September 5, 1983.

"Bobby 'Blue' Bland." Interviews. www.pbs.org/klru/austin/interviews/bblandinterview .html.

Bobby "Blue" Bland: Long Beach 1983. CD liner notes, Lelystad, Holland: Blues Factory, 2008.

"Bobby 'Blue' Bland." Rock and Roll Hall of Fame + Museum. www.rockhall.com/ inductee/bobby-blue-bland.

Bogdanov, Vladimir, Chris Woodstra, and Stephen Thomas Erlewine, eds. *All Music Guide to the Blues*, 3rd ed. San Francisco: Backbeat, 2003.

Booth, Phillip. "Time Is Right For Bobby Bland." Sarasota *Herald Tribune*, September 26, 1997.

Bowman, Rob. "The Malaco Story." www.malaco.com/story.php.

———. *Malaco Records: The Last Soul Company.* Jackson, MS: Malaco Records, 1999.

———. *Soulsville, U.S.A.: The Story of Stax Records.* New York: Schirmer, 1997.

Brisbin, John Anthony. "B.B. and Bobby vs. Dylan." *Living Blues* 41, November–December 1978.

———. "Jay McShann: I Always Thought Blues and Jazz Went Together." *Living Blues* 149, January–February 2000.

———. "Texas Johnny Brown: I Just Want to Do it All Well." *Living Blues* 167, March–May 2003.

Broven, John. *Rhythm & Blues in New Orleans.* Gretna, LA: Pelican, 1988.

Brown, Ryan. "Band Leader & Male Lead Vocals: Ryan Brown." www.k2band.com/ singer-band.html.

Burk, Bill E. "'Sunbeam' Mitchell Is Puzzled at 75." Memphis *Press-Scimitar*, November 5, 1981.

Byrd, Bobby. *White Panties, Dead Friends & Other Bits & Pieces of Love.* El Paso, TX: Cinco Puntos, 2006.

Camarigg, Mark. "All the King's Men," *Living Blues* 200, April 2009.

Cantor, Louis. *Wheelin' on Beale: How WDIA-Memphis Became the Nation's First All-Black Radio Station and Created the Sound That Changed America.* New York: Pharos, 1992.

Chadbourne, Eugene. "Ernie Fields, Jr. On Fathers." *All Music Guide.* www.foundersacad emy.org/Gallery_EFJ/ABOUT%20EFJ.html.

Chase, Alan. "The Blues Will Be Smokin' in Portsmouth This Weekend." archive.seacoast line.com/calendar/2000/8_17coverstory.htm.

Cheseborough, Steve. *Blues Traveling: The Holy Sites of Delta Blues.* Jackson: University Press of Mississippi, 2001.

Clayton, Rose. "Third Annual Ceremony: Bland Wins Three Blues Awards." *Billboard* vol. 94, no. 49, December 11, 1982.

Cohn, David L. "Sing No Blues for Memphis." *New York Times*, September 4, 1955.

Collier, Aldore. "B.B. and Bobby Bland—Royal Blues." Memphis *Press-Scimitar*, August 3, 1979.

Concord Music Group. "About Frederick Knight." www.concordmusicgroup.com/artists/ Frederick-Knight/

Connell, Mary Ann Strong. *The Peabody Hotel.* Thesis, University of Mississippi, 1959.

Daguerre, Pierre, and Kurt Mohr. "Bobby Bland Discography." *Soul Bag* 115, 1989.

Dahl, Bill. "Bobby 'Blue' Bland: Soulful Seduction." *Blues Revue* 88, June/July 2004.

———. Liner notes for *Bobby Bland: Greatest Hits Vol. Two*, MCA Records, 1998.

———. Liner notes for *Bobby "Blue" Bland: The Anthology*, MCA Records, 2001.

———. Liner notes for *Bobby "Blue" Bland: The Definitive Collection*, Geffen Records, 2007.

———. "Relaxed Blues Master Bobby 'Blue' Bland Continues to be the Man." Chicago *Tribune*, November 15, 1996.

Danchin, Sebastian. "The Many Sides of Wayne Bennett." *Soul Bag* 115, 1989.

"Darrel Andrews: Spider Soul." cdbaby.com/cd/darrel13.

Davis, Francis. *The History of the Blues.* New York: Hyperion, 1995.

Davis, Hank. "Bobby 'Blue' Bland," in Bogdanov.

———. "Living Blues Interview: Roscoe Gordon." *Living Blues* 49, Winter 1980–81.

Davis, John T. "A Farewell to the Man Behind the Blues." *XL Music.* www.austin360.com/ music/content/music/stories/xl/2006/05/2.

Dawson, Walter. "Bobby 'Blue' Bland Keeps On Steppin'." Memphis *Commercial Appeal*, April 29, 1979.

Dolby, Ray. "Some Musings on Progress in Audio: A Quest for Better Sound at Affordable Prices." Heyser Memorial Lecture, AES 112th Convention, M.O.C.-Center, Munchen, Germany, May 11, 2005.

Downing, Stanley. "Bland's Tour Bus to Be Sold Friday." Memphis *Commercial Appeal*, November 1, 1989.

Eagle, Robert. "Duke," in Komara.

"Early Sixties in Hollywood." www.hollywoodhangover.com/early_sixties_in_hollywood .htm.

Elder, Sean. "Brilliant Careers: Bobby 'Blue' Bland." cobrand.salon.com/people/ bc/2000/03/14/bland/.

Eliot, Marc. *Rockonomics: The Money Behind the Music.* New York: Franklin Watts, 1989.

Ellis, Bill. "The Golden Voice of the Blues." Memphis *Commercial Appeal*, May 21, 1997.

Erlewine, Stephen Thomas. "Bobby 'Blue' Bland," in Bogdanov.

Escott, Colin, with Martin Hawkins. *Good Rockin' Tonight: Sun Records and the Birth of Rock 'n' Roll.* New York: St. Martin's, 1991.

Evans, David. *The NPR Curious Listener's Guide to Blues.* New York: Penguin, 2005.

Fancourt, Leslie, and Bob McGrath. *The Blues Discography 1943–70*. West Vancouver, BC, Canada: Eyeball Productions, 2006.

Figi, J. B. "Time for Bobby Bland." *Down Beat*, August 7, 1969.

Fisher, Bob. "Bobby Bland: Dreamer." *NME*, November, 1974.

Floyd, John. "Black Nights." Memphis *Flyer*, May 10, 1999.

Foster, Stella. "We're All Blue." Chicago *Sun-Times*, June 28, 2007.

Frith, Simon. "All That Glitters," London *Sunday Times*, May 30, 1982.

Fullylove, Kaye. "Bobby Bland Proclaimed Master of the Blues." www.theboogiereport .net/jboogiemasononline/id73.html.

Gart, Galen, and Roy C. Ames. *Duke/Peacock Records: An Illustrated History and Discography*. Milford, NH: Big Nickel, 1990.

George, Nelson. "Bobby 'Blue' Bland: Storm Warnings." Unattributed article in the Bobby Bland file at the University of Mississippi's Blues Archives.

———. *The Death of Rhythm & Blues*. New York: Pantheon, 1988.

"Gibson Guitar Hero Video: Johnny Jones on Bobby Blue Bland—The Bend of the String." www.blip.tv/file/495532.

"Gibson Memphis to Host Blues Ball Gala Saturday Night." Press release, September 21, 2000.

Giddins, Gary. "Bobby Blue Bland Meets the White Folks." *Village Voice*, September 1, 1975.

"Gil Caple." Discography. www.discogs.com/artist/Gil+Caple.

Gillett, Charlie. "Junior Parker: Junior's Last Stand." *Creem*, January 1972.

Goins, Kevin L. Liner notes for *Sippin' Sorrow (With a Spoon)*. New York: Night Train International, 2004.

Goldman, Albert. *Elvis*. New York: McGraw-Hill, 1981.

Gordon, Robert. "Bobby 'Blue' Bland." *Rolling Stone*, May 28, 1998.

———. "Bobby 'Blue' Bland: Love Throat of the Blues." In Guralnick, Peter, Robert Santelli, Holly George-Warren, and Christopher John Farley. *Martin Scorsese Presents the Blues: A Musical Journey*. New York: HarperCollins, 2003.

Govenar, Alan. "Al 'TNT' Braggs." *Living Blues* 83, November–December 1988.

———. *The Early Years of Rhythm & Blues: Focus on Houston*. Houston: Rice University Press, 1990.

———. "Evelyn Johnson." *Living Blues* 83, November–December 1988.

———. *Living Texas Blues*. Dallas: Dallas Museum of Art, 1985.

———. *Meeting the Blues*. Dallas: Taylor, 1988.

———. *Texas Blues: The Rise of a Contemporary Sound*. College Station: Texas A&M University Press, 2008.

Graham, Bonnie D. "Concert Review: B.B. King with Bobby 'Blue' Bland." *The Improper Magazine*, May 2005.

Gray, Christopher. "Blues for Clifford." Austin *Chronicle*, May 26, 2006, Music Section.

Grendysa, Pete. "The Making of Rhythm & Blues." *Collecting Magazine*, 1985.

Guralnick, Peter. *Dream Boogie: The Triumph of Sam Cooke*. New York: Little Brown, 2005.

———. "Farther Up the Road." *Real Paper*, April 30, 1975.

———. *Last Train to Memphis: The Rise of Elvis Presley*. Boston: Little Brown, 1994.

———. *Lost Highway: Journeys and Arrivals of American Musicians*. New York: Perennial, 1989.

————. *Sweet Soul Music: Rhythm and Blues and the Southern Dream of Freedom.* New York: Harper & Row, 1986.

Hannusch, Jeff. "Bobby 'Blue' Bland: Storied Blues Singer Anything but Bland." *Goldmine,* October 31, 2003.

————. "Mel Brown." *Living Blues* 154, November-December 2000.

Haralambos, Michael *Right On: From Blues to Soul in Black America.* New York: Drake, 1975.

Harrington, Richard. "The Guitar Stars: Hall of Fame Inducts Yardbirds, Hendrix, Fender." Washington *Post,* January 16, 1992.

Harris, Sheldon. *Blues Who's Who.* New York: Da Capo, 1981.

Hendricks, Jon. "Responding to the Blues." Unattributed article in the Bobby Bland file at the University of Mississippi's Blues Archives.

"Henry Boozier: Credits." music.msn.com/artist?artist=16113848&menu=credits&ipp=10.

Hillinger, Charles. "Thousands Attend Rites for Singer Sam Cooke." Los Angeles *Times,* December 20, 1964.

"History: The Lineups." The Ann Arbor Blues & Jazz Festival. a2.blues.jazzfest.org/history/lineup.html.

Hobson, Charles. "Following the Stars." *Black Stars,* May 1978.

Hoekstra, Dave "Bland Through the Years." Chicago *Sun-Times,* December 26, 2003.

————. "Bluesman Bennett Dies Waiting for Transplant." Chicago *Sun-Times,* December 2, 1992.

————. "New Regal Picks 'Blue' Bland for 2 Holiday Shows." Chicago *Sun-Times,* November 22, 1989.

————. "Revues Bring Distinct Styles of Music to Town." Chicago *Sun-Times,* March 23, 1990.

————. "True 'Blue' WVON's Pervis Spann and Legendary Bobby Bland Make Beautiful Music." Chicago *Sun-Times,* December 23, 2003.

Hoffman, Larry. "Bobby Bland Honored in Memphis." *Living Blues* 128, July-August 1996.

Hogan, Ed. "Deadric Malone: Biography." All Music Guide. shopping.yahoo.com/p:Deadric%20Malone:1927158802:page=biography.

Holsey, Steve. "Bobby 'Blue' Bland, One Night Only." *Michigan Chronicle,* July 5, 1994.

Hoskyns, Barney. "Malaco: Soul's Retirement Home." London *Times,* July 10, 1989.

————. "Rock's Backpages Audio Interview with Bobby Bland." July 8, 1989. www.rocksbackpages.com.

————. "Two Steps from the Blues: The Gospel According to Bobby 'Blue' Bland." In *From a Whisper to a Scream.* London: Fontana, 1991.

Hoskyns, Barney, and James Maycock. "'Rocket 88' and the Birth of Rock & Roll." *Mojo,* February 2002.

Jackson, George. Profile. www.myspace.com/legendarygeorgejackson.

"Jimmy Beck." All Music Guide. www.allgame.com/cg/amg.dll?p=amg&sql=11:acfoxqr51dje~T4.

"Joe Scott." All Music Guide. wc03.allmusic.com/cg/amg.dll?p=amg&sql=11:f9fpxqrkldoe~T4.

"Joe Scott," Obituary, *Living Blues* 43, Summer 1979.

"Johnny Board." All Music Guide. www.allgame.com/cg/amg.dll?p=amg&sql 11:hcfwxqy51dae~T4.

Johnson, Greg. "Joe 'Guitar' Hughes." In Cascade Blues Association, *BluesNotes*. November 1988.

Johnson, Robert. "Good Evening!" Memphis *Press-Scimitar*, March 18, 1965.

Jordan, Mark. "Casino Scene: Doobies Leader Says Modern Lineup Rocks Out Better Than Ever." Memphis *Commercial Appeal*, February 15, 2008.

Joyce, Mike. "Bobby 'Blue' Bland's Soulful Sound." Washington *Post*, August 21, 2008.

Kain, John F. "Postwar Metropolitan Development: Housing Preferences and Auto Ownership." *American Economic Review* vol. 57, no. 2, May 1967.

"Kansas City's Classic Theatres." members.aol.com/screenviews/theatres.html.

Keil, Charles. *Urban Blues*. Chicago: University of Chicago Press, 1966.

Kelly, Red. "George Jackson—My Desires Are Getting the Best of Me (Fame 1457)." The B Side, December 6, 2006. redkelly.blogspot.com/2006/12/george-jackson-my-desires-are-getting.html.

King, B.B., with David Ritz. *Blues All Around Me: The Autobiography of B.B. King*. New York: Avon, 1996.

Klanac, Bob. "Bobby Blue Bland." Klanac Industries. klanac.blogspot.com/2006/09/bobby-blue-bland.html.

Klibanoff, Hank. "Ernest C. Withers: The Eye on the Prize." *New York Times Magazine*, December 30, 2007.

Komara, Edward. "Blues." In Komara, Edward, ed., *Encyclopedia of the Blues*. New York: Routledge, 2006.

"Korean War." *Wikipedia*.

Kreiser, Christine M. "Don Robey and Duke—Peacock Records." Year of the Blues 2003, www.yearoftheblues.org/features.

Kubernik, Harvey. "Tell 'Em Willie Boy Was Here." *Mojo*, undated article in the Willie Mitchell file at the University of Mississippi's Blues Archives.

Lang, Joe. "Rock and Roll Hall of Fame Week at Dakota Club on 8/7/07." *How Was the Show*, August 22, 2007.

Larkin, Colin. *The Virgin Encyclopedia of R&B and Soul*. London: Virgin, 1998.

Lauterback, Preston. "Chitlin' Circuit." *Memphis: The City Magazine*, August 6, 2005.

Leadbitter, Mike, *Delta Country Blues*, Bexhill-on-Sea (Sussex), Blues Unlimited, 1968.

Leatherwood, Tom, Shelby County Register of Deeds: Instr. #S20152, "Notice of Federal Tax Lien Under Internal Revenue Laws," January 15, 1981. Death Records 1949–2005.

Lee, George W. *Beale Street: Where the Blues Began*. New York: Robert O. Ballou, 1934.

Leopold, Todd. "When the Beatles Hit America." Cable News Network, 2007. www.cnn.com.

Lewis, Julius. "Birthday Wishes From Julius Lewis." *Bobby "Blue" Bland Official Program*. Memphis, TN: Heritage Entertainment, 2010.

Lisle, Andria. Liner notes for *Hucknall: Tribute to Bobby*. simplyred.com ltd., 2008.

———. "The Soul of a Man." *Mojo* 175, June 2008.

Lofgren, Tommy. "Bobby Blue Bland: Ain't Doing Too Bad." *Jefferson* no. 27, 1974.

"Long Beach Boasts Big Blues Bash On Labor Day Weekend." Los Angeles *Sentinel*, August 29, 2001.

Long, Ron. "Bobby Bland, Top Blues Singer, Says 'You've Still Got To Mind.'" *Jet*, October 20, 1977.

Lumb, Lisa. "Turn Up That Noise." Memphis *Flyer*, November 22, 1999.

Maddix, Jacquie. "Interview: Bobby 'Blue' Bland." *Blues On Stage*, KFAI Radio, Minneapolis. October 1, 2002. www.mnblues.com/review/2002/bobbybluebland-intv-11-02-jm.html.

Manheim, James M. "Blue Bland." www.answers.com/topic/blue-bland.

Marion, J. C. "I Smell Trouble: Bobby 'Blue' Bland." *JammUpp* 24, 2002.

———. "Mystery Train: Little Junior Parker." *JammUpp* 24, 2002.

Marsh, Dave. *The Heart of Rock & Soul: The 1001 Greatest Singles Ever Made*. New York: New American Library, 1989.

Martin, Gavin. "Arts: The Main Event—None More Blue Van Morrison/Bobby 'Blue' Bland Royal Albert Hall London," *The Independent*, March 23, 2000.

———. "Bobby Bland: The Best Of (MCA)." *NME*, June 1982.

McClusky, Dan. Audio interview with Bobby Bland. Tom Mazzolini's *Blues by the Bay*, KPFA, San Francisco. February 17 and 24, 2007 kpfa.org/archives/index .php?arch=19033.

McKee, Margaret, and Fred Chisenhall. *Beale Black & Blue: Life and Music on Black America's Main Street*. Baton Rouge: Louisiana State University Press, 1981.

"Mel Brown: Artist Bios." *Electro-Fi*. www.electrofi.com/melbrown_bio.htm.

"Mel Brown." Obituary. *Living Blues* 201, June 2009.

Merrill, Hugh. *The Blues Route*. New York: William Morrow, 1990.

"Michael Omartian." *Wikipedia.*

"Mike 'Monk' Bruce." *Tulsa Area Music Archives*. 2005. www.preservemusic.org/tributes .htm.

Miller, Kelly. Memphis *World*, September 18, 1931.

"Milton Bland, 50, Music Producer." Obituary. Chicago *Sun-Times*, July 13, 1986.

Minutaglio, Bill. "Texas Claims Its Rightful Rank in History of Blues." *Corpus Christi Caller Times*. Undated article in the Bobby Bland file at the University of Mississippi's Blues Archives.

"Mitchell Hotel Business Card." The Beale Street Collection of the Memphis/Shelby County Room of the Memphis/Shelby County Public Library and Information Center.

Mohair Slim. "Rosco Gordon Interview." May, 2001. www.bluejuice.org.au/rosco_inter view.html.

———. "The Rosco Gordon Story." www.bluejuice.org.au/rosco_story.html.

Mohr, Kurt. "Les Hommes de Bobby Bland." *Soul Bag* 115, 1989.

"Moohah" [A. C. Williams]. "What's Happening in the Big M." *Tri-State Defender*, November 24, 1951.

Moonoogian, George, and Roger Meeden. "Duke Records: The Early Years. An Interview with David J. Mattis." *Whiskey, Women, and . . .* 14, June 1984.

Morris, Chris Liner notes for *Bobby Bland: Greatest Hits, Vol. One*, MCA Records, 1998.

Morthland, John. "Everybody Comes to Antone's." *eMusic Spotlight*. www.emusic.com/ features/spotlight/292_200606.html.

———. "Royal Blue." *Texas Monthly* vol. 5, no. 8, August 1997.

"Muscle Shoals Sound Studio." *Wikipedia.*

Murray, Charles Shaar. *Blues on CD: The Essential Guide*. London: Kyle Cathie, 1993.

———. "Talkin' Blues: John Lee Hooker/B.B. King/Bobby 'Blue' Bland." *NME*, June 5, 1982.

Myers, Leslie R. "Bland Leads Jackson Music Awards Slate With 8 Nominations." *Jackson Clarion-Ledger*, July 11, 1986.

Nager, Larry. "Rock Honors Surprise Bland." Memphis *Commercial Appeal*, January 15, 1992.

"The National Academy of Blues Awards." *Living Blues* 51, Summer 1981.

"Night Life: Rock and Pop." *The New Yorker*, August 25, 2008.

O, Don. "Lucky Dallas: Lucky Peterson Interview 3/19/98." www.geocities.com/bluesdfw/lucky.htm.

Office of Public Affairs, Smithsonian Institution. "B.B. King, Bobby Blue Bland and Memphis Slim Star in April 29–May 1 Smithsonian Program Celebrating the Memphis Blues." Press release, December 17, 1982.

O'Neal, Amy. "Bobby Bland! Onstage." *Living Blues* 4, Winter 1970–71.

O'Neal, Jim. "Bobby Bland! Backstage." *Living Blues* 4, Winter 1970–71.

———. "Junior Wells." *Living Blues* 119, February 1995.

———. "Living Blues Interview: Z.Z. Hill." *Living Blues* 53, Summer/Autumn 1982.

Osteen, Faye Ellis. *Millington, The First Hundred Years*. Southhaven, MS: King's Press, 2002.

"Other Deaths: Ernest Withers." Obituary. *Living Blues* 194, February 2008.

Palmer, Robert. *Deep Blues*. New York: Penguin, 1982.

Pareles, Jon. "Blues Review: A Wounded Man, Still Singing That Sad Old Song at 72." *New York Times*, January 23, 2003.

———. "Concert: Country and Blues." *New York Times*, August 20, 1984.

———. "Review/Blues: Despair Dotted by Smiles." *New York Times*, August 19, 1988.

Patoski, Joe Nick. "Okie Dokie Stomp." Austin *Chronicle*, May 26, 2006, Music Section.

Patterson, Dale R. "Radio's Jackie Robinson: Nat D. Williams." *Rock Radio Scrapbook*. rockradioscrapbook.ca/natd.html.

Paul, Mike "Don Robey." Obituary. *Living Blues* 23, September-October 1975.

Payne, Jim. *Give the Drummers Some!* Katanoh, NY: Face the Music, 1996.

Perlich, Tim. "Bland At His Best: Soul-Blues Icon Roars Back . . . Again." *Now Toronto*, January 16, 2003.

Peterson, Clark. "B.B. King, Bobbie Blue Bland Knock 'em at Winterland." *Berkeley Barb*, January 17–23, 1975.

"Phillips Celebrates its 142nd Church Anniversary." www.phillipscme.org/Welcom.html.

Point, Michael. "Ace, Buddy." In Komara.

———. "Bennett, Wayne T." In Komara

———. "Hill, Z.Z." In Kormara.

———. "Holliman, Clarence." In Komara.

———. "Murphy, Matt 'Guitar,'" In Komara.

Polk's Memphis (Shelby County, Tenn.) City Directory. 1945, 1946, 1948, 1950, 1955, 1960, 1961, 1967.

"Pop/Sneak Peek: Zappa, Bland Honored for Musical Contributions." Los Angeles *Daily News*, January 3, 1997.

Prudhomme, Chester. "Bobby 'Blue' Bland." *DISCoveries*, December 1989.

Quick, Barney. "The All-Time Top 100 R&B Tunes—Part 1: The Top Ten." *suite101.com*. March 3, 2001. www.suite101.com/article.cfm/r&b_history/62034.

Raum, Tom. "Obama Proclaims Himself the Democratic Nominee." Associated Press, June 3, 2008.

Reagoso, Joe. Liner notes for *Bobby Bland: Blues & Ballads*. MCA Records, 1999.

Roberts, Kimberly C. "Bland Brings Down the House at Blues Fest." Philadelphia *Tribune*, October 12, 2004.

Robertson, Rebecca L. *City on the Bluff: History and Heritage of Memphis*. Memphis: St. Luke's Press, 1987.

Robinson, Louie. "The Tragic Death of Sam Cooke." *Ebony* 20, February 1965.

Robson, Britt. "True Blue." Minneapolis *Star Tribune*, August 5, 2007.

Rooster. "Rooster Pickin's." *Blues Access* 41, Spring 2000.

"Rosco Gordon." *Wikipedia*.

Rosenberg, Merri. "Making Records Far from the Urban Beat." *New York Times*, February 4, 1996.

Rowe, Mike. *Chicago Blues: The City and the Music*. New York: Da Capo, 1981.

"Roy Gaines—The Legendary Blues Guitarist and Musician." www.roygaines.com.

Rutkoff, Peter, and Will Scott. "Preaching the Blues: The Mississippi Delta of Muddy Waters." *Kenyon Review*, New Series vol. XXVII, no. 2, Spring 2005.

Rye, Howard. "Ace (United Kingdom)." In Komara.

Salem, James M. *The Late, Great Johnny Ace and the Transition from R&B to Rock 'n' Roll*. Urbana: University of Illinois Press, 1999.

"Sam Phillips' Sun Records." www.history-of-rock.com/sam_phillips_sun_records.htm.

"Sam Phillips." *Wikipedia*.

Santelli, Robert. *The Big Book of Blues: A Biographical Encyclopedia*. New York: Penguin, 1993.

Sawyer, Charles. *The Arrival of B.B. King*. Garden City, NY: Doubleday, 1980.

Schoemer, Karen. "Bobby (Blue) Bland, Honored at Last." *New York Times*, January 22, 1992.

Schoenherr, Neil. "Korean War Had Major Impact on Race Relations in the United States." *Washington University in St. Louis News & Information*. July 25, 2003.

Scruggs, Afi-Odelia. "Elegant Bobby Bland Wears a New Style," Jackson *Clarion-Ledger*. Undated article in the Bobby Bland file at the University of Mississippi's Blues Archives.

Shaw, Arnold. *Honkers and Shouters: The Golden Years of Rhythm and Blues*. New York: Macmillan, 1978.

Shurman, Dick. Liner notes for *That Did It! The Duke Recordings, Vol. 3*. MCA Records, 1996.

Shurman, Dick, Jim O'Neal, and Amy O'Neal. "Living Blues Interview: Otis Rush." *Living Blues* 28, July–August 1976.

Sigafoos, Robert A. *Cotton Row to Beale Street: A Business History of Memphis*. Memphis: Memphis State University Press, 1979.

"Since I Fell for You." *Wikipedia*.

Sinclair, John. "Scott, Joe." In Komara.

Sisario, Ben. "Tyrone Davis, Singer of Soul Songs Tinged with the Blues, 66." Obituary. *New York Times*, February 14, 2005.

———. "Willie Mitchell, Soul Music Producer, Dies at 81." Obituary. *New York Times*, January 6, 2010.

Snowden, Don. Liner notes for *Bobby Bland: I Pity the Fool, The Duke Recordings, Vol. 1*. MCA Records, 1992.

Snowden, Don. "Malaco: Rhythm & Business." Los Angeles *Times*, May 9, 1987.

Snyder, Mike. "With Its Rich History, Fourth Ward Is Strong in Symbolism." Houston *Chronicle*, January 9, 2000.

Sontag, Deborah. "Out of Exile, Back in Soulville." *New York Times*, August 16, 2009.

Spann, Purvis, and Jim O'Neal. "Junior Parker." Obituary. *Living Blues* 7, Winter 1971–72.

Spencer, Paul. *Simply Blue*. DVD. Documentary recorded in Memphis, Tennessee, November, 2007, and included as part of the album *Hucknall: Tribute to Bobby.*

Spitzer, Nick. "Bobby 'Blue' Bland Interview." Audio interview. 2003. www.yearofthe blues.org/features.asp?type=4&id=%7B024252EB-DB9.

Standifer, Jim. "Bobby Blue Bland." Interview for African American Music Collection. www.umich.edu/~afroammu/standifer/bland.html.

Stapleton-Corcoran, Erin. "Clark, Dave." In Komara.

State of Tennessee Marriage License, County of Shelby. I. J. Brooks and Mary Lee Smith. September 26, 1929.

Stephenson, Wolf. Liner notes for *Blues at Midnight*. Malaco Records, 1998.

"Steve Barri: Biography." *Golden Grass—The Grass Roots Fan Page.* home.att. net/~souldeep69/biosbarri.html.

Stites, Sara. "Rock 'n' Roll Band to be Inducted into Kansas Hall of Fame." Kansas City *Star*, December 10, 2006.

Streissguth, Mike. "From Memphis to Malaco: Bobby 'Blue' Bland Turns on Your Lovelight." *Goldmine* 139, July 21, 1995.

Summers, Lynn S., and Bob Scheir. "Living Blues Interview: Little Milton." *Living Blues* 18, Autumn 1974.

Tennessee Department of Health. Certificate of Death for Mary Bland. January 12, 2001.

———. Certificate of Death for Isaac J. Brooks. January 24, 1992.

Tennessee Department of Health Office of Vital Records. Verification of Birth Facts for Robert Calvin Bland. September 17, 2007.

———. Verification of Birth Facts for Roderick Cornelius Bland. May 7, 2008.

———. Verification of Marriage Facts for Robert Calvin Bland and Willie Mae Martin. December 7, 2007.

Thrasher, Don. "Bobby Bland Is Here To Stay." Dayton *Daily News*, July 19, 2003.

Tipaldi, Art. *Children of the Blues*. San Francisco: Backbeat, 2002.

"Tommy Tate." *Wikipedia*.

Topping, Ray. Liner notes for *Bobby "Blue" Bland: The "3B" Blues Boy.* Ace Records, 1990.

Tosches, Nick. *Unsung Heroes of Rock 'n' Roll*. New York: Charles Scribner's Sons, 1984.

Tschmuck, Peter. *Creativity and Innovation in the Music Industry*. New York: Springer, 2006.

U.S. Department of Defense. "United States of America Korean War Commemoration." www.korea.50.army.mil/history/factsheets/afroamer.shtml.

Vera, Billy. Liner notes for *Junior's Blues*. MCA Records, 1992.

"Vinyl Statistics: Bobby Bland." Undated press release from ABC Records, [YEAR].

Ward, Ed. "Buried Alive in the Blues." Austin *Chronicle*, May 25, 2006, Music Section.

Wasserzieher, Bill. "The Lion in Winter: Clarence 'Gatemouth' Brown." *Blues Revue*, January 2002.

Webb, Arthur. "Bobby Blue Bland." *The Downtowner Magazine*, August. 1997.

Welch, Chris. "Legendary Blues Man Has No Plans to Slow Down." Huntsville *Times*, February 14, 2008.

West, Hollie. "Records." *Rolling Stone*, May 31, 1969.

Wexler, Jerry, and David Ritz. *Rhythm and the Blues: A Life in American Music.* New York: Alfred A. Knopf, 1993.

Whitburn, Joel. *The Billboard Book of Top 40 R&B and Hip-Hop Hits.* New York: Billboard, 2006.

Whiteis, David. "Ike Turner." Obituary. *Living Blues* 194, April 2008.

Williams, Mark. "Blues Worth the Drive—R&B Legend Bland Plays Houston Tonight." *The Bulletin*, July 13, 2001.

Wiser, Donna Rae. "Bobby Bland: It's All 'Biscuits' and Gravy, Baby." *Beaumont Journal,* October 25, 2006.

Wood, Roger. "Clarence 'Gatemouth' Brown." Obituary. *Living Blues* 181, November–December 2005.

———. *Down in Houston: Bayou City Blues.* Austin: University of Texas Press, 2003.

———. "Hamp W. Simmons, Jr." Obituary. *Living Blues* 156, March–April 2001.

———. "Joe 'Guitar' Hughes." Obituary. *Living Blues* 169, September–October 2003.

———. "Teddy Reynolds." *The Handbook of Texas Online.* www.tsha.utexas.edu/hand book/online/articles/RR/fre67.html.

Worley, William S. *Beale Street: Crossroads of America's Music.* Lenexa, KS: Addax, 1998.

Worsham, Doris. "The Saga of Bobby Bland." Oakland *Tribune*, March 8, 1975.

Wynn, Ron. "Bobby 'Blue' Bland." In Bogdanov.

Zugna, Daniel. *FortiFi@Public Journal.* February 8, 2007. journals.aol.com/kingbing1/ FortiFi/entries/2007/02/08/motown-pianist-joe-hunter-die.

Interviews

Except where noted, the following interviews were conducted in person by the author. Locations indicate where interviews were conducted. All transcripts and notes are in the author's files.

Bland, Roderick. Crossroads Music Hall, Huntsville, AL. February 17, 2008.

Hardin, Joseph, Jr. Telephone interview. August 4, 2008.

King, B.B. Von Braun Concert Hall, Huntsville, AL. September 21, 2008.

Latimore, Benny. Sunflower Blues and Gospel Festival, Clarksdale, MS. August 8, 2008.

Mitchell, Willie. Royal Recording Studio, Memphis, TN. August 8, 2008.

Stephenson, Gerald "Wolf." Malaco Records, Jackson, MS. July 30, 2008.

Permission Acknowledgments

Grateful acknowledgment is made to the following for permission to reprint previously published material:

Alfred Publishing Co., Inc. Excerpts from "A Change is Gonna Come" by Sam Cooke, Copyright © 1964; and "Stormy Monday Blues" by B. Crowder/ Earl Hines/Billy Eckstine, Copyright © 1947 by Alfred Publishing Co., Inc. International Rights Secured. All Rights Reserved. Used by permission.

Cinco Puntos Press. Excerpt from "Why I am a Poet, #7," in *White Panties, Dead Friends & Other Bits & Pieces of Love.* Copyright © 2006 by Bobby Byrd (1942), a poet who lives in El Paso, TX. He grew up in Memphis during the golden years of that city's music scene. All Rights Reserved. Used by permission.

Hal Leonard Corporation. Excerpts from "Lead Me On" by Deadric Malone, Copyright © 1967; and "Poverty" by Dave Clark and Pearl Woods, Copyright © 1966, by Hal Leonard Corporation. International Rights Secured. All Rights Reserved. Used by permission.

Malaco Music Co. and Peermusic III, Ltd. Excerpt from "I'm a Blues Man" by Joseph Shamwell/Walter Godbold/AD Prestage. Copyright © 1983 by Malaco Music Co. and Peermusic III, Ltd. International Rights Secured. All Rights Reserved. Used by permission.

Index